America and the World
Debating the New Shape
of International Politics

Books from
FOREIGN AFFAIRS

America and the World: Debating the New Shape of International Politics *(2002)*

The Clash of Civilizations? The Debate (1996)

How Did This Happen? Terrorism and the New War
Edited by James F. Hoge, Jr. and Gideon Rose *(2001) PublicAffairs*

The American Encounter:
The United States and the Making of the Modern World
Edited by James F. Hoge, Jr. and Fareed Zakaria *(1997) BasicBooks*

FOREIGN AFFAIRS
Editors' Choice

Globalization: Challenge and Opportunity *(2002)*

The Middle East in Crisis *(2002)*

The Rise of China *(2002)*

The War on Terror *(2002)*

Closing the Great Divide: Development and the Eradication of Poverty *(2001)*

Intervention and American Foreign Policy *(2001)*

The New Terrorism *(2001)*

The New Trade Agenda *(2001)*

The United States and the Persian Gulf *(2001)*

The United States and Russia *(2001)*

Weapons of Mass Destruction: Threat and Response *(2001)*

Foreign Affairs Agenda: The New Shape of World Politics *(1999)*

Is Global Capitalism Working ?*(1999)*

Competitiveness: An International Economics Reader (1994)

For additional information visit
www.foreignaffairs.org/reader/reader.html

FOREIGN AFFAIRS

America and the World
Debating the New Shape
of International Politics

A Council on Foreign Relations Book

NEW YORK

Distributed by
W.W. Norton and Company
500 Fifth Avenue
New York, New York 10110

Founded in 1921, the Council on Foreign Relations is a nonpartisan membership organization, research center, and publisher. It is dedicated to increasing America's understanding of the world and contributing ideas to U.S. foreign policy. The Council accomplishes this mainly by promoting constructive discussions and by publishing *Foreign Affairs*, the leading journal on global issues. The Council is host to the widest possible range of views, but an advocate of none, though its research fellows and Independent Task Forces do take policy stands. From time to time, books and reports written by members of the Council's research staff or others are published as a "Council on Foreign Relations Book."

The Council takes no institutional position on policy issues and has no affiliation with the U.S. government. All statements of fact and expressions of opinion contained in all its publications are the sole responsibility of the author or authors.

The Council's bimonthly magazine, *Foreign Affairs*, has been America's leading publication on international affairs and foreign policy for 80 years. With a circulation of 115,000 worldwide, *Foreign Affairs* has long been the most influential forum for important new ideas, analysis, and debate on significant global issues. To subscribe, or for more information, visit www.foreignaffairs.org.

Foreign Affairs books are distributed by W.W. Norton & Company (www.wwnorton.com).

Contents

Introduction

Gideon Rose

THE END OF THE COLD WAR and the collapse of the Soviet Union ushered in a new era of international politics, one that people have been trying to get a handle on ever since. A decade on its contours still seemed vague, and it was still labeled with reference to what it was not—its predecessor—rather than for any quality of its own. Then came the attacks of September 11, 2001, which seemed to begin yet another chapter in the history of the United States, the world, and the relations between them. All were utterly changed. Or were they?

The truth is that our understanding of such matters is always partial and subjective, with clarity emerging less from reality itself than from our need to impose some kind of intellectual order on the bloomin', buzzin' confusion around us. This collection is a record of the best attempts at that task over the last dozen years. It brings together many powerful and well-stocked minds, all trying to figure out what forces are driving world events and how Americans should respond.

Which is more important, ideology, culture, or power? What lies ahead, order or chaos? What is democracy? How strong is the United States, and for what purposes should it use its strength? How vulnerable is it, and what must it do for protection? The authors gathered here address these and many other questions, often directly engaging each other's arguments and educating the rest of us in the process. Originally published in Foreign Affairs and eight other leading journals and magazines, the articles constitute an essential reading list for anyone interested in contemporary international relations.

GIDEON ROSE is Managing Editor of *Foreign Affairs*.

Gideon Rose

Francis Fukuyama kicked off the first great debate of the post-Cold War era by arguing in a now-legendary 1989 essay that what had arrived was nothing less than the end of history, by which he meant the culmination of the ideological evolution of humanity. The debate over the ideal form of government was over, and liberal democracy had won; large ideological questions were a thing of the past, and large conflicts eventually would be too. Among the most compelling of the responses to Fukuyama came from Samuel P. Huntington, who pointed to the reversibility of all political trends and the weakness and irrationality of human nature as crucial reasons why the traumas of history would continue.

Huntington himself would then kick off the second great debate a few years later, arguing in a 1993 essay (now just as legendary as Fukuyama's) that the fault lines of future conflict would not be ideological, economic, or political but cultural, as the world's major civilizations clashed with each other. This time one of the most powerful responses came from Fouad Ajami, who argued that Huntington overestimated the clarity and significance of civilizational identities and underestimated the tenacity and slyness of states, which would continue to find ways to retain their influence over their citizens and over the course of events.

Yet another prognostication soon came from Robert D. Kaplan, who published a 1994 essay predicting that Africa's present would become the world's future, as population growth, environmental devastation, and political decay spread anarchy across the globe. Taking on both this kind of apocalyptic vision and the arguments predicting a return to war among the great powers, in 1996 G. John Ikenberry stressed the enduring sources of international stability. Properly understood, he argued, the end of the Cold War represented not the beginning of a fundamentally new era but simply the extension of the American-sponsored post–World War II liberal order from the West to the world at large.

Many developing countries, however, were finding it increasingly difficult to follow the path forward, Fareed Zakaria noted in 1997, and had gotten trapped in an unpleasant way station that he called "illiberal democracy." They had the forms and trappings of democratic regimes but not the political or legal substance,—and were not likely to acquire the latter any time soon. It would be best for all concerned, he claimed, if the world recognized that constitutional liberalism without democratic representation was likely to produce better results in the long run than would democratic procedures without liberal protections. Marc F. Plattner agreed about the need to distinguish liberal democracy's two components but considered Zakaria's conclusions misguided: illiberal democracies could eventually improve, he argued, whereas liberal authoritarianism was rare and unreliable.

By the second half of the 1990s, the mounting evidence that the world's economic integration was proceeding apace produced an explosion of debates over the nature, merits, and challenges of this phenomenon, termed "globalization. In 1997 Dani Rodrik offered a clear-eyed guide to thinking through various aspects of the subject, combining the perspective of a mainstream economist with sympathy for many of the concerns raised by the antiglobalization movement. Four years later, David Dollar and Aart Kraay argued that it was precisely those who cared about the poor who should be globalization's biggest fans, since by improving the lot of the Chinese and Indian masses, economic integration had reversed a centuries-old trend toward greater global economic inequality.

As the millennium approached, the lopsided nature of the international distribution of power had not only failed to slide towards multipolarity, but if anything had grown more exaggerated. Questions surrounding the extent and future prospects of American hegemony thus came to the fore, and were given new urgency by the post-September 11 crisis and the unilateralist instincts of the new Bush administration. In 1999 Charles A. Kupchan argued that American primacy was bound to fade as Europe coalesced into an opposing pole of the international system and the American public grew tired of bearing the burdens of global leadership. The wisest course, therefore, was to anticipate such developments and plan for a graceful transition of power while there was still time. Three years later, Robert Kagan, and Stephen G. Brooks and William C. Wohlforth, disagreed; writing in the wake of the Afghan campaign's stunning success, they analyzed the United States' historically unprecedented international position and its implications for transatlantic relations and American foreign policy more generally.

Gideon Rose

The devastating terrorist attacks on the World Trade Center and the Pentagon brought home with a vengeance the realization that the new century had come accompanied by new enemies and new dangers, and Americans found themselves enrolled willy-nilly in a crash course on contemporary Muslim politics. Three outstanding efforts to provide intellectual context for the attacks and subsequent events were turned in by Fareed Zakaria, Michael Scott Doran, and Ladan and Roya Boroumand, who together offered a sobering portrait of the intersection of terrorism, religion, and repression. Stephen M. Walt, meanwhile, sketched out some potential implications of the crisis for American foreign policy.

The still-mysterious anthrax mailings, finally, have revealed just how ill prepared is the United States, along with everybody else, to cope with a world in which weapons of mass destruction are more widely available and more potentially deadly than ever before. Richard K. Betts presciently highlighted these dangers several years earlier and offered suggestions on how to rise to the challenge. And in his 2002 commencement address at West Point, President Bush set out his own bold vision of the need for preventive action to head off such problems. But just what that approach might look like and in which cases it might be applied remained unclear, not least because of the international repercussions that G. John Ikenberry noted are likely should the new policy be put into practice.

A dozen years after the end of the Cold War, in short, some of the most important features of the strategic landscape have yet to be determined. Secretary of Defense Donald Rumsfeld may have best described the situation facing scholars and practitioners alike when he observed: "There are things we know that we know. ... there are things we now know we don't know. But there are also ... things we do not know we don't know." We hope readers will agree that this collection at least helps summarize and advance the discussion.✪

The End of History?

Francis Fukuyama

IN WATCHING the flow of events over the past decade or so, it is hard to avoid the feeling that something very fundamental has happened in world history. The past year has seen a flood of articles commemorating the end of the Cold War, and the fact that "peace" seems to be breaking out in many regions of the world. Most of these analyses lack any larger conceptual framework for distinguishing between what is essential and what is contingent or accidental in world history and are predictably superficial. If Mr. Gorbachev were ousted from the Kremlin or a new Ayatollah proclaimed the millennium from a desolate Middle Eastern capital, these same commentators would scramble to announce the rebirth of a new era of conflict.

And yet, all of these people sense dimly that there is some larger process at work, a process that gives coherence and order to the daily headlines. The twentieth century saw the developed world descend into a paroxysm of ideological violence, as liberalism contended first with the remnants of absolutism, then bolshevism and fascism, and finally an updated Marxism that threatened to lead to the ultimate apocalypse of nuclear war. But the century that began full of self-confidence in the ultimate triumph of Western liberal democracy seems at its close to be returning full circle to where it started: not to an "end of ideology" or a convergence

FRANCIS FUKUYAMA is Dean of Faculty and Bernard L. Schwartz Professor of International Political Economy at the Paul H. Nitze School of Advanced International Studies of Johns Hopkins University. This article orginally appeared in the Summer 1989 issue of *The National Interest*. Reprinted by permission of International Creative Management, Inc. Copyright © 1989 by Francis Fukuyama.

between capitalism and socialism, as earlier predicted, but to an unabashed victory of economic and political liberalism.

The triumph of the West, of the Western *idea,* is evident first of all in the total exhaustion of viable systematic alternatives to Western liberalism. In the past decade, there have been unmistakable changes in the intellectual climate of the world's two largest communist countries, and the beginnings of significant reform movements in both. But this phenomenon extends beyond high politics and it can be seen also in the ineluctable spread of consumerist Western culture in such diverse contexts as the peasants' markets and color television sets now omnipresent throughout China, the cooperative restaurants and clothing stores opened in the past year in Moscow, the Beethoven piped into Japanese department stores, and the rock music enjoyed alike in Prague, Rangoon, and Tehran.

What we may be witnessing is not just the end of the Cold War, or the passing of a particular period of postwar history; but the end of history as such: that is, the end point of mankind's ideological evolution and the universalization of Western liberal democracy as the final form of human government. This is not to say that there will no longer be events to fill the pages of *Foreign Affairs'* yearly summaries of international relations, for the victory of liberalism has occurred primarily in the realm of ideas or consciousness and is as yet incomplete in the real or material world. But there are powerful reasons for believing that it is the ideal that will govern the material world *in the long run.* To understand how this is so, we must first consider some theoretical issues concerning the nature of historical change.

I

THE NOTION of the end of history is not an original one. Its best known propagator was Karl Marx, who believed that the direction of historical development was a purposeful one determined by the interplay of material forces, and would come to an end only with the achievement of a communist utopia that would finally resolve all prior contradictions. But the concept of history as a dialectical process with a beginning, a middle, and an end was borrowed by Marx from his great German predecessor Georg Wilhelm Friedrich Hegel.

The End of History?

For better or worse, much of Hegel's historicism has become part of our contemporary intellectual baggage. The notion that mankind has progressed through a series of primitive stages of consciousness on his path to the present, and that these stages corresponded to concrete forms of social organization, such as tribal, slave-owning, theocratic, and finally democratic-egalitarian societies, has become inseparable from the modern understanding of man. Hegel was the first philosopher to speak the language of modern social science, insofar as man for him was the product of his concrete historical and social environment and not, as earlier natural right theorists would have it, a collection of more or less fixed "natural" attributes. The mastery and transformation of man's natural environment through the application of science and technology was originally not a Marxist concept, but a Hegelian one. Unlike later historicists whose historical relativism degenerated into relativism *tout court*, however, Hegel believed that history culminated in an absolute moment—a moment in which a final, rational form of society and state became victorious.

It is Hegel's misfortune to be known now primarily as Marx's precursor, and it is our misfortune that few of us are familiar with Hegel's work from direct study, but only as it has been filtered through the distorting lens of Marxism. In France, however, there has been an effort to save Hegel from his Marxist interpreters and to resurrect him as the philosopher who most correctly speaks to our time. Among those modern French interpreters of Hegel, the greatest was certainly Alexandre Kojève, a brilliant Russian émigré who taught a highly influential series of seminars in Paris in the 1930s at the *Ecole Practique des Hautes Etudes*.[1] While largely unknown in the United States, Kojève had a major impact on the intellectual life of the continent. Among his students ranged such future luminaries as

---

1. Kojève's best-known work is his *Introduction ala lecture de Hegel* (Paris: Editions Gallimard, 1947), which is a transcript of the Ecole Practique lectures from the 1930s. This book is available in English entitled *Introduction to the Reading of Hegel* arranged by Raymond Queneau, edited by Allan Bloom, and translated by James Nichols (New York: Basic Books, 1969).

Jean-Paul Sartre on the Left and Raymond Aron on the Right; postwar existentialism borrowed many of its basic categories from Hegel via Kojève.

Kojève sought to resurrect the Hegel of the *Phenomenology of Mind*, the Hegel who proclaimed history to be at an end in 1806. For as early as this Hegel saw in Napoleon's defeat of the Prussian monarchy at the Battle of Jena the victory of the ideals of the French Revolution, and the imminent universalization of the state incorporating the principles of liberty and equality. Kojève, far from rejecting Hegel in light of the turbulent events of the next century and a half, insisted that the latter had been essentially correct.[2] The Battle of Jena marked the end of history because it was at that point that the vanguard of humanity (a term quite familiar to Marxists) actualized the principles of the French Revolution. While there was considerable work to be done after 1806—abolishing slavery and the slave trade, extending the franchise to workers, women, blacks, and other racial minorities, etc.—the basic *principles* of the liberal democratic state could not be improved upon. The two world wars in this century and their attendant revolutions and upheavals simply had the effect of extending those principles spatially, such that the various provinces of human civilization were brought up to the level of its most advanced outposts, and of forcing those societies in Europe and North America at the vanguard of civilization to implement their liberalism more Fully.

The state that emerges at the end of history is liberal insofar as it recognizes and protects through a system of law man's universal right to freedom, and democratic insofar as it exists only with the consent of the governed. For Kojève, this so-called "universal homogenous state" found real-life embodiment in the countries of postwar Western Europe—precisely those flabby, prosperous, self-satisfied, inward-looking, weak-willed states whose grandest project was nothing more heroic than the creation

2. In this respect Kojève stands in sharp contrast to contemporary German interpreters of Hegel like Herbert Marcuse who, being more sympathetic to Marx, regarded Hegel ultimately as an historically bound and incomplete philosopher.

of the Common Market.[3] But this was only to be expected. For human history and the conflict that characterized it was based on the existence of "contradictions": primitive man's quest for mutual recognition, the dialectic of the master and slave, the transformation and mastery of nature, the struggle for the universal recognition of rights, and the dichotomy between proletarian and capitalist. But in the universal homogenous state, all prior contradictions are resolved and all human needs are satisfied. There is no struggle or conflict over "large" issues, and consequently no need for generals or statesmen; what remains is primarily economic activity And indeed, Kojève's life was consistent with his teaching. Believing that there was no more work for philosophers as well, since Hegel (correctly understood) had already achieved absolute knowledge, Kojève left teaching after the war and spent the remainder of his life working as a bureaucrat in the European Economic Community until his death in 1968.

To his contemporaries at mid-century, Kojève's proclamation of the end of history must have seemed like the typical eccentric solipsism of a French intellectual, coming as it did on the heels of World War II and at the very height of the Cold War. To comprehend how Kojève could have been so audacious as to assert that history has ended, we must first of all understand the meaning of Hegelian idealism.

II

FOR HEGEL, the contradictions that drive history exist first of all in the realm of human consciousness, i.e. on the level of ideas[4]-not the trivial election year proposals of American politicians, but ideas in the sense of large unifying world views that might best be understood under the rubric of ideology. Ideology in this sense

---

3. Kojève alternatively identified the end of history with the postwar "American way of life," toward which he thought the Soviet Union was moving as well.

4. This notion was expressed in the famous aphorism from the preface to the *Philosophy of History* to the effect that "everything that is rational is real, and every thing that is real is rational."

is not restricted to the secular and explicit political doctrines we usually associate with the term, but can include religion, culture, and the complex of moral values underlying any society as well.

Hegel's view of the relationship between the ideal and the real or material worlds was an extremely complicated one, beginning with the fact that for him the distinction between the two was only apparent.[5] He did not believe that the real world conformed or could be made to conform to ideological preconceptions of philosophy professors in any simple-minded way, or that the "material" world could not impinge on the ideal. Indeed, Hegel the professor was temporarily thrown out of work as a result of a very material event, the Battle of Jena. But while Hegel's writing and thinking could be stopped by a bullet from the material world, the hand on the trigger of the gun was motivated in turn by the ideas of liberty and equality that had driven the French Revolution.

For Hegel, all human behavior in the material world, and hence all human history, is rooted in a prior state of consciousness—an idea similar to the one expressed by John Maynard Keynes when he said that the views of men of affairs were usually derived from defunct economists and academic scribblers of earlier generations. This consciousness may not be explicit and self-aware, as are modern political doctrines, but may rather take the form of religion or simple cultural or moral habits. And yet this realm of consciousness in the long run necessarily becomes manifest in the material world, indeed creates the material world in its own image. Consciousness is cause and not effect, and can develop autonomously from the material world; hence the real subtext underlying the apparent jumble of current events is the history of ideology.

Hegel's idealism has fared poorly at the hands of later thinkers. Marx reversed the priority of the real and the ideal completely, relegating the entire realm of consciousness—religion, art, culture, philosophy itself—to a "superstructure" that was determined entirely by the prevailing material mode of production. Yet another

---

5. Indeed, for Hegel the very dichotomy between the ideal and material worlds was itself only an apparent one that was ultimately overcome by the self-conscious subject; in his system, the material world is itself only an aspect of mind.

unfortunate legacy of Marxism is our tendency to retreat into materialist or utilitarian explanations of political or historical phenomena, and our disinclination to believe in the autonomous power of ideas. A recent example of this is Paul Kennedy's hugely successful *The Rise and Fall of the Great Powers*, which ascribes the decline of great powers to simple economic overextension. Obviously, this is true on some level: an empire whose economy is barely above the level of subsistence cannot bankrupt its treasury indefinitely. But whether a highly productive modern industrial society chooses to spend 3 or 7 percent of its GNP on defense rather than consumption is entirely a matter of that society's political priorities, which are in turn determined in the realm of consciousness.

The materialist bias of modern thought is characteristic not only of people on the Left who may be sympathetic to Marxism, but of many passionate anti-Marxists as well. Indeed, there is on the Right what one might label the *Wall Street Journal* school of deterministic materialism that discounts the importance of ideology and culture and sees man as essentially a rational, profit-maximizing individual. It is precisely this kind of individual and his pursuit of material incentives that is posited as the basis for economic life as such in economic textbooks.[6] One small example will illustrate the problematic character of such materialist views.

Max Weber begins his famous book, *The Protestant Ethic and the Spirit of Capitalism*, by noting the different economic performance of Protestant and Catholic communities throughout Europe and America, summed up in the proverb that Protestants eat well while Catholics sleep well. Weber notes that according to any economic theory that posited man as a rational profit-maximizer, raising the piece-work rate should increase labor productivity. But in fact, in many traditional peasant communities, raising the piece-work rate actually had the opposite effect of *lowering* labor productivity: at the higher rate, a peasant accustomed to earning

---

6. In fact, modern economists, recognizing that man does not always behave as a profit-maximizer, posit a "utility" function, utility being either income or some other good that can be maximized: leisure, sexual satisfaction, or the pleasure of philosophizing. That profit must be replaced with a value like utility indicates the cogency of the idealist perspective.

two and one-half marks per day found he could earn the same amount by working less, and did so because he valued leisure more than income. The choices of leisure over income, or of the militaristic life of the Spartan hoplite over the wealth of the Athenian trader, or even the ascetic life of the early capitalist entrepreneur over that of a traditional leisured aristocrat, cannot possibly be explained by the impersonal working of material forces, but come preeminently out of the sphere of consciousness—what we have labeled here broadly as ideology. And indeed, a central theme of Weber's work was to prove that contrary to Marx, the material mode of production, far from being the "base," was itself a "superstructure" with roots in religion and culture, and that to understand the emergence of modern capitalism and the profit motive one had to study their antecedents in the realm of the spirit.

As we look around the contemporary world, the poverty of materialist theories of economic development is all too apparent. The *Wall Street Journal* school of deterministic materialism habitually points to the stunning economic success of Asia in the past few decades as evidence of the viability of free market economics, with the implication that all societies would see similar development were they simply to allow their populations to pursue their material self-interest freely. Surely free markets and stable political systems are a necessary precondition to capitalist economic growth. But just as surely the cultural heritage of those Far Eastern societies, the ethic of work and saving and family, a religious heritage that does not, like Islam, place restrictions on certain forms of economic behavior, and other deeply ingrained moral qualities, are equally important in explaining their economic performance.[7] And yet the intellectual weight of materialism is such that not a single respectable contemporary theory of economic development addresses consciousness and culture seriously as the matrix within which economic behavior is formed.

---

7. One need look no further than the recent performance of Vietnamese immigrants in the U.S. school system when compared to their black or Hispanic classmates to realize that culture and consciousness are absolutely crucial to explain not only economic behavior but virtually every other important aspect of life as well.

FAILURE TO understand that the roots of economic behavior lie in the realm of consciousness and culture leads to the common mistake of attributing material causes to phenomena that are essentially ideal in nature. For example, it is commonplace in the West to interpret the reform movements first in China and most recently in the Soviet Union as the victory of the material over the ideal—that is, a recognition that ideological incentives could not replace material ones in stimulating a highly productive modern economy, and that if one wanted to prosper one had to appeal to baser forms of self-interest. But the deep defects of socialist economies were evident thirty or forty years ago to anyone who chose to look. Why was it that these countries moved away from central planning only in the 1980s? The answer must be found in the consciousness of the elites and leaders ruling them, who decided to opt for the "Protestant" life of wealth and risk over the "Catholic" path of poverty and security.[8] That change was in no way made inevitable by the material conditions in which either country found itself on the eve of the reform, but instead came about as the result of the victory of one idea over another.[9]

For Kojève, as for all good Hegelians, understanding the underlying processes of history requires understanding developments in the realm of consciousness or ideas, since consciousness will ultimately remake the material world in its own image. To say that history ended in 1806 meant that mankind's ideological evolution ended in the ideals of the French or American Revolutions: while particular regimes in the real world might not implement these ideals fully, their theoretical truth is absolute and consciousness of the postwar generation of Europeans had not been univer-

---

8. I understand that a full explanation of the origins of the reform movements in China and Russia is a good deal more complicated than this simple formula would suggest. The Soviet reform, for example, was motivated in good measure by Moscow's sense of insecurity in the technological-military realm. Nonetheless, neither country on the eve of its reforms was in such a state of material crisis that one could have predicted the surprising reform paths ultimately taken.

9. It is still not clear whether the Soviet peoples are as "Protestant" as Gorbachev and will follow him down that path.

salized throughout the world; if ideological development had in fact ended, the homogenous state would eventually become victorious throughout the material world.

I have neither the space nor, frankly, the ability to defend in depth Hegel's radical idealist perspective. The issue is not whether Hegel's system was right, but whether his perspective might uncover the problematic nature of many materialist explanations we often take for granted. This is not to deny the role of material factors as such. To a literal-minded idealist, human society can be built around any arbitrary set of principles regardless of their relationship to the material world. And in fact men have proven themselves able to endure the most extreme material hardships in the name of ideas that exist in the realm of the spirit alone, be it the divinity of cows or the nature of the Holy Trinity.[10]

But while man's very perception of the material world is shaped by his historical consciousness of it, the material world can clearly affect in return the viability of a particular state of consciousness. In particular, the spectacular abundance of advanced liberal economies and the infinitely diverse consumer culture made possible by them seem to both foster and preserve liberalism in the political sphere. I want to avoid the materialist determinism that says that liberal economics inevitably produces liberal politics, because I believe that both economics and politics presuppose an autonomous prior state of consciousness that makes them possible. But that state of consciousness that permits the growth of liberalism seems to stabilize in the way one would expect at the end of history if it is underwritten by the abundance of a modern free market economy. We might summarize

---

10. The internal politics of the Byzantine Empire at the time of Justinian revolved around a conflict between the so-called monophysites and monothelites, who believed that the unity of the Holy Trinity was alternatively one of nature or of will. This conflict corresponded to some extent to one between proponents of different racing teams in the Hippodrome in Byzantium and led to a not insignificant level of political violence. Modern historians would tend to seek the roots of such conflicts in antagonisms between social classes or some other modern economic category, being unwilling to believe that men would kill each other over the nature of the Trinity.

the content of the universal homogenous state as liberal democracy in the political sphere combined with easy access to VCRs and stereos in the economic.

III

HAVE WE in fact reached the end of history? Are there, in other words, any fundamental "contradictions" in human life that cannot be resolved in the context of modern liberalism, that would be resolvable by an alternative political-economic structure? If we accept the idealist premises laid out above, we must seek an answer to this question in the realm of ideology and consciousness. Our task is not to answer exhaustively the challenges to liberalism promoted by every crackpot messiah around the world, but only those that are embodied in important social or political forces and movements, and which are therefore part of world history. For our purposes, it matters very little what strange thoughts occur to people in Albania or Burkina Faso, for we are interested in what one could in some sense call the common ideological heritage of mankind.

In the past century, there have been two major challenges to liberalism, those of fascism and of communism. The former[11] saw the political weakness, materialism, anomie, and lack of community of the West as fundamental contradictions in liberal societies that could only be resolved by a strong state that forged a new "people" on the basis of national exclusiveness. Fascism was destroyed as a living ideology by World War II. This was a defeat, of course, on a very material level, but it amounted to a defeat of

11. I am not using the term "fascism" here in its most precise sense, fully aware of the frequent misuse of this term to denounce anyone to the right of the user. "Fascism" here denotes any organized ultra-nationalist movement with universalistic pretensions—not universalistic with regard to its nationalism, of course, since the latter is exclusive by definition, but with regard to the movement's belief in its right to rule other people. Hence Imperial Japan would qualify as fascist while former strongman Stoessner's Paraguay or Pinochet's Chile would not. Obviously fascist ideologies cannot be universalistic in the sense of Marxism or liberalism, but the structure of the doctrine can be transferred from country to country.

the idea as well. What destroyed fascism as an idea was not universal moral revulsion against it, since plenty of people were willing to endorse the idea as long as it seemed the wave of the future, but its lack of success. After the war, it seemed to most people that German fascism as well as its other European and Asian variants were bound to self-destruct. There was no material reason why new fascist movements could not have sprung up again after the war in other locales, but for the fact that expansionist ultranationalism, with its promise of unending conflict leading to disastrous military defeat, had completely lost its appeal. The ruins of the Reich chancellery as well as the atomic bombs dropped on Hiroshima and Nagasaki killed this ideology on the level of consciousness as well as materially, and all of the protofascist movements spawned by the German and Japanese examples like the Peronist movement in Argentina or Subhas Chandra Bose's Indian National Army withered after the war.

The ideological challenge mounted by the other great alternative to liberalism, communism, was far more serious. Marx, speaking Hegel's language, asserted that liberal society contained a fundamental contradiction that could not be resolved within its context, that between capital and labor, and this contradiction has constituted the chief accusation against liberalism ever since. But surely, the class issue has actually been successfully resolved in the West. As Kojève (among others) noted, the egalitarianism of modern America represents the essential achievement of the classless society envisioned by Marx. This is not to say that there are not rich people and poor people in the United States, or that the gap between them has not grown in recent years. But the root causes of economic inequality do not have to do with the underlying legal and social structure of our society, which remains fundamentally egalitarian and moderately redistributionist, so much as with the cultural and social characteristics of the groups that make it up, which are in turn the historical legacy of premodern conditions. Thus black poverty in the United States is not the inherent product of liberalism, but is rather the "legacy of slavery and racism" which persisted long after the formal abolition of slavery.

As a result of the receding of the class issue, the appeal of communism in the developed Western world, it is safe to say, is lower today than any time since the end of the First World War. This can be measured in any number of ways: in the declining membership and electoral pull of the major European communist parties, and their overtly revisionist programs; in the corresponding electoral success of conservative parties from Britain and Germany to the United States and Japan, which are unabashedly pro-market and antistatist; and in an intellectual climate whose most "advanced" members no longer believe that bourgeois society is something that ultimately needs to be overcome. This is not to say that the opinions of progressive intellectuals in Western countries are not deeply pathological in any number of ways. But those who believe that the future must inevitably be socialist tend to be very old, or very marginal to the real political discourse of their societies.

ONE MAY argue that the socialist alternative was never terribly plausible for the North Atlantic world, and was sustained for the last several decades primarily by its success outside of this region. But it is precisely in the non-European world that one is most struck by the occurrence of major ideological transformations. Surely the most remarkable changes have occurred in Asia. Due to the strength and adaptability of the indigenous cultures there, Asia became a battleground for a variety of imported Western ideologies early in this century. Liberalism in Asia was a very weak reed in the period after World War I; it is easy today to forget how gloomy Asia's political future looked as recently as ten or fifteen years ago. It is easy to forget as well how momentous the outcome of Asian ideological struggles seemed for world political development as a whole.

The first Asian alternative to liberalism to be decisively defeated was the fascist one represented by Imperial Japan. Japanese fascism (like its German version) was defeated by the force of American arms in the Pacific war, and liberal democracy was imposed on Japan by a victorious United States. Western capitalism and political liberalism when transplanted to Japan were adapted and transformed by the Japanese in such a way as to be scarcely recognizable.[12] Many Americans are now aware that Japanese industrial organization is very different from that prevailing in the United States or Europe, and it is questionable what relationship the factional maneuvering that takes place with the governing Liberal Democratic Party bears to democracy. Nonetheless, the very fact that the essential elements of economic and political liberalism have been so successfully grafted onto uniquely Japanese traditions and institutions guarantees their survival in the long run. More important is the contribution that Japan has made in turn to world history by following in the footsteps of the United States to create a truly universal consumer culture that has become both a symbol and an underpinning of the universal homogenous state. V.S. Naipaul traveling in Khomeini's Iran shortly after the revolution noted the omnipresent signs advertising the products of Sony, Hitachi, and JVC, whose appeal remained virtually irresistible and gave the lie to the regime's pretensions of restoring a state based on the rule of the *Shariah*. Desire for access to the consumer culture, created in large measure by Japan, has played a crucial role in fostering the spread of economic liberalism throughout Asia, and hence in promoting political liberalism as well.

The economic success of the other newly industrializing countries (NICs) in Asia following on the example of Japan is by now a familiar story. What is important from a Hegelian standpoint is that political liberalism has been following economic liberalism, more slowly than many had hoped but with seeming inevitability. Here again we see the victory of the idea of the universal homogenous state. South Korea had developed into a modern, urbanized society with an increasingly large and well-educated middle class that could not possibly be isolated from the larger democratic trends around them. Under these circumstances it seemed intolerable to a large part of this population that it

---

12. I use the example of Japan with some caution, since Kojève late in his life came to conclude that Japan, with its culture based on purely formal arts, proved that the universal homogenous state was not victorious and that history had perhaps not ended. See the long note at the end of the second edition of *Introduction a Ia Lecture de Hegel*, 462-3.

should be ruled by an anachronistic military regime while Japan, only a decade or so ahead in economic terms, had parliamentary institutions for over forty years. Even the former socialist regime in Burma, which for so many decades existed in dismal isolation from the larger trends dominating Asia, was buffeted in the past year by pressures to liberalize both its economy and political system. It is said that unhappiness with strongman Ne Win began when a senior Burmese officer went to Singapore for medical treatment and broke down crying when he saw how far socialist Burma had been left behind by its ASEAN neighbors.

BUT THE power of the liberal idea would seem much less impressive if it had not infected the largest and oldest culture in Asia, China. The simple existence of communist China created an alternative pole of ideological attraction, and as such constituted a threat to liberalism. But the past fifteen years have seen an almost total discrediting of Marxism-Leninism as an economic system. Beginning with the famous third plenum of the Tenth Central Committee in 1978, the Chinese Communist party set about decollectivizing agriculture for the 800 million Chinese who still lived in the countryside. The role of the state in agriculture was reduced to that of a tax collector, while production of consumer goods was sharply increased in order to give peasants a taste of the universal homogenous state and thereby an incentive to work. The reform doubled Chinese grain output in only five years, and in the process created for Deng Xiao-ping a solid political base from which he was able to extend the reform to other parts of the economy. Economic statistics do not begin to describe the dynamism, initiative, and openness evident in China since the reform began.

China could not now be described in any way as a liberal democracy. At present, no more than 20 percent of its economy has been marketized, and most importantly it continues to be ruled by a self-appointed Communist party which has given no hint of wanting to devolve power. Deng has made none of Gorbachev's promises regarding democratization of the political system and there is no Chinese equivalent of *glasnost*. The Chinese leadership has in fact been much more circumspect in criticizing Mao and Maoism than Gorbachev with respect to Brezhnev and Stalin, and the regime continues to pay lip service to Marxism-Leninism as its ideological underpinning. But anyone familiar with the outlook and behavior of the new technocratic elite now governing China knows that Marxism and ideological principle have become virtually irrelevant as guides to policy, and that bourgeois consumerism has a real meaning in that country for the first time since the revolution. The various slowdowns in the pace of reform, the campaigns against "spiritual pollution" and crackdowns on political dissent are more properly seen as tactical adjustments made in the process of managing what is an extraordinarily difficult political transition. By ducking the question of political reform while putting the economy on a new footing, Deng has managed to avoid the breakdown of authority that has accompanied Gorbachev's *perestroika*. Yet the pull of the liberal idea continues to be very strong as economic power devolves and the economy becomes more open to the outside world. There are currently over 20,000 Chinese students studying in the U.S. and other Western countries, almost all of them the children of the Chinese elite. It is hard to believe that when they return home to run the country they will be content for China to be the only country in Asia unaffected by the larger democratizing trend. The student demonstrations in Beijing that broke out first in December 1986 and recurred recently on the occasion of Hu Yao-bang's death were only the beginning of what will inevitably be mounting pressure for change in the political system as well.

What is important about China from the standpoint of world history is not the present state of the reform or even its future prospects. The central issue is the fact that the People's Republic of China can no longer act as a beacon for illiberal forces around the world, whether they be guerrillas in some Asian jungle or middle class students in Paris. Maoism, rather than being the pattern for Asia's future, became an anachronism, and it was the mainland Chinese who in fact were decisively influenced by the prosperity and dynamism of their overseas co-ethnics—the ironic ultimate victory of Taiwan.

Important as these changes in China have been, however, it is developments in the Soviet Union—the original "homeland of the world proletariat"—that have put the final nail in the coffin of the Marxist-Leninist alternative to liberal democracy. It should be clear that in terms of formal institutions, not much has changed in the four years since Gorbachev has come to power: free markets and the cooperative movement represent only a small part of the Soviet economy, which remains centrally planned; the political system is still dominated by the Communist party which has only begun to democratize internally and to share power with other groups; the regime continues to assert that it is seeking only to modernize socialism and that its ideological basis remains Marxism-Leninism; and, finally, Gorbachev faces a potentially powerful conservative opposition that could undo many of the changes that have taken place to date. Moreover, it is hard to be too sanguine about the chances for success of Gorbachev's proposed reforms, either in the sphere of economics or politics. But my purpose here is not to analyze events in the short-term, or to make predictions for policy purposes, but to look at underlying trends in the sphere of ideology and consciousness. And in that respect, it is clear that an astounding transformation has occurred.

Émigrés from the Soviet Union have been reporting for at least the last generation now that virtually nobody in that country truly believed in Marxism-Leninism any longer, and that this was nowhere more true than in the Soviet elite, which continued to mouth Marxist slogans out of sheer cynicism. The corruption and decadence of the late Brezhnev-era Soviet state seemed to matter little, however for as long as the state itself refused to throw into question any of the fundamental principles underlying Soviet society, the system was capable of functioning adequately out of sheer inertia and could even muster some dynamism in the realm of foreign and defense policy. Marxism-Leninism was like a magical incantation which, however absurd and devoid of meaning, was the only common basis on which the elite could agree to rule Soviet society.

WHAT HAS happened in the four years since Gorbachev's coming to power is a revolutionary assault on the most fundamental institutions and principles of Stalinism, and their replacement by other principles which do not amount to liberalism per se but whose only connecting thread is liberalism. This is most evident in the economic sphere, where the reform economists around Gorbachev have become steadily more radical in their support for free markets, to the point where some like Nikolai Shmelev do not mind being compared in public to Milton Friedman. There is a virtual consensus among the currently dominant school of Soviet economists now that central planning and the command system of allocation are the root cause of economic inefficiency, and that if the Soviet system is ever to heal itself, it must permit free and decentralized decision-making with respect to investment, labor, and prices. After a couple of initial years of ideological confusion, these principles have finally been incorporated into policy with the promulgation of new laws on enterprise autonomy, cooperatives, and finally in 1988 on lease arrangements and family farming. There are, of course, a number of fatal flaws in the current implementation of the reform, most notably the absence of a thoroughgoing price reform. But the problem is no longer a *conceptual* one: Gorbachev and his lieutenants seem to understand the economic logic of marketization well enough, but like the leaders of a Third World country facing the IMF, are afraid of the social consequences of ending consumer subsidies and other forms of dependence on the state sector.

In the political sphere, the proposed changes to the Soviet constitution, legal system, and party rules amount to much less than the establishment of a liberal state. Gorbachev has spoken of democratization primarily in the sphere of internal party affairs, and has shown little intention of ending the Communist party's monopoly of power; indeed, the political reform seeks to legitimize and therefore strengthen the CPSU's rule.[13]

Nonetheless, the general principles underlying many of the reforms—that the "people" should be truly responsible for their own affairs, that higher political bodies should be answerable to

---

13 This is not true in Poland and Hungary, however, whose Communist parties have taken moves toward true power-sharing and pluralism.

lower ones, and not vice versa, that the rule of law should prevail over arbitrary police actions, with separation of powers and an independent judiciary that there should be legal protection for property rights, the need for open discussion of public issues and the right of public dissent, the empowering of the Soviets as a forum in which the whole Soviet people can participate, and of a political culture that is more tolerant and pluralistic—come from a source fundamentally alien to the USSR's Marxist-Leninist tradition, even if they are incompletely articulated and poorly implemented in practice.

Gorbachev's repeated assertions that he is doing no more than trying to restore the original meaning of Leninism are themselves a kind of Orwellian doublespeak. Gorbachev and his allies have consistently maintained that intraparty democracy was somehow the essence of Leninism, and that the various liberal practices of open debate, secret ballot elections, and rule of law were all part of the Leninist heritage, corrupted only later by Stalin. While almost anyone would look good compared to Stalin, drawing so sharp a line between Lenin and his successor is questionable. The essence of Lenin's democratic centralism was centralism, not democracy; that is, the absolutely rigid, monolithic, and disciplined dictatorship of a hierarchically organized vanguard Communist party, speaking in the name of the *demos*. All of Lenin's vicious polemics against Karl Kautsky, Rosa Luxemburg, and various other Menshevik and Social Democratic rivals, not to mention his contempt for "bourgeois legality" and freedoms, centered around his profound conviction that a revolution could not be successfully made by a democratically run organization.

Gorbachev's claim that he is seeking to return to the true Lenin is perfectly easy to understand: having fostered a thorough denunciation of Stalinism and Brezhnevism as the root of the USSR's present predicament, he needs some point in Soviet history on which to anchor the legitimacy of the CPSU's continued rule. But Gorbachev's tactical requirements should not blind us to the fact that the democratizing and decentralizing principles which he has enunciated in both the economic and political spheres are highly subversive of some of the most fundamental precepts of both Marxism and Leninism. Indeed, if the bulk of the present economic reform proposals were put into effect, it is hard to know how the Soviet economy would be more socialist than those of other Western countries with large public sectors.

The Soviet Union could in no way be described as a liberal or democratic country now, nor do I think that it is terribly likely that *perestroika* will succeed such that the label will be thinkable any time in the near future. But at the end of history it is not necessary that all societies become successful liberal societies, merely that they end their ideological pretensions of representing different and higher forms of human society. And in this respect I believe that something very important has happened in the Soviet Union in the past few years: the criticisms of the Soviet system sanctioned by Gorbachev have been so thorough and devastating that there is very little chance of going back to either Stalinism or Brezhnevism in any simple way. Gorbachev has finally permitted people to say what they had privately understood for many years, namely, that the magical incantations of Marxism-Leninism were nonsense, that Soviet socialism was not superior to the West in any respect but was in fact a monumental failure. The conservative opposition in the USSR, consisting both of simple workers afraid of unemployment and inflation and of party officials fearful of losing their jobs and privileges, is outspoken and may be strong enough to force Gorbachev's ouster in the next few years. But what both groups desire is tradition, order, and authority; they manifest no deep commitment to Marxism—Leninism, except insofar as they have invested much of their own lives in it.[14] For authority to be restored in the Soviet Union after Gorbachev's demolition work, it must be on the basis of some new and vigorous ideology which has not yet appeared on the horizon.

IF WE ADMIT for the moment that the fascist and communist challenges to liberalism are dead, are there any other ideological

14. This is particularly true of the leading Soviet conservative, former Second Secretary Yegor Ligachev, who has publicly recognized many of the deep defects of the Brezhnev period.

competitors left? Or put another way, are there contradictions in liberal society beyond that of class that are not resolvable? Two possibilities suggest themselves, those of religion and nationalism.

The rise of religious fundamentalism in recent years within the Christian, Jewish, and Muslim traditions has been widely noted. One is inclined to say that the revival of religion in some way attests to a broad unhappiness with the impersonality and spiritual vacuity of liberal consumerist societies. Yet while the emptiness at the core of liberalism is most certainly a defect in the ideology—indeed, a flaw that one does not need the perspective of religion to recognize[15]—it is not at all clear that it is remediable through politics. Modern liberalism itself was historically a consequence of the weakness of religiously-based societies which, failing to agree on the nature of the good life, could not provide even the minimal preconditions of peace and stability. In the contemporary world only Islam has offered a theocratic state as a political alternative to both liberalism and communism. But the doctrine has little appeal for non-Muslims, and it is hard to believe that the movement will take on any universal significance. Other less organized religious impulses have been successfully satisfied within the sphere of personal life that is permitted in liberal societies.

The other major "contradiction" potentially unresolvable by liberalism is the one posed by nationalism and other forms of racial and ethnic consciousness. It is certainly true that a very large degree of conflict since the Battle of Jena has had its roots in nationalism. Two cataclysmic world wars in this century have been spawned by the nationalism of the developed world in various guises, and if those passions have been muted to a certain extent in postwar Europe, they are still extremely powerful in the Third World. Nationalism has been a threat to liberalism historically in Germany, and continues to be one in isolated parts of "posthistorical" Europe like Northern Ireland.

But it is not clear that nationalism represents an irreconcilable

---

15 I am thinking particularly of Rousseau and the Western philosophical tradition that flows from him that was highly critical of Lockean or Hobbesian liberalism, though one could criticize liberalism from the standpoint of classical political philosophy as well.

contradiction in the heart of liberalism. In the first place, nationalism is not one single phenomenon but several, ranging from mild cultural nostalgia to the highly organized and elaborately articulated doctrine of National Socialism. Only systematic nationalisms of the latter sort can qualify as a formal ideology on the level of liberalism or communism. The vast majority of the world's nationalist movements do not have a political program beyond the negative desire of independence from some other group or people, and do not offer anything like a comprehensive agenda for socioeconomic organization. As such, they are compatible with doctrines and ideologies that do offer such agendas. While they may constitute a source of conflict for liberal societies, this conflict does not arise from liberalism itself so much as from the fact that the liberalism in question is incomplete. Certainly a great deal of the world's ethnic and nationalist tension can be explained in terms of peoples who are forced to live in unrepresentative political systems that they have not chosen.

While it is impossible to rule out the sudden appearance of new ideologies or previously unrecognized contradictions in liberal societies, then, the present world seems to confirm that the fundamental principles of socio-political organization have not advanced terribly far since 1806. Many of the wars and revolutions fought since that time have been undertaken in the name of ideologies which claimed to be more advanced than liberalism, but whose pretensions were ultimately unmasked by history. In the meantime, they have helped to spread the universal homogenous state to the point where it could have a significant effect on the overall character of international relations.

IV

WHAT ARE the implications of the end of history for international relations? Clearly, the vast bulk of the Third World remains very much mired in history, and will be a terrain of conflict for many years to come. But let us focus for the time being on the larger and more developed states of the world who after all account for the greater part of world politics. Russia and China are not likely to join the developed nations of the West as liberal societies any time in the foreseeable future, but suppose for a moment that Marxism-Leninism ceases to be a factor driving the foreign policies of these states—a prospect which, if not yet here, the last few years have made a real possibility. How will the overall characteristics of a de-ideologized world differ from those of the one with which we are familiar at such a hypothetical juncture?

The most common answer is—not very much. For there is a very widespread belief among many observers of international relations that underneath the skin of ideology is a hard core of great power national interest that guarantees a fairly high level of competition and conflict between nations.

Indeed, according to one academically popular school of international relations theory, conflict inheres in the international system as such, and to understand the prospects for conflict one must look at the shape of the system—for example, whether it is bipolar or multipolar—rather than at the specific character of the nations and regimes that constitute it. This school in effect applies a Hobbesian view of politics to international relations, and assumes that aggression and insecurity are universal characteristics of human societies rather than the product of specific historical circumstances.

Believers in this line of thought take the relations that existed between the participants in the classical nineteenth-century European balance of power as a model for what a de-ideologized contemporary world would look like. Charles Krauthammer, for example, recently explained that if as a result of Gorbachev's reforms the USSR is shorn of Marxist-Leninist ideology, its behavior will revert to that of nineteenth century imperial Russia.[16] While he finds this more reassuring than the threat posed by a communist Russia, he implies that there will still be a substantial degree of competition and conflict in the international system, just as there was say between Russia and Britain or Wilhelmine Germany in the last century. This is, of course, a convenient point of view for people who want to admit that

---

16. See his article, "Beyond the Cold War," *New Republic*, December 19, 1988.

something major is changing in the Soviet Union, but do not want to accept responsibility for recommending the radical policy redirection implicit in such a view. But is it true?

In fact, the notion that ideology is a superstructure imposed on a substratum of permanent great power interest is a highly questionable proposition. For the way in which any state defines its national interest is not universal but rests on some kind of prior ideological basis, just as we saw that economic behavior is determined by a prior state of consciousness. In this century, states have adopted highly articulated doctrines with explicit foreign policy agendas legitimizing expansionism, like Marxism-Leninism or National Socialism.

THE EXPANSIONIST and competitive behavior of nineteenth-century European states rested on no less ideal a basis; it just so happened that the ideology driving it was less explicit than the doctrines of the twentieth century. For one thing, most "liberal" European societies were illiberal insofar as they believed in the legitimacy of imperialism, that is, the right of one nation to rule over other nations without regard for the wishes of the ruled. The justifications for imperialism varied from nation to nation, from a crude belief in the legitimacy of force, particularly when applied to non-Europeans, to the White Man's Burden and Europe's Christianizing mission, to the desire to give people of color access to the culture of Rabelais and Molière. But whatever the particular ideological basis, every "developed" country believed in the acceptability of higher civilizations ruling lower ones—including, incidentally, the United States with regard to the Philippines. This led to a drive for pure territorial aggrandizement in the latter half of the century and played no small role in causing the Great War.

The radical and deformed outgrowth of nineteenth-century imperialism was German fascism, an ideology which justified Germany's right not only to rule over non-European peoples, but over *all* non-German ones. But in retrospect it seems that Hitler represented a diseased by-path in the general course of European development, and since his fiery defeat, the legitimacy of any kind of territorial aggrandizement has been thoroughly discredited.[17] Since the Second World War, European nationalism has been defanged and shorn of any real relevance to foreign policy, with the consequence that the nineteenth-century model of great power behavior has become a serious anachronism. The most extreme form of nationalism that any Western European state has mustered since 1945 has been Gaullism, whose self-assertion has been confined largely to the realm of nuisance politics and culture. International life for the part of the world that has reached the end of history is far more preoccupied with economics than with politics or strategy.

The developed states of the West do maintain defense establishments and in the postwar period have competed vigorously for influence to meet a worldwide communist threat. This behavior has been driven, however, by an external threat from states that possess overtly expansionist ideologies, and would not exist in their absence. To take the "neo-realist" theory seriously, one would have to believe that "natural" competitive behavior would reassert itself among the OECD states were Russia and China to disappear from the face of the earth. That is, West Germany and France would arm themselves against each other as they did in the 1930s, Australia and New Zealand would send military advisers to block each others' advances in Africa, and the U.S.-Canadian border would become fortified. Such a prospect is, of course, ludicrous: minus Marxist-Leninist ideology we are far more likely to see the "Common Marketization" of world politics than the disintegration of the EEC into nineteenth-century competitiveness. Indeed, as our experience in dealing with Europe on matters such as terrorism or Libya prove, they are much further gone than we down the road that denies the legitimacy of the use of force in international politics, even in self-defense.

The automatic assumption that Russia shorn of its expansionist communist ideology should pick up where the czars left off just prior to the Bolshevik Revolution is therefore a curious one. It assumes that the evolution of human consciousness has stood still in the meantime,

---

17. It took European colonial powers like France several years after the war to admit the illegitimacy of their empires, but decolonialization was an inevitable consequence of the Allied victory, which had been based on the promise of a restoration of democratic freedoms.

Francis Fukuyama

and that the Soviets, while picking up currently fashionable ideas in the realm of economics, will return to foreign policy views a century out of date in the rest of Europe. This is certainly not what happened to China after it began its reform process. Chinese competitiveness and expansionism on the world scene have virtually disappeared: Beijing no longer sponsors Maoist insurgencies or tries to cultivate influence in distant African countries as it did in the 1960s. This is not to say that there are not troublesome aspects to contemporary Chinese foreign policy, such as the reckless sale of ballistic missile technology in the Middle East; and the PRC continues to manifest traditional great power behavior in its sponsorship of the Khmer Rouge against Vietnam. But the former is explained by commercial motives and the latter is a vestige of earlier ideologically-based rivalries. The new China far more resembles Gaullist France than pre-World War I Germany.

The real question for the future, however, is the degree to which Soviet elites have assimilated the consciousness of the universal homogenous state that is post-Hitler Europe. From their writings and from my own personal contacts with them, there is no question in my mind that the liberal Soviet intelligentsia rallying around Gorbachev has arrived at the end-of-history view in a remarkably short time, due in no small measure to the contacts they have had since the Brezhnev era with the larger European civilization around them. "New political thinking," the general rubric for their views, describes a world dominated by economic concerns, in which there are no ideological grounds for major conflict between nations, and in which, consequently, the use of military force becomes less legitimate. As Foreign Minister Shevardnadze put it in mid-1988:

> The struggle between two opposing systems is no longer a determining tendency of the present-day era. At the modern stage, the ability to build up material wealth at an accelerated rate on the basis of front-ranking science and high-level techniques and technology, and to distribute it fairly, and through joint efforts to restore and protect the resources necessary for mankind's survival acquires decisive importance.[18]

18. *Vestnik Ministertva Inostrannikh Del SSSR* no.15 (August 1988), pp.27-46. "New thinking" does of course serve a propagandistic purpose in persuading Western audiences of Soviet good intentions. But the fact that it is good propaganda does not mean that its formulators do not take many of its ideas seriously.

THE POST-HISTORICAL CONSCIOUSNESS represented by "new thinking" is only one possible future for the Soviet Union, however. There has always been a very strong current of great Russian chauvinism in the Soviet Union, which has found freer expression since the advent of glasnost. It may be possible to return to traditional Marxism-Leninism for a while as a simple rallying point for those who want to restore the authority that Gorbachev has dissipated. But as in Poland, Marxism-Leninism is dead as a mobilizing ideology: under its banner people cannot be made to work harder, and its adherents have lost confidence in themselves. Unlike the propagators of traditional Marxism-Leninism, however, ultranationalists in the USSR believe in their Slavophile cause passionately, and one gets the sense that the fascist alternative is not one that has played itself out entirely there.

The Soviet Union, then, is at a fork in the road: it can start down the path that was staked out by Western Europe forty-five years ago, a path that most of Asia has followed, or it can realize its own uniqueness and remain stuck in history. The choice it makes will be highly important for us, given the Soviet Union's size and military strength, for that power will continue to preoccupy us and slow our realization that we have already emerged on the other side of history.

V

THE PASSING OF MARXISM-LENINISM first from China and then from the Soviet Union will mean its death as a living ideology of world historical significance. For while there may be some isolated true believers left in places like Managua, Pyongyang, or Cambridge, Massachusetts, the fact that there is not a single large state in which it is a going concern undermines completely its pretensions to being in the vanguard of human history. And the death of this ideology means the growing "Common Marketization" of international relations, and the diminution of the likelihood of large-scale conflict between states.

This does not by any means imply the end of international conflict *per se*. For the world at that point would be divided between a part that was historical and a part that was post-histori-cal. Conflict between states still in history and between those states and those at the end of history, would still be possible. There would still be a high and perhaps rising level of ethnic and nation-alist violence, since those are impulses incompletely played out, even in parts of the post-historical world. Palestinians and Kurds, Sikhs and Tamils, Irish Catholics and Walloons, Armenians and Azeris, will continue to have their unresolved grievances. This implies that terrorism and wars of national liberation will continue to be an important item on the international agenda. But large-scale conflict must involve large states still caught in the grip of history, and they are what appear to be passing from the scene.

The end of history will be a very sad time. The struggle for recognition, the willingness to risk one's life for a purely abstract goal, the worldwide ideological struggle that called forth daring, courage, imagination, and idealism, will be replaced by economic calculation, the endless solving of technical problems, environmen-tal concerns, and the satisfaction of sophisticated consumer demands. In the post-historical period there will be neither art nor philosophy, just the perpetual caretaking of the museum of human history. I can feel in myself, and see in others around me, a power-ful nostalgia for the time when history existed. Such nostalgia, in fact, will continue to fuel competition and conflict even in the post-historical world for some time to come. Even though I recog-nize its inevitability, I have the most ambivalent feelings for the civilization that has been created in Europe since 1945, with its north Atlantic and Asian offshoots. Perhaps this very prospect of centuries of boredom at the end of history will serve to get history started once again.

No Exit:
The Errors of Endism

Samuel P. Huntington

FOR A SECOND YEAR serious discussion of international affairs has been dominated by a major theoretical and academic issue. In 1988 the issue was American declines. The theory of declinism, articulated by many thinkers, but most notably by Paul Kennedy, became the focus of extended and intense debate. Was the United States following in the path of Great Britain and declining as a great power? To what extent was its economic base being undermined by spending too much on defense and/or too much on consumption?

The major issue in 1989 is very different. The theory of declinism has been displaced by the theory of endism. Its central element is that bad things are coming to an end.[1] Endism manifests itself in at least three ways. At its most specific level, endism hails the end of the Cold War. In the spring of 1989 the *New York Times* and International Institute for Strategic Studies, George Kennan and George Bush, all set forth this proposition in one form or another. The end of the Cold War became the Foreign Policy Establishment's Established Truth.

At a second level, endism manifested itself in the more academic and more general proposition that wars among nation states, or at least among some types of nation states, were coming to an end. Many scholars pointed to the historical absence of wars

SAMUEL P. HUNTINGTON is the Eaton Professor of the Science of Government and Director of the John M. Olin Institute for Strategic Studies at Harvard University. This article originally appeared in the Fall 1989 issue of *The National Interest* Copyright © 1989 by National Affairs, Inc.

between democratic countries and saw the multiplication of democratic regimes since 1974 as evidence that the probability of war was declining. In a related but somewhat different version of this proposition, Michael Doyle argued that wars were impossible between liberal states. In a still more sweeping formulation, John Mueller contended that the advance of civilization was making war obsolescent and that it would disappear the same way that slavery and dueling had disappeared in advanced societies.[2] Wars still might occur among backward third world countries, but among developed countries, communist or capitalist, war was unthinkable.

The third and most extreme formulation of endism was advanced by Francis Fukuyama in a brilliant essay called "The End of History?" in the Summer issue of this journal. Fukuyama celebrates not just the end of the Cold War or the end of wars among developed nation states, but instead "the end of history as such." This results from the "unabashed victory of economic and political liberalism" and the exhaustion of viable systematic alternatives." Like Mueller, Fukuyama concedes that wars may occur among Third World states still caught up in the historical process. But for the developed countries, the Soviet Union, and China, history is at an end.

1. Some have raised the question as to what extent endist writers are really serious in their arguments. The time and intellectual effort they have devoted to elaborating those arguments suggest that they are, and I will assume this to be the case. The arguments also deserve to be taken seriously because of their widespread popularity.

2. Michael W. Doyle, "Kant, Liberal Legacies, and Foreign Affairs," *Philosophy and Public Affairs,* vol. 12 (Summer, Fall 1983), pp.205-235, 323-353, and "Liberalism and World Politics," *American Political Science Review,* vol. 80 (December 1986), pp.1151-1169; John Mueller, *Retreat from Doomsday; The Obsolescence of Major War* (New York: Basic Books, 1989). Also see Dean V. Babst, "A Force for Peace," *Industrial Research,* vol. 14 (April 1972), pp.55-58; R.J. Rummel, "Libertarianism and International Violence, "*Journal of Conflict Resolution,* vol. 27 (March 1983), pp.27-71; Ze'ev Maoz and Nasrin Abdolali, "Regime Types and International Conflict, 1816-1976, *Journal of Conflict Resolution,* vol. 33 (March 1989), pp.3-35; Bruce Russett, "The Politics of an Alternative Security System: Toward a More Democratic and Therefore More Peaceful World," in Burns Weston, ed., *Alternatives to Nuclear Deterrence* (Boulder: Westview Press, 1989).

No Exit: The Errors of Endism

Endism—the intellectual fad of 1989—contrasts rather dramatically with declinism—the intellectual fad of 1988. Declinism is conditionally pessimistic. It is rooted in the study of history and draws on the parallels between the United States in the late twentieth century, Britain in the late nineteenth century, and France, Spain, and other powers in earlier centuries. Its proponents and its critics debate the relevance of these parallels and argue over detailed, historical data concerning economic growth, productivity, defense spending, savings, and investment.[3] Endism, on the other hand, is oriented to the future rather than the past and is unabashedly optimistic. In its most developed form, as with Fukuyama, it is rooted in philosophical speculation rather than historical analysis. It is based not so much on evidence from history as on assumptions about history. In its extreme form, declinism is historically deterministic: nations naturally, and perhaps inevitably, evolve through phases of rise, expansion, and decline. They are caught in the inexorable grip of history. In the extreme form of endism, in contrast, nations escape from history.

The message of declinism for Americans is "We're losing"; the message of endism is "We've won!" Despite or perhaps even because of its deterministic strand, declinism performs a useful historical function. It provides a warning and a goad to action in order to head off and reverse the decline that it says is taking place. It serves that purpose now as it did in its earlier manifestations in the 1950s, 1960s, and 1970s. Endism, in contrast, provides not a warning of danger but an illusion of well-being. It invites not corrective action but relaxed complacency. The consequences of its thesis being in error, hence, are far more dangerous and subversive than those that would result if the declinist thesis should be wrong.

"The Cold War is over" was the prevailing cry in the spring of 1989. What does this mean? It is typically referred to two related developments: the changes usually referred to as *glasnost* and *perestroika* in the Soviet Union and the improvements that were occur-

---

3. For a careful analysis of the evidence and arguments on this issue, see Joseph S. Nye, Jr.'s forthcoming book, *American Power: Past and Future* (New York: Basic Books).

Samuel P. Huntington

ring in Soviet-American relations. "The cold war," as the *New York Times* put it, "of poisonous Soviet-American feelings, of domestic political hysteria, of events enlarged and distorted by East-West confrontation, of almost perpetual diplomatic deadlock is over."[4] Several questions can be raised about this proposition.

First, is it really true? The easing in Soviet-American relations in the late 1950s was followed by the Berlin and Cuban crises; détente in the early 1970s was followed by Angola and Afghanistan. How do we know that the current relaxation is not simply another swing of the cycle? One answer is that the changes occurring within the Soviet Union are far more fundamental than those that have occurred in the past, and this is certainly the case. The opening up of political debate, limited but real competition in elections, the formation of political groups outside the Party, the virtual abandonment, indeed, of the idea of a monolithic party, the assertion of power by the Supreme Soviet—all these will, if continued, lead to a drastically different Soviet political system. The price of attempting to reverse them increase daily, but it would be rash to conclude that they are as yet irreversible, and the costs of reversing them could decline in the future. On the international level, the Soviets have cooperated in resolving regional conflicts in the Persian Gulf, southern Africa, and Indochina. They have promised to reduce their overall military forces and their deployments in Eastern Europe. As yet, however, no perceptible changes have taken place in Soviet force structure, Soviet deployments, or Soviet output of military equipment. Even if these do occur, the competition between the United States and the Soviet Union for influence and power in world affairs will still go on. It has been continuing as President Bush and President Gorbachev attempt to woo Eastern and Western European publics. Europe, it is well to remember, is where the Cold War started. It is the overwhelming preeminent stake in the Cold War, and Gorbachev's public relations can be as much a threat to American interests in Europe as were Brezhnev's tanks (which, for the moment at any rate, Gorbachev also has).

---

4. "The Cold War Is Over," *The New York Times*, April 2, 1989, p. E30.

No Exit: The Errors of Endism

Let us, however concede that in some meaningful and not transitory sense the Cold War is over and that a real change has occurred in Soviet-American relations. How do the proponents of this thesis see the post-Cold War world? The "we-they world" that has existed, the editors of the *New York Times* assure us, is giving way "to the more traditional struggles of great powers." In a similar vein, George Kennan alleges that the Soviet Union "should now be regarded essentially as another great power, like other great powers." Its interests may differ from ours but these differences can be "adjusted by the normal means of compromise and accommodation."[5]

Russia was, however, just "another great power" for several centuries before it became a communist state. As a great power, Russia frequently deployed its armies into Europe and repeatedly crushed popular uprisings in central Europe. Soviet troops bloodily suppressed the Hungarian Revolution in 1956 and trampled the embryonic Czech democracy in 1968. Russian troops bloodily suppressed the Hungarian revolution of 1848-49 and violently put down uprisings in Poland in 1831 and again in 1863-4. Soviet forces occupied Berlin in 1945; Russian troops occupied and burnt Berlin in 1760. In pursuit of Russia's interests as a great power, Russian troops appeared many places where as yet Soviet troops have not. In 1799 Russian troops occupied Milan and Turin and fought a battle on the outskirts of Zurich. The same year, they occupied the Ionian islands off Greece and stayed there until 1907. These excursions preceded Napoleon's invasion of Russian. As a great power, Russia regularly participated in the partitions of Poland. In 1914 Nicholas II directly ruled more of Europe (including most of Poland) than Gorbachev does today.

The past record of Russia as a "normal" great power, therefore, is not reassuring for either the liberty of Eastern Europe or the security of Western Europe. Some suggest that the liberalizing and democratizing trends in the Soviet Union will prevent that country from bludgeoning other countries in the manner of the tsars. One cannot assume, Fukuyama argues, that "the evolution of

---

5. "Just Another Great Power," *The New York Times*, April 9, 1989 p. E25.

human consciousness has stood still" and that "the Soviets will return to foreign policy views a century out of date in the rest of Europe." Fukuyama is right: one cannot assume that the Soviets will revert to the bad old ways of the past. One also cannot assume that they will not. Gorbachev may be able to discard communism but he cannot discard geography and the geopolitical imperatives that have shaped Russian and Soviet behavior for centuries. And, as any Latin American will quickly point out, even a truly democratic superpower is capable of intervening militarily in the affairs of its smaller neighbors.

The era of the Cold War, John Lewis Gaddis reminds us, has also been the ear of the Long Peace, the longest period in history without hot war between major powers. Does the end of the Cold War mean the end of the Long Peace? Two central elements of both have been bipolarity and nuclear weapons: they have in considerable measure defined both the Soviet-American rivalry and its limits. The end of the Cold War will mean a loosening of bipolarity even if it does not mean, as some declinists predict, a world of five or more roughly equal major powers. The delegitimation of nuclear weapons and the increasing constraints on their deployment and potential use could increase the probability of conventional war.

Active American involvement in world affairs has been substantially limited to two world wars and one prolonged and ideologically drive cold war. In the absence of Kaiser, Hitler, Stalin, and Brezhnev, the American inclination may well be to relax and to assume that peace, goodwill, and international cooperation will prevail: that if the Cold War is over, American relations with the Soviet Union will be similar to its relations with Canada, France, or Japan. Americans tend to see competition and conflict as normal and even desirable features of the domestic economy and politics and yet perversely assume them to be abnormal and undesirable in relations among states. In fact, however, the history of the relations among great powers, when it has not been the history of hot wars, has usually been the history of cold wars.

The end of the Cold War does not mean the end of political, ideological, diplomatic, economic, technological, or even military rivalry among nations. It does not mean the end of the struggle for power and influence. It very probably does mean increased insta-bility, unpredictability, and violence in international affairs. It could mean the end of the Long Peace.

THE END OF WAR

A SECOND manifestation of endism postulates the end of war between certain types of nation states. A number of authors, includ-ing Dean V. Babst, R.J. Rummel, and Bruce Russett, have pointed to the fact that no significant interstate wars have occurred between democratic regimes since the emergence of such regimes in the early nineteenth century. Michael Doyle has similarly argued that a "pacific union" exists among liberal regimes (which includes and is slightly broader that the class of democratic regimes, as defined by most scholars. *"[C]onstitutionally secure liberal states,"* he says, *have yet to engage in war with each other. Even threats of war have been regarded as illegitimate."*

Given the large number of wars between non-democratic regimes and between democratic regimes and non-democratic regimes, the almost total absence of armed conflict between demo-cratic regimes is indeed striking. It is, as Bruce Russett says, "per-haps the strongest non-trivial or non-tautological statement that can be made about international relations." It is also plausible to believe that this absence of war may stem from the nature of the regime. Democracy is a means for the peaceful resolution of dis-putes, involving negotiation and compromise as well as elections and voting. The leaders of democracies may well expect that they ought to be able to resolve through peaceful means their differences with the leaders of other democracies. In the years since World War II, for instance, several conflicts which could or did lead to war between countries tended to moderate when the countries became democratic. The controversies between Britain and Argentina, Guatemala, and Spain over the remnants of empire (one of deploy-ment) moderated considerably when those three countries became democratic. The conflict between Greece and Turkey similarly seemed to ease in the 1980s after both countries had democratically elected regimes.

The democratic "zone of peace" is a dramatic historical phenomenon. If that relationship continues to hold and if democracy continues to spread, wars should become less frequent in the future than they have been in the past. This is one endist argument that has a strong empirical base. Three qualifications have to be noted, however, to its implications for the end of war.

First, democracies are still a minority among the world's regimes. The 1989 Freedom House survey classified 60 out of 167 sovereign states as "free" according to its rather generous definition of freedom. Multiple possibilities for war thus continue to exist among the 197 states that are not free, and between those states and the democratic states.

Second, the number of democratic states has been growing, but it tends to grow irregularly in a two-step forward, one-step backward pattern. A major wave of democratization occurred in the nineteenth century, but then significant reversals to authoritarianism took place in the 1920s and 1930s. A second wave of democratization after World War II was followed by several reversals in the 1960s and 1970s. A third wave of democratization began in 1974, with fifteen to twenty countries shifting in a democratic direction since then. If the previous pattern prevails, some of these new democracies are likely to revert to authoritarianism. Hence, the possibility of war could increase rather than decrease in the immediate future, although still remaining less than it was prior to 1974.

Finally, peace among democratic states could be related to extraneous accidental factors and not to the nature of democracy. In the nineteenth century, for instance, wars tended to occur between geographical neighbors. Democratic states were few in number and seldom bordered on each other. Hence the absence of war could be caused by the absence of propinquity.[6] Since World War II most democratic countries have been members of the alliance system led by the United States, which has been directed against an alliance of non-democratic regimes and within which

6. See J. David Singer and Melvin Small, "The War-Proneness of Democratic Regimes, 1815-1965," *Jerusalem Journal of International Relations*, vol. I (Summer 1976), p.67.

the hegemonic position of the U.S. has precluded war between other alliance members (e.g., between Greece and Turkey). If American leadership weakens and the alliance system loosens, the probability of war between its erstwhile members, democratic or otherwise, could well increase.

The "democratic zone of peace" argument is thus valid as far as it goes, but it may not go all that far. In his book, *Retreat from Doomsday*, John Mueller argues for the growing obsolescence of war on more general grounds. He sees the Long Peace since 1945 not as the result of bipolarity or nuclear weapons but rather as the result of a learning experience that wars do not pay and that there are few conflicts of interest among countries where it would be reasonable for either side to resort to war to achieve its goals. World War II was an aberration from the twentieth-century trend away from war due largely to the idiosyncratic and irrational personality of Hitler. As countries become more developed and civilized, they will become more peaceful. Denmark is the future model for individual countries, U.S.-Canadian relations the future model for relations between countries.

Mueller make much of the argument that war will become "obsolete, subrationally unthinkable," and unacceptable in civilized society in the way slavery and dueling have become. Why not murder? Murder has been unacceptable in civilized societies for millennia, and yet it seems unlikely that the murder rate in twentieth-century New York is less than it was in fifth-century Athens. While major wars between developed countries have not occurred since World War II, interstate and intrastate violence has been widespread with casualties numbering in the tens of millions.

Mueller himself substantially qualifies his case. He agrees that wars will continue among less developed countries. He also concedes that irrational leaders on the Hitler model could involve their countries in future wars. Economic considerations motivate strongly against war, he says, but economic prosperity "is not always an overriding goal even now." Territorial issues exist even in the developed world that "could lead to wars of expansion or territorial readjustments." The Cold War is being resolved peacefully, "but there is no firm guarantee that this trend will continue."

A more general problem may also exist with the end-of-war or even a decline-in-war thesis. As Michimi Muranushi of Yale has pointed out, peace can be self-limiting rather than cumulative. If relations between two countries become more peaceful, this may, in some circumstances, increase the probability that either or both of those countries will go to war with a third country. The Hitler-Stalin pact paves the way for the attacks on Poland; normalization of U.S.-China relations precipitates China's war with Vietnam. If the Soviet threat disappears so also does an inhibitor of Greek-Turkish war.

In addition, if more countries become like Denmark, forswearing war and committing themselves to material comfort, that in itself may produce a situation which other countries will wish to exploit. History is full of examples of leaner, meaner societies overrunning richer, less martial ones.

THE END OF HISTORY

"The end of history" is a sweeping, dramatic, and provocative phrase. What does Fukuyama mean by it? The heart of Fukuyama's argument is an alleged change in political consciousness throughout the principal societies in the world and the emergence of a pervasive consensus on liberal-democratic principles. It posits the triumph of one ideology and the consequent end of ideology and ideological conflict as significant factors in human existence. His choice of language suggests, however, that he may have something more sweeping in mind that simply the obsolescence of war highlighted by Mueller or the end of ideology predicted by Daniel Bell twenty-five years ago.

Insofar as it is focused on war, Fukuyama's argument suffers all the weakness that Mueller's does. He admits that "conflict between states still in history, and between those states and those at the end of history, would still be possible." At the same time he includes China and the Soviet Union among those states that are out of history. Current Soviet leaders, he says, have arrived at the "end-of-history view" and "assimilated the consciousness of the universal homogenous state that is post-Hitler Europe"; yet he also admits that the Soviet Union could turn to Slavophile Russian chauvinism and thus remain stuck in history.

No Exit: The Errors of Endism

Fukuyama ridicules the idea that Germany and France might fight each other again. That is a valid but irrelevant point. A hundred years ago one could have validly made the point the Pennsylvania and Virginia would not fight each other again. That did not prevent the United States, of which each was a part, from engaging in world wars in the subsequent century. One trend in history is the amalgamation of smaller units into larger ones. The probability of war between the smaller unit declines but the probability of war between the larger amalgamated units does not necessarily change. A united European community may end the possibility of Franco-German; war it does not end the possibility of war between that community and other political units.

With respect to China, Fukuyama argues that "Chinese competitiveness and expansionism on the world scene have virtually disappeared" and, he implies strongly, will not reappear. A more persuasive argument, however, could be made for exactly the opposite proposition that Chinese expansionism has yet to appear on the world scene. Britain and France, Germany and Japan, the United States and the Soviet Union, all became expansionist and imperialist powers in the course of industrialization. China is just beginning seriously to develop its industrial strength Maybe China will be different from all the other major powers and not attempt to expand its influence and control as it industrializes. But how can one be confident that it will pursue this deviant course? And if it follows the more familiar pattern, a billion Chinese engaged in imperial expansion are likely to impose a lot of history on the rest of the world.

Fukuyama quite appropriately emphasizes the role of consciousness, ideas, and ideology in motivating and shaping the actions of men and nations. He is also right in pointing to the virtual end of the appeal of communism as an ideology. Ideologically, communism has been "the grand failure" that Brzezinski labels it. It is erroneous, however, to jump from the decline of communism to the global triumph of liberalism and the disappearance of ideology as a force in world affairs.

First, revivals are possible. A set of ideas or an ideology may fade from the scene in one generation only to reappear with renewed strength a generation or two later. From the 1940s to the 1960s, dominant currents in economic thinking were Keynesianism, welfare statism, social democracy, and planning. It was hard to find much support for classical economic liberalism. By the late 1970s, however, the latter had staged an amazing comeback: economists and economic institutions were devoted to The Plan in the 1950s; they have been devoted to The Market in the 1980s. Somewhat similarly, social scientists in the decades immediately after World War II argued that religion, ethnic consciousness, and nationalism would all be done in by economic development and modernization. But in the 1980s these have been the dominant bases of political action in most societies. The revival of religion is now a global phenomenon. Communism maybe be down for the moment, but it is rash to assume that it is out for all time.

Second, the universal acceptance of liberal democracy does not preclude conflicts within liberalism. The history of ideology is the history of schism. Struggles between those who profess different versions of a common ideology are often more intense and vicious than struggles between those espousing entirely different ideologies. To a believer the heretic is worse than the nonbeliever. An ideological consensus on Christianity existed in Europe in 1500 but that did not prevent Protestants and Catholics from slaughtering each other for the next century and a half. Socialists and communists, Trotskyites and Leninists, Shi'ites and Sunnis have treated each other in similar fashion.

Third, the triumph of one ideology does not preclude the emergence of new ideologies. Nations and societies presumably will continue to evolve. New challenges to human well-being will emerge, and people will develop new concepts, theories, and ideologies as to how those challenges should be met. Unless all social, economic and political distinctions disappear, people will also develop belief systems that legitimatize what they have and justify their getting more. Among its other functions, for instance, communism historically legitimized the power of intellectuals and bureaucrats. If it is gone for good, it seems highly likely that intellectuals and bureaucrats will develop new sets of ideas to rationalize their claims to power and wealth.

Fourth, has liberal democracy really triumphed? Fukuyama admits that it has not won out in the Third World. To what extent, however, has it really been accepted in the Soviet Union and China? Between them these societies encompass well over one quarter of the world's population. If any one trend is operative in the world today it is for societies to turn back toward their traditional cultures, values, and patterns of behavior. This trend is manifest in the revival of traditional identities and characters of Eastern European countries, escaping from the deadly uniformity of Soviet-imposed communism and also in the increasing differentiation among the republics within the Soviet Union itself. Russia and China do not lack elements of liberalism and democracy in their histories. These are, however, minor chords, and their subordinate importance is underlined by the contemporary problems facing economic liberalism in the Soviet Union and political democracy in communist China.

More generally, Fukuyama's thesis itself reflects not the disappearance of Marxism but its pervasiveness. His image of the end of history is straight from Marx. Fukuyama speaks of the "universal homogenous state," in which "all prior contradictions are resolved and all human needs are satisfied." What is this but the Marxist image of a society without class conflict or other contradictions organized on the basis of from each according to his abilities and to each according to his needs? The struggles of history, Fukuyama says, "will be replaced by economic calculation, the endless solving of technical problems, environmental concerns, and the satisfaction of sophisticated consumer demands." Engels said it even more succinctly: "The government of persons is replaced by the administration of things and the direction of the process of production." Fukuyama says liberalism is the end of history. Marx says communism "is the solution to the riddle of history." They are basically saying the same thing and, most importantly, they are thinking the same way. Marxist ideology is alive and well in Fukuyama's arguments to refute it.

TWO FALLACIES

THE SOVIET UNION is increasingly preoccupied with its own problems and a significant political loosening has occurred in that country. The ideological intensity of the early Cold War has virtually disappeared, and the probability of hot war between the two superpowers is as low as it has ever been. War is even more unlikely between any of the advanced industrialized democracies. On these points, endist propositions are accurate. The more extensive formulations of the endist argument, however, suffer from two basic fallacies.

First, endism overemphasizes the predictability of history and the permanence of the moment. Current trends may or may not continue into the future. Past experience certainly suggests that they are unlikely to do so. The record of past predictions by social scientists is not a happy one. Fifteen years ago, just as the democratic wave was beginning, political analysts were elaborating fundamental reasons why authoritarianism had to prevail in the Third World. Ten years ago foreign policy journals filled with warnings of the rise of Soviet military power and political influence throughout the world. Five years ago what analyst of the Soviet Union predicted the extent of the political changes that have occurred in that country? Given the limitations of human foresight, endist predictions of the end of the war and ideological conflict deserve a heavy dose of skepticism. Indeed, in the benign atmosphere of the moment, it is sobering to speculate on the possible future horrors that social analysts are now failing to predict.

Second, endism tends to ignore the weakness and irrationality of human nature. Endist arguments often assume that because it would be rational for human beings to focus on their economic well-being, they will act in that way, and therefore they will not engage in wars that do not meet the tests of cost-benefit analysis or in ideological conflicts that are much ado about nothing. Human beings are at times rational, generous, creative, and wise, but they are also stupid, selfish, cruel, and sinful. The struggle that is history began with the eating of the forbidden fruit and is rooted in human nature. In history there maybe total defeats, but there are no final solutions. So long as human beings exist, there is no exits from the traumas of history.

To hope for the benign end of history is human. To expect it to happen is unrealistic. To plan on it happening is disastrous.

The Clash of Civilizations?

Samuel P. Huntington

THE NEXT PATTERN OF CONFLICT

WORLD POLITICS IS entering a new phase, and intellectuals have not hesitated to proliferate visions of what it will be—the end of history, the return of traditional rivalries between nation states, and the decline of the nation state from the conflicting pulls of tribalism and globalism, among others. Each of these visions catches aspects of the emerging reality. Yet they all miss a crucial, indeed a central, aspect of what global politics is likely to be in the coming years.

It is my hypothesis that the fundamental source of conflict in this new world will not be primarily ideological or primarily economic. The great divisions among humankind and the dominating source of conflict will be cultural. Nation states will remain the most powerful actors in world affairs, but the principal conflicts of global politics will occur between nations and groups of different civilizations. The clash of civilizations will dominate global politics. The fault lines between civilizations will be the battle lines of the future.

Conflict between civilizations will be the latest phase in the evolution of conflict in the modern world. For a century and a half after the emergence of the modern international system with the Peace of Westphalia, the conflicts of the Western world were

SAMUEL P. HUNTINGTON is the Eaton Professor of the Science of Government and Director of the John M. Olin Institute for Strategic Studies at Harvard University. This article is the product of the Olin Institute's project on "The Changing Security Environment and American National Interests." This article originally published in the Summer 1993 issue of *Foreign Affairs* © 1993 by the Council on Foreign Relations.

largely among princes—emperors, absolute monarchs and constitutional monarchs attempting to expand their bureaucracies, their armies, their mercantilist economic strength and, most important, the territory they ruled. In the process they created nation states, and beginning with the French Revolution the principal lines of conflict were between nations rather than princes. In 1793, as R. R. Palmer put it, "The wars of kings were over; the wars of peoples had begun." This nineteenth-century pattern lasted until the end of World War I. Then, as a result of the Russian Revolution and the reaction against it, the conflict of nations yielded to the conflict of ideologies, first among communism, fascism-Nazism and liberal democracy, and then between communism and liberal democracy. During the Cold War, this latter conflict became embodied in the struggle between the two superpowers, neither of which was a nation state in the classical European sense and each of which defined its identity in terms of its ideology.

These conflicts between princes, nation states and ideologies were primarily conflicts within Western civilization, "Western civil wars," as William Lind has labeled them. This was as true of the Cold War as it was of the world wars and the earlier wars of the seventeenth, eighteenth and nineteenth centuries. With the end of the Cold War, international politics moves out of its Western phase, and its centerpiece becomes the interaction between the West and non-Western civilizations and among non-Western civilizations. In the politics of civilizations, the peoples and governments of non-Western civilizations no longer remain the objects of history as targets of Western colonialism but join the West as movers and shapers of history.

THE NATURE OF CIVILIZATIONS

DURING THE COLD WAR the world was divided into the First, Second and Third Worlds. Those divisions are no longer relevant. It is far more meaningful now to group countries not in terms of their political or economic systems or in terms of their level of economic development but rather in terms of their culture and civilization.

The Clash of Civilizations?

What do we mean when we talk of a civilization? A civilization is a cultural entity. Villages, regions, ethnic groups, nationalities, religious groups, all have distinct cultures at different levels of cultural heterogeneity. The culture of a village in southern Italy may be different from that of a village in northern Italy, but both will share in a common Italian culture that distinguishes them from German villages. European communities, in turn, will share cultural features that distinguish them from Arab or Chinese communities. Arabs, Chinese and Westerners, however, are not part of any broader cultural entity. They constitute civilizations. A civilization is thus the highest cultural grouping of people and the broadest level of cultural identity people have short of that which distinguishes humans from other species. It is defined both by common objective elements, such as language, history, religion, customs, institutions, and by the subjective self-identification of people. People have levels of identity: a resident of Rome may define himself with varying degrees of intensity as a Roman, an Italian, a Catholic, a Christian, a European, a Westerner. The civilization to which he belongs is the broadest level of identification with which he intensely identifies. People can and do redefine their identities and, as a result, the composition and boundaries of civilizations change.

Civilizations may involve a large number of people, as with China ("a civilization pretending to be a state," as Lucian Pye put it), or a very small number of people, such as the Anglophone Caribbean. A civilization may include several nation states, as is the case with Western, Latin American and Arab civilizations, or only one, as is the case with Japanese civilization. Civilizations obviously blend and overlap, and may include subcivilizations. Western civilization has two major variants, European and North American, and Islam has its Arab, Turkic and Malay subdivisions. Civilizations are nonetheless meaningful entities, and while the lines between them are seldom sharp, they are real. Civilizations are dynamic; they rise and fall; they divide and merge. And, as any student of history knows, civilizations disappear and are buried in the sands of time.

Westerners tend to think of nation states as the principal actors in global affairs. They have been that, however, for only a few centuries. The broader reaches of human history have been the history of civilizations. In *A Study of History*, Arnold Toynbee identified 21 major civilizations; only six of them exist in the contemporary world.

WHY CIVILIZATIONS WILL CLASH

CIVILIZATION IDENTITY will be increasingly important in the future, and the world will be shaped in large measure by the interactions among seven or eight major civilizations. These include Western, Confucian, Japanese, Islamic, Hindu, Slavic-Orthodox, Latin American and possibly African civilization. The most important conflicts of the future will occur along the cultural fault lines separating these civilizations from one another.

Why will this be the case?

First, differences among civilizations are not only real; they are basic. Civilizations are differentiated from each other by history, language, culture, tradition and, most important, religion. The people of different civilizations have different views on the relations between God and man, the individual and the group, the citizen and the state, parents and children, husband and wife, as well as differing views of the relative importance of rights and responsibilities, liberty and authority, equality and hierarchy. These differences are the product of centuries. They will not soon disappear. They are far more fundamental than differences among political ideologies and political regimes. Differences do not necessarily mean conflict, and conflict does not necessarily mean violence. Over the centuries, however, differences among civilizations have generated the most prolonged and the most violent conflicts.

Second, the world is becoming a smaller place. The interactions between peoples of different civilizations are increasing; these increasing interactions intensify civilization consciousness and awareness of differences between civilizations and commonalities within civilizations. North African immigration to France generates hostility among Frenchmen and at the same time increased receptivity to immigration by "good" European Catholic Poles. Americans react far more negatively to Japanese investment than to larger investments from Canada and European countries. Similarly, as Donald Horowitz has pointed out, "An Ibo may be... an Owerri Ibo or an Onitsha Ibo in what was the Eastern region of Nigeria. In Lagos, he is simply an Ibo. In London, he is a Nigerian. In New York, he is an African." The interactions among peoples of different civilizations enhance the civilization-consciousness of people that, in turn, invigorates differences and animosities stretching or thought to stretch back deep into history.

Third, the processes of economic modernization and social change throughout the world are separating people from long-standing local identities. They also weaken the nation state as a source of identity. In much of the world religion has moved in to fill this gap, often in the form of movements that are labeled "fundamentalist." Such movements are found in Western Christianity, Judaism, Buddhism and Hinduism, as well as in Islam. In most countries and most religions the people active in fundamentalist movements are young, college-educated, middle-class technicians, professionals and business persons. The "unsecularization of the world," George Weigel has remarked, "is one of the dominant social facts of life in the late twentieth century." The revival of religion, "la revanche de Dieu," as Gilles Kepel labeled it, provides a basis for identity and commitment that transcends national boundaries and unites civilizations.

Fourth, the growth of civilization-consciousness is enhanced by the dual role of the West. On the one hand, the West is at a peak of power. At the same time, however, and perhaps as a result, a return to the roots phenomenon is occurring among non-Western civilizations. Increasingly one hears references to trends toward a turning inward and "Asianization" in Japan, the end of the Nehru legacy and the "Hinduization" of India, the failure of Western ideas of socialism and nationalism and hence "re-Islamization" of the Middle East, and now a debate over Westernization versus Russianization in Boris Yeltsin's country. A West at the peak of its power confronts non-Wests that increasingly have the desire, the will and the resources to shape the world in non-Western ways.

In the past, the elites of non-Western societies were usually the people who were most involved with the West, had been educated at Oxford, the Sorbonne or Sandhurst, and had absorbed Western attitudes and values. At the same time, the populace in non-Western countries often remained deeply imbued with the indigenous culture. Now, however, these relationships are being reversed. A de-Westernization and indigenization of elites is occurring in many non-Western countries at the same time that Western, usually American, cultures, styles and habits become more popular among the mass of the people.

Fifth, cultural characteristics and differences are less mutable and hence less easily compromised and resolved than political and economic ones. In the former Soviet Union, communists can become democrats, the rich can become poor and the poor rich, but Russians cannot become Estonians and Azeris cannot become Armenians. In class and ideological conflicts, the key question was "Which side are you on?" and people could and did choose sides and change sides. In conflicts between civilizations, the question is "What are you?" That is a given that cannot be changed. And as we know, from Bosnia to the Caucasus to the Sudan, the wrong answer to that question can mean a bullet in the head. Even more than ethnicity, religion discriminates sharply and exclusively among people. A person can be half-French and half-Arab and simultaneously even a citizen of two countries. It is more difficult to be half-Catholic and half-Muslim.

Finally, economic regionalism is increasing. The proportions of total trade that were intraregional rose between 1980 and 1989 from 51 percent to 59 percent in Europe, 33 percent to 37 percent in East Asia, and 32 percent to 36 percent in North America. The importance of regional economic blocs is likely to continue to increase in the future. On the one hand, successful economic regionalism will reinforce civilization-consciousness. On the other hand, economic regionalism may succeed only when it is rooted in a common civilization. The European Community rests on the shared foundation of European culture and Western Christianity. The success of the North American Free Trade Area depends on the convergence now underway of Mexican, Canadian and American cultures. Japan, in contrast, faces difficulties in creating a comparable economic entity in East Asia because Japan is a society and civilization unique to itself. However strong the trade and investment links Japan may develop with other East Asian countries, its cultural differences with those countries inhibit and perhaps preclude its promoting regional economic integration like that in Europe and North America.

Common culture, in contrast, is clearly facilitating the rapid expansion of the economic relations between the People's Republic of China and Hong Kong, Taiwan, Singapore and the overseas Chinese communities in other Asian countries. With the Cold War over, cultural commonalities increasingly overcome ideological differences, and mainland China and Taiwan move closer together. If cultural commonality is a prerequisite for economic integration, the principal East Asian economic bloc of the future is likely to be centered on China. This bloc is, in fact, already coming into existence. As Murray Weidenbaum has observed,

> Despite the current Japanese dominance of the region, the Chinese-based economy of Asia is rapidly emerging as a new epicenter for industry, commerce and finance. This strategic area contains substantial amounts of technology and manufacturing capability (Taiwan), outstanding entrepreneurial, marketing and services acumen (Hong Kong), a fine communications network (Singapore), a tremendous pool of financial capital (all three), and very large endowments of land, resources and labor (mainland China)... From Guangzhou to Singapore, from Kuala Lumpur to Manila, this influential network—often based on extensions of the traditional clans—has been described as the backbone of the East Asian economy.[1]

Culture and religion also form the basis of the Economic Co-operation Organization, which brings together ten non-Arab Muslim countries: Iran, Pakistan, Turkey, Azerbaijan, Kazakhstan, Kyrgyzstan, Turkmenistan, Tadjikistan, Uzbekistan and Afghanistan. One impetus to the revival and expansion of this organization, founded originally in the 1960s by Turkey, Pakistan and Iran, is the realization by the leaders of several of these countries that they had no chance of admission to the European Community.

---

1. Murray Weidenbaum, *Greater China: The Next Economic Superpower?*, St. Louis: Washington University Center for the Study of American Business, Contemporary Issues, Series 57, February 1993, pp. 2-3.

Similarly, Caricom, the Central American Common Market and Mercosur rest on common cultural foundations. Efforts to build a broader Caribbean-Central American economic entity bridging the Anglo-Latin divide, however, have to date failed.

As people define their identity in ethnic and religious terms, they are likely to see an "us" versus "them" relation existing between themselves and people of different ethnicity or religion. The end of ideologically defined states in Eastern Europe and the former Soviet Union permits traditional ethnic identities and animosities to come to the fore. Differences in culture and religion create differences over policy issues, ranging from human rights to immigration to trade and commerce to the environment. Geographical propinquity gives rise to conflicting territorial claims from Bosnia to Mindanao. Most important, the efforts of the West to promote its values of democracy and liberalism as universal values, to maintain its military predominance and to advance its economic interests engender countering responses from other civilizations. Decreasingly able to mobilize support and form coalitions on the basis of ideology, governments and groups will increasingly attempt to mobilize support by appealing to common religion and civilization identity.

The clash of civilizations thus occurs at two levels. At the micro- level, adjacent groups along the fault lines between civilizations struggle, often violently, over the control of territory and each other. At the macro-level, states from different civilizations compete for relative military and economic power, struggle over the control of international institutions and third parties, and competitively promote their particular political and religious values.

THE FAULT LINES BETWEEN CIVILIZATIONS

THE FAULT LINES between civilizations are replacing the political and ideological boundaries of the Cold War as the flash points for crisis and bloodshed. The Cold War began when the Iron Curtain divided Europe politically and ideologically. The Cold War ended with the end of the Iron Curtain. As the ideological division of Europe has disappeared, the cultural division of Europe between

Western Christianity, on the one hand, and Orthodox Christianity and Islam, on the other, has reemerged. The most significant dividing line in Europe, as William Wallace has suggested, may well be the eastern boundary of Western Christianity in the year 1500. This line runs along what are now the boundaries between Finland and Russia and between the Baltic states and Russia, cuts through Belarus and Ukraine separating the more Catholic western Ukraine from Orthodox eastern Ukraine, swings westward separating Transylvania from the rest of Romania, and then goes through Yugoslavia almost exactly along the line now separating Croatia and Slovenia from the rest of Yugoslavia. In the Balkans this line, of course, coincides with the historic boundary between the Hapsburg and Ottoman empires. The peoples to the north and west of this line are Protestant or Catholic; they shared the common experiences of Euro-pean history—feudalism, the Renaissance, the Reformation, the Enlightenment, the French Revolution, the Industrial Revo-lution; they are generally economically better off than the peoples to the east; and they may now look forward to increasing involvement in a common European economy and to the consolidation of democratic political systems. The peoples to the east and south of this line are Orthodox or Muslim; they historically belonged to the Ottoman or Tsarist empires and were only lightly touched by the shaping events in the rest of Europe; they are generally less advanced economically; they seem much less likely to develop stable democratic political systems. The Velvet Curtain of culture has replaced the Iron Curtain of ideology as the most significant dividing line in Europe. As the events in Yugoslavia show, it is not only a line of difference; it is also at times a line of bloody conflict.

Conflict along the fault line between Western and Islamic civilizations has been going on for 1,300 years. After the founding of Islam, the Arab and Moorish surge west and north only ended at Tours in 732. From the eleventh to the thirteenth century the Crusaders attempted with temporary success to bring Christianity and Christian rule to the Holy Land. From the fourteenth to the seventeenth century, the Ottoman Turks reversed the balance, extended their sway over the Middle East and the Balkans, captured Constantinople, and twice laid siege to Vienna. In the nineteenth and early twentieth centuries as Ottoman power declined Britain, France, and Italy established Western control over most of North Africa and the Middle East.

After World War II, the West, in turn, began to retreat; the colonial empires disappeared; first Arab nationalism and then Islamic fundamentalism manifested themselves; the West became heavily dependent on the Persian Gulf countries for its energy; the oil-rich Muslim countries became money-rich and, when they wished to, weapons-rich. Several wars occurred between Arabs and Israel (created by the West). France fought a bloody and ruthless war in Algeria for most of the 1950s; British and French forces invaded Egypt in 1956; American forces went into Lebanon in 1958; subsequently American forces returned to Lebanon, attacked Libya, and engaged in various military encounters with Iran; Arab and Islamic terrorists, supported by at least three Middle Eastern governments, employed the weapon of the weak and bombed Western planes and installations and seized Western hostages. This warfare between Arabs and the West culminated in 1990, when the United States sent a massive army to the Persian Gulf to defend some Arab countries against aggression by another. In its aftermath NATO planning is increasingly directed to potential threats and instability along its "southern tier."

This centuries-old military interaction between the West and Islam is unlikely to decline. It could become more virulent. The Gulf War left some Arabs feeling proud that Saddam Hussein had attacked Israel and stood up to the West. It also left many feeling humiliated and resentful of the West's military presence in the Persian Gulf, the West's overwhelming military dominance, and their apparent inability to shape their own destiny. Many Arab countries, in addition to the oil exporters, are reaching levels of economic and social development where autocratic forms of government become inappropriate and efforts to introduce democracy become stronger. Some openings in Arab political systems have already occurred. The principal beneficiaries of these openings have been Islamist movements. In the Arab world, in short, Western democracy strengthens anti-

Western political forces. This may be a passing phenomenon, but it surely complicates relations between Islamic countries and the West.

Those relations are also complicated by demography. The spectacular population growth in Arab countries, particularly in North Africa, has led to increased migration to Western Europe. The movement within Western Europe toward minimizing internal boundaries has sharpened political sensitivities with respect to this development. In Italy, France and Germany, racism is increasingly open, and political reactions and violence against Arab and Turkish migrants have become more intense and more widespread since 1990.

On both sides the interaction between Islam and the West is seen as a clash of civilizations. The West's "next confrontation," observes M. J. Akbar, an Indian Muslim author, "is definitely going to come from the Muslim world. It is in the sweep of the Islamic nations from the Maghreb to Pakistan that the struggle for a new world order will begin." Bernard Lewis comes to a similar conclusion:

> We are facing a mood and a movement far transcending the level of issues and policies and the governments that pursue them. This is no less than a clash of civilizations—the perhaps irrational but surely historic reaction of an ancient rival against our Judeo-Christian heritage, our secular present, and the worldwide expansion of both.[2]

Historically, the other great antagonistic interaction of Arab Islamic civilization has been with the pagan, animist, and now increasingly Christian black peoples to the south. In the past, this antagonism was epitomized in the image of Arab slave dealers and black slaves. It has been reflected in the on-going civil war in the Sudan between Arabs and blacks, the fighting in Chad between Libyan-supported insurgents and the government, the tensions between Orthodox Christians and Muslims in the Horn of Africa, and the political conflicts, recurring riots and communal

---

2. Bernard Lewis, "The Roots of Muslim Rage," *The Atlantic Monthly*, vol. 266, September 1990, p. 60; *Time*, June 15, 1992, pp. 24-28.

violence between Muslims and Christians in Nigeria. The modernization of Africa and the spread of Christianity are likely to enhance the probability of violence along this fault line. Symptomatic of the intensification of this conflict was the Pope John Paul II's speech in Khartoum in February 1993 attacking the actions of the Sudan's Islamist government against the Christian minority there.

On the northern border of Islam, conflict has increasingly erupted between Orthodox and Muslim peoples, including the carnage of Bosnia and Sarajevo, the simmering violence between Serb and Albanian, the tenuous relations between Bulgarians and their Turkish minority, the violence between Ossetians and Ingush, the unremitting slaughter of each other by Armenians and Azeris, the tense relations between Russians and Muslims in Central Asia, and the deployment of Russian troops to protect Russian interests in the Caucasus and Central Asia. Religion reinforces the revival of ethnic identities and restimulates Russian fears about the security of their southern borders. This concern is well captured by Archie Roosevelt:

> Much of Russian history concerns the struggle between the Slavs and the Turkic peoples on their borders, which dates back to the foundation of the Russian state more than a thousand years ago. In the Slavs' millennium-long confrontation with their eastern neighbors lies the key to an understanding not only of Russian history, but Russian character. To understand Russian realities today one has to have a concept of the great Turkic ethnic group that has preoccupied Russians through the centuries.[3]

The conflict of civilizations is deeply rooted elsewhere in Asia. The historic clash between Muslim and Hindu in the subcontinent manifests itself now not only in the rivalry between Pakistan and India but also in intensifying religious strife within India between increasingly militant Hindu groups and India's substantial Muslim minority. The destruction of the Ayodhya mosque in December 1992 brought to the fore the issue of whether India will remain

---

3. Archie Roosevelt, *For Lust of Knowing*, Boston: Little, Brown, 1988, pp. 332-333.

a secular democratic state or become a Hindu one. In East Asia, China has outstanding territorial disputes with most of its neighbors. It has pursued a ruthless policy toward the Buddhist people of Tibet, and it is pursuing an increasingly ruthless policy toward its Turkic-Muslim minority. With the Cold War over, the underlying differences between China and the United States have reasserted themselves in areas such as human rights, trade and weapons proliferation. These differences are unlikely to moderate. A "new cold war," Deng Xaioping reportedly asserted in 1991, is under way between China and America.

The same phrase has been applied to the increasingly difficult relations between Japan and the United States. Here cultural difference exacerbates economic conflict. People on each side allege racism on the other, but at least on the American side the antipathies are not racial but cultural. The basic values, attitudes, behavioral patterns of the two societies could hardly be more different. The economic issues between the United States and Europe are no less serious than those between the United States and Japan, but they do not have the same political salience and emotional intensity because the differences between American culture and European culture are so much less than those between American civilization and Japanese civilization.

The interactions between civilizations vary greatly in the extent to which they are likely to be characterized by violence. Economic competition clearly predominates between the American and European subcivilizations of the West and between both of them and Japan. On the Eurasian continent, however, the proliferation of ethnic conflict, epitomized at the extreme in "ethnic cleansing," has not been totally random. It has been most frequent and most violent between groups belonging to different civilizations. In Eurasia the great historic fault lines between civilizations are once more aflame. This is particularly true along the boundaries of the crescent-shaped Islamic bloc of nations from the bulge of Africa to central Asia. Violence also occurs between Muslims, on the one hand, and Orthodox Serbs in the Balkans, Jews in Israel, Hindus in India, Buddhists in Burma and Catholics in the Philippines. Islam has bloody borders.

Samuel P. Huntington

CIVILIZATION RALLYING: THE KIN-COUNTRY SYNDROME

GROUPS OR STATES belonging to one civilization that become involved in war with people from a different civilization naturally try to rally support from other members of their own civilization. As the post-Cold War world evolves, civilization commonality, what H. D. S. Greenway has termed the "kin-country" syndrome, is replacing political ideology and traditional balance of power considerations as the principal basis for cooperation and coalitions. It can be seen gradually emerging in the post-Cold War conflicts in the Persian Gulf, the Caucasus and Bosnia. None of these was a full-scale war between civilizations, but each involved some elements of civilizational rallying, which seemed to become more important as the conflict continued and which may provide a foretaste of the future.

First, in the Gulf War one Arab state invaded another and then fought a coalition of Arab, Western and other states. While only a few Muslim governments overtly supported Saddam Hussein, many Arab elites privately cheered him on, and he was highly popular among large sections of the Arab publics. Islamic fundamentalist movements universally supported Iraq rather than the Western-backed governments of Kuwait and Saudi Arabia. Forswearing Arab nationalism, Saddam Hussein explicitly invoked an Islamic appeal. He and his supporters attempted to define the war as a war between civilizations. "It is not the world against Iraq," as Safar Al-Hawali, dean of Islamic Studies at the Umm Al-Qura University in Mecca, put it in a widely circulated tape. "It is the West against Islam." Ignoring the rivalry between Iran and Iraq, the chief Iranian religious leader, Ayatollah Ali Khamenei, called for a holy war against the West: "The struggle against American aggression, greed, plans and policies will be counted as a jihad, and anybody who is killed on that path is a martyr." "This is a war," King Hussein of Jordan argued, "against all Arabs and all Muslims and not against Iraq alone."

The rallying of substantial sections of Arab elites and publics behind Saddam Hussein caused those Arab governments in the anti-Iraq coalition to moderate their activities and temper their public statements. Arab governments opposed or distanced themselves from subsequent Western efforts to apply pressure on Iraq, including enforcement of a no-fly zone in the summer of 1992 and the bombing of Iraq in January 1993. The Western-Soviet-Turkish-Arab anti-Iraq coalition of 1990 had by 1993 become a coalition of almost only the West and Kuwait against Iraq.

Muslims contrasted Western actions against Iraq with the West's failure to protect Bosnians against Serbs and to impose sanctions on Israel for violating U.N. resolutions. The West, they alleged, was using a double standard. A world of clashing civilizations, however, is inevitably a world of double standards: people apply one standard to their kin-countries and a different standard to others.

Second, the kin-country syndrome also appeared in conflicts in the former Soviet Union. Armenian military successes in 1992 and 1993 stimulated Turkey to become increasingly supportive of its religious, ethnic and linguistic brethren in Azerbaijan. "We have a Turkish nation feeling the same sentiments as the Azerbaijanis," said one Turkish official in 1992. "We are under pressure. Our newspapers are full of the photos of atrocities and are asking us if we are still serious about pursuing our neutral policy. Maybe we should show Armenia that there's a big Turkey in the region." President Turgut Özal agreed, remarking that Turkey should at least "scare the Armenians a little bit." Turkey, Özal threatened again in 1993, would "show its fangs." Turkish Air Force jets flew reconnaissance flights along the Armenian border; Turkey suspended food shipments and air flights to Armenia; and Turkey and Iran announced they would not accept dismemberment of Azerbaijan. In the last years of its existence, the Soviet government supported Azerbaijan because its government was dominated by former communists. With the end of the Soviet Union, however, political considerations gave way to religious ones. Russian troops fought on the side of the Armenians, and Azerbaijan accused the "Russian government of turning 180 degrees" toward support for Christian Armenia.

Third, with respect to the fighting in the former Yugoslavia, Western publics manifested sympathy and support for the Bosnian Muslims and the horrors they suffered at the hands of the Serbs.

Relatively little concern was expressed, however, over Croatian attacks on Muslims and participation in the dismemberment of Bosnia-Herzegovina. In the early stages of the Yugoslav breakup, Germany, in an unusual display of diplomatic initiative and muscle, induced the other 11 members of the European Community to follow its lead in recognizing Slovenia and Croatia. As a result of the pope's determination to provide strong backing to the two Catholic countries, the Vatican extended recognition even before the Community did. The United States followed the European lead. Thus the leading actors in Western civilization rallied behind their coreligionists. Subsequently Croatia was reported to be receiving substantial quantities of arms from Central European and other Western countries. Boris Yeltsin's government, on the other hand, attempted to pursue a middle course that would be sympathetic to the Orthodox Serbs but not alienate Russia from the West. Russian conservative and nationalist groups, however, including many legislators, attacked the government for not being more forthcoming in its support for the Serbs. By early 1993 several hundred Russians apparently were serving with the Serbian forces, and reports circulated of Russian arms being supplied to Serbia.

Islamic governments and groups, on the other hand, castigated the West for not coming to the defense of the Bosnians. Iranian leaders urged Muslims from all countries to provide help to Bosnia; in violation of the U.N. arms embargo, Iran supplied weapons and men for the Bosnians; Iranian-supported Lebanese groups sent guerrillas to train and organize the Bosnian forces. In 1993 up to 4,000 Muslims from over two dozen Islamic countries were reported to be fighting in Bosnia. The governments of Saudi Arabia and other countries felt under increasing pressure from fundamentalist groups in their own societies to provide more vigorous support for the Bosnians. By the end of 1992, Saudi Arabia had reportedly supplied substantial funding for weapons and supplies for the Bosnians, which significantly increased their military capabilities vis-à-vis the Serbs.

In the 1930s the Spanish Civil War provoked intervention from countries that politically were fascist, communist and democratic. In the 1990s the Yugoslav conflict is provoking intervention from countries that are Muslim, Orthodox and Western Christian. The parallel has not gone unnoticed. "The war in Bosnia-Herzegovina has become the emotional equivalent of the fight against fascism in the Spanish Civil War," one Saudi editor observed. "Those who died there are regarded as martyrs who tried to save their fellow Muslims."

Conflicts and violence will also occur between states and groups within the same civilization. Such conflicts, however, are likely to be less intense and less likely to expand than conflicts between civilizations. Common membership in a civilization reduces the probability of violence in situations where it might otherwise occur. In 1991 and 1992 many people were alarmed by the possibility of violent conflict between Russia and Ukraine over territory, particularly Crimea, the Black Sea fleet, nuclear weapons and economic issues. If civilization is what counts, however, the likelihood of violence between Ukrainians and Russians should be low. They are two Slavic, primarily Orthodox peoples who have had close relationships with each other for centuries. As of early 1993, despite all the reasons for conflict, the leaders of the two countries were effectively negotiating and defusing the issues between the two countries. While there has been serious fighting between Muslims and Christians elsewhere in the former Soviet Union and much tension and some fighting between Western and Orthodox Christians in the Baltic states, there has been virtually no violence between Russians and Ukrainians.

Civilization rallying to date has been limited, but it has been growing, and it clearly has the potential to spread much further. As the conflicts in the Persian Gulf, the Caucasus and Bosnia continued, the positions of nations and the cleavages between them increasingly were along civilizational lines. Populist politicians, religious leaders and the media have found it a potent means of arousing mass support and of pressuring hesitant governments. In the coming years, the local conflicts most likely to escalate into major wars will be those, as in Bosnia and the Caucasus, along the fault lines between civilizations. The next world war, if there is one, will be a war between civilizations.

Samuel P. Huntington

THE WEST VERSUS THE REST

THE WEST IS NOW at an extraordinary peak of power in relation to other civilizations. Its superpower opponent has disappeared from the map. Military conflict among Western states is unthinkable, and Western military power is unrivaled. Apart from Japan, the West faces no economic challenge. It dominates international political and security institutions and with Japan international economic institutions. Global political and security issues are effectively settled by a directorate of the United States, Britain and France, world economic issues by a directorate of the United States, Germany and Japan, all of which maintain extraordinarily close relations with each other to the exclusion of lesser and largely non-Western countries. Decisions made at the U.N. Security Council or in the International Monetary Fund that reflect the interests of the West are presented to the world as reflecting the desires of the world community. The very phrase "the world community" has become the euphemistic collective noun (replacing "the Free World") to give global legitimacy to actions reflecting the interests of the United States and other Western powers.[4] Through the IMF and other international economic institutions, the West promotes its economic interests and imposes on other nations the economic policies it thinks appropriate. In any poll of non-Western peoples, the IMF undoubtedly would win the support of finance ministers and a few others, but get an overwhelmingly unfavorable rating from just about everyone else, who would agree with Georgy Arbatov's characterization of IMF officials as "neo-Bolsheviks who love expropriating other people's money, imposing undemocratic and alien rules of economic and political conduct and stifling economic freedom."

Western domination of the U.N. Security Council and its decisions, tempered only by occasional abstention by China, produced U.N. legitimation of the West's use of force to drive Iraq out of Kuwait

---

4. Almost invariably Western leaders claim they are acting on behalf of "the world community." One minor lapse occurred during the run-up to the Gulf War. In an interview on "Good Morning America," Dec. 21, 1990, British Prime Minister John Major referred to the actions "the West" was taking against Saddam Hussein. He quickly corrected himself and subsequently referred to "the world community." He was, however, right when he erred.

and its elimination of Iraq's sophisticated weapons and capacity to produce such weapons. It also produced the quite unprecedented action by the United States, Britain and France in getting the Security Council to demand that Libya hand over the Pan Am 103 bombing suspects and then to impose sanctions when Libya refused. After defeating the largest Arab army, the West did not hesitate to throw its weight around in the Arab world. The West in effect is using international institutions, military power and economic resources to run the world in ways that will maintain Western predominance, protect Western interests and promote Western political and economic values.

That at least is the way in which non-Westerners see the new world, and there is a significant element of truth in their view. Differences in power and struggles for military, economic and institutional power are thus one source of conflict between the West and other civilizations. Differences in culture, that is basic values and beliefs, are a second source of conflict. V. S. Naipaul has argued that Western civilization is the "universal civilization" that "fits all men." At a superficial level much of Western culture has indeed permeated the rest of the world. At a more basic level, however, Western concepts differ fundamentally from those prevalent in other civilizations. Western ideas of individualism, liberalism, constitutionalism, human rights, equality, liberty, the rule of law, democracy, free markets, the separation of church and state, often have little resonance in Islamic, Confucian, Japanese, Hindu, Buddhist or Orthodox cultures. Western efforts to propagate such ideas produce instead a reaction against "human rights imperialism" and a reaffirmation of indigenous values, as can be seen in the support for religious fundamentalism by the younger generation in non-Western cultures. The very notion that there could be a "universal civilization" is a Western idea, directly at odds with the particularism of most Asian societies and their emphasis on what distinguishes one people from another. Indeed, the author of a review of 100 comparative studies of values in different societies concluded that "the values that are most important in the West are least important worldwide."[5] In the political realm,

5. Harry C. Triandis, *The New York Times*, Dec. 25, 1990, p. 41, and "Cross-Cultural Studies of Individualism and Collectivism," Nebraska Symposium on Motivation, vol. 37, 1989, pp. 41-133.

of course, these differences are most manifest in the efforts of the United States and other Western powers to induce other peoples to adopt Western ideas concerning democracy and human rights. Modern democratic government originated in the West. When it has developed in non-Western societies it has usually been the product of Western colonialism or imposition.

The central axis of world politics in the future is likely to be, in Kishore Mahbubani's phrase, the conflict between "the West and the Rest" and the responses of non-Western civilizations to Western power and values.[6] Those responses generally take one or a combination of three forms. At one extreme, non-Western states can, like Burma and North Korea, attempt to pursue a course of isolation, to insulate their societies from penetration or "corruption" by the West, and, in effect, to opt out of participation in the Western-dominated global community. The costs of this course, however, are high, and few states have pursued it exclusively. A second alternative, the equivalent of "band-wagoning" in international relations theory, is to attempt to join the West and accept its values and institutions. The third alternative is to attempt to "balance" the West by developing economic and military power and cooperating with other non-Western societies against the West, while preserving indigenous values and institutions; in short, to modernize but not to Westernize.

THE TORN COUNTRIES

IN THE FUTURE, as people differentiate themselves by civilization, countries with large numbers of peoples of different civilizations, such as the Soviet Union and Yugoslavia, are candidates for dismemberment. Some other countries have a fair degree of cultural homogeneity but are divided over whether their society belongs to one civilization or another. These are torn countries. Their leaders typically wish to pursue a bandwagoning strategy and to make their countries members of the West, but the history,

---

6. Kishore Mahbubani, "The West and the Rest," *The National Interest*, Summer 1992, pp. 3-13.

culture and traditions of their countries are non-Western. The most obvious and prototypical torn country is Turkey. The late twentieth-century leaders of Turkey have followed in the Attatürk tradition and defined Turkey as a modern, secular, Western nation state. They allied Turkey with the West in NATO and in the Gulf War; they applied for membership in the European Community. At the same time, however, elements in Turkish society have supported an Islamic revival and have argued that Turkey is basically a Middle Eastern Muslim society. In addition, while the elite of Turkey has defined Turkey as a Western society, the elite of the West refuses to accept Turkey as such. Turkey will not become a member of the European Community, and the real reason, as President Özal said, "is that we are Muslim and they are Christian and they don't say that." Having rejected Mecca, and then being rejected by Brussels, where does Turkey look? Tashkent may be the answer. The end of the Soviet Union gives Turkey the opportunity to become the leader of a revived Turkic civilization involving seven countries from the borders of Greece to those of China. Encouraged by the West, Turkey is making strenuous efforts to carve out this new identity for itself.

During the past decade Mexico has assumed a position somewhat similar to that of Turkey. Just as Turkey abandoned its historic opposition to Europe and attempted to join Europe, Mexico has stopped defining itself by its opposition to the United States and is instead attempting to imitate the United States and to join it in the North American Free Trade Area. Mexican leaders are engaged in the great task of redefining Mexican identity and have introduced fundamental economic reforms that eventually will lead to fundamental political change. In 1991 a top adviser to President Carlos Salinas de Gortari described at length to me all the changes the Salinas government was making. When he finished, I remarked: "That's most impressive. It seems to me that basically you want to change Mexico from a Latin American country into a North American country." He looked at me with surprise and exclaimed: "Exactly! That's precisely what we are trying to do, but of course we could never say so publicly." As his remark indicates, in Mexico as in

Turkey, significant elements in society resist the redefinition of their country's identity. In Turkey, European oriented leaders have to make gestures to Islam (Özal's pilgrimage to Mecca); so also Mexico's North American-oriented leaders have to make gestures to those who hold Mexico to be a Latin American country (Salinas' Ibero-American Guadalajara summit).

Historically Turkey has been the most profoundly torn country. For the United States, Mexico is the most immediate torn country. Globally the most important torn country is Russia. The question of whether Russia is part of the West or the leader of a distinct Slavic-Orthodox civilization has been a recurring one in Russian history. That issue was obscured by the communist victory in Russia, which imported a Western ideology, adapted it to Russian conditions and then challenged the West in the name of that ideology. The dominance of communism shut off the historic debate over Westernization versus Russification. With communism discredited Russians once again face that question.

President Yeltsin is adopting Western principles and goals and seeking to make Russia a "normal" country and a part of the West. Yet both the Russian elite and the Russian public are divided on this issue. Among the more moderate dissenters, Sergei Stankevich argues that Russia should reject the "Atlanticist" course, which would lead it "to become European, to become a part of the world economy in rapid and organized fashion, to become the eighth member of the Seven, and to put particular emphasis on Germany and the United States as the two dominant members of the Atlantic alliance." While also rejecting an exclusively Eurasian policy, Stankevich nonetheless argues that Russia should give priority to the protection of Russians in other countries, emphasize its Turkic and Muslim connections, and promote "an appreciable redistribution of our resources, our options, our ties, and our interests in favor of Asia, of the eastern direction." People of this persuasion criticize Yeltsin for subordinating Russia's interests to those of the West, for reducing Russian military strength, for failing to support traditional friends such as Serbia, and for pushing economic and political reform in ways injurious to the Russian people. Indicative of this trend is the new popularity of the ideas of Petr Savitsky, who in the 1920s argued that Russia was a unique Eurasian civilization.[7] Anti-Western and anti-Semitic views, and urge Russia to redevelop its military strength and to establish closer ties with China and Muslim countries. The people of Russia are as divided as the elite. An opinion survey in European Russia in the spring of 1992 revealed that 40 percent of the public had positive attitudes toward the West and 36 percent had negative attitudes. As it has been for much of its history, Russia in the early 1990s is truly a torn country.

To redefine its civilization identity, a torn country must meet three requirements. First, its political and economic elite has to be generally supportive of and enthusiastic about this move. Second, its public has to be willing to acquiesce in the redefinition. Third, the dominant groups in the recipient civilization have to be willing to embrace the convert. All three requirements in large part exist with respect to Mexico. The first two in large part exist with respect to Turkey. It is not clear that any of them exist with respect to Russia's joining the West. The conflict between liberal democracy and Marxism-Leninism was between ideologies which, despite their major differences, ostensibly shared ultimate goals of freedom, equality and prosperity. A traditional, authoritarian, nationalist Russia could have quite different goals. A Western democrat could carry on an intellectual debate with a Soviet Marxist. It would be virtually impossible for him to do that with a Russian traditionalist. If, as the Russians stop behaving like Marxists, they reject liberal democracy and begin behaving like Russians but not like Westerners, the relations between Russia and the West could again become distant and conflictual.[8]

---

7. Sergei Stankevich, "Russia in Search of Itself," *The National Interest*, Summer 1992, pp. 47-51; Daniel Schneider, "A Russian Movement Rejects Western Tilt," *Christian Science Monitor*, Feb. 5, 1993, pp. 5-7.

8. Owen Harries has pointed out that Australia is trying (unwisely in his view) to become a torn country in reverse. Although it has been a full member not only of the West but also of the ABCA military and intelligence core of the West, its current leaders are in effect proposing that it defect from the West, redefine itself as an Asian country and cultivate close ties with its neighbors. Australia's future, they argue, is with the dynamic economies of East Asia. But, as I have suggested, close economic cooperation normally requires a common cultural base. In addition, none of the three conditions necessary for a torn country to join another civilization is likely to exist in Australia's case.

Samuel P. Huntington

THE CONFUCIAN-ISLAMIC CONNECTION

THE OBSTACLES TO non-Western countries joining the West vary considerably. They are least for Latin American and East European countries. They are greater for the Orthodox countries of the former Soviet Union. They are still greater for Muslim, Confucian, Hindu and Buddhist societies. Japan has established a unique position for itself as an associate member of the West: it is in the West in some respects but clearly not of the West in important dimensions. Those countries that for reason of culture and power do not wish to, or cannot, join the West compete with the West by developing their own economic, military and political power. They do this by promoting their internal development and by cooperating with other non-Western countries. The most prominent form of this cooperation is the Confucian-Islamic connection that has emerged to challenge Western interests, values and power.

Almost without exception, Western countries are reducing their military power; under Yeltsin's leadership so also is Russia. China, North Korea and several Middle Eastern states, however, are significantly expanding their military capabilities. They are doing this by the import of arms from Western and non-Western sources and by the development of indigenous arms industries. One result is the emergence of what Charles Krauthammer has called "Weapon States," and the Weapon States are not Western states. Another result is the redefinition of arms control, which is a Western concept and a Western goal. During the Cold War the primary purpose of arms control was to establish a stable military balance between the United States and its allies and the Soviet Union and its allies. In the post-Cold War world the primary objective of arms control is to prevent the development by non-Western societies of military capabilities that could threaten Western interests. The West attempts to do this through international agreements, economic pressure and controls on the transfer of arms and weapons technologies.

The conflict between the West and the Confucian-Islamic states focuses largely, although not exclusively, on nuclear, chemical and biological weapons, ballistic missiles and other sophisticated means for delivering them, and the guidance, intelligence and other electronic capabilities for achieving that goal. The West promotes nonproliferation as a universal norm and nonproliferation treaties and inspections as means of realizing that norm. It also threatens a variety of sanctions against those who promote the spread of sophisticated weapons and proposes some benefits for those who do not. The attention of the West focuses, naturally, on nations that are actually or potentially hostile to the West.

The non-Western nations, on the other hand, assert their right to acquire and to deploy whatever weapons they think necessary for their security. They also have absorbed, to the full, the truth of the response of the Indian defense minister when asked what lesson he learned from the Gulf War: "Don't fight the United States unless you have nuclear weapons." Nuclear weapons, chemical weapons and missiles are viewed, probably erroneously, as the potential equalizer of superior Western conventional power. China, of course, already has nuclear weapons; Pakistan and India have the capability to deploy them. North Korea, Iran, Iraq, Libya and Algeria appear to be attempting to acquire them. A top Iranian official has declared that all Muslim states should acquire nuclear weapons, and in 1988 the president of Iran reportedly issued a directive calling for development of "offensive and defensive chemical, biological and radiological weapons."

Centrally important to the development of counter-West military capabilities is the sustained expansion of China's military power and its means to create military power. Buoyed by spectacular economic development, China is rapidly increasing its military spending and vigorously moving forward with the modernization of its armed forces. It is purchasing weapons from the former Soviet states; it is developing long-range missiles; in 1992 it tested a one-megaton nuclear device. It is developing power-projection capabilities, acquiring aerial refueling technology, and trying to purchase an aircraft carrier. Its military buildup and assertion of sovereignty over the South China Sea are provoking a multilateral regional arms race in East Asia. China is also a major exporter of arms and weapons technology. It has exported materials to Libya and Iraq that could be used to manufacture nuclear weapons and nerve gas. It has helped Algeria build a reactor suitable for nuclear weapons research and production. China has sold to Iran nuclear technology that American officials believe could only be used to create weapons and apparently has shipped components of 300-mile-range missiles to Pakistan. North Korea has had a nuclear weapons program under way for some while and has sold advanced missiles and missile technology to Syria and Iran. The flow of weapons and weapons technology is generally from East Asia to the Middle East. There is, however, some movement in the reverse direction; China has received Stinger missiles from Pakistan.

A Confucian-Islamic military connection has thus come into being, designed to promote acquisition by its members of the weapons and weapons technologies needed to counter the military power of the West. It may or may not last. At present, however, it is, as Dave McCurdy has said, "a renegades' mutual support pact, run by the proliferators and their backers." A new form of arms competition is thus occurring between Islamic-Confucian states and the West. In an old-fashioned arms race, each side developed its own arms to balance or to achieve superiority against the other side. In this new form of arms competition, one side is developing its arms and the other side is attempting not to balance but to limit and prevent that arms build-up while at the same time reducing its own military capabilities.

IMPLICATIONS FOR THE WEST

THIS ARTICLE DOES not argue that civilization identities will replace all other identities, that nation states will disappear, that each civilization will become a single coherent political entity, that groups within a civilization will not conflict with and even fight each other. This paper does set forth the hypotheses that differences between civilizations are real and important; civilization-consciousness is increasing; conflict between civilizations will supplant ideological and other forms of conflict as the dominant global form of conflict; international relations, historically a game played out within Western civilization, will increasingly be de-Westernized and become a game in which non-Western civilizations are actors and not simply objects; successful political, security and economic international institutions are more likely to develop within civilizations than across civilizations; conflicts between groups in different civilizations will be more frequent, more sustained and more violent than conflicts between groups in the same civilization; violent conflicts between groups in different civilizations are the most likely and most dangerous source of escalation that could lead to global wars; the paramount axis of world politics will be the relations between "the West and the Rest"; the elites in some torn non-Western countries will try to make their countries part of the West, but in most cases face major obstacles to accomplishing this; a central focus of conflict for the immediate future will be between the West and several Islamic-Confucian states.

This is not to advocate the desirability of conflicts between civilizations. It is to set forth descriptive hypotheses as to what the future may be like. If these are plausible hypotheses, however, it is necessary to consider their implications for Western policy. These implications should be divided between short-term advantage and long-term accommodation. In the short term it is clearly in the interest of the West to promote greater cooperation and unity within its own civilization, particularly between its European and North American components; to incorporate into the West societies in Eastern Europe and Latin America whose cultures are close to those of the West; to promote and maintain cooperative relations with Russia and Japan; to prevent escalation of local inter-civilization conflicts into major inter-civilization wars; to limit the expansion of the military strength of Confucian and Islamic states; to moderate the reduction of Western military capabilities and maintain military superiority in East and Southwest Asia; to exploit differences and conflicts among Confucian and Islamic states; to support in other civilizations groups sympathetic to Western values and interests; to strengthen international institutions that reflect and legitimate Western interests and values and to promote the involvement of non-Western states in those institutions.

multilateralism

> coop w/E u p

In the longer term other measures would be called for. Western civilization is both Western and modern. Non-Western civilizations have attempted to become modern without becoming Western. To date only Japan has fully succeeded in this quest. Non-Western civilizations will continue to attempt to acquire the wealth, technology, skills, machines and weapons that are part of being modern. They will also attempt to reconcile this modernity with their traditional culture and values. Their economic and military strength relative to the West will increase. Hence the West will increasingly have to accommodate these non-Western modern civilizations whose power approaches that of the West but whose values and interests differ significantly from those of the West. This will require the West to maintain the economic and military power necessary to protect its interests in relation to these civilizations. It will also, however, require the West to develop a more profound understanding of the basic religious and philosophical assumptions underlying other civilizations and the ways in which people in those civilizations see their interests. It will require an effort to identify elements of commonality between Western and other civilizations. For the relevant future, there will be no universal civilization, but instead a world of different civilizations, each of which will have to learn to coexist with the others.

The Summoning

'But They Said, We Will Not Hearken.'
JEREMIAH 6:17

Fouad Ajami

IN JOSEPH CONRAD's *Youth*, a novella published at the turn of the century, Marlowe, the narrator, remembers when he first encountered "the East":

> And then, before I could open my lips, the East spoke to me, but it was in a Western voice. A torrent of words was poured into the enigmatical, the fateful silence; outlandish, angry words mixed with words and even whole sentences of good English, less strange but even more surprising. The voice swore and cursed violently; it riddled the solemn peace of the bay by a volley of abuse. It began by calling me Pig, and from that went crescendo into unmentionable adjectives —in English.

The young Marlowe knew that even the most remote civilization had been made and remade by the West, and taught new ways.

Not so Samuel P. Huntington. In a curious essay, "The Clash of Civilizations," Huntington has found his civilizations whole and intact, watertight under an eternal sky. Buried alive, as it were, during the years of the Cold War, these civilizations (Islamic, Slavic-Orthodox, Western, Confucian, Japanese, Hindu, etc.) rose as soon as the stone was rolled off, dusted themselves off, and proceeded to claim the loyalty of their adherents. For this student of history and culture, civilizations have always seemed messy creatures. Furrows run across

---

FOUAD AJAMI is Majid Khadduri Professor and Director of Middle East Studies at the School of Advanced International Studies, Johns Hopkins University. This article originally appeared in the September/October 1993 issue of *Foreign Affairs* © 1993 by the Council on Foreign Relations.

whole civilizations, across individuals themselves—that was modernity's verdict. But Huntington looks past all that. The crooked and meandering alleyways of the world are straightened out. With a sharp pencil and a steady hand Huntington marks out where one civilization ends and the wilderness of "the other" begins.

More surprising still is Huntington's attitude toward states, and their place in his scheme of things. From one of the most influential and brilliant students of the state and its national interest there now comes an essay that misses the slyness of states, the unsentimental and cold-blooded nature of so much of what they do as they pick their way through chaos. Despite the obligatory passage that states will remain "the most powerful actors in world affairs," states are written off, their place given over to clashing civilizations. In Huntington's words, "The next world war, if there is one, will be a war between civilizations."

THE POWER OF MODERNITY

HUNTINGTON'S MEDITATION IS occasioned by his concern about the state of the West, its power and the terms of its engagement with "the rest."[1] "He who gives, dominates," the great historian Fernand Braudel observed of the traffic of civilizations. In making itself over the centuries, the West helped make the others as well. We have come to the end of this trail, Huntington is sure. He is impressed by the "de-Westernization" of societies, their "indigenization" and apparent willingness to go their own way. In his view of things such phenomena as the "Hinduization" of India and Islamic fundamentalism are ascendant. To these detours into "tradition" Huntington has assigned great force and power.

But Huntington is wrong. He has underestimated the tenacity of modernity and secularism in places that acquired these ways against great odds, always perilously close to the abyss, the darkness never far.

---

1. The West itself is unexamined in Huntington's essay. No fissures run through it. No multiculturalists are heard from. It is orderly within its ramparts. What doubts Huntington has about the will within the walls, he has kept within himself. He has assumed that his call to unity will be answered, for outside flutter the banners of the Saracens and the Confucians.

India will not become a Hindu state. The inheritance of Indian secularism will hold. The vast middle class will defend it, keep the order intact to maintain India's—and its own—place in the modern world of nations. There exists in that anarchic polity an instinctive dread of playing with fires that might consume it. Hindu chauvinism may coarsen the public life of the country, but the state and the middle class that sustains it know that a detour into religious fanaticism is a fling with ruin. A resourceful middle class partakes of global culture and norms. A century has passed since the Indian bourgeoisie, through its political vehicle the Indian National Congress, set out to claim for itself and India a place among nations. Out of that long struggle to overturn British rule and the parallel struggle against "communalism," the advocates of the national idea built a large and durable state. They will not cede all this for a political kingdom of Hindu purity.

We have been hearing from the traditionalists, but we should not exaggerate their power, for traditions are often most insistent and loud when they rupture, when people no longer really believe and when age-old customs lose their ability to keep men and women at home. The phenomenon we have dubbed as Islamic fundamentalism is less a sign of resurgence than of panic and bewilderment and guilt that the border with "the other" has been crossed. Those young urban poor, half-educated in the cities of the Arab world, and their Sorbonne-educated lay preachers, can they be evidence of a genuine return to tradition? They crash Europe's and America's gates in search of liberty and work, and they rail against the sins of the West. It is easy to understand Huntington's frustration with this kind of complexity, with the strange mixture of attraction and repulsion that the West breeds, and his need to simplify matters, to mark out the borders of civilizations.

Tradition-mongering is no proof, though, that these civilizations outside the West are intact, or that their thrashing about is an indication of their vitality, or that they present a conventional threat of arms. Even so thorough and far-reaching an attack against Western hegemony as Iran's theocratic revolution could yet fail to wean that society from the culture of the West. That country's cruel revolution was born of the realization of the "armed Imam" that his people were being seduced by America's ways. The gates had been thrown wide open in the 1970s, and the high walls Ayatollah Khomeini built around his polity were a response to that cultural seduction. Swamped, Iran was "rescued" by men claiming authenticity as their banner. One extreme led to another.

"We prayed for the rain of mercy and received floods," was the way Mehdi Bazargan, the decent modernist who was Khomeini's first prime minister, put it. But the millennium has been brought down to earth, and the dream of a pan-Islamic revolt in Iran's image has vanished into the wind. The terror and the shabbiness have caught up with the utopia. Sudan could emulate the Iranian "revolutionary example." But this will only mean the further pauperization and ruin of a desperate land. There is no rehabilitation of the Iranian example.

A battle rages in Algeria, a society of the Mediterranean, close to Europe—a wine-producing country for that matter—and in Egypt between the secular powers that be and an Islamic alternative. But we should not rush to print with obituaries of these states. In Algeria the nomenklatura of the National Liberation Front failed and triggered a revolt of the young, the underclass and the excluded. The revolt raised an Islamic banner. Caught between a regime they despised and a reign of virtue they feared, the professionals and the women and the modernists of the middle class threw their support to the forces of "order." They hailed the army's crackdown on the Islamicists; they allowed the interruption of a democratic process sure to bring the Islamicists to power; they accepted the "liberties" protected by the repression, the devil you know rather than the one you don't.

The Algerian themes repeat in the Egyptian case, although Egypt's dilemma over its Islamicist opposition is not as acute. The Islamicists continue to hound the state, but they cannot bring it down. There is no likelihood that the Egyptian state—now riddled with enough complacency and corruption to try the celebrated patience and good humor of the Egyptians—will go under. This is an old and skeptical country. It knows better than to trust its fate to enforcers of radical religious dogma. These are not deep and secure structures of order that the national middle classes have put in place. But they will not be blown away overnight.

Nor will Turkey lose its way, turn its back on Europe and chase after some imperial temptation in the scorched domains of Central Asia. Huntington sells that country's modernity and secularism short when he writes that the Turks—rejecting Mecca and rejected by Brussels—are likely to head to Tashkent in search of a Pan-Turkic role. There is no journey to that imperial past. Ataturk severed that link with fury, pointed his country westward, embraced the civilization of Europe and did it without qualms or second thoughts. It is on Frankfurt and Bonn—and Washington—not on Baku and Tashkent that the attention of the Turks is fixed. The inheritors of Ataturk's legacy are too shrewd to go chasing after imperial glory, gathering about them the scattered domains of the Turkish peoples. After their European possessions were lost, the Turks clung to Thrace and to all that this link to Europe represents.

Huntington would have nations battle for civilizational ties and fidelities when they would rather scramble for their market shares, learn how to compete in a merciless world economy, provide jobs, move out of poverty. For their part, the "management gurus" and those who believe that the interests have vanquished the passions in today's world tell us that men want Sony, not soil.[2] There is a good deal of truth in what they say, a terrible exhaustion with utopias, a reluctance to set out on expeditions of principle or belief. It is hard to think of Russia, ravaged as it is by inflation, taking up the grand cause of a "second Byzantium," the bearer of the orthodox-Slavic torch.

And where is the Confucian world Huntington speaks of? In the busy and booming lands of the Pacific Rim, so much of politics and ideology has been sublimated into finance that the nations of East Asia have turned into veritable workshops. The civilization of Cathay is dead; the Indonesian archipelago is deaf to the call of the religious radicals in Tehran as it tries to catch up with Malaysia and Singapore. A different wind blows in the lands of the Pacific. In that world economics, not politics, is in command. The world is far less antiseptic than Lee Kuan Yew, the sage of Singapore, would want it to be. A

---

2. Kenichi Ohmae, "Global Consumers Want Sony, Not Soil," *New Perspectives Quarterly*, Fall 1991.

Fouad Ajami

nemesis could lie in wait for all the prosperity that the 1980s brought to
the Pacific. But the lands of the Pacific Rim—protected, to be sure, by
an American security umbrella—are not ready for a great falling out
among the nations. And were troubles to visit that world they would
erupt within its boundaries, not across civilizational lines.

The things and ways that the West took to "the rest"—those
whole sentences of good English that Marlowe heard a century
ago—have become the ways of the world. The secular idea, the
state system and the balance of power, pop culture jumping tariff
walls and barriers, the state as an instrument of welfare, all these
have been internalized in the remotest places. We have stirred up
the very storms into which we now ride.

THE WEAKNESS OF TRADITION

NATIONS "CHEAT": THEY juggle identities and interests. Their
ways meander. One would think that the traffic of arms from North
Korea and China to Libya and Iran and Syria shows this—that
states will consort with any civilization, however alien, as long as the
price is right and the goods are ready. Huntington turns this routine
act of selfishness into a sinister "Confucian-Islamic connection."
There are better explanations: the commerce of renegades, plain
piracy, an "underground economy" that picks up the slack left by the
great arms suppliers (the United States, Russia, Britain and France).
Contrast the way Huntington sees things with Braudel's depic-
tion of the traffic between Christendom and Islam across the
Mediterranean in the sixteenth century—and this was in a religious
age, after the fall of Constantinople to the Turks and of Granada to
the Spanish: "Men passed to and fro, indifferent to frontiers, states
and creeds. They were more aware of the necessities for shipping and
trade, the hazards of war and piracy, the opportunities for complici-
ty or betrayal provided by circumstances."[3]

Those kinds of "complicities" and ambiguities are missing in
Huntington's analysis. Civilizations are crammed into the nooks and

3. Ferdinand Braudel, *The Mediterranean and the Mediterranean World in
the Age of Philip II*, Vol. II, New York: Harper & Row, 1976, p. 759.

crannies—and checkpoints—of the Balkans. Huntington goes where only the brave would venture, into that belt of mixed populations stretching from the Adriatic to the Baltic. Countless nationalisms make their home there, all aggrieved, all possessed of memories of a fabled past and equally ready for the demagogues vowing to straighten a messy map. In the thicket of these pan-movements he finds the line that marked "the eastern boundary of Western Christianity in the year 1500." The scramble for turf between Croatian nationalism and its Serbian counterpart, their "joint venture" in carving up Bosnia, are made into a fight of the inheritors of Rome, Byzantium and Islam.

But why should we fall for this kind of determinism? "An outsider who travels the highway between Zagreb and Belgrade is struck not by the decisive historical fault line which falls across the lush Slavonian plain but by the opposite. Serbs and Croats speak the same language, give or take a few hundred words, have shared the same village way of life for centuries."[4] The cruel genius of Slobodan Milosevic and Franjo Tudjman, men on horseback familiar in lands and situations of distress, was to make their bids for power into grand civilizational undertakings—the ramparts of the Enlightenment defended against Islam or, in Tudjman's case, against the heirs of the Slavic-Orthodox faith. Differences had to be magnified. Once Tito, an equal opportunity oppressor, had passed from the scene, the balancing act among the nationalities was bound to come apart. Serbia had had a measure of hegemony in the old system. But of the world that loomed over the horizon—privatization and economic reform— the Serbs were less confident. The citizens of Sarajevo and the Croats and the Slovenes had a head start on the rural Serbs. And so the Serbs hacked at the new order of things with desperate abandon.

Some Muslim volunteers came to Bosnia, driven by faith and zeal. Huntington sees in these few stragglers the sweeping power of "civilizational rallying," proof of the hold of what he calls the "kin-country syndrome." This is delusion. No Muslim cavalry was ever going to ride to the rescue. The Iranians may have railed about holy warfare, but the Chetniks went on with their work. The

---

4. Michael Ignatieff, "The Balkan Tragedy," *New York Review of Books*, May 13, 1993.

work of order and mercy would have had to be done by the United States if the cruel utopia of the Serbs was to be contested.

It should have taken no powers of prophecy to foretell where the fight in the Balkans would end. The abandonment of Bosnia was of a piece with the ways of the world. No one wanted to die for Srebrenica. The Europeans averted their gaze, as has been their habit. The Americans hesitated for a moment as the urge to stay out of the Balkans did battle with the scenes of horror. Then "prudence" won out. Milosevic and Tudjman may need civilizational legends, but there is no need to invest their projects of conquest with this kind of meaning.

In his urge to find that relentless war across Islam's "bloody borders," Huntington buys Saddam Hussein's interpretation of the Gulf War. It was, for Saddam and Huntington, a civilizational battle. But the Gulf War's verdict was entirely different. For if there was a campaign that laid bare the interests of states, the lengths to which they will go to restore a tolerable balance of power in a place that matters, this was it. A local despot had risen close to the wealth of the Persian Gulf, and a Great Power from afar had come to the rescue. The posse assembled by the Americans had Saudi, Turkish, Egyptian, Syrian, French, British and other riders.

True enough, when Saddam Hussein's dream of hegemony was shattered, the avowed secularist who had devastated the *ulama*, the men of religion in his country, fell back on Ayatollah Khomeini's language of fire and brimstone and borrowed the symbolism and battle cry of his old Iranian nemesis. But few, if any, were fooled by this sudden conversion to the faith. They knew the predator for what he was: he had a Christian foreign minister (Tariq Aziz); he had warred against the Iranian revolution for nearly a decade and had prided himself on the secularism of his regime. Prudent men of the social and political order, the *ulama* got out of the way and gave their state the room it needed to check the predator at the Saudi/Kuwaiti border.[5] They knew this was one

---

5. Huntington quotes one Safar al Hawali, a religious radical at Umm al Qura University in Mecca, to the effect that the campaign against Iraq was another Western campaign against Islam. But this can't do as evidence. Safar al Hawali was a crank. Among the *ulama* class and the religious scholars in Saudi Arabia he was, for all practical purposes, a loner.

of those moments when purity bows to necessity. Ten days after Saddam swept into Kuwait, Saudi Arabia's most authoritative religious body, the Council of Higher Ulama, issued a *fatwa*, or a ruling opinion, supporting the presence of Arab and Islamic and "other friendly forces." All means of defense, the ulama ruled, were legitimate to guarantee the people "the safety of their religion, their wealth, and their honor and their blood, to protect what they enjoy of safety and stability." At some remove, in Egypt, that country's leading religious figure, the Shaykh of Al Ashar, Shaykh Jadd al Haqq, denounced Saddam as a tyrant and brushed aside his Islamic pretensions as a cover for tyranny.

Nor can the chief Iranian religious leader Ayatollah Ali Khamenei's rhetoric against the Americans during the Gulf War be taken as evidence of Iran's disposition toward that campaign. Crafty men, Iran's rulers sat out that war. They stood to emerge as the principal beneficiaries of Iraq's defeat. The American-led campaign against Iraq held out the promise of tilting the regional balance in their favor. No tears were shed in Iran for what befell Saddam Hussein's regime.

It is the mixed gift of living in hard places that men and women know how to distinguish between what they hear and what there is: no illusions were thus entertained in vast stretches of the Arab Muslim world about Saddam, or about the campaign to thwart him for that matter. The fight in the gulf was seen for what it was: a bid for primacy met by an imperial expedition that laid it to waste. A circle was closed in the gulf: where once the order in the region "east of Suez" had been the work of the British, it was now provided by Pax Americana. The new power standing sentry in the gulf belonged to the civilization of the West, as did the prior one. But the American presence had the anxious consent of the Arab lands of the Persian Gulf. The stranger coming in to check the kinsmen.

The world of Islam divides and sub-divides. The battle lines in the Caucasus, too, are not coextensive with civilizational fault lines. The lines follow the interests of states. Where Huntington sees a civilizational duel between Armenia and Azerbaijan, the Iranian state has cast religious zeal and fidelity to the wind. Indeed, in that battle the Iranians have tilted toward Christian Armenia.

Fouad Ajami

THE WRIT OF STATES

WE HAVE BEEN delivered into a new world, to be sure. But it is not a world where the writ of civilizations runs. Civilizations and civilizational fidelities remain. There is to them an astonishing measure of permanence. But let us be clear: civilizations do not control states, states control civilizations. States avert their gaze from blood ties when they need to; they see brotherhood and faith and kin when it is in their interest to do so.

We remain in a world of self-help. The solitude of states continues; the disorder in the contemporary world has rendered that solitude more pronounced. No way has yet been found to reconcile France to Pax Americana's hegemony, or to convince it to trust its security or cede its judgment to the preeminent Western power. And no Azeri has come up with a way the lands of Islam could be rallied to the fight over Nagorno Karabakh. The sky has not fallen in Kuala Lumpur or in Tunis over the setbacks of Azerbaijan in its fight with Armenia.

The lesson bequeathed us by Thucydides in his celebrated dialogue between the Melians and the Athenians remains. The Melians, it will be recalled, were a colony of the Lacedaemonians. Besieged by Athens, they held out and were sure that the Lacedaemonians were "bound, if only for very shame, to come to the aid of their kindred." The Melians never wavered in their confidence in their "civilizational" allies: "Our common blood insures our fidelity."[6] We know what became of the Melians. Their allies did not turn up, their island was sacked, their world laid to waste.

---

6. Thucydides, *The Peloponnesian War*, New York: The Modern American Library, 1951, pp. 334-335.

The Coming Anarchy

Robert D. Kaplan

THE MINISTER'S EYES were like egg yolks, an aftereffect of some of the many illnesses, malaria especially, endemic in his country. There was also an irrefutable sadness in his eyes. He spoke in a slow and creaking voice, the voice of hope about to expire. Flame trees, coconut palms, and a ballpoint-blue Atlantic compose the background. None of it seemed beautiful, though. "In forty-five years I have never seen things so bad. We did not manage ourselves well after the British departed. But what we have now is something worse—the revenge of the poor, of the social failures, of the people least able to bring up children in a modern society." Then he referred to the recent coup in the West African country Sierra Leone. "The boys who took power in Sierra Leone come from houses like this." The Minister jabbed his finger at a corrugated metal shack teeming with children. "In three months these boys confiscated all the official Mercedes, Volvos, and BMWs and willfully wrecked them on the road." The Minister mentioned one of the coup's leaders, Solomon Anthony Joseph Musa, who shot the people who had paid for his schooling, "in order to erase the humiliation and mitigate the power his middle-class sponsors held over him."

Tyranny is nothing new in Sierra Leone or in the rest of West Africa. But it is now part and parcel of an increasing lawlessness that is far more significant than any coup, rebel incursion, or episodic experiment in democracy. Crime was what my friend—a

---

top-ranking African official whose life would be threatened were I to identify him more precisely—really wanted to talk about. Crime is what makes West Africa a natural point of departure for my report on what the political character of our planet is likely to be in the twenty-first century.

The cities of West Africa at night are some of the unsafest places in the world. Streets are unlit; the police often lack gasoline for their vehicles; armed burglars, carjackers, and muggers proliferate. "The government in Sierra Leone has no writ after dark," says a foreign resident, shrugging. When I was in the capital, Freetown, last September, eight men armed with AK-47s broke into the house of an American man. They tied him up and stole everything of value. Forget Miami: direct flights between the United States and the Murtala Muhammed Airport, in neighboring Nigeria's largest city, Lagos, have been suspended by order of the U.S. Secretary of Transportation because of ineffective security at the terminal and its environs. A State Department report cited the airport for "extortion by law-enforcement and immigration officials." This is one of the few times that the U.S. government has embargoed a foreign airport for reasons that are linked purely to crime. In Abidjan, effectively the capital of the Cote d'Ivoire, or Ivory Coast, restaurants have stick-and gun-wielding guards who walk you the fifteen feet or so between your car and the entrance, giving you an eerie taste of what American cities might be like in the future. An Italian ambassador was killed by gunfire when robbers invaded an Abidjan restaurant. The family of the Nigerian ambassador was tied up and robbed at gunpoint in the ambassador's residence. After university students in the Ivory Coast caught bandits who had been plaguing their dorms, they executed them by hanging tires around their necks and setting the tires on fire. In one instance Ivorian policemen stood by and watched the "necklacings," afraid to intervene. Each time I went to the Abidjan bus terminal, groups of young men with restless, scanning eyes surrounded my taxi, putting their hands all over the windows, demanding "tips" for carrying my luggage even though I had only a rucksack. In cities in six West African countries I saw similar young men everywhere—hordes of them. They were like loose molecules in a very unstable social fluid, a fluid that was clearly on the verge of igniting.

"You see," my friend the Minister told me, "in the villages of Africa it is perfectly natural to feed at any table and lodge in any hut. But in the cities this communal existence no longer holds. You must pay for lodging and be invited for food. When young men find out that their relations cannot put them up, they become lost. They join other migrants and slip gradually into the criminal process."

"In the poor quarters of Arab North Africa," he continued, "there is much less crime, because Islam provides a social anchor: of education and indoctrination. Here in West Africa we have a lot of superficial Islam and superficial Christianity. Western religion is undermined by animist beliefs not suitable to a moral society, because they are based on irrational spirit power. Here spirits are used to wreak vengeance by one person against another, or one group against another." Many of the atrocities in the Liberian civil war have been tied to belief in *juju* spirits, and the BBC has reported, in its magazine *Focus on Africa*, that in the civil fighting in adjacent Sierra Leone, rebels were said to have "a young woman with them who would go to the front naked, always walking backwards and looking in a mirror to see where she was going. This made her invisible, so that she could cross to the army's positions and there bury charms… to improve the rebels' chances of success."

Finally my friend the Minister mentioned polygamy. Designed for a pastoral way of life, polygamy continues to thrive in sub-Saharan Africa even though it is increasingly uncommon in Arab North Africa. Most youths I met on the road in West Africa told me that they were from "extended" families, with a mother in one place and a father in another. Translated to an urban environment, loose family structures are largely responsible for the world's highest birth rates and the explosion of the HIV virus on the continent. Like the communalism and animism, they provide a weak shield against the corrosive social effects of life in cities. In those cities African culture is being redefined while desertification and deforestation—also tied to overpopulation—drive more and more African peasants out of the countryside.

Robert D. Kaplan

A PREMONITION OF THE FUTURE

WEST AFRICA IS becoming the symbol of worldwide demographic, environmental, and societal stress, in which criminal anarchy emerges as the real "strategic" danger. Disease, overpopulation, unprovoked crime, scarcity of resources, refugee migrations, the increasing erosion of nation-states and international borders, and the empowerment of private armies, security firms, and international drug cartels are now most tellingly demonstrated through a West African prism. West Africa provides an appropriate introduction to the issues, often extremely unpleasant to discuss, that will soon confront our civilization. To remap the political earth the way it will be a few decades hence—as I intend to do in this article—I find I must begin with West Africa.

There is no other place on the planet where political maps are so deceptive—where, in fact, they tell such lies—as in West Africa. Start with Sierra Leone. According to the map, it is a nation-state of defined borders, with a government in control of its territory. In truth the Sierra Leonian government, run by a twenty-seven-year-old army captain, Valentine Strasser, controls Freetown by day and by day also controls part of the rural interior. In the government's territory the national army is an unruly rabble threatening drivers and passengers at most checkpoints. In the other part of the country units of two separate armies from the war in Liberia have taken up residence, as has an army of Sierra Leonian rebels. The government force fighting the rebels is full of renegade commanders who have aligned themselves with disaffected village chiefs. A premodern formlessness governs the battlefield, evoking the wars in medieval Europe prior to the 1648 Peace of Westphalia, which ushered in the era of organized nation-states.

As a consequence, roughly 400,000 Sierra Leonians are internally displaced, 280,000 more have fled to neighboring Guinea, and another 100,000 have fled to Liberia, even as 400,000 Liberians have fled to Sierra Leone. The third largest city in Sierra Leone, Gondama, is a displaced-persons camp. With an additional 600,000 Liberians in Guinea and 250,000 in the Ivory Coast, the borders dividing these four countries have become largely meaningless. Even in quiet zones none of the governments except the Ivory Coast's maintains the schools, bridges, roads, and police forces in a manner necessary for functional sovereignty. The Koranko ethnic group in northeastern Sierra Leone does all its trading in Guinea. Sierra Leonian diamonds are more likely to be sold in Liberia than in Freetown. In the eastern provinces of Sierra Leone you can buy Liberian beer but not the local brand.

In Sierra Leone, as in Guinea, as in the Ivory Coast, as in Ghana, most of the primary rain forest and the secondary bush is being destroyed at an alarming rate. I saw convoys of trucks bearing majestic hardwood trunks to coastal ports. When Sierra Leone achieved its independence, in 1961, as much as 60 percent of the country was primary rain forest. Now six percent is. In the Ivory Coast the proportion has fallen from 38 percent to eight percent. The deforestation has led to soil erosion, which has led to more flooding and more mosquitoes. Virtually everyone in the West African interior has some form of malaria.

Sierra Leone is a microcosm of what is occurring, albeit in a more tempered and gradual manner, throughout West Africa and much of the underdeveloped world: the withering away of central governments, the rise of tribal and regional domains, the unchecked spread of disease, and the growing persuasiveness of war. West Africa is reverting to the Africa of the Victorian atlas. It consists now of a series of coastal trading posts, such as Freetown and Conakry, and an interior that, owing to violence, volatility, and disease, is again becoming, as Graham Greene once observed, "blank" and "unexplored." However, whereas Greene's vision implies a certain romance, as in the somnolent and charmingly seedy Freetown of his celebrated novel *The Heart of the Matter*, it is Thomas Malthus, the philosopher of demographic doomsday, who is now the prophet of West Africa's future. And West Africa's future, eventually, will also be that of most the rest of the world.

Consider "Chicago." I refer not to Chicago, Illinois, but to a slum district of Abidjan, which the young toughs in the area have named after the American city. ("Washington" is another poor section of Abidjan.) Although Sierra Leone is widely regarded as beyond salvage, the Ivory Coast has been considered an African success story, and Abidjan has been called "the Paris of West Africa." Success, however, was built on two artificial factors: the high price of cocoa, of which the Ivory Coast is the world's leading producer, and the talents of a French expatriate community, whose members have helped run the government and the private sector. The expanding cocoa economy made the Ivory Coast a magnet for migrant workers from all over West Africa: between a third and a half of the country's population is now non-Ivorian, and the figure could be as high as 75 percent in Abidjan. During the 1980s cocoa prices fell and the French began to leave. The skyscrapers of the Paris of West Africa are a facade. Perhaps 15 percent of Abidjan's population of three million people live in shantytowns like Chicago and Washington, and the vast majority live in places that are not much better. Not all of these places appear on any of the readily available maps. This is another indication of how political maps are the products of tired conventional wisdom and, in the Ivory Coast's case, of an elite that will ultimately be forced to relinquish power.

Chicago, like more and more of Abidjan, is a slum in the bush: a checkerwork of corrugated zinc roofs and walls made of cardboard and black plastic wrap. It is located in a gully teeming with coconut palms and oil palms, and is ravaged by flooding. Few residents have easy access to electricity, a sewage system, or a clean water supply. The crumbly red laterite earth crawls with foot-long lizards both inside and outside the shacks. Children defecate in a stream filled with garbage and pigs, droning with malarial mosquitoes. In this stream women do the washing. Young unemployed men spend their time drinking beer, palm wine, and gin while gambling on pinball games constructed out of rotting wood and rusty nails. These are the same youths who rob houses in more prosperous Ivorian neighborhoods at night. One man I met, Damba Tesele, came to Chicago from Burkina Faso in 1963. A cook by profession, he has four wives and thirty-two children, not one of whom has made it to high school. He has seen his shanty community destroyed by municipal authorities seven times since coming to the area. Each time he and his neighbors rebuild. Chicago is the latest incarnation.

Fifty-five percent of the Ivory Coast's population is urban, and the proportion is expected to reach 62 percent by 2000. The yearly net population growth is 3.6 percent. This means that the Ivory Coast's 13.5 million people will become 39 million by 2025, when much of the population will consist of urbanized peasants like those of Chicago. But don't count on the Ivory Coast's still existing then. Chicago, which is more indicative of Africa's and the Third World's demographic present—and even more of the future—than any idyllic junglescape of women balancing earthen jugs on their heads, illustrates why the Ivory Coast, once a model of Third World success, is becoming a case study in Third World catastrophe.

President Félix Houphouët-Boigny, who died last December at the age of about ninety, left behind a weak cluster of political parties and a leaden bureaucracy that discourages foreign invest- ment. Because the military is small and the non-Ivorian population large, there is neither an obvious force to maintain order nor a sense of nationhood that would lessen the need for such enforce- ment. The economy has been shrinking since the mid-1980s. Though the French are working assiduously to preserve stability, the Ivory Coast faces a possibility worse than a coup: an anarchic implosion of criminal violence—an urbanized version of what has already happened in Somalia. Or it may become an African Yugoslavia, but one without mini-states to replace the whole.

Because the demographic reality of West Africa is a country- side draining into dense slums by the coast, ultimately the region's rulers will come to reflect the values of these shanty-towns. There are signs of this already in Sierra Leone—and in Togo, where the dictator Etienne Eyadema, in power since 1967, was nearly toppled in 1991, not by democrats but by thousands of youths whom the London-based magazine *West Africa* described as "Soweto-like stone-throwing adolescents." Their behavior may herald a regime more brutal than Eyadema's repressive one.

The fragility of these West African "countries" impressed itself on me when I took a series of bush taxis along the Gulf of Guinea, from the Togolese capital of Lome, across Ghana, to Abidjan. The 400-mile journey required two full days of driving, because of stops at two border crossings and an additional eleven customs stations, at each of which my fellow passengers had their bags searched. I had to change money twice and repeatedly fill in currency-declaration forms. I had to bribe a Togolese immigration official with the equivalent of eighteen dollars before he would agree to put an exit stamp on my passport. Nevertheless, smuggling across these borders is rampant. *The London Observer* has reported that in 1992 the equivalent of $856 million left West Africa for Europe in the form of "hot cash" assumed to be laundered drug money. International cartels have discovered the utility of weak, financially strapped West African regimes.

The more fictitious the actual sovereignty, the more severe border authorities seem to be in trying to prove otherwise. Getting visas for these states can be as hard as crossing their borders. The Washington embassies of Sierra Leone and Guinea—the two poorest nations on earth, according to a 1993 United Nations report on "human development"—asked for letters from my bank (in lieu of prepaid round-trip tickets) and also personal references, in order to prove that I had sufficient means to sustain myself during my visits. I was reminded of my visa and currency hassles while traveling to the communist states of Eastern Europe, particularly East Germany and Czechoslovakia, before those states collapsed.

Ali A. Mazrui, the director of the Institute of Global Cultural Studies at the State University of New York at Binghamton, predicts that West Africa—indeed, the whole continent—is on the verge of large-scale border upheaval. Mazrui writes,

> In the 21st century France will be withdrawing from West Africa as she gets increasingly involved in the affairs [of Europe]. France's West African sphere of influence will be filled by Nigeria—a more natural hegemonic power... It will be under those circumstances that Nigeria's own boundaries are likely to expand to incorporate the Republic of Niger (the Hausa link), the Republic of Benin (the Yoruba link), and conceivably Cameroon.

The future could be more tumultuous, and bloodier, than Mazrui dares to say. France will withdraw from former colonies like Benin, Togo, Niger, and the Ivory Coast, where it has been propping up local currencies. It will do so not only because its attention will diverted to new challenges in Europe and Russia but also because younger French officials lack the older generation's emotional ties to the ex-colonies. However, even as Nigeria attempts to expand, it, too, is likely to split into several pieces. The State Department's Bureau of Intelligence and Research recently made the following points in an analysis of Nigeria:

> Prospects for a transition to civilian rule and democratization are slim... The repressive apparatus of the state security service... will be difficult for any future civilian government to control... The country is becoming increasingly ungovernable... Ethnic and regional splits are deepening, a situation made worse by an increase in the number of states from 19 to 30 and a doubling in the number of local governing authorities; religious cleavages are more serious; Muslim fundamentalism and evangelical Christian militancy are on the rise; and northern Muslim anxiety over southern [Christian] control of the economy is intense... the will to keep Nigeria together is now very weak.

prob-lems

Given that oil-rich Nigeria is a bellwether for the region—its population of roughly 90 million equals the populations of all the other West African states combined—it is apparent that Africa faces cataclysms that could make the Ethiopian and Somalian famines pale in comparison. This is especially so because Nigeria's population, including that of its largest city, Lagos, whose crime, pollution, and overcrowding make it the clichè par excellence of Third World urban dysfunction, is set to double during the next twenty-five years, while the country continues to deplete its natural resources.

Part of West Africa's quandary is that although its population belts are horizontal, with habitation densities increasing as one travels south away from the Sahara and toward the tropical abundance of the Atlantic littoral, the borders erected by European colonialists are vertical, and therefore at cross-purposes with demography and topography. Satellite photos depict the same reality I experienced in the bush taxi: the Lomé-Abidjan coastal corridor—indeed, the entire stretch of coast from Abidjan eastward to Lagos—is one burgeoning megalopolis that by any rational economic and geographical standard should constitute a single sovereignty, rather than the five (the Ivory Coast, Ghana, Togo, Benin, and Nigeria) into which it is currently divided.

As many internal African borders begin to crumble, a more impenetrable boundary is being erected that threatens to isolate the continent as a whole: the wall of disease. Merely to visit West Africa in some degree of safety, I spent about $500 for a hepatitis B vaccination series and other disease prophylaxis. Africa may today be more dangerous in this regard than it was in 1862, before antibiotics, when the explorer Sir Richard Francis Burton described the health situation on the continent as "deadly, a Golgotha, a Jehannum." Of the approximately 12 million people worldwide whose blood is HIV-positive, 8 million are in Africa. In the capital of the Ivory Coast, whose modern road system only helps to spread the disease, 10 percent of the population is HIV-positive. And war and refugee movements help the virus break through to more-remote areas of Africa. Alan Greenberg, M.D., a representative of the Centers for Disease Control in Abidjan, explains that in Africa the HIV virus and tuberculosis are now "fast-forwarding each other." Of the approximately 4,000 newly diagnosed tuberculosis patients in Abidjan, 45 percent were also found to be HIV-positive. As African birth rates soar and slums proliferate, some experts worry that viral mutations and hybridizations might, just conceivably, result in a form of the AIDS virus that is easier to catch than the present strain.

It is malaria that is most responsible for the disease wall that threatens to separate Africa and other parts of the Third World from more-developed regions of the planet in the twenty-first century. Carried by mosquitoes, malaria, unlike AIDS, is easy to catch. Most people in sub-Saharan Africa have recurring bouts of the disease throughout their entire lives, and it is mutating into increasingly deadly forms. "The great gift of Malaria is utter apathy," wrote Sir Richard Burton, accurately portraying the situation in much of the Third World today. Visitors to malaria-afflicted parts of the planet are protected by a new drug, mefloquine, a side effect of which is vivid, even violent, dreams. But a strain of cerebral malaria resistant to mefloquine is now on the offensive. Consequently, defending oneself against malaria in Africa is becoming more and more like defending oneself against violent crime. You engage in "behavior modification": not going out at dusk, wearing mosquito repellent all the time.

And the cities keep growing. I got a general sense of the future while driving from the airport to downtown Conakry, the capital of Guinea. The forty-five-minute journey in heavy traffic was through one never-ending shantytown: a nightmarish Dickensian spectacle to which Dickens himself would never have given credence. The corrugated metal shacks and scabrous walls were coated with black slime. Stores were built out of rusted shipping containers, junked cars, and jumbles of wire mesh. The streets were one long puddle of floating garbage. Mosquitoes and flies were everywhere. Children, many of whom had protruding bellies, seemed as numerous as ants. When the tide went out, dead rats and the skeletons of cars were exposed on the mucky beach. In twenty-eight years Guinea's population will double if growth goes on at current rates. Hardwood logging continues at a madcap speed, and people flee the Guinean countryside for Conakry. It seemed to me that here, as elsewhere in Africa and the Third World, man is challenging nature far beyond its limits, and nature is now beginning to take its revenge.

AFRICA MAY BE as relevant to the future character of world politics as the Balkans were a hundred years ago, prior to the two Balkan wars and the First World War. Then the threat was the collapse of empires and the birth of nations based solely on tribe. Now the threat is more elemental: nature unchecked. Africa's immediate future could be very bad. The coming upheaval, in which foreign embassies are shut down, states collapse, and contact with the outside world takes place through dangerous, disease-ridden coastal trading posts, will loom large in the century we are entering. (Nine of twenty-one U.S. foreign-aid missions to be closed over the next three years are in Africa—a prologue to a consolidation of U.S. embassies themselves.) Precisely because much of Africa is set to go over the edge at a time when the Cold War has ended, when environmental and demographic stress in other parts of the globe is becoming critical, and when the post-First World War system of nation-states—not just in the Balkans but perhaps also in the Middle East—is about to be toppled, Africa suggests what war, borders, and ethnic politics will be like a few decades hence.

Europe?

To understand the events of the next fifty years, then, one must understand environmental scarcity, cultural and racial clash, geographic destiny, and the transformation of war. The order in which I have named these is not accidental. Each concept except the first relies partly on the one or ones before it, meaning that the last two—new approaches to mapmaking and to warfare—are the most important. They are also the least understood. I will now look at each idea, drawing upon the work of specialists and also my own travel experiences in various parts of the globe besides Africa, in order to fill in the blanks of a new political atlas.

THE ENVIRONMENT AS A HOSTILE POWER

FOR A WHILE the media will continue to ascribe riots and other violent upheavals abroad mainly to ethnic and religious conflict. But as these conflicts multiply, it will become apparent that something else is afoot, making more and more places like Nigeria, India, and Brazil ungovernable.

Mention "the environment" or "diminishing natural resources" in foreign-policy circles and you meet a brick wall of skepticism or boredom. To conservatives especially, the very terms seem flaky. Public-policy foundations have contributed to the lack of interest, by funding narrowly focused environmental studies replete with technical jargon which foreign-affairs experts just let pile up on their desks.

It is time to understand "the environment" for what it is: the national-security issue of the early twenty-first century. The political and strategic impact of surging populations, spreading disease, deforestation and soil erosion, water depletion, air pollution, and, possibly, rising sea levels in critical, overcrowded regions like the Nile Delta and Bangladesh-developments that will prompt mass migrations and, in turn, incite group conflicts—will be the core foreign-policy challenge from which most others will ultimately emanate, arousing the public and uniting assorted interests left over from the Cold War. In the twenty-first century water will be in dangerously short supply in such diverse locales as Saudi Arabia, Central Asia, and the southwestern United States. A war could erupt between Egypt and Ethiopia over Nile River water. Even in Europe tensions have arisen between Hungary and Slovakia over the damming of the Danube, a classic case of how environmental disputes fuse with ethnic and historical ones. The political scientist and erstwhile Clinton adviser Michael Mandelbaum has said, "We have a foreign policy today in the shape of a doughnut—lots of peripheral interests but nothing at the center." The environment, I will argue, is part of a terrifying array of problems that will define a new threat to our security, filling the hole in Mandelbaum's doughnut and allowing a postCold War foreign policy to emerge inexorably by need rather than by design.

Our Cold War foreign policy truly began with George F. Kennan's famous article, signed "X," published in *Foreign Affairs* in July of 1947, in which Kennan argued for a "firm and vigilant containment" of a Soviet Union that was imperially, rather than ideologically, motivated. It may be that our post-Cold War foreign policy will one day be seen to have had its beginnings in an even bolder and more detailed piece of written analysis: one that appeared in the journal *International Security*. The article, published in the fall of 1991 by Thomas Fraser Homer-Dixon, who is the head of the Peace and Conflict Studies Program at the University of Toronto, was titled "On the Threshold: Environmental Changes as Causes of Acute Conflict." Homer-Dixon has, more successfully than other analysts, integrated two hitherto separate fields—military-conflict studies and the study of the physical environment.

In Homer-Dixon's view, future wars and civil violence will often arise from scarcities of resources such as water, cropland, forests, and fish. Just as there will be environmentally driven wars and refugee flows, there will be environmentally induced praetorian regimes—or, as he puts it, "hard regimes." Countries with the highest probability of acquiring hard regimes, according to Homer-Dixon, are those that are threatened by a declining resource base yet also have "a history of state [read 'military'] strength." Candidates include Indonesia, Brazil, and, of course, Nigeria. Though each of these nations has exhibited democratizing tendencies of late, Homer-Dixon argues that such tendencies are likely to be superficial "epiphenomena" having nothing to do with long-term processes that include soaring populations and shrinking raw materials. Democracy is problematic; scarcity is more certain.

Indeed, the Saddam Husseins of the future will have more, not fewer, opportunities. In addition to engendering tribal strife, scarcer resources will place a great strain on many peoples who never had much of a democratic or institutional tradition to begin with. Over the next fifty years the earth's population will soar from 5.5 billion to more than nine billion. Though optimists have hopes for new resource technologies and free-market development in the global village, they fail to note that, as the National Academy of Sciences has pointed out, 95 percent of the population increase will be in the poorest regions of the world, where governments now—just look at Africa—show little ability to function, let alone to implement even marginal improvements. Homer-Dixon writes, ominously, "Neo-Malthusians may underestimate human adaptability in today's environmental-social system, but as time passes their analysis may become ever more compelling."

While a minority of the human population will be, as Francis Fukuyama would put it, sufficiently sheltered so as to enter a "posthistorical" realm, living in cities and suburbs in which the environment has been mastered and ethnic animosities have been quelled by bourgeois prosperity, an increasingly large number of people will be stuck in history, living in shantytowns where attempts to rise above poverty, cultural dysfunction, and ethnic strife will be doomed by a lack of water to drink, soil to till, and space to survive in. In the developing world environmental stress will present people with a choice that is increasingly among totalitarianism (as in Iraq), fascist-tending mini-states (as in Serb-held Bosnia), and road-warrior cultures (as in Somalia). Homer-Dixon concludes that "as environmental degradation proceeds, the size of the potential social disruption will increase."

Tad Homer-Dixon is an unlikely Jeremiah. Today a boyish thirty-seven, he grew up amid the sylvan majesty of Vancouver Island, attending private day schools. His speech is calm, perfectly even, and crisply enunciated. There is nothing in his background or manner that would indicate a bent toward pessimism. A Canadian Anglican who spends his summers canoeing on the lakes of northern Ontario, and who talks about the benign mountains, black bears, and Douglas firs of his youth, he is the opposite of the intellectually severe neoconservative, the kind at home with conflict scenarios. Nor is he an environmentalist who opposes development. "My father was a logger who thought about ecologically safe forestry before others," he says. "He logged, planted, logged, and planted. He got out of the business just as the issue was being polarized by environmentalists. They hate changed ecosystems. But human beings, just by carrying seeds around, change the natural world." As an only child whose playground was a virtually untouched wilderness and seacoast, Homer-Dixon has a familiarity with the natural world that permits him to see a reality that most policy analysts—children of suburbia and city streets—are blind to.

"We need to bring nature back in," he argues. "We have to stop separating politics from the physical world—the climate, public health, and the environment." Quoting Daniel Deudney, another pioneering expert on the security aspects of the environment, Homer-Dixon says that "for too long we've been prisoners of 'social-social' theory, which assumes there are only social causes for social and political changes, rather than natural causes, too. This social-social mentality emerged with the Industrial Revolution, which separated us from nature. But nature is coming back with a vengeance, tied to population growth. It will have incredible security implications.

"Think of a stretch limo in the potholed streets of New York City, where homeless beggars live. Inside the limo are the air-conditioned post-industrial regions of North America, Europe, the emerging Pacific Rim, and a few other isolate places, with their trade summitry and computer-information highways. Outside is the rest of mankind, going in a completely different direction."

We are entering a bifurcated world. Part of the globe is inhabited by Heysel's and Fukuyama's Last Man, healthy, well fed; and pampered by technology. The other, larger, part is inhabited by Hobbes's First Man, condemned to a life that is "poor, nasty, brutish, and short." Although both parts will be threatened by environmental stress, the Last Man will be able to master it; the First Man will not.

The Last Man will adjust to the loss of underground water tables in the western United States. He will build dikes to save Cape Hatteras and the Chesapeake beaches from rising sea levels, even as the Maldive Islands, off the coast of India, sink into oblivion, and the shorelines of Egypt, Bangladesh, and Southeast Asia recede, driving tens of millions of people inland where there is no room for them, and thus sharpening ethnic divisions.

Homer-Dixon points to a world map of soil degradation in his Toronto office. "The darker the map color, the worse the degradation," he explains. The West African coast, the Middle East, the Indian subcontinent, China, and Central America have the darkest shades, signifying all manner of degradation, related to winds, chemicals, and water problems. "The worst degradation is generally where the population is highest. The population is generally highest where the soil is the best. So we're degrading earth's best soil."

China, in Homer-Dixon's view, is the quintessential example of environmental degradation. Its current economic "success" masks deeper problems. "China's fourteen percent growth rate does not mean it's going to be a world power. It means that coastal China, where the economic growth is taking place, is joining the rest of the Pacific Rim. The disparity with inland China is intensifying." Referring to the environmental research of his colleague, the Czech-born ecologist Vaclav Smil, Homer-Dixon explains how the per capita availability of arable land in interior China has rapidly declined at the same time that the quality of that land has been destroyed by deforestation, loss of topsoil, and salinization. He mentions the loss and contamination of water supplies, the exhaustion of wells, the plugging of irrigation systems and reservoirs with eroded silt, and a population of 1.54 billion by the year 2025: it is a misconception that China has gotten its population under control. Large-scale population movements are under way, from inland China to coastal China and from villages to cities, leading to a crime surge like the one in Africa and to growing regional disparities and conflicts in a land with a strong tradition of warlordism and a weak tradition of central government—again as in Africa. "We will probably see the center challenged and fractured, and China will not remain the same on the map," Homer-Dixon says.

Environmental scarcity will inflame existing hatreds and affect power relationships, at which we now look.

SKINHEAD COSSACKS, JUJU WARRIORS

IN THE SUMMER, 1993, issue of *Foreign Affairs*, Samuel P. Huntington, of Harvard's Olin Institute for Strategic Studies, published a thought-provoking article called "The Clash of Civilizations?" The world, he argues, has been moving during the course of this century from nation state conflict to ideological conflict to, finally, cultural conflict. I would add that as refugee flows increase and as peasants continue migrating to cities around the world—turning them into sprawling villages—national borders will mean less, even as more power will fall into the hands of less educated, less sophisticated groups. In the eyes of these uneducated but newly empowered millions, the real borders are the most tangible and intractable ones: those of culture and tribe. Huntington writes, "First, differences among civilizations are not only real; they are basic," involving, among other things, history, language, and religion. "Second... interactions between peoples of different civilizations are increasing; these increasing interactions intensify civilization consciousness." Economic modernization is not necessarily a panacea, since it fuels individual and group ambitions while weakening traditional loyalties to the state. It is worth noting, for example, that it is precisely the wealthiest and fastest-developing city in India, Bombay, that has seen the worst intercommunal violence between Hindus and Muslims. Consider that Indian cities, like African and Chinese ones, are ecological time bombs—Delhi and Calcutta, and also Beijing, suffer the worst air quality of any cities in the world—and it is apparent how surging populations, environmental degradation, and ethnic conflict are deeply related.

Huntington points to interlocking conflicts among Hindu, Muslim, Slavic Orthodox, Western, Japanese, Confucian, Latin

American, and possibly African civilizations: for instance, Hindus clashing with Muslims in India, Turkic Muslims clashing with Slavic Orthodox Russians in Central Asian cities, the West clashing with Asia. (Even in the United States, African-Americans find themselves besieged by an influx of competing Latinos.) Whatever laws, refugees find a way to crash official borders, bringing their passions with them, meaning that Europe and the United States will be weakened by cultural disputes.

Because Huntington's brush is broad, his specifics are vulnerable to attack. In a rebuttal of Huntington's argument, the Johns Hopkins professor Fouad Ajami, a Lebanese-born Shi'ite who certainly knows the world beyond suburbia, writes in the September-October, 1993, issue of *Foreign Affairs,*

> The world of Islam divides and subdivides. The battle lines in the Caucasus are not coextensive with civilizational fault lines. The lines follow the interests of states. Where Huntington sees a civilizational duel between Armenia and Azerbaijan, the Iranian state has cast religious zeal... to the wind... in that battle the Iranians have tilted toward Christian Armenia.

True, Huntington's hypothesized war between Islam and Orthodox Christianity is not borne out by the alliance network in the Caucasus. But that is only because he has misidentified which cultural war is occurring there. A recent visit to Azerbaijan made clear to me that Azeri Turks, the world's most secular Shi'ite Muslims, see their cultural identity in terms not of religion but of their Turkic race. The Armenians, likewise, fight the Azeris not because the latter are Muslims but because they are Turks, related to the same Turks who massacred Armenians in 1915. Turkic culture (secular and based on languages employing a Latin script) is battling Iranian culture (religiously militant as defined by Tehran, and wedded to an Arabic script) across the whole swath of Central Asia and the Caucasus. The Armenians are, therefore, natural allies of their fellow Indo-Europeans the Iranians.

Huntington is correct that the Caucasus is a flashpoint of cultural and racial war. But, as Ajami observes, Huntington's plate tectonics are too simple. Two months of recent travel throughout Turkey revealed to me that although the Turks are developing a deep distrust, bordering on hatred, of fellow-Muslim Iran, they are also, especially in the shantytowns that are coming to dominate Turkish public opinion, revising their group identity, increasingly seeing themselves as Muslims being deserted by a West that does little to help besieged Muslims in Bosnia and that attacks Turkish Muslims in the streets of Germany.

In other words, the Balkans, a powder keg for nation-state war at the beginning of the twentieth century, could be a powder keg for cultural war at the turn of the twenty-first: between Orthodox Christianity (represented by the Serbs and a classic Byzantine configuration of Greeks, Russians, and Romanians) and the House of Islam. Yet in the Caucasus that House of Islam is falling into a clash between Turkic and Iranian civilizations. Ajami asserts that this very subdivision, not to mention all the divisions within the Arab world, indicates that the West, including the United States, is not threatened by Huntington's scenario. As the Gulf War demonstrated, the West has proved capable of playing one part of the House of Islam against another.

True. However, whether he is aware of it or not, Ajami is describing a world even more dangerous than the one Huntington envisions, especially when one takes into account Homer-Dixon's research on environmental scarcity. Outside the stretch limo would be a rundown, crowded planet of skinhead Cossacks and *juju* warriors, influenced by the worst refuse of Western pop culture and ancient tribal hatreds, and battling over scraps of overused earth in guerrilla conflicts that ripple across continents and intersect in no discernible pattern—meaning there's no easy-to-define threat. Kennan's world of one adversary seems as distant as the world of Herodotus.

Most people believe that the political earth since 1989 has undergone immense change. But it is minor compared with what is yet to come. The breaking apart and remaking of the atlas is only now beginning. The crack-up of the Soviet empire and the coming end of Arab-Israeli military confrontation are merely prologues to the really big changes that lie ahead. Michael Vlahos, a long-range thinker for the U.S. Navy, warns, "We are not in charge of the environment and the world is not following us. It is going in many directions. Do not assume that democratic capitalism is the last word in human social evolution."

Before addressing the questions of maps and of warfare, I want to take a closer look at the interaction of religion, culture, demographic shifts, and the distribution of natural resources in a specific area of the world: the Middle East.

THE PAST IS DEAD

BUILT ON STEEP, muddy hills, the shantytowns of Ankara, the Turkish capital, exude visual drama. Altindag, or "Golden Mountain," is a pyramid of dreams, fashioned from cinder blocks and corrugated iron, rising as though each shack were built on top of another, all reaching awkwardly and painfully toward heaven—the heaven of wealthier Turks who live elsewhere in the city. Nowhere else on the planet have I found such a poignant architectural symbol of man's striving, with gaps in house walls plugged with rusted cans, and leeks and onions growing on verandas assembled from planks of rotting wood. For reasons that I will explain, the Turkish shacktown is a psychological universe away from the African one.

To see the twenty-first century truly, one's eyes must learn a different set of aesthetics. One must reject the overly stylized images of travel magazines, with their inviting photographs of exotic villages and glamorous downtowns. There are far too many millions whose dreams are more vulgar, more real—whose raw energies and desires will overwhelm the visions of the elites, remaking the future into something frighteningly new. But in Turkey I learned that shantytowns are not all bad.

Slum quarters in Abidjan terrify and repel the outsider. In Turkey it is the opposite. The closer I got to Golden Mountain the better it looked, and the safer I felt. I had $1,500 worth of Turkish lira in one pocket and $1,000 in traveler's checks in the other, yet I felt no fear. Golden Mountain was a real neighborhood. The inside of one house told the story: The architectural bedlam of cinder block and sheet metal and cardboard walls was deceiving. Inside was a home—order, that is, bespeaking dignity. I saw a working refrigerator, a television, a wall cabinet with a few books and lots of family pictures, a few plants by a window, and a stove. Though the streets become rivers of mud when it rains, the floors inside this house were spotless.

Other houses were like this too. Schoolchildren ran along with briefcases strapped to their backs, trucks delivered cooking gas, a few men sat inside a cafe sipping tea. One man sipped beer. Alcohol is easy to obtain in Turkey, a secular state where 99 percent of the population is Muslim. Yet there is little problem of alcoholism. Crime against persons is infinitesimal. Poverty and illiteracy are watered-down versions of what obtains in Algeria and Egypt (to say nothing of West Africa), making it that much harder for religious extremists to gain a foothold.

My point in bringing up a rather wholesome, crime-free slum is this: its existence demonstrates how formidable is the fabric of which Turkish Muslim culture is made. A culture this strong has the potential to dominate the Middle East once again. Slums are litmus tests for innate cultural strengths and weaknesses. Those peoples whose cultures can harbor extensive slum life without decomposing will be, relatively speaking, the future's winners. Those whose cultures cannot will be the future's victims. Slums— in the sociological sense—do not exist in Turkish cities. The mortar between people and family groups is stronger here than in Africa. Resurgent Islam and Turkic cultural identity have produced a civilization with natural muscle tone. Turks, history's perennial nomads, take disruption in stride.

The future of the Middle East is quietly being written inside the heads of Golden Mountain's inhabitants. Think of an Ottoman military encampment on the eve of the destruction of Greek Constantinople in 1453. That is Golden Mountain. "We brought the village here. But in the village we worked harder—in the field, all day. So we couldn't fast during [the holy month of] Ramadan. Here we fast. Here we are more religious." Aishe Tanrikulu, along with half a dozen other women, was stuffing rice into vine leaves from a crude plastic bowl. She asked me to join her under the shade of a piece of sheet metal. Each of these women had her hair covered by a kerchief. In the city they were encountering television for the first time. "We are traditional, religious people. The programs offend us," Aishe said. Another woman complained about the schools. Though her children had educational options unavailable in the village, they had to compete with wealthier, secular Turks. "The kids from rich families with connections—they get all the places." More opportunities, more tensions, in other words.

My guidebook to Golden Mountain was an untypical one: *Tales From the Garbage Hills,* a brutally realistic novel by a Turkish writer, Latife Tekin, about life in the shantytowns, which in Turkey are called *gecekondus* ("built in a night"). "He listened to the earth and wept unceasingly for water, for work and for the cure of the illnesses spread by the garbage and the factory waste," Tekin writes. In the most revealing passage of *Tales From the Garbage Hills* the squatters are told "about a certain 'Ottoman Empire'... that where they now lived there had once been an empire of this name." This history "confounded" the squatters. It was the first they had heard of it. Though one of them knew "that his grandfather and his dog died fighting the Greeks," nationalism and an encompassing sense of Turkish history are the province of the Turkish middle and upper classes, and of foreigners like me who feel required to have a notion of "Turkey."

But what did the Golden Mountain squatters know about the armies of Turkish migrants that had come before their own—namely, Seljuks and Ottomans? For these recently urbanized peasants, and their counterparts in Africa, the Arab world, India, and so many other places, the world is new, to adapt V. S. Naipau's phrase. As Naipaul wrote of urban refugees in *India: A Wounded Civilization,* "They saw themselves at the beginning of things: unaccommodated men making a claim on their land for the first time, and out of chaos evolving their own philosophy of community and self-help. For them the past was dead; they had left it behind in the villages."

Everywhere in the developing world at the turn of the twenty-first century these new men and women, rushing into the cities, are remaking civilizations and redefining their identities in terms of religion and tribal ethnicity which do not coincide with the borders of existing states.

IN TURKEY SEVERAL things are happening at once. In 1980, 44 percent of Turks lived in cities; in 1990 it was 61 percent. By the year 2000 the figure is expected to be 67 percent. Villages are emptying out as concentric rings of *gecekondu* developments grow around Turkish cities. This is the real political and demographic revolution in Turkey and elsewhere, and foreign correspondents usually don't write about it.

Whereas rural poverty is age-old and almost a "normal" part of the social fabric, urban poverty is socially destabilizing. As Iran has shown, Islamic extremism is the psychological defense mechanism of many urbanized peasants threatened with the loss of traditions in pseudo-modern cities where their values are under attack, where basic services like water and electricity are unavailable, and where they are assaulted by a physically unhealthy environment. The American ethnologist and orientalist Carleton Stevens Coon wrote in 1951 that Islam "has made possible the optimum survival and happiness of millions of human beings in an increasingly impoverished environment over a fourteen-hundred-year period." Beyond its stark, clearly articulated message, Islam's very militancy makes it attractive to the downtrodden. It is the one religion that is prepared to fight. A political era driven by environmental stress, increased cultural sensitivity, unregulated urbanization, and refugee migrations is an era divinely created for the spread and intensification of Islam, already the world's fastest-growing religion. (Though Islam is spreading in West Africa, it is being hobbled by syncretization with animism: this makes new converts less apt to become anti-Western extremists, but it also makes for a weakened version of the faith, which is less effective as an antidote to crime.)

In Turkey, however, Islam is painfully and awkwardly forging a consensus with modernization, a trend that is less apparent in the Arab and Persian worlds (and virtually invisible in Africa). In Iran the oil boom—because it put development and urbanization on a fast track, making the culture shock more intense—fueled the 1978 Islamic Revolution. But Turkey, unlike Iran and the Arab world, has little oil. Therefore its development and urbanization have been more gradual. Islamists have been integrated into the parliamentary system for decades. The tensions I noticed in Golden Mountain are natural, creative ones: the kind immigrants face the world over. While the world has focused on religious perversity in Algeria, a nation rich in natural gas, and in Egypt, parts of whose capital city, Cairo, evince worse crowding than I have seen even in Calcutta, Turkey has been living through the Muslim equivalent of the Protestant Reformation.

Resource distribution is strengthening Turks in another way vis-à-vis Arabs and Persians. Turks may have little oil, but their Anatolian heartland has lots of water—the most important fluid of the twenty-first century. Turkey's Southeast Anatolia Project, involving twenty-two major dams and irrigation systems, is impounding the waters of the Tigris and Euphrates rivers. Much of the water that Arabs and perhaps Israelis will need to drink in the future is controlled by Turks. The project's centerpiece is the mile-wide, sixteen-story Atatürk Dam, upon which are emblazoned the words of modern Turkey's founder: "Ne Mutlu Turkum Diyene" ("Lucky is the one who is a Turk").

Unlike Egypt's Aswan High Dam, on the Nile, and Syria's Revolution Dam, on the Euphrates, both of which were built largely by Russians, the Atatürk Dam is a predominantly Turkish affair, with Turkish engineers and companies in charge. On a recent visit my eyes took in the immaculate offices and their gardens, the high-voltage electric grids and phone switching stations, the dizzying sweep of giant humming transformers, the poured-concrete spillways, and the prim unfolding suburbia, complete with schools, for dam employees. The emerging power of the Turks was palpable.

Erduhan Bayindir, the site manager at the dam, told me that "while oil can be shipped abroad to enrich only elites, water has to be spread more evenly within the society... It is true, we can stop the flow of water into Syria and Iraq for up to eight months without the same water overflowing our arms, in order to regulate their political behavior."

Power is certainly moving north in the Middle East, from the oil fields of Dhahran, on the Persian Gulf, to the water plain of Hanan, in southern Anatolia—near the site of the Atatürk Dam.

But will the nation-state of Turkey, as presently constituted, be the inheritor of this wealth?

I very much doubt it.

THE LIES OF MAPMAKERS

WHEREAS WEST AFRICA represents the least stable part of political reality outside Homer-Dixon's stretch limo, Turkey, an organic outgrowth of two Turkish empires that ruled Anatolia for 850 years, has been among the most stable. Turkey's borders were established not by colonial powers but in a war of independence, in the early 1920s. Kemal Atatürk provided Turkey with a secular nation-building myth that most Arab and African states, burdened by artificially drawn borders, lack. That lack will leave many Arab states defenseless against a wave of Islam that will eat away at their legitimacy and frontiers in coming years. Yet even as regards Turkey, maps deceive.

It is not only African shantytowns that don't appear on urban maps. Many shantytowns in Turkey and elsewhere are also missing—as are the considerable territories controlled by guerrilla armies and urban mafias. Traveling with Eritrean guerrillas in what, according to the map, was northern Ethiopia, traveling in "northern Iraq" with Kurdish guerrillas, and staying in a hotel in the Caucasus controlled by a local mafia—to say nothing of my experiences in West Africa—led me to develop a healthy skepticism toward maps, which, I began to realize, create a conceptual barrier that prevents us from comprehending the political crack-up just beginning to occur worldwide.

Consider the map of the world, with its 190 or so countries, each signified by a bold and uniform color: this map, with which all of us have grown up, is generally an invention of modernism, specifically of European colonialism. Modernism, in the sense of which I speak, began with the rise of nation states in Europe and was confirmed by the death of feudalism at the end of the Thirty Years' War—an event that was interposed between the Renaissance and the Enlightenment, which together gave birth to modern science. People were suddenly flush with an enthusiasm to categorize, to define. The map, based on scientific techniques of measurement,

Robert D. Kaplan

offered a way to classify new national organisms, making a jigsaw puzzle of neat pieces without transition zones between them. "Frontier" is itself a modern concept that didn't exist in the feudal mind. And as European nations carved out far-flung domains at the same time that print technology was making the reproduction of maps cheaper, cartography came into its own as a way of creating facts by ordering the way we look at the world.

In his book *Imagined Communities: Reflections on the Origin and Spread of Nationalism*, Benedict Anderson, of Cornell University, demonstrates that the map enabled colonialists to think about their holdings in terms of a "totalizing classificatory grid… It was bounded, determinate, and therefore—in principle—countable." To the colonialist, country maps were the equivalent of an accountant's ledger books. Maps, Anderson explains, "shaped the grammar" that would make possible such questionable concepts as Iraq, Indonesia, Sierra Leone, and Nigeria. The state, recall, is a purely Western notion, one that until the twentieth century applied to countries covering only three percent of the earth's land area. Nor is the evidence compelling that the state, as a governing ideal, can be successfully transported to areas outside the industrialized world. Even the United States of America, in the words of one of our best living poets, Gary Snyder, consists of "arbitrary and inaccurate impositions on what is really here."

Yet this inflexible, artificial reality staggers on, not only in the United Nations but in various geographic and travel publications (themselves by-products of an age of elite touring which colonialism made possible) that still report on and photograph the world according to "country." Newspapers, this magazine, and this writer are not innocent of the tendency.

According to the map, the great hydropower complex emblematized by the Atatürk Dam is situated in Turkey. Forget the map. This southeastern region of Turkey is populated almost completely by Kurds. About half of the world's 20 million Kurds live in "Turkey." The Kurds are predominant in an ellipse of territory that overlaps not only with Turkey but also with Iraq, Iran, Syria, and the former Soviet Union. The Western-enforced Kurdish enclave in northern Iraq, a consequence of the 1991 Gulf War, has already exposed the fictitious nature of that supposed nation-state.

fiction

The Coming Anarchy

On a recent visit to the Turkish-Iranian border, it occurred to me what a risky idea the nation-state is. Here I was on the legal fault line between two clashing civilizations, Turkic and Iranian. Yet the reality was more subtle: as in West Africa, the border was porous and smuggling abounded, but here the people doing the smuggling, on both sides of the border, were Kurds. In such a moonscape, over which peoples have migrated and settled in patterns that obliterate borders, the end of the Cold War will bring on a cruel process of natural selection among existing states. No longer will these states be so firmly propped up by the West or the Soviet Union. Because the Kurds overlap with nearly everybody in the Middle East, on account of their being cheated out of a state in the post-First World War peace treaties, they are emerging, in effect, as the natural selector—the ultimate reality check. They have destabilized Iraq and may continue to disrupt states that do not offer them adequate breathing space, while strengthening states that do.

Because the Turks, owing to their water resources, their growing economy, and the social cohesion evinced by the most crime-free slums I have encountered, are on the verge of big-power status, and because the 10 million Kurds within Turkey threaten that status, the outcome of the Turkish-Kurdish dispute will be more critical to the future of the Middle East than the eventual outcome of the recent Israeli-Palestinian agreement. *conflict.*

AMERICA'S FASCINATION WITH the Israeli-Palestinian issue, coupled with its lack of interest in the Turkish-Kurdish one, is a function of its own domestic and ethnic obsessions, not of the cartographic reality that is about to transform the Middle East. The diplomatic process involving Israelis and Palestinians will, I believe, have little effect on the early and mid-twenty-first-century map of the region. Israel, with a 6.6 percent economic growth rate based increasingly on high-tech exports, is about to enter Homer-Dixon's stretch limo, fortified by a well-defined political community that is an organic outgrowth of history and ethnicity. Like prosperous and peaceful Japan on the one hand, and war-torn and poverty wracked Armenia on the other, Israel is a classic national-ethnic organism. Much of the Arab world, however, will undergo alteration, as Islam spreads across artificial frontiers, fueled by mass migrations into the cities and a soaring birth rate of more than 3.2 percent. Seventy percent of the Arab population has been born since 1970—youths with little historical memory of anticolonial independence struggles, postcolonial attempts at nation-building, or any of the Arab-Israeli Wars. The most distant recollection of these youths will be the West's humiliation of colonially invented Iraq in 1991. Today seventeen out of twenty-two Arab states have a declining gross national product; in the next twenty years, at current growth rates, the population of many Arab countries will double. These states, like most African ones, will be ungovernable through conventional secular ideologies. The Middle East analyst Christine M. Helms explains,

> Declaring Arab nationalism "bankrupt," the political "disinherited" are not rationalizing the failure of Arabism… or reformulating it. Alternative solutions are not contemplated. They hare simply opted for the political paradigm at the other end of the political spectrum with which they are familiar—Islam.

Like the borders of West Africa, the colonial borders of Syria, Iraq, Jordan, Algeria, and other Arab states are often contrary to cultural and political reality. As state control mechanisms wither in the face of environmental and demographic stress, "hard" Islamic city-states or shantytown states are likely to emerge. The fiction that the impoverished city of Algiers, on the Mediterranean, controls Tamanrasset, deep in the Algerian Sahara, cannot obtain forever. Whatever the outcome of the peace process, Israel is destined to be a Jewish ethnic fortress amid a vast and volatile realm of Islam. In that realm, the violent youth culture of the Gaza shantytowns may be indicative of the coming era.

The destiny of Turks and Kurds is far less certain, but far more relevant to the kind of map that will explain our future world. The Kurds suggest a geographic reality that cannot be shown in two-dimensional space. The issue in Turkey is not simply a matter of giving autonomy or even independence to Kurds in the southeast. This isn't the Balkans or the Caucasus, where regions are merely subdividing into smaller units, Abkhazia breaking off from Georgia, and so on. Federalism is not the answer. Kurds are found everywhere in Turkey, including the shanty districts of Istanbul and Ankara. Turkey's problem is that its Anatolian land mass is the home of two cultures and languages, Turkish and Kurdish. Identity in Turkey, as in India, Africa, and elsewhere, is more complex and subtle than conventional cartography can display.

A NEW KIND OF WAR

TO APPRECIATE FULLY the political and cartographic implications of postmodernism—an epoch of themeless juxtapositions, in which the classificatory grid of nation-states is going to be replaced by a jagged-glass pattern of city-states, shanty-states, nebulous and anarchic regionalisms—it is necessary to consider, finally, the whole question of war.

"Oh, what a relief to fight, to fight enemies who defend themselves, enemies who are awake!" André Malraux wrote in *Man's Fate*. I cannot think of a more suitable battle cry for many combatants in the early decades of the twenty-first century. The intense savagery of the fighting in such diverse cultural settings as Liberia, Bosnia, the Caucasus, and Sri Lanka—to say nothing of what obtains in American inner cities—indicates something very troubling that those of us inside the stretch limo, concerned with issues like middle-class entitlements and the future of interactive cable television, lack the stomach to contemplate. It is this: a large number of people on this planet, to whom the comfort and stability of a middle-class life is utterly unknown, find war and a barracks existence a step up rather than a step down.

"Just as it makes no sense to ask 'why people eat' or 'what they sleep for," writes Martin van Creveld, a military historian at the Hebrew University in Jerusalem, in *The Transformation of War*, "so fighting in many ways is not a means but an end. Throughout history, for every person who has expressed his horror of war there is another who found in it the most marvelous of all the experiences that are vouchsafed to man, even to the point that he later spent a lifetime boring his descendants by recounting his exploits." When

I asked Pentagon officials about the nature of war in the twenty-first century, the answer I frequently got was "Read Van Creveld." The top brass are enamored of this historian not because his writings justify their existence but, rather, the opposite: Van Creveld warns them that huge state military machines like the Pentagon's are dinosaurs about to go extinct, and that something far more terrible awaits us.

The degree to which Van Creveld's *Transformation of War* complements Homer-Dixon's work on the environment, Huntington's thoughts on cultural clash, my own realizations in traveling by foot, bus, and bush taxi in more than sixty countries, and America's sobering comeuppances in intractable-culture zones like Haiti and Somalia is startling. The book begins by demolishing the notion that men don't like to fight. "By compelling the senses to focus themselves on the here and now," Van Creveld writes, war "can cause a man to take his leave of them." As anybody who has had experience with Chetniks in Serbia, "technicals" in Somalia, Tontons Macoutes in Haiti, or soldiers in Sierra Leone can tell you, in places where the Western Enlightenment has not penetrated and where there has always been mass poverty, people find liberation in violence. In Afghanistan and elsewhere, I vicariously experienced this phenomenon: worrying about mines and ambushes frees you from worrying about mundane details of daily existence. If my own experience is too subjective, there is a wealth of data showing the sheer frequency of war, especially in the developing world since the Second World War. Physical aggression is a part of being human. Only when people attain a certain economic, educational, and cultural standard is this trait tranquilized. In light of the fact that 95 percent of the earth's population growth will be in the poorest areas of the globe, the question is not whether there will be war (there will be a lot of it) but what kind of war. And who will fight whom?

Debunking the great military strategist Carl von Clausewitz, Van Creveld, who may be the most original thinker on war since that early-nineteenth-century Prussian, writes, "Clausewitz's ideas... were wholly rooted in the fact that, ever since 1648, war had been waged overwhelmingly by states." But, as Van Creveld explains, the period of nation-states and, therefore, of state conflict is now ending, and with it the clear "threefold division into government, army, and people" which state-directed wars enforce. Thus, to see the future, the first step is to look back to the past immediately prior to the birth of modernism the wars in medieval Europe which began during the Reformation and reached their culmination in the Thirty Years' War.

Van Creveld writes,

> In all these struggles political, social, economic, and religious motives were hopelessly entangled. Since this was an age when armies consisted of mercenaries, all were also attended by swarms of military entrepreneurs... Many of them paid little but lip service to the organizations for whom they had contracted to fight. Instead, they robbed the countryside on their own behalf...

> Given such conditions, any fine distinctions... between armies on the one hand and peoples on the other were bound to break down. Engulfed by war, civilians suffered terrible atrocities.

BACK THEN, IN other words, there was no "politics" as we have come to understand the term, just as there is less and less "politics" today in Liberia, Sierra Leone, Somalia, Sri Lanka, the Balkans, and the Caucasus, among other places.

Because, as Van Creveld notes, the radius of trust within tribal societies is narrowed to one's immediate family and guerrilla comrades, truces arranged with one Bosnian commander, say, may be broken immediately by another Bosnian commander. The plethora of short-lived ceasefires in the Balkans and the Caucasus constitute proof that we are no longer in a world where the old rules of state warfare apply. More evidence is provided by the destruction of medieval monuments in the Croatian port of Dubrovnik: when cultures, rather than states, fight, then cultural and religious monuments are weapons of war, making them fair game.

Also, war-making entities will no longer be restricted to a specific territory. Loose and shadowy organisms such as Islamic terrorist organizations suggest why borders will mean increasingly little and sedimentary layers of tribalistic identity and control will mean more. "From the vantage point of the present, there appears every prospect that religious... fanaticisms will play a larger role in the motivation of armed conflict" in the West than at any time "for the last 300 years," Van Creveld writes. This is why analysts like Michael Vlahos are closely monitoring religious cults. Vlahos says, "An ideology that challenges us may not take familiar form, like the old Nazis or Commies. It may not even engage us initially in ways that fit old threat markings." Van Creveld concludes, "Armed conflict will be waged by men on earth, not robots in space. It will have more in common with the struggles of primitive tribes than with large-scale conventional war." While another military historian, John Keegan, in his new book *A History of Warfare*, draws a more benign portrait of primitive man, it is important to point out that what Van Creveld really means is *re-primitivized man*: warrior societies operating at a time of unprecedented resource capacity and planetary overcrowding.

Van Creveld's pre-Westphalian vision of worldwide low-intensity conflict is not a superficial "back to the future" scenario. First of all, technology will be used toward primitive ends. In Liberia the guerrilla leader Prince Johnson didn't just cut off the ears of President Samuel Doe before Doe was tortured to death in 1990—Johnson made a video of it which has circulated throughout West Africa. In December of 1992, when plotters of a failed coup against the Strasser regime in Sierra Leone had their ears cut off at Freetown's Hamilton Beach prior to being killed, it was seen by many to be a copycat execution. Considering, as I've explained earlier, that the Strasser regime is not really a government and that Sierra Leone is not really a nation-state, listen closely to Van Creveld: "Once the legal monopoly of armed force long claimed by the state, is wrested out of its hands, existing distinctions between war and crime will break down much as is already the case today in... Lebanon, Sri Lanka, El Salvador, Peru, or Colombia."

If crime and war become indistinguishable, then "national defense" may in the future be viewed as a local concept. As crime continues to grow in our cities and the ability of state governments and criminal-justice systems to protect their citizens diminishes, urban crime may, according to Van Creveld, "develop into low-intensity conflict by coalescing along racial, religious, social, and political lines." As small-scale violence multiplies at home and abroad, state armies will continue to shrink, being gradually replaced by a booming private security business, as in West Africa, and by urban mafias, especially in the former communist world, who may be better equipped than municipal police forces to grant physical protection to local inhabitants.

Future wars will be those of communal survival, aggravated or, in many cases, caused by environmental scarcity. These wars will be subnational, meaning that it will be hard for states and local governments to protect their own citizens physically. This is how many states will ultimately die. As state power fades—and with it the state's ability to help weaker groups within society, not to mention other states—peoples and cultures around the world will be thrown back upon their own strengths and weaknesses, with fewer equalizing mechanisms to protect them. Whereas the distant future will probably see the emergence of a racially hybrid, globalized man, the coming decades will see us more aware of our differences than of our similarities. To the average person, political values will mean less, personal security more. The belief that we are all equal is liable to be replaced by the overriding obsession of the ancient Greek travelers: Why the differences between peoples?

THE LAST MAP

IN *GEOGRAPHY AND THE HUMAN SPIRIT*, Anne Buttimer, a professor at University College, Dublin, recalls the work an early-nineteenth-century German geographer, Carl Ritter, whose work implied "a divine plan for humanity" based on regionalism and a constant, living flow of forms. The map of the future, to the extent that a map is even possible, will represent a perverse twisting of Ritter's vision. Imagine cartography in three dimensions, as if in a hologram. In this hologram would be the overlapping sediments of group and other identities atop the merely two-dimensional color markings of city-states and the remaining nations, themselves confused in places by shadowy tentacles, hovering overhead, indicating the power of drug cartels, mafias, and private security agencies.

Instead of borders, there would be moving "centers" of power, as in the Middle Ages. Many of these layers would be in motion. Replacing fixed and abrupt lines on a flat space would be a shifting pattern of buffer entities, like the Kurdish and Azeri buffer entities between Turkey and Iran, the Turkic Uighur buffer entity between Central Asia and Inner China (itself distinct from coastal China), and the Latino buffer entity replacing a precise U.S.-Mexican border. To this protean cartographic hologram one must add other factors, such as migrations of populations, explosions of birth rates, vectors of disease. Henceforward the map of the world will never be static. This future map—in a sense, the "Last Map"—will be an ever-mutating representation of chaos.

The Indian subcontinent offers examples of what is happening. For different reasons, both India and Pakistan are increasingly dysfunctional. The argument over democracy in these places is less and less relevant to the larger issue of governability. In India's case the question arises, Is one unwieldy bureaucracy in New Delhi the best available mechanism for promoting the lives of 866 million people of diverse languages, religions, and ethnic groups? In 1950, when the Indian population was much less than half as large and nation-building idealism was still strong, the argument for democracy was more impressive than it is now. Given that in 2025 India's population could be close to 1.5 billion, that much of its economy rests on a shrinking natural-resource base, including dramatically declining water levels, and that communal violence and urbanization are spiraling upward, it is difficult to imagine that the Indian state will survive the next century. India's oft-trumpeted Green Revolution has been achieved by overworking its croplands and depleting its watershed. Norman Myers, a British development consultant, worries that Indians have "been feeding themselves today by borrowing against their children's food sources."

Pakistan's problem is more basic still: like much of Africa, the country makes no geographic or demographic sense. It was founded as a homeland for the Muslims of the subcontinent, yet there are more subcontinental Muslims outside Pakistan than within it. Like Yugoslavia, Pakistan is a patchwork of ethnic groups, increasingly in violent conflict with one another. While the Western media gushes over the fact that the country has a woman Prime Minister, Benazir Bhutto, Karachi is becoming a subcontinental version of Lagos. In eight visits to Pakistan, I have never gotten a sense of a cohesive national identity. With as much as 65 percent of its land dependent on intensive irrigation, with wide-scale deforestation, and with a yearly population growth of 2.7 percent (which ensures that the amount of cultivated land per rural inhabitant will plummet), Pakistan is becoming a more and more desperate place. As irrigation in the Indus River basin intensifies to serve two growing populations, Muslim-Hindu strife over falling water tables may be unavoidable.

"India and Pakistan will probably fall apart," Homer-Dixon predicts. "Their sector governments have less and less legitimacy as well as less management ability over people and resources." Rather than one bold line dividing the subcontinent into two parts, the future will likely see a lot of thinner lines and smaller parts, with the ethnic entities of Pakhtunistan and Punjab gradually replacing Pakistan in the space between the Central Asian plateau and the heart of the subcontinent.

None of this even takes into account climatic change, which, if it occurs in the next century, will further erode the capacity of existing states to cope. India, for instance, receives 70 percent of its precipitation from the monsoon cycle, which planetary warming could disrupt.

Not only will the three-dimensional aspects of the Last Map be in constant motion, but its two-dimensional base may change too. The National Academy of Sciences reports that as many as one billion people, or 20 per cent of the world's population, live on lands likely to be inundated or dramatically changed by rising waters... Low-lying countries in the developing world such as Egypt and Bangladesh, where rivers are large and the deltas extensive and densely populated, will be hardest hit... Where the rivers are dammed, as in the case of the Nile, the effects... will be especially severe.

Egypt could be where climatic upheaval—to say nothing of the more immediate threat of increasing population—will incite religious upheaval in truly biblical fashion. Natural catastrophes, such as the October 1992 Cairo earthquake, in which the government failed to deliver relief aid and slum residents were in many instances helped by their local mosques, can only strengthen the position of Islamic factions. In a statement about greenhouse warming which could refer to any of a variety of natural catastrophes, the environmental expert Jessica Tuchman Matthews warns that many of us underestimate the extent to which political systems, in affluent societies as well as in places like Egypt, "depend on the underpinning of natural systems." She adds, "The fact that one can move with ease from Vermont to Miami has nothing to say about the consequences of Vermont acquiring Miami's climate."

Indeed, it is not clear that the United States will survive the next century in exactly its present form. Because America is a multiethnic society, the nation-state has always been more fragile here than it is in more homogeneous societies like Germany and Japan. James Kurth, in an article published in *The National Interest* in 1992, explains that whereas nation-state societies tend to be built around a mass-conscription army and a standardized public school system, "multicultural regimes" feature a high-tech, all-volunteer army (and, I would add, private schools that teach competing values), operating in a culture in which the international media and entertainment industry has more influence than the "national political class." In other words, a nation-state is a place where everyone has been educated along similar lines, where people take their cue from national leaders, and where everyone (every male, at least) has gone through the crucible of military service, making patriotism a simpler issue. Writing about his immigrant family in turn-of-the-century Chicago, Saul Bellow states, "The country took us over. It was a country then, not a collection of "cultures."

During the Second World War and the decade following it, the United States reached its apogee as a classic nation-state. During the 1960s, as is now clear, America began a slow but unmistakable process of transformation. The signs hardly need belaboring: racial polarity, educational dysfunction, social fragmentation of many and various kinds. William Irwin Thompson, in *Passages About Earth: An Exploration of the New Planetary Culture*, writes, "The educational system that had worked on the Jews or the Irish could no longer work on the blacks; and when Jewish teachers in New York tried to take black children away from their parents exactly in the way they had been taken from theirs, they were shocked to encounter a violent affirmation of negritude."

Issues like West Africa could yet emerge as a new kind of foreign-policy issue, further eroding America's domestic peace. The spectacle of several West African nations collapsing at once could reinforce the worst racial stereotypes here at home. That is another reason why Africa matters. We must not kid ourselves: the sensitivity factor is higher than ever. The Washington, D.C., public school system is already experimenting with an Afrocentric curriculum. Summits between African leaders and prominent African-Americans are becoming frequent, as are Pollyanna-ish prognostications about multiparty elections in Africa that do not factor in crime, surging birth rates, and resource depletion. The Congressional Black Caucus was among those urging U.S. involvement in Somalia and in Haiti. At the Los Angeles Times minority staffers have protested against, among other things, what they allege to be the racist tone of the newspaper's Africa coverage, allegations that the editor of the "World Report" section, Dan Fisher, denies, saying essentially that Africa should be viewed through the same rigorous analytical lens as other parts of the world. Africa may be marginal in terms of conventional late twentieth-century conceptions of strategy, but in an age of cultural and racial clash, when national defense is increasingly local, Africa's distress will exert a destabilizing influence on the United States.

This and many other factors will make the United States less of a nation than it is today, even as it gains territory following the peaceful dissolution of Canada. Quebec, based on the bedrock of Roman Catholicism and Francophone ethnicity, could yet turn out to be North America's most cohesive and crime-free nation-state. (It may be a smaller Quebec, though, since aboriginal peoples may lop off northern parts of the province.) "Patriotism" will become increasingly regional as people in Alberta and Montana discover that they have far more in common with each other than they do with Ottawa or Washington, and Spanish-speakers in the Southwest discover a greater commonality with Mexico City. (*The Nine Nations of North America*, by Joel Garreau, a book about the continent's regionalization, is more relevant now than when it was published, in 1981.) As Washington's influence wanes, and with it the traditional symbols of American patriotism, North Americans will take psychological refuge in their insulated communities and cultures.

RETURNING FROM WEST AFRICA last fall was an illuminating ordeal. After leaving Abidjan, my Air Afrique flight landed in Dakar, Senegal, where all passengers had to disembark in order to go through another security check, this one demanded by U.S. authorities before they would permit the flight to set out for New York. Once we were in New York, despite the midnight hour, immigration officials at Kennedy Airport held up disembarkation by conducting quick interrogations of the aircraft's passengers— this was in addition to all the normal immigration and customs procedures. It was apparent that drug smuggling, disease, and other factors had contributed to the toughest security procedures I have ever encountered when returning from overseas.

Then, for the first time in over a month, I spotted business-people with attaché cases and laptop computers. When I had left New York for Abidjan, all the businesspeople were boarding planes for Seoul and Tokyo, which departed from gates near Air Afrique's. The only non-Africans off to West Africa had been relief workers in T-shirts and khakis. Although the borders within West Africa are increasingly unreal, those separating West Africa from the outside world are in various ways becoming more impenetrable.

But Afrocentrists are right in one respect: we ignore this dying region at our own risk. When the Berlin Wall was falling, in November of 1989, I happened to be in Kosovo, covering a riot between Serbs and Albanians. The future was in Kosovo, I told myself that night, not in Berlin. The same day that Yitzhak Rabin and Yasser Arafat clasped hands on the White House lawn, my Air Afrique plane was approaching Bamako, Mali, revealing corrugated-zinc shacks at the edge of an expanding desert. The real news wasn't at the White House, I realized. It was right below.

The Myth of
Post–Cold War Chaos

G. John Ikenberry

THE 1945 ORDER LIVES ON

A GREAT DEAL of ink has been shed in recent years describing various versions of the post–Cold War order. These attempts have all failed, because there is no such creature. The world order created in the 1940s is still with us, and in many ways stronger than ever. The challenge for American foreign policy is not to imagine and build a new world order but to reclaim and renew an old one—an innovative and durable order that has been hugely successful and largely unheralded.

The end of the Cold War, the common wisdom holds, was a historical watershed. The collapse of communism brought the collapse of the order that took shape after World War II. While foreign policy theorists and officials scramble to design new grand strategies, the United States is rudderless on uncharted seas.

The common wisdom is wrong. What ended with the Cold War was bipolarity, the nuclear stalemate, and decades of containment of the Soviet Union—seemingly the most dramatic and consequential features of the postwar era. But the world order created in the middle to late 1940s endures, more extensive and in some respects more robust than during its Cold War years. Its basic principles, which deal with organization and relations among the Western liberal democracies, are alive and well.

G. JOHN IKENBERRY is Peter F. Krogh Professor of Geopolitics and Global Justice, with a joint affiliation in the Department of Government, at the Edmund A. Walsh School of Foreign Service, Georgetown University. This article originally appeared in the May/June 1996 issue of *Foreign Affairs* © 1996 by the Council on Foreign Relations.

G. John Ikenberry

These less celebrated, less heroic, but more fundamental principles and policies—the real international order—include the commitment to an open world economy and its multilateral management, and the stabilization of socioeconomic welfare. And the political vision behind the order was as important as the anticipated economic gains. The major industrial democracies took it upon themselves to "domesticate" their dealings through a dense web of multilateral institutions, intergovernmental relations, and joint management of the Western and world political economies. Security and stability in the West were seen as intrinsically tied to an array of institutions—the United Nations and its agencies and the General Agreement on Tariffs and Trade (GATT) only some among many—that bound the democracies together, constrained conflict, and facilitated political community. Embracing common liberal democratic norms and operating within interlocking multilateral institutions, the United States, Western Europe, and, later, Japan built an enduring postwar order.

The end of the Cold War has been so disorienting because it ended the containment order—40 years of policies and bureaucratic missions and an entire intellectual orientation. But the watershed of postwar order predated hostilities with the Soviet Union. The turning point was not a Cold War milestone such as the announcement of the Truman Doctrine in 1947 or the creation of the Atlantic alliance in 1948-49. It might have come as early as 1941, when Roosevelt and Churchill issued the Atlantic Charter declaring the liberal principles that were to guide the postwar settlement. The process became irreversible in 1944, when representatives at the Bretton Woods conference laid down the core principles and mechanisms of the postwar Western economic order and those at Dumbarton Oaks gave the political aspect of the vision concrete form in their proposals for a United Nations. The Cold War may have reinforced the liberal democratic order, by hastening the reintegration of Germany and Japan and bringing the United States much more directly into the management of the system. But it did not call it forth.

In world historical terms, the end of the Cold War is an overrated event. Former Secretary of State James A. Baker III observes in his 1995 memoir, *The Politics of Diplomacy,* "In three and a half years [from the late 1980s to the early 1990s]... the very nature of the international system as we know it was transformed." To be sure, large parts of the non-Western world are undergoing a tremendous and difficult transformation. A great human drama is playing itself out in the former communist states, and the future there hangs in the balance. But the system the United States led the way in creating after World War II has not collapsed; on the contrary, it remains the core of world order. The task today is not to discover or define some mythic new order but to reclaim the policies, commitments, and strategies of the old.

A TALE OF TWO DOCTRINES

WORLD WAR II produced two postwar settlements. One, a reaction to deteriorating relations with the Soviet Union, led to the containment order, which was based on the balance of power, nuclear deterrence, and political and ideological competition. The other, a reaction to the economic rivalry and political turmoil of the 1930s and the resulting world war, can be called the liberal democratic order. It culminated in a wide range of new institutions and relations among the Western industrial democracies, built around economic openness, political reciprocity, and multilateral management of an American-led liberal political system.

Distinct political visions and intellectual rationales animated the two settlements, and at key moments the American president gave voice to each. On March 12, 1947, President Truman delivered his celebrated speech before Congress announcing aid to Greece and Turkey, wrapping it in an American commitment to support the cause of freedom worldwide. The declaration of the Truman Doctrine was a founding moment of the containment order, rallying Americans to a new great struggle, this one against what was thought to be Soviet communism's quest for world domination. A "fateful hour" had struck, Truman said, and the people of the world "must choose between two alternate ways of life." If the United States failed to exercise leadership, he warned, "we may endanger the peace of the world."

It is often forgotten that six days before, Truman had delivered an equally sweeping speech at Baylor University. On this occasion he spoke of the lessons the world must learn from the disasters of the 1930s. "As each battle of the economic war of the Thirties was fought, the inevitable tragic result became more and more apparent," said Truman. "From the tariff policy of Hawley and Smoot, the world went on to Ottawa and the system of imperial preferences, from Ottawa to the kind of elaborate and detailed restrictions adopted by Nazi Germany." Truman reaffirmed America's commitment to "economic peace," which would involve tariff reductions and rules and institutions of trade and investment. When economic differences arose, he said, "the interests of all will be considered, and a fair and just solution will be found." Conflicts would be captured and tamed in a cage of multilateral rules, standards, safeguards, and procedures for dispute resolution. According to Truman, "This is the way of a civilized community."

But it was the containment order that impressed itself on the popular imagination. In celebrated American accounts of the early years after World War II, intrepid officials struggled to make sense of Soviet military power and geopolitical intentions. A few "wise men" fashioned a reasoned and coherent response to the global challenge of Soviet communism, and their containment strategy gave clarity and purpose to several decades of American foreign policy. Over those decades, sprawling bureaucratic and military organizations were built around containment. The bipolar division of the world, nuclear weapons of growing size and sophistication, the ongoing clash of two expansive ideologies—all these gave life to and reinforced the centrality of the containment order.

By comparison, the thinking behind the liberal democratic order was more diffuse. The liberal democratic agenda was less obviously a grand strategy designed to advance American security interests, and it was inevitably viewed during the Cold War as secondary, a preoccupation of economists and businessmen. The policies and institutions that supported free trade among the advanced industrial societies seemed the stuff of low politics. But the liberal democratic agenda was actually built on a robust yet sophisticated set of ideas about American security interests, the causes of war and depression, and a desirable postwar political order. Although containment over-shadowed it, the postwar liberal democratic order was more deeply rooted in the American experience and an understanding of history, economics, and the sources of political stability.

The proper foundations of political order have preoccupied American thinkers from the nation's founding onward, and innovative institutions and practices were developed in response to independence, continental expansion, civil war, economic depression, and world war. The liberal ideal was held high: open and decentralized political institutions could limit and diffuse conflict while integrating diverse peoples and interests. Moreover, a stable and legitimate political order was assured by its grounding in the Constitution, which specified rights, guarantees, and an institutionalized political process. When American officials began to contemplate postwar order, they were drawing on a wellspring of ideas, experiments, and historical lessons and sifting these with an abiding liberal belief in the possibility of peaceful and mutually beneficial international relations.

The most basic conviction underlying the postwar liberal agenda was that the closed autarkic regions that had contributed to the worldwide depression and split the globe into competing blocs before the war must be broken up and replaced by an open, nondiscriminatory economic system. Peace and security, proponents had decided, were impossible in the face of exclusive economic regions. The challengers of liberal multilateralism, however, occupied almost every corner of the advanced industrial world. Germany and Japan were the most overtly hostile; both had pursued a dangerous path that combined authoritarian capitalism with military dictatorship and coercive regional autarky. But the British Commonwealth and its imperial preference system also challenged liberal multilateral order.

The hastily drafted Atlantic Charter was an American effort to ensure that Britain signed on to its liberal democratic war aims.[1]

---

1. Churchill insisted that the charter not mandate the dismantling of the British Empire and its system of trade preferences, and only last-minute sidestepping of this controversial issue made agreement possible.

The joint statement of principles affirmed free trade, equal access to natural resources for all interested buyers, and international economic collaboration to advance labor standards, employment security, and social welfare. Roosevelt and Churchill declared before the world that they had learned the lessons of the interwar years—and those lessons were fundamentally about the proper organization of the Western political economy. America's enemies, its friends, and even America itself had to be reformed and integrated into the postwar economic system.

THE LIBERAL MANIFESTO

THE POSTWAR LIBERAL democratic order was designed to solve the internal problems of Western industrial capitalism. It was not intended to fight Soviet communism, nor was it simply a plan to get American business back on its feet after the war by opening up the world to trade and investment. It was a strategy to build Western solidarity through economic openness and joint political governance. Four principles pursued in the 1940s gave shape to this order.

The most obvious principle was economic openness, which would ideally take the form of a system of nondiscriminatory trade and investment. As American strategic thinkers of the 1930s watched the world economy collapse and the German and Japanese blocs emerge, they pondered whether the United States could remain a great industrial power within the confines of the western hemisphere. What were the minimum geographical requirements for the country's economic and military viability? For all practical purposes they had their answer by the time the United States entered the war. An American hemispheric bloc would not be sufficient; the United States needed secure markets and supplies of raw materials in Asia and Europe. Experts in a Council on Foreign Relations study group reached a similar conclusion when considering the necessary size of the area on which the United States depended for economic vitality.

American thinking was that economic openness was an essential element of a stable and peaceful world political order.

"Prosperous neighbors are the best neighbors," remarked Roosevelt administration Treasury official Harry Dexter White. But officials were convinced that American economic and security interests demanded it as well. Great liberal visionaries and hard-nosed geopolitical strategists could agree on the notion of open markets; it united American postwar planners and was the seminal idea informing the work of the Bretton Woods conference on postwar economic cooperation. In his farewell remarks to the conference, Secretary of the Treasury Henry Morgenthau asserted that the agreements creating the International Monetary Fund and the World Bank marked the end of economic nationalism, by which he meant not that countries would give up pursuit of their national interest but that trade blocs and economic spheres of influence would no longer be their vehicles.

The second principle was joint management of the Western political-economic order. The leading industrial democratic states must not only lower barriers to trade and the movement of capital but must govern the system. This also was a lesson from the 1930s: institutions, rules, and active mutual management by governments were necessary to avoid unproductively competitive and conflictual economic practices. Americans believed such cooperation necessary in a world where national economies were increasingly at the mercy of developments abroad. The unwise or untoward policies of one country threatened contagion, undermining the stability of all. As Roosevelt said at the opening of Bretton Woods, "The economic health of every country is a proper matter of concern to all its neighbors, near and far."

The belief in cooperative economic management also drew inspiration from the government activism of Roosevelt's New Deal. The postwar Western system was organized at a high tide of optimism about the capability of experts, economic and technical knowledge, and government intervention. The rise of Keynesian economics in Europe in the 1930s had begun to encourage an activist role for the state in the economy and society. International economic governance was a natural and inevitable extension of the policies being tried in individual Western industrial societies.

A third principle of liberal democratic order held that the rules and institutions of the Western world economy must be organized to support domestic economic stability and social security. This new commitment was foreshadowed in the Atlantic Charter's call for postwar international collaboration to ensure employment stability and social welfare. It was a sign of the times that Churchill, a conservative Tory, could promise a historic expansion of the government's responsibility for the people's well-being. In their schemes for postwar economic order, both Britain and the United States sought a system that would aid and protect their nascent social and economic commitments. They wanted an open world economy, but one congenial to the emerging welfare state as well as business.

The discovery of a middle way between old political alternatives was a major innovation of the postwar Western economic order. British and American planners began their discussion in 1942 deadlocked, Britain's desire for full employment and economic stabilization after the war running up against the American desire for free trade. The breakthrough came in 1944 with the Bretton Woods agreements on monetary order, which secured a more or less open system of trade and payments while providing safeguards for domestic economic stability through the International Monetary Fund. The settlement was a synthesis that could attract a new coalition of conservative free traders and the liberal prophets of economic planning.

A final element of the liberal democratic system might be termed "constitutionalism"—meaning simply that the Western nations would make systematic efforts to anchor their joint commitments in principled and binding institutional mechanisms. In fact, this may be the order's most basic aspect, encompassing the other principles and policies and giving the whole its distinctive domestic character. Governments might ordinarily seek to keep their options open, cooperating with other states but retaining the possibility of disengagement. The United States and the other Western nations after the war did exactly the opposite. They built long-term economic, political, and security commitments that were difficult to retract, and locked in the relationships, to the extent that sovereign states can. Insofar as the participating governments attempted to construct a political order based on commonly embraced norms and principles along with institutional mechanisms for resolving conflicts and reaching specific agreements, they practiced constitutionalism.

Democracies are particularly capable of making constitutional commitments to each other. For self-regarding states to agree to pursue their interests within binding institutions, they must perceive in their partners a credible sense of commitment—an assurance that they will not exit at the least sign of disagreement. Because policymaking in democracies tends to be decentralized and open, the character of commitments can be more clearly determined and there are opportunities to lobby policymakers in the other democracies. Democracies do not just sign agreements; they create political processes that reduce uncertainty and build confidence in mutual commitments.

A CONSTITUTION FOR THE WEST

THE CONSTITUTIONAL POLITICAL order was constructed in the West around economic, political, and security institutions. In the economic realm, the Bretton Woods accords were the first permanent international arrangements for cooperation between states. Rules and institutions were proposed to ensure a stable and expansionary world economy and an orderly exchange rate system. Many of the original agreements for a rule-based monetary order gave way to ad hoc arrange-ments based more on the American dollar, but the vision of jointly managed, multilateral order remained. The organization of postwar trade relations also had an uncertain start, but ultimately an elaborate system of rules and obligations was developed, with quasi-judicial procedures for adjudicating disputes. In effect, the Western governments created an array of transnational political arenas organized by function. The postwar years were filled with economic disputes, but they were largely contained within these arenas.

The constitutional vision informed the creation of the United Nations, which combined political, economic, and security aspirations. To be sure, the U.N. system preserved the sovereign rights of member states. Intent on avoiding the failures of the League of Nations, the architects of the new international body drafted a charter under which the great powers would retain their freedom of action. But despite its weak rules and obligations, the United Nations reflected American and European desires to insure against a relapse of American isolation, to establish principles and mechanisms of conflict resolution, and to mute conflicts between states within a semi-institutionalized political process.

Cold War security structures provided additional constitutional architecture. Lord Ismay's observation that NATO was created to keep the Russians out, the Germans down, and the Americans in encapsulates the alliance's importance in locking in long-term commitments and expectations. The American-Japanese security pact had a similar dual-containment character. These institutions not only served as alliances in the ordinary sense of organized efforts to balance external threats, but offered mechanisms and venues for building relations, conducting business, and regulating conflict. The recent French decision to rejoin NATO can be understood only in this light. If NATO were simply a balancing alliance, the organization would be in an advanced stage of decay. It is NATO's broader political function—binding the democracies together and reinforcing political community—that explains its remarkable durability.

The democratic character of the United States and its partners facilitated construction of these dense interstate connections. The decentralized and open character of domestic institutions encouraged political give-and-take across the advanced industrial world. Thus the Western liberal democratic order was not only defined by a set of institutions and agreements but made for a particular kind of politics—transnational, pluralistic, reciprocal, legitimate.

The constitutional features of the Western order have been especially important for Germany and Japan. Both countries were reintegrated into the advanced industrial world as semisovereign powers that had accepted unprecedented constitutional limits on their military capacity and independence. As such, they became unusually reliant on Western regional and multilateral economic and security institutions. The Western order in which they were embedded was integral to their stability and their very functioning. The Christian Democratic politician Walther Leisler Kiep argued in 1972 that "the German-American alliance... is not merely one aspect of modern German history, but a decisive element as a result of its preeminent place in our politics. In effect, it provides a second constitution for our country." Western economic and security institutions were and are for Germany and Japan a political bulwark that provides stability and transcends those institutions' more immediate purposes.

WHAT ENDURES

FOR THOSE WHO thought cooperation among the advanced industrial democracies was driven primarily by Cold War threats, the last few years must appear puzzling. Relations between the major Western countries have not broken down. Germany has not rearmed, nor has Japan. What the Cold War focus misses is an appreciation of the other, less heralded, postwar American project—the building of a liberal order in the West. Archaeologists remove one stratum only to discover an older one beneath; the end of the Cold War allows us to see a deeper and more enduring layer of the postwar political order that was largely obscured by the more dramatic struggles between East and West.

Fifty years after its founding, the Western liberal democratic world is robust, and its principles and policies remain the core of world order. The challenges to liberal multilateralism both from within and from outside the West have mainly disappeared. Although regional experiments abound, they are fundamentally different from the autarkic blocs of the 1930s. The forces of business and financial integration are moving the globe inexorably toward a more tightly interconnected system that ignores regional as well as national borders. Recent proposals for an Atlantic free trade agreement and a Transatlantic Treaty, whatever their economic merits, reflect the trend toward increased integration across regions. The successful conclusion of the Uruguay Round

G. John Ikenberry

of international trade talks in 1994 and the launching of the World Trade Organization on January 1, 1995, testify to the vigor of liberal multilateral principles.

Some aspects of the vision of the 1940s have faded. The optimism about government activism and economic management that animated the New Deal and Keynesianism has been considerably tempered. Likewise, the rule-based, quasi-judicial functions of liberal multilateralism have eroded, particularly in monetary relations. Paradoxically, although the rules of cooperation have become less coherent, cooperation itself has increased. Formal rules governing the Western world economy have gradually been replaced by a convergence of thinking on economic policy. The consensus on the broad outlines of desirable domestic and international economic policies has both reflected and promoted increased economic growth and the incorporation of emerging economies into the system.

The problems the liberal democratic order confronts are mostly problems of success, foremost among them the need to integrate the newly developing and post-communist countries. Here one sees most clearly that the post–Cold War order is really a continuation and extension of the Western order forged during and after World War II. The difference is its increasingly global reach. The world has seen an explosion in the desire of countries and peoples to move toward democracy and capitalism. When the history of the late twentieth century is written, it will be the struggle for more open and democratic polities throughout the world that will mark the era, rather than the failure of communism.

Other challenges to the system are boiling up in its leading states. In its early years, rapid and widely shared economic growth buoyed the system, as working- and middle-class citizens across the advanced industrial world rode the crest of the boom. Today economic globalization is producing much greater inequality between the winners and the losers, the wealthy and the poor. How the subsequent dislocations, dashed expectations, and political grievances are dealt with—whether the benefits are shared and the system as a whole is seen as socially just—will affect the stability of the liberal world order more than regional conflict, however tragic, in places like the Balkans.

The Myth of Post–Cold War Chaos

To be sure, the Cold War reinforced solidarity and a sense of common identity among the liberal democracies, so it would be a mistake to take these binding forces for granted now. Trade disputes, controversies over burden-sharing, and regional conflict will test the durability of the liberal order. Without a Cold War threat to unite their countries, leaders in the advanced democracies will have to work harder to manage the inevitable conflicts and fissures. An agenda of reform and renewal would be an intelligent move to protect 50 years of investment in stable and thriving relations. Policies, institutions, and political symbols can all be directed at reinforcing liberal order, just as they are in individual liberal polities. At the very least, Western leaders could spend much more time acknowledging and celebrating the political space they share.

It is fashionable to say that the United States after the Cold War faces its third try at forging a durable world order, at reinventing the basic rules of world politics, just as after both world wars. But this view is more rhetorically compelling than historically valid. The end of the Cold War was less the end of a world order than the collapse of the communist world into an expanding Western order. If that order is to be defended and strengthened, its historical roots and accomplishments must be reclaimed. The United States built and then managed the containment order for 40 years, but it also built and continues to enjoy the rewards of an older liberal democratic order. America is not adrift in uncharted seas. It is at the center of a world of its own making.

The Rise of
Illiberal Democracy

Fareed Zakaria

THE NEXT WAVE

THE AMERICAN DIPLOMAT Richard Holbrooke pondered a problem on the eve of the September 1996 elections in Bosnia, which
were meant to restore civic life to that ravaged country. "Suppose the
election was declared free and fair," he said, and those elected are
"racists, fascists, separatists, who are publicly opposed to [peace and
reintegration]. That is the dilemma." Indeed it is, not just in the former Yugoslavia, but increasingly around the world. Democratically
elected regimes, often ones that have been reelected or reaffirmed
through referenda, are routinely ignoring constitutional limits on

their power and depriving their citizens of basic rights and freedoms.
From Peru to the Palestinian Authority, from Sierra Leone to
Slovakia, from Pakistan to the Philippines, we see the rise of a dis-
turbing phenomenon in international life—illiberal democracy.

It has been difficult to recognize this problem because for
almost a century in the West, democracy has meant *liberal*
democracy—a political system marked not only by free and fair
elections, but also by the rule of law, a separation of powers,
and the protection of basic liberties of speech, assembly,
religion, and property. In fact, this latter bundle of freedoms—
what might be termed constitutional liberalism—is theoretically different and historically distinct from democracy. As

FAREED ZAKARIA is Editor of *Newsweek* magazine's overseas editions. This article originally appeared in the November/December 1997
issue of *Foreign Affairs* © 1997 by the Council on Foreign Relations.

the political scientist Philippe Schmitter has pointed out, "Liberalism, either as a conception of political liberty, or as a doctrine about economic policy, may have coincided with the rise of democracy. But it has never been immutably or unambiguously linked to its practice." Today the two strands of liberal democracy, interwoven in the Western political fabric, are coming apart in the rest of the world. Democracy is flourishing; constitutional liberalism is not.

Today, 118 of the world's 193 countries are democratic, encompassing a majority of its people (54.8 percent, to be exact), a vast increase from even a decade ago. In this season of victory, one might have expected Western statesmen and intellectuals to go one further than E. M. Forster and give a rousing three cheers for democracy. Instead there is a growing unease at the rapid spread of multiparty elections across south-central Europe, Asia, Africa, and Latin America, perhaps because of what happens *after* the elections. Popular leaders like Russia's Boris Yeltsin and Argentina's Carlos Menem bypass their parliaments and rule by presidential decree, eroding basic constitutional practices. The Iranian parliament—elected more freely than most

Putin

in the Middle East—imposes harsh restrictions on speech, assembly, and even dress, diminishing that country's already meager supply of liberty. Ethiopia's elected government turns its security forces on journalists and political opponents, doing permanent damage to human rights (as well as human beings).

Naturally there is a spectrum of illiberal democracy, ranging from modest offenders like Argentina to near-tyrannies like Kazakhstan and Belarus, with countries like Romania and Bangladesh in between. Along much of the spectrum, elections are rarely as free and fair as in the West today, but they do reflect the reality of popular participation in politics and support for those elected. And the examples are not isolated or atypical. Freedom House's 1996-97 survey, *Freedom in the World*, has separate rankings for political liberties and civil liberties, which correspond roughly with democracy and constitutional liberalism, respectively. Of the countries that lie between confirmed dictatorship and consolidated *f* democracy, 50 percent do better on political liberties than on civil ones. In other words, half of the "democratizing" countries in the world today are illiberal democracies.[1]

Illiberal democracy is a growth industry. Seven years ago only 22 percent of democratizing countries could have been so categorized; five years ago that figure had risen to 35 percent.[2] And to date few illiberal democracies have matured into liberal democracies; if anything, they are moving toward heightened illiberalism.

---

1. Roger Kaplan, ed., *Freedom Around the World, 1997*, New York: Freedom House, 1997, pp. 21-22. The survey rates countries on two 7-point scales, for political rights and civil liberties (lower is better). I have considered all countries with a combined score of between 5 and 10 to be democratizing. The percentage figures are based on Freedom House's numbers, but in the case of individual countries I have not adhered strictly to its ratings. While the *Survey* is an extraordinary feat—comprehensive and intelligent—its methodology conflates certain constitutional rights with democratic procedures, which confuses matters. In addition, I use as examples (though not as part of the data set) countries like Iran, Kazakhstan, and Belarus, which even in procedural terms are semi-democracies at best. But they are worth highlighting as interesting problem cases since most of their leaders were elected, reelected, and remain popular.

2. *Freedom in the World: The Annual Survey of Political Rights and Civil Liberties, 1992-1993*, pp. 620-26; *Freedom in the World, 1989-1990*, pp. 312-19.

Far from being a temporary or transitional stage, it appears that many countries are settling into a form of government that mixes a substantial degree of democracy with a substantial degree of illiberalism. Just as nations across the world have become comfortable with many variations of capitalism, they could well adopt and sustain varied forms of democracy. Western liberal democracy might prove to be not the final destination on the democratic road, but just one of many possible exits.

DEMOCRACY AND LIBERTY

FROM THE TIME of Herodotus democracy has meant, first and foremost, the rule of the people. This view of democracy as a process of selecting governments, articulated by scholars ranging from Alexis de Tocqueville to Joseph Schumpeter to Robert Dahl, is now widely used by social scientists. In *The Third Wave*, Samuel P. Huntington explains why:

> Elections, open, free and fair, are the essence of democracy, the inescapable sine qua non. Governments produced by elections may be inefficient, corrupt, shortsighted, irresponsible, dominated by special interests, and incapable of adopting policies demanded by the public good. These qualities make such governments undesirable but they do not make them undemocratic. Democracy is one public virtue, not the only one, and the relation of democracy to other public virtues and vices can only be understood if democracy is clearly distinguished from the other characteristics of political systems.

This definition also accords with the commonsense view of the term. If a country holds competitive, multiparty elections, we call it democratic. When public participation in politics is increased, for example through the enfranchisement of women, it is seen as more democratic. Of course elections must be open and fair, and this requires some protections for freedom of speech and assembly. But to go beyond this minimalist definition and label a country democratic only if it guarantees a comprehensive catalog of social, political, economic, and religious rights turns the word democracy into a badge of honor rather than a descriptive category. After all, Sweden has an economic system that many argue curtails individual property rights, France until recently had a state monopoly on television, and England has an established religion. But they are all clearly and identifiably democracies. To have democracy mean, subjectively, "a good government" renders it analytically useless.

Constitutional liberalism, on the other hand, is not about the procedures for selecting government, but rather government's goals. It refers to the tradition, deep in Western history, that seeks to protect an individual's autonomy and dignity against coercion, whatever the source—state, church, or society. The term marries two closely connected ideas. It is *liberal* because it draws on the philosophical strain, beginning with the Greeks, that emphasizes individual liberty.[3] It is *constitutional* because it rests on the tradition, beginning with the Romans, of the rule of law. Constitutional liberalism developed in Western Europe and the United States as a defense of the individual's right to life and property, and freedom of religion and speech. To secure these rights, it emphasized checks on the power of each branch of government, equality under the law, impartial courts and tribunals, and separation of church and state. Its canonical figures include the poet John Milton, the jurist William Blackstone, statesmen such as Thomas Jefferson and James Madison, and philosophers such as Thomas Hobbes, John Locke, Adam Smith, Baron de Montesquieu, John Stuart Mill, and Isaiah Berlin. In almost all of its variants, constitutional liberalism argues that human beings have certain natural (or "inalienable") rights and that governments must accept a basic law, limiting its own powers, that secures them. Thus in 1215 at Runnymede, England's barons forced the king to abide by the settled and customary law of the land. In the American colonies these laws were made explicit, and in 1638 the town of Hartford adopted the first written constitution in modern history. In the 1970s, Western nations codified standards of behavior for regimes across the globe. The Magna Carta, the Fundamental

---

3. The term "liberal" is used here in its older, European sense, now often called classical liberalism. In America today the word has come to mean something quite different, namely policies upholding the modern welfare state.

Orders of Connecticut, the American Constitution, and the Helsinki Final Act are all expressions of constitutional liberalism.

THE ROAD TO LIBERAL DEMOCRACY

SINCE 1945 Western governments have, for the most part, embodied both democracy and constitutional liberalism. Thus it is difficult to imagine the two apart, in the form of either illiberal democracy or liberal autocracy. In fact both have existed in the past and persist in the present. Until the twentieth century, most countries in Western Europe were liberal autocracies or, at best, semi-democracies. The franchise was tightly restricted, and elected legislatures had little power. In 1830 Great Britain, in some ways the most democratic European nation, allowed barely 2 percent of its population to vote for one house of Parliament; that figure rose to 7 percent after 1867 and reached around 40 percent in the 1880s. Only in the late 1940s did most Western countries become full-fledged democracies, with universal adult suffrage. But one hundred years earlier, by the late 1840s, most of them had adopted important aspects of constitutional liberalism—the rule of law, private property rights, and increasingly, separated powers and free speech and assembly. For much of modern history, what characterized governments in Europe and North America, and differentiated them from those around the world, was not democracy but constitutional liberalism. The "Western model" is best symbolized not by the mass plebiscite but the impartial judge.

The recent history of East Asia follows the Western itinerary. After brief flirtations with democracy after World War II, most East Asian regimes turned authoritarian. Over time they moved from autocracy to liberalizing autocracy, and, in some cases, toward liberalizing semi-democracy.[4] Most of the regimes in East Asia remain only semi-democratic, with patriarchs or one-party systems

---

4. Indonesia, Singapore, and Malaysia are examples of liberalizing autocracies, while South Korea, Taiwan, and Thailand are liberal semi-democracies. Both groups, however, are more liberal than they are democratic, which is also true of the region's only liberal democracy, Japan; Papua New Guinea, and to a lesser extent the Philippines, are the only examples of illiberal democracy in East Asia.

that make their elections ratifications of power rather than genuine contests. But these regimes have accorded their citizens a widening sphere of economic, civil, religious, and limited political rights. As in the West, liberalization in East Asia has included economic liberalization, which is crucial in promoting both growth and liberal democracy. Historically, the factors most closely associated with full-fledged liberal democracies are capitalism, a bourgeoisie, and a high per capita GNP. Today's East Asian governments are a mix of democracy, liberalism, capitalism, oligarchy, and corruption—much like Western governments circa 1900.

Constitutional liberalism has led to democracy, but democracy does not seem to bring constitutional liberalism. In contrast to the Western and East Asian paths, during the last two decades in Latin America, Africa, and parts of Asia, dictatorships with little background in constitutional liberalism have given way to democracy. The results are not encouraging. In the western hemisphere, with elections having been held in every country except Cuba, a 1993 study by the scholar Larry Diamond determined that 10 of the 22 principal Latin American countries "have levels of human rights abuse that are incompatible with the consolidation of [liberal] democracy."[5] In Africa, democratization has been extraordinarily rapid. Within six months in 1990 much of Francophone Africa lifted its ban on multiparty politics. Yet although elections have been held in most of the 45 sub-Saharan states since 1991 (18 in 1996 alone), there have been setbacks for freedom in many countries. One of Africa's most careful observers, Michael Chege, surveyed the wave of democratization and drew the lesson that the continent had "overemphasized multiparty elections... and correspondingly neglected the basic tenets of liberal governance." In Central Asia, elections, even when reasonably free, as in Kyrgyzstan and Kazakstan, have resulted in strong executives, weak legislatures and judiciaries, and few civil and economic liberties. In the Islamic world, from the Palestinian Authority to Iran to Pakistan,

---

5. Larry Diamond, "Democracy in Latin America," in Tom Farer, ed., *Beyond Sovereignty: Collectively Defending Democracy in a World of Sovereign States,* Baltimore: The Johns Hopkins University Press, 1996, p. 73.

democratization has led to an increasing role for theocratic politics, eroding long-standing traditions of secularism and tolerance. In many parts of that world, such as Tunisia, Morocco, Egypt, and some of the Gulf States, were elections to be held tomorrow, the resulting regimes would almost certainly be more illiberal than the ones now in place.

Many of the countries of Central Europe, on the other hand, have moved successfully from communism to liberal democracy, having gone through the same phase of liberalization without democracy as other European countries did during the nineteenth century. Indeed, the Austro-Hungarian empire, to which most belonged, was a classic liberal autocracy. Even outside Europe, the political scientist Myron Weiner detected a striking connection between a constitutional past and a liberal democratic present. He pointed out that, as of 1983, "every single country in the Third World that emerged from colonial rule since the Second World War with a population of at least one million (and almost all the smaller colonies as well) with a continuous democratic experience is a former British colony."[6] British rule meant not democracy—colonialism is by definition undemocratic—but constitutional liberalism. Britain's legacy of law and administration has proved more beneficial than France's policy of enfranchising some of its colonial populations.

While liberal autocracies may have existed in the past, can one imagine them today? Until recently, a small but powerful example

---

6. Myron Weiner, "Empirical Democratic Theory," in Myron Weiner and Ergun Ozbudun, eds., *Competitive Elections in Developing Countries*, Durham: Duke University Press, 1987, p. 20. Today there are functioning democracies in the Third World that are not former British colonies, but the majority of the former are the latter.

Liberal autonomy (handwritten margin note)

flourished off the Asian mainland—Hong Kong. For 156 years, until July 1, 1997, Hong Kong was ruled by the British Crown through an appointed governor general. Until 1991 it had never held a meaningful election, but its government epitomized constitutional liberalism, protecting its citizens' basic rights and administering a fair court system and bureaucracy. A September 8, 1997, editorial on the island's future in *The Washington Post* was titled ominously, "Undoing Hong Kong's Democracy." Actually, Hong Kong has precious little democracy to undo; what it has is a framework of rights and laws. Small islands may not hold much practical significance in today's world, but they do help one weigh the relative value of democracy and constitutional liberalism. Consider, for example, the question of where you would rather live, Haiti, an illiberal democracy, or Antigua, a liberal semi-democracy. Your choice would probably relate not to the weather, which is pleasant in both, but to the political climate, which is not.

ABSOLUTE SOVEREIGNTY

JOHN STUART MILL opened his classic *On Liberty* by noting that as countries became democratic, people tended to believe that "too much importance had been attached to the limitation of power itself. That... was a response against rulers whose interests were opposed to those of the people." Once the people were themselves in charge, caution was unnecessary. "The nation did not need to be protected against its own will." As if confirming Mill's fears, consider the words of Alexandr Lukashenko after being elected president of Belarus with an overwhelming majority in a free election in 1994, when asked about limiting his powers: "There will be no dictatorship. I am of the people, and I am going to be for the people."

The tension between constitutional liberalism and democracy centers on the scope of governmental authority. Constitutional liberalism is about the limitation of power, democracy about its accumulation and use. For this reason, many eighteenth- and nineteenth-century liberals saw in democracy a force that could undermine liberty. James Madison explained in *The Federalist* that "the danger of oppression" in a democracy came from "the majority of the community." Tocqueville warned of the "tyranny of the majority," writing, "The very essence of democratic government consists in the absolute sovereignty of the majority."

The tendency for a democratic government to believe it has absolute sovereignty (that is, power) can result in the centralization of authority, often by extraconstitutional means and with grim results. Over the last decade, elected governments claiming to represent the people have steadily encroached on the powers and rights of other elements in society, a usurpation that is both horizontal (from other branches of the national government) and vertical (from regional and local authorities as well as private businesses and other nongovernmental groups). Lukashenko and Peru's Alberto Fujimori are only the worst examples of this practice. (While Fujimori's actions—disbanding the legislature and suspending the constitution, among others—make it difficult to call his regime democratic, it is worth noting that he won two elections and was extremely popular until recently.) Even a bona fide reformer like Carlos Menem has passed close to 300 presidential decrees in his eight years in office, about three times as many as all previous Argentinean presidents put together, going back to 1853. Kyrgyzstan's Askar Akayev, elected with 60 percent of the vote, proposed enhancing his powers in a referendum that passed easily in 1996. His new powers include appointing all top officials except the prime minister, although he can dissolve parliament if it turns down three of his nominees for the latter post.

Horizontal usurpation, usually by presidents, is more obvious, but vertical usurpation is more common. Over the last three decades, the Indian government has routinely disbanded state legislatures on flimsy grounds, placing regions under New Delhi's direct rule. In a less dramatic but typical move, the elected government of the Central African Republic recently ended the long-standing independence of its university system, making it part of the central state apparatus.

Usurpation is particularly widespread in Latin America and the states of the former Soviet Union, perhaps because both regions mostly have presidencies. These systems tend to produce strong leaders who believe that they speak for the people—even when they have been elected by no more than a plurality. (As Juan Linz points out, Salvador Allende was elected to the Chilean presidency in 1970 with only 36 percent of the vote. In similar circumstances, a prime minister would have had to share power in a coalition government.) Presidents appoint cabinets of cronies, rather than senior party figures, maintaining few internal checks on their power. And when their views conflict with those of the legislature, or even the courts, presidents tend to "go to the nation," bypassing the dreary tasks of bargaining and coalition-building. While scholars debate the merits of presidential versus parliamentary forms of government, usurpation can occur under either, absent well-developed alternate centers of power such as strong legislatures, courts, political parties, regional governments, and independent universities and media. Latin America actually combines presidential systems with proportional representation, producing populist leaders and multiple parties—an unstable combination.

Many Western governments and scholars have encouraged the creation of strong and centralized states in the Third World. Leaders in these countries have argued that they need the authority to break down feudalism, split entrenched coalitions, override vested interests, and bring order to chaotic societies. But this confuses the need for a legitimate government with that for a powerful one. Governments that are seen as legitimate can usually maintain order and pursue tough policies, albeit slowly, by building coalitions. After all, few claim that governments in developing countries should not have adequate police powers; the trouble comes from all the other political, social, and economic powers that they accumulate. In crises like civil wars, constitutional governments might not be able to rule effectively, but the alternative—states with vast security apparatuses that suspend constitutional rights—has usually produced neither order nor good government. More often, such states have become predatory, maintaining some order but also arresting opponents, muzzling dissent, nationalizing industries, and confiscating property. While anarchy has its dangers, the greatest threats to human liberty and happiness in this century have been caused not by disorder but by brutally strong, centralized states, like Nazi Germany, Soviet

Russia, and Maoist China. The Third World is littered with the bloody handiwork of strong states.

Historically, unchecked centralization has been the enemy of liberal democracy. As political participation increased in Europe over the nineteenth century, it was accommodated smoothly in countries such as England and Sweden, where medieval assemblies, local governments, and regional councils had remained strong. Countries like France and Prussia, on the other hand, where the monarchy had effectively centralized power (both horizontally and vertically), often ended up illiberal and undemocratic. It is not a coincidence that in twentieth-century Spain, the beachhead of liberalism lay in Catalonia, for centuries a doggedly independent and autonomous region. In America, the presence of a rich variety of institutions—state, local, and private—made it much easier to accommodate the rapid and large extensions in suffrage that took place in the early nineteenth century. Arthur Schlesinger Sr. has documented how, during America's first 50 years, virtually every state, interest group and faction tried to weaken and even break up the federal government.[7] More recently, India's semi-liberal democracy has survived because of, not despite, its strong regions and varied languages, cultures, and even castes. The point is

7. Arthur Schlesinger, Sr., *New Viewpoints in American History*, New York: Macmillan, 1922, pp. 220-40.

logical, even tautological: pluralism in the past helps ensure political pluralism in the present.

Fifty years ago, politicians in the developing world wanted extraordinary powers to implement then-fashionable economic doctrines, like nationalization of industries. Today their successors want similar powers to privatize those very industries. Menem's justification for his methods is that they are desperately needed to enact tough economic reforms. Similar arguments are made by Abdalá Bucarem of Ecuador and by Fujimori. Lending institutions, such as the International Monetary Fund and the World Bank, have been sympathetic to these pleas, and the bond market has been positively exuberant. But except in emergencies like war, illiberal means are in the long run incompatible with liberal ends. Constitutional government is in fact the key to a successful economic reform policy. The experience of East Asia and Central Europe suggests that when regimes—whether authoritarian, as in East Asia, or liberal democratic, as in Poland, Hungary, and the Czech Republic—protect individual rights, including those of property and contract, and create a framework of law and administration, capitalism and growth will follow. In a recent speech at the Woodrow Wilson International Center in Washington, explaining what it takes for capitalism to flourish, Federal Reserve chairman Alan Greenspan concluded that, "The guiding mechanism of a free market economy... is a bill of rights, enforced by an impartial judiciary."

Finally, and perhaps more important, power accumulated to do good can be used subsequently to do ill. When Fujimori disbanded parliament, his approval ratings shot up to their highest ever. But recent opinion polls suggest that most of those who once approved of his actions now wish he were more constrained. In 1993 Boris Yeltsin famously (and literally) attacked the Russian parliament, prompted by parliament's own unconstitutional acts. He then suspended the constitutional court, dismantled the system of local governments, and fired several provincial governors. From the war in Chechnya to his economic programs, Yeltsin has displayed a routine lack of concern for constitutional procedures and limits. He may well be a liberal democrat at heart, but Yeltsin's actions have created a Russian super-presidency. We can only hope his successor will not abuse it.

For centuries Western intellectuals have had a tendency to view constitutional liberalism as a quaint exercise in rule-making, mere formalism that should take a back seat to battling larger evils in society. The most eloquent counterpoint to this view remains an exchange in Robert Bolt's play *A Man For All Seasons*. The fiery young William Roper, who yearns to battle evil, is exasperated by Sir Thomas More's devotion to the law. More gently defends himself.

> MORE: What would you do? Cut a great road through the law to get after the Devil?

> ROPER: I'd cut every law in England to do that!

> MORE: And when the last law was down, and the Devil turned on you—where would you hide Roper, the laws all being flat?

ETHNIC CONFLICT AND WAR

ON DECEMBER 8, 1996, Jack Lang made a dramatic dash to Belgrade. The French celebrity politician, formerly minister of culture, had been inspired by the student demonstrations involving tens of thousands against Slobodan Miloševic, a man Lang and many Western intellectuals held responsible for the war in the Balkans. Lang wanted to lend his moral support to the Yugoslav opposition. The leaders of the movement received him in their offices—the philosophy department—only to boot him out, declare him "an enemy of the Serbs," and order him to leave the country. It turned out that the students opposed Miloševic not for starting the war, but for failing to win it.

Lang's embarrassment highlights two common, and often mistaken, assumptions—that the forces of democracy are the forces of ethnic harmony and of peace. Neither is necessarily true. Mature liberal democracies can usually accommodate ethnic divisions without violence or terror and live in peace with other liberal democracies. But without a background in constitutional liberalism, the introduction of democracy in divided societies has actually fomented nationalism, ethnic conflict, and even war. The spate of elections held immediately after the collapse of communism were won in the Soviet Union and Yugoslavia by nationalist separatists and resulted in the breakup of those countries. This was not in and of itself bad, since those countries had been bound together by force. But the rapid secessions, without guarantees, institutions, or political power for the many minorities living within the new countries, have caused spirals of rebellion, repression, and, in places like Bosnia, Azerbaijan, and Georgia, war.

Elections require that politicians compete for peoples' votes. In societies without strong traditions of multiethnic groups or assimilation, it is easiest to organize support along racial, ethnic, or religious lines. Once an ethnic group is in power, it tends to exclude other ethnic groups. Compromise seems impossible; one can bargain on material issues like housing, hospitals, and handouts, but how does one split the difference on a national religion? Political competition that is so divisive can rapidly degenerate into violence. Opposition movements, armed rebellions, and coups in Africa have often been directed against ethnically based regimes, many of which came to power through elections. Surveying the breakdown of African and Asian democracies in the 1960s, two scholars concluded that democracy "is simply not viable in an environment of intense ethnic preferences." Recent studies, particularly of Africa and Central Asia, have confirmed this pessimism. A distinguished expert on ethnic conflict, Donald Horowitz, concluded, "In the face of this rather dismal account... of the concrete failures of democracy in divided societies... one is tempted to throw up one's hands. What is the point of holding elections if all they do in the end is to substitute a Bemba-dominated regime for a Nyanja regime in Zambia, the two equally narrow, or a southern regime for a northern one in Benin, neither incorporating the other half of the state?"[8]

---

8. Alvin Rabushka and Kenneth Shepsle, *Politics in Plural Societies: A Theory of Democratic Instability*, Columbus: Charles E. Merill, pp. 62-92; Donald Horowitz, "Democracy in Divided Societies," in Larry Diamond and Mark F. Plattner, eds., *Nationalism, Ethnic Conflict and Democracy*, Baltimore: The Johns Hopkins University Press, 1994, pp. 35-55.

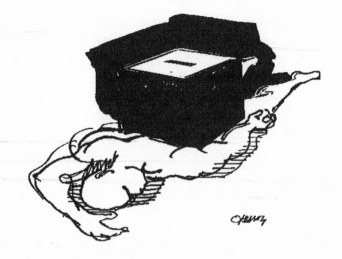

Over the past decade, one of the most spirited debates among scholars of international relations concerns the "democratic peace"—the assertion that no two modern democracies have gone to war with each other. The debate raises interesting substantive questions (does the American Civil War count? do nuclear weapons better explain the peace?) and even the statistical findings have raised interesting dissents. (As the scholar David Spiro points out, given the small number of both democracies and wars over the last two hundred years, sheer chance might explain the absence of war between democracies. No member of his family has ever won the lottery, yet few offer explanations for this impressive correlation.) But even if the statistics are correct, what explains them? Kant, the original proponent of the democratic peace, contended that in democracies, those who pay for wars—that is, the public—make the decisions, so they are understandably cautious. But that claim suggests that democracies are more pacific than other states. Actually they are more warlike, going to war more often and with greater intensity than most states. It is only with other democracies that the peace holds.

When divining the cause behind this correlation, one thing becomes clear: the democratic peace is actually the liberal peace. Writing in the eighteenth century, Kant believed that democracies were tyrannical, and he specifically excluded them from his conception of "republican" governments, which lived in a zone of peace. Republicanism, for Kant, meant a separation of powers, checks and balances, the rule of law, protection of individual rights, and some level of representation in government (though nothing close to universal suffrage). Kant's other explanations for the "perpetual peace" between republics are all closely linked to their constitutional and liberal character: a mutual respect for the rights of each other's citizens, a system of checks and balances assuring that no single leader can drag his country into war, and classical liberal economic policies—most importantly, free trade—which create an interdependence that makes war costly and cooperation useful. Michael Doyle, the leading scholar on the subject, confirms in his 1997 book *Ways of War and Peace* that without constitutional liberalism, democracy itself has no peace-inducing qualities:

> Kant distrusted unfettered, democratic majoritarianism, and his argument offers no support for a claim that all participatory polities—democracies—should be peaceful, either in general or between fellow democracies. Many participatory polities have been non-liberal. For two thousand years before the modern age, popular rule was widely associated with aggressiveness (by Thucydides) or imperial success (by Machiavelli)... The decisive preference of [the] median voter might well include "ethnic cleansing" against other democratic polities.

THE DISTINCTION BETWEEN liberal and illiberal democracies sheds light on another striking statistical correlation. Political scientists Jack Snyder and Edward Mansfield contend, using an impressive data set, that over the last 200 years democratizing states went to war significantly more often than either stable autocracies or liberal democracies. In countries not grounded in constitutional liberalism, the rise of democracy often brings with it hyper-nationalism and war-mongering. When the political system is opened up, diverse groups with incompatible interests gain access to power and press their demands. Political and military leaders, who are often embattled remnants of the old authoritarian order, realize that to succeed that they must rally the masses behind a national cause. The result is invariably aggressive rhetoric and policies, which often drag countries into confrontation and war. Noteworthy examples range from Napoleon III's France, Wilhelmine Germany, and

Taisho Japan to those in today's newspapers, like Armenia and Azerbaijan and Milošević's Serbia. The democratic peace, it turns out, has little to do with democracy.

THE AMERICAN PATH

AN AMERICAN SCHOLAR recently traveled to Kazakstan on a U.S. government-sponsored mission to help the new parliament draft its electoral laws. His counterpart, a senior member of the Kazak parliament, brushed aside the many options the American expert was outlining, saying emphatically, "We want our parliament to be just like your Congress." The American was horrified, recalling, "I tried to say something other than the three words that had immediately come screaming into my mind: 'No you don't!'" This view is not unusual. Americans in the democracy business tend to see their own system as an unwieldy contraption that no other country should put up with. In fact, the adoption of some aspects of the American constitutional framework could ameliorate many of the problems associated with illiberal democracy. The philosophy behind the U.S. Constitution, a fear of accumulated power, is as relevant today as it was in 1789. Kazakstan, as it happens, would be particularly well-served by a strong parliament—like the American Congress—to check the insatiable appetite of its president.

It is odd that the United States is so often the advocate of elections and plebiscitary democracy abroad. What is distinctive about the American system is not how democratic it is but rather how undemocratic it is, placing as it does multiple constraints on electoral majorities. Of its three branches of government, one—arguably paramount—is headed by nine unelected men and women with life tenure. Its Senate is the most unrepresentative upper house in the world, with the lone exception of the House of Lords, which is powerless. (Every state sends two senators to Washington regardless of its population—California's 30 million people have as many votes in the Senate as Arizona's 3.7 million—which means that senators representing about 16 percent of the country can block any proposed law.)

Similarly, in legislatures all over the United States, what is striking is not the power of majorities but that of minorities. To further check national power, state and local governments are strong and fiercely battle every federal intrusion onto their turf. Private businesses and other nongovernmental groups, what Tocqueville called intermediate associations, make up another stratum within society.

The American system is based on an avowedly pessimistic conception of human nature, assuming that people cannot be trusted with power. "If men were angels," Madison famously wrote, "no government would be necessary." The other model for democratic governance in Western history is based on the French Revolution. The French model places its faith in the goodness of human beings. Once the people are the source of power, it should be unlimited so that they can create a just society. (The French revolution, as Lord Acton observed, is not about the limitation of sovereign power but the abrogation of all intermediate powers that get in its way.) Most non-Western countries have embraced the French model—not least because political elites like the prospect of empowering the state, since that means empowering themselves—and most have descended into bouts of chaos, tyranny, or both. This should have come as no surprise. After all, since its revolution France itself has run through two monarchies, two empires, one proto-fascist dictatorship, and five republics.[9]

Of course cultures vary, and different societies will require different frameworks of government. This is not a plea for the wholesale adoption of the American way but rather for a more variegated conception of liberal democracy, one that emphasizes both parts of that phrase. Before new policies can be adopted, there lies an intellectual task of recovering the constitutional liberal tradition, central to the Western experience and to the development of good government throughout the world. Political progress in Western history has been the result of a growing recognition

---

9 Bernard Lewis, "Why Turkey Is the Only Muslim Democracy," *Middle East Quarterly*, March 1994, pp. 47-48.

over the centuries that, as the Declaration of Independence puts it, human beings have "certain inalienable rights" and that "it is to secure these rights that governments are instituted." If a democracy does not preserve liberty and law, that it is a democracy is a small consolation.

LIBERALIZING FOREIGN POLICY

A PROPER APPRECIATION of constitutional liberalism has a variety of implications for American foreign policy. First, it suggests a certain humility. While it is easy to impose elections on a country, it is more difficult to push constitutional liberalism on a society. The process of genuine liberalization and democratization is gradual and long-term, in which an election is only one step. Without appropriate preparation, it might even be a false step. Recognizing this, governments and nongovernmental organizations are increasingly promoting a wide array of measures designed to bolster constitutional liberalism in developing countries. The National Endowment for Democracy promotes free markets, independent labor movements, and political parties. The U.S. Agency for International Development funds independent judiciaries. In the end, however, elections trump everything. If a country holds elections, Washington and the world will tolerate a great deal from the resulting government, as they have with Yeltsin, Akayev, and Menem. In an age of images and symbols, elections are easy to capture on film. (How do you televise the rule of law?) But there is life after elections, especially for the people who live there.

Conversely, the absence of free and fair elections should be viewed as one flaw, not the definition of tyranny. Elections are an important virtue of governance, but they are not the only virtue. Governments should be judged by yardsticks related to constitutional liberalism as well. Economic, civil, and religious liberties are at the core of human autonomy and dignity. If a government with limited democracy steadily expands these freedoms, it should not be branded a dictatorship. Despite the limited political choice they offer, countries like Singapore, Malaysia, and Thailand provide a better environment for the life, liberty, and happiness of their citizens than do either dictatorships like Iraq and Libya or illiberal democracies like Slovakia or Ghana. And the pressures of global capitalism can push the process of liberalization forward. Markets and morals can work together. Even China, which remains a deeply repressive regime, has given its citizens more autonomy and economic liberty than they have had in generations. Much more needs to change before China can even be called a liberalizing autocracy, but that should not mask the fact that much has changed.

Finally, we need to revive constitutionalism. One effect of the overemphasis on pure democracy is that little effort is given to creating imaginative constitutions for transitional countries. Constitutionalism, as it was understood by its greatest eighteenth century exponents, such as Montesquieu and Madison, is a complicated system of checks and balances designed to prevent the accumulation of power and the abuse of office. This is done not by simply writing up a list of rights but by constructing a system in which government will not violate those rights. Various groups must be included and empowered because, as Madison explained, "ambition must be made to counteract ambition." Constitutions were also meant to tame the passions of the public, creating not simply democratic but also deliberative government. Unfortunately, the rich variety of unelected bodies, indirect voting, federal arrangements, and checks and balances that characterized so many of the formal and informal constitutions of Europe are now regarded with suspicion. What could be called the Weimar syndrome—named after interwar Germany's beautifully constructed constitution, which failed to avert fascism—has made people regard constitutions as simply paperwork that cannot make much difference. (As if any political system in Germany would have easily weathered military defeat, social revolution, the Great Depression, and hyperinflation.) Procedures that inhibit direct democracy are seen as inauthentic, muzzling the voice of the people. Today around the world we see variations on the same majoritarian theme. But the trouble with these winner-take-all systems is that, in most democratizing countries, the winner really does take all.

DEMOCRACY'S DISCONTENTS

WE LIVE IN a democratic age. Through much of human history the danger to an individual's life, liberty and happiness came from the absolutism of monarchies, the dogma of churches, the terror of dictatorships, and the iron grip of totalitarianism. Dictators and a few straggling totalitarian regimes still persist, but increasingly they are anachronisms in a world of global markets, information, and media. There are no longer respectable alternatives to democracy; it is part of the fashionable attire of modernity. Thus the problems of governance in the 21st century will likely be problems *within* democracy. This makes them more difficult to handle, wrapped as they are in the mantle of legitimacy.

Illiberal democracies gain legitimacy, and thus strength, from the fact that they are reasonably democratic. Conversely, the greatest danger that illiberal democracy poses—other than to its own people—is that it will discredit liberal democracy itself, casting a shadow on democratic governance. This would not be unprecedented. Every wave of democracy has been followed by setbacks in which the system was seen as inadequate and new alternatives were sought by ambitious leaders and restless masses. The last such period of disenchantment, in Europe during the interwar years, was seized upon by demagogues, many of whom were initially popular and even elected. Today, in the face of a spreading virus of illiberalism, the most useful role that the international community, and most importantly the United States, can play is—instead of searching for new lands to democratize and new places to hold elections—to consolidate democracy where it has taken root and to encourage the gradual development of constitutional liberalism across the globe. Democracy without constitutional liberalism is not simply inadequate, but dangerous, bringing with it the erosion of liberty, the abuse of power, ethnic divisions, and even war. Eighty years ago, Woodrow Wilson took America into the twentieth century with a challenge, to make the world safe for democracy. As we approach the next century, our task is to make democracy safe for the world.

Response

Liberalism and Democracy

Can't Have One Without the Other

Marc F. Plattner

LESS THAN A QUARTER-CENTURY ago, democracy appeared to be confined, with a few exceptions, to North America and Western Europe. These nations had advanced industrial economies, sizable middle classes, and high literacy rates—factors that many political scientists regarded as prerequisites for successful democracy. They were home not only to free and competitive multiparty elections but also to the rule of law and the protection of individual liberties. In short, they were what had come to be called "liberal democracies."

In the rest of the world, by contrast, most countries were neither liberal nor democratic. They were ruled by a variety of dictatorships—military, single-party, revolutionary, Marxist-Leninist—that rejected free, multiparty elections (in practice, if not always in principle). By the early 1990s, however, this situation had changed dramatically, as an astonishing number of autocratic regimes around the world fell from power. They were generally succeeded by regimes that at least aspired to be democratic, giving rise to the phenomenon that Samuel P. Huntington termed the "third wave" of democratization. Today, well over a hundred countries, in every continent in the world, can plausibly claim to have freely elected governments.

MARC A. PLATTNER is Co-Director of the International Forum for Democratic Studies at the National Endowment for Democracy. This article originally appeared in the March/April 1998 issue of *Foreign Affairs* © 1998 by the Council on Foreign Relations.

Outside of Africa, few of these aspiring new democracies have suffered outright reversions to authoritarianism. But many, even among those that hold unambiguously free and fair elections, fall short of providing the protection of individual liberties and adherence to the rule of law commonly found in the long-established democracies. As Larry Diamond has put it, many of the new regimes are "electoral democracies" but not "liberal democracies." Citing Diamond's distinction, Huntington has argued that the introduction of elections in non-Western societies may often lead to victory by antiliberal forces. And Fareed Zakaria has contended that the promotion of elections around the world has been responsible for "the rise of illiberal democracy"—that is, of freely elected governments that fail to safeguard basic liberties. "Constitutional liberalism," Zakaria argues, "is theoretically different and historically distinct from democracy.... Today the two strands of liberal democracy, interwoven in the Western political fabric, are coming apart in the rest of the world. Democracy is flourishing; constitutional liberalism is not." Drawing upon this distinction, Zakaria recommends that Western policymakers not only increase their efforts to foster constitutional liberalism but diminish their support for elections, and suggests that "liberal autocracies" are preferable to illiberal democracies.

DECONSTRUCTING DEMOCRACY

THE BASIC DISTINCTION made by all these authors is both valid and important. Liberal democracy—which is what most people mean today when they speak of democracy—is indeed an interweaving of two different elements, one democratic in a stricter sense and the other liberal. As its etymological derivation suggests, the most basic meaning of the word "democracy" is the rule of the people. As the rule of the many, it is distinguished from monarchy (the rule of one person), aristocracy (the rule of the best), and oligarchy (the rule of the few). In the modern world, where the sheer size of states has rendered impossible the direct democracy once practiced by some ancient republics, the election of legislative representatives and other public officials is the chief mechanism by which the people exercise their rule. Today it is further presumed that democracy implies virtually universal adult suffrage and eligibility to run for office. Elections, then, are regarded as embodying the popular or majoritarian aspect of contemporary liberal democracy.

The word "liberal" in the phrase liberal democracy refers not to the matter of who rules but to the matter of how that rule is exercised. Above all, it implies that government is limited in its powers and its modes of acting. It is limited first by the rule of law, and especially by a fundamental law or constitution, but ultimately it is limited by the rights of the individual. The idea of natural or inalienable rights, which today are most commonly called "human rights," originated with liberalism. The primacy of individual rights means that the protection of the private sphere, along with the plurality and diversity of ends that people seek in their pursuit of happiness, is a key element of a liberal political order.

The fact that democracy and liberalism are not inseparably linked is proven by the historical existence both of nonliberal democracies and of liberal nondemocracies. The democracies of the ancient world, although their citizens were incomparably more involved in governing themselves than we are today, did not provide freedom of speech or religion, protection of private property, or constitutional government. On the other side, the birthplace of liberalism, modern England, retained a highly restricted franchise well into the nineteenth century. As Zakaria points out, England offers the classic example of democratization by a gradual extension of suffrage well after the essential institutions of constitutional liberalism were already in place. In our own time, Zakaria offers Hong Kong under British colonial rule as an example of a flourishing of liberalism in the absence of democracy.

ALL MEN ARE CREATED EQUAL

ALTHOUGH "unpacking" the component elements of modern liberal democracy is a crucial first step toward comprehending its character, overstating the disjunction between liberalism and democracy can easily lead to new misunderstanding. While many new electoral democracies fall short of liberalism, on the whole, countries that hold free elections are overwhelmingly more liberal than those that do not, and countries that protect civil liberties are overwhelmingly more likely to hold free elections than those that do not. This is not simply an accident. It is the result of powerful intrinsic links between electoral democracy and a liberal order.

Some of these links are immediately apparent. Starting from the democratic side, elections would seem to require the guarantee of certain civil liberties—the freedoms of speech, association, and assembly—if they are to be genuinely free and fair. Thus even minimalist definitions of democracy offered by political scientists usually include a stipulation that such liberties must be maintained at least to the extent necessary to make possible open electoral competition. If we begin instead with the human rights mandated by the liberal tradition, these are generally held today to include some kind of right to electoral participation. Thus Article 21 of the U.N. Universal Declaration of Human Rights states: "Everyone has the right to take part in the government of his country, directly or through freely chosen representatives . . . The will of the people shall be the basis of the authority of the government; this will shall be expressed in periodic and genuine elections which shall be by universal and equal suffrage and shall be held by secret vote or by equivalent free voting procedures." One may regard this as a formal or even merely definitional link between liberalism and electoral democracy, but it points to a more profound kinship.

For the political doctrine at the source of liberalism also contains a deeply egalitarian and majoritarian dimension. This is the doctrine that all legitimate political power is derived from the consent of individuals, who are by nature not only free but equal. In the opening pages of his *Second Treatise of Government*, John Locke states that men are naturally in "a state of perfect freedom," which is "a state also of equality, wherein all the power and jurisdiction is reciprocal, no one having more than another: there being nothing more evident, than that Creatures of the same species and rank promiscuously born to all the same advantages of Nature, and the use of the same faculties, should be equal one amongst another without Subordination or Subjection." The essential point is that no man has a natural claim to rule over another, and its clear corollary is that the rule of man over man can be justified only on the basis of a mutual agreement or "compact."

Now it is true that neither Locke nor his immediate successors concluded from this that democracy was the only legitimate form of government. For while they held that the consent of all is essential to the original compact that forms a political community, they also contended that the political community is free to decide where it chooses to bestow legislative power—whether it is in a democracy, an oligarchy, a monarchy, or a mix, as it was among the King, Lords, and Commons in England. Liberalism did not originally insist on democracy as a form of government, but it unequivocally insisted upon the ultimate sovereignty of the people. Thus Locke argues that if the legislature is dissolved or violates its trust, the power to institute a new one reverts to the majority of the people.

In order to grasp the distinctive character of liberal egalitarianism, it is necessary to appreciate how different modern liberal democracy is from the premodern (and truly illiberal) democracy of the ancient city. Reliance on elected representation in the legislature, the key political institution of modern liberal democracy, was understood by its proponents as a decisive departure from ancient democracy. The authors of *The Federalist* frequently contrast two very different kinds of "popular government." They write in favor of a "republic" ("a government in which the scheme of representation takes place"), which they argue need not be subject to the infirmities of "a pure democracy" ("a society consisting of a small number of citizens who assemble and administer the government in person," *Federalist* 10). In pure or direct democracies, they contend, "there is nothing to check the inducements to sacrifice the weaker party or an obnoxious individual," and therefore they "have ever been found incompatible with personal security or the rights of property." Later, in *Federalist* 63, acknowledging that the principle of representation was not unknown to the ancients, Madison states: "The true distinction between [ancient democracies] and the American governments *lies in the total exclusion of the people in their collective capacity*, from any share in the *latter*, and not in the *total exclusion of the representatives of the people* from the administration of the *former*" (italics in original). In short, modern liberal democracy from the outset was inclined to minimize the direct political role of the people. In this sense, Zakaria is on solid ground in stressing the anti-majoritarian aspects of liberalism.

In part, of course, the substitution of representative government for direct democracy was justified by the larger size of modern states, which made it impractical for the whole people to assemble. But this very fact had led thinkers like Montesquieu and Rousseau to conclude that democratic or republican government was possible only in a small state, and Rousseau to assert that "the moment that a people gives itself representatives, it is no longer free." There was, however, another ground used to justify representative government. In Madison's words, it "would refine and enlarge the public views by passing them through the medium of a chosen body of citizens, whose wisdom may best discern the true interest of their country and whose patriotism and love of justice will be least likely to sacrifice it to temporary or partial considerations." In other words, elected representatives are expected to be superior to the average citizen. In the ancient democracies, by contrast, most public officials were chosen by lot. In *The Politics*, Aristotle characterizes lot as the democratic mode of choosing officials, and election as the oligarchic mode. Montesquieu reiterates this judgment, adding, "The suffrage by lot is a method of electing that offends no one, but animates each citizen with the pleasing hope of serving his country." Where elections are used instead, those chosen tend to be richer, better educated, and more talented than most of their fellow citizens. In this light, representative or electoral democracy, besides largely eliminating the people from direct participation in self-government, also seems to constitute an aristocratic deviation from political equality.

BY AND FOR THE PEOPLE

YET THERE IS ANOTHER SENSE in which modern liberal, representative democracy is much more egalitarian than was ancient democracy. In the latter, the citizens entitled to participate in public affairs invariably represented a relatively small percentage of the overall population. Not only were large numbers of slaves and resident aliens excluded, but women had no role in political affairs. Pre-liberal democracy, the direct democracy of the ancient city, was not based on any concept of the fundamental, natural equality of all human beings. It is true, of course, that modern representative government for a long time excluded the poor and all women from political participation, and in the United States even coexisted with slavery. But it is no less true that these kinds of exclusions were always in tension with the underlying principle of liberalism—namely, that all human beings are by nature free and equal. The historical development of this principle inevitably transformed liberalism into liberal democracy.

It is one thing to claim that the majority of people in a traditional and hierarchical society have somehow given their tacit consent to a political arrangement in which they are excluded from having any voice. Popular sentiment in seventeenth-century England, if there had been a way of measuring it, might well have approved of a monarchical political system. But as the principle that all men are created equal gained currency, and as the educational and economic situation of the common people continued to improve, it was only to be expected that some of them would begin to demand the vote. And once they began to do so, how could it any longer be claimed that they consented to a political order in which they had no say? Popular sovereignty without popular government may be coherent in theory and even sustainable in practice for a time. Over the long run, however, popular sovereignty can hardly fail to lead to popular government.

Thus it is not surprising that throughout the Western world, liberal, constitutional regimes became more and more democratic during the nineteenth and twentieth centuries. The share of legislative power wielded by monarchs or unelected bodies receded until it had virtually disappeared. At the same time, suffrage was gradually broadened. Property qualifications and exclusions on the basis of race or sex were eliminated, to the point where "universal and equal suffrage" was endorsed by the world community in 1948 as a human right.

The moral grounds for extending suffrage are succinctly stated by John Stuart Mill in his *Considerations on Representative Government*, published in 1861. "It is a personal injustice," Mill argues, "to withhold from anyone, unless for the prevention of greater evils, the ordinary privilege of having his voice reckoned in the disposal of affairs in which he has the same interest as other people . . . No arrangement of the suffrage, therefore, can be permanently satisfactory in which any person or class is peremptorily excluded, in which the electoral privilege is not open to all persons of full age who desire to obtain it." On these grounds Mill also argues for the extension of the franchise to women. Yet this does not prevent him from arguing against granting the vote to illiterates and to recipients of parish relief (i.e., welfare); he also proposes that multiple votes be allotted to the educated and professional classes. Today, such departures from universality and equality in the allocation of the franchise seem shockingly "elitist." No arguments for "the prevention of greater evils" are reckoned as sufficiently powerful to overbalance the injustice of denying any citizen an equal vote.

MAKING DEMOCRACY WORK

THERE IS ANOTHER RESPECT in which Mill's *Representative Government* is repugnant to contemporary sensibilities—namely, its justification of colonialism. For Mill, representative government "is the ideal type of a perfect government," but it is not applicable under all social conditions. In particular, it is ill suited to "barbarous" or "backward" peoples, who are likely to need some form of monarchical or (preferably) external rule to bring them toward the state of civilization in which they might become fit for representative government.

In part, Mill's argument in favor of colonialism is grounded in a dubious doctrine of historical progress (or of "modernization," as we would say today). Yet there is another basis for Mill's contention that representative government is not applicable under all conditions that is not easily dismissed. As he puts it, "representative, like any other government, must be unsuitable in any case in which it cannot permanently subsist." If people do not value representative government, if they are unwilling to defend it, if they are unable to do what it requires, then they will not be able to maintain it. Thus it would be vain to expect that it would serve them well.

Marc F. Plattner

The concern with making democracy able to maintain itself, with training and spurring the people to do what is needed to make democracy work, is certainly not outdated. It is at the heart of most programs of "democracy assistance" now being provided to new democracies by Western governments, international and regional organizations, and nongovernmental organizations alike. It is at the root of the central concern today of political scientists who study new democracies—the problem of consolidation, or how to bring a democratic regime to the point where its breakdown becomes extremely unlikely. And it explains the widespread attention to issues of citizenship and civil society today, not only in new democracies but in long-established ones as well. These concerns reflect the irreducible fact that making self-government work is not easy. A democratic government can be given to any people, but not every people can maintain it. But what is to be done in the case of a people that is not, at least for the time being, capable of making democracy work? Mill's answer to this question was colonial rule. What is ours? That is the question implicitly raised by Zakaria's article.

The difficulty in answering it points to an acute tension within the modern democratic tradition between the liberal doctrine of just or legitimate government and the practical requirements of popular government. (In *The Social Contract*, Rousseau says that "all legitimate government is republican." But later in the same work he says that "freedom is not a fruit of every climate, and it is not therefore within the capacity of every people.") The principle that all men are born free and equal, and that no one has a right to rule them without their consent, has now swept the world. As I have argued above, this has inevitably come to be understood as meaning that they cannot be ruled without their clearly expressed consent, in the form of an election. Yet the experience of past ages and of many lands suggests that this principle cannot be effectively put into practice everywhere and immediately. The failure in the 1960s of so many of the democracies bequeathed by the departing colonial powers once again demonstrated the fact that under certain conditions democracy is unlikely to endure. But if democratic government is required everywhere in principle, what course can a good liberal democrat follow where it appears unable to work in practice? This conundrum largely accounts for the alternating cycles of euphoria and despair about the prospects for the spread of liberal democracy.

How does Zakaria suggest that this dilemma be resolved? He contends, first, that constitutionalism, the rule of law, and the protection of individual liberty are more essential than representative government. Accordingly, he recommends that, rather than encouraging the introduction of elections in many developing countries, Western policy should favor the establishment of "liberal autocracy." As noted above, the prime example of liberal autocracy that he presents is nineteenth-century Europe, where the introduction of constitutional liberalism by monarchical governments preceded democratization. It has often been remarked that the sequence of first liberal constitutionalism, then gradual democratization, can have advantages in accustoming people to the requirements of self-government. But is this a practical strategy today?

During the nineteenth and early twentieth centuries, democratization proceeded in a context in which more traditional principles of social hierarchy still had a considerable hold over the popular imagination. The idea of equality had not been fully accepted as the preeminent principle of political legitimacy. Monarchy and aristocracy still prevailed in most of Europe, so that even a limited legislative role for an assembly elected with a restricted suffrage could seem like progress toward popular government. Today the situation is dramatically different. There are only a few countries—principally Islamic monarchies—in which anything like traditional rule still holds sway. In these cases, perhaps the nineteenth-century European model can to some extent be emulated. Elsewhere, existing autocracies—or the regimes that aspiring democracies have replaced—are generally ideological rather than traditional regimes and espouse some kind of egalitarian doctrine of their own. In a post- communist or formerly one-party socialist regime, what principle could be accepted as a basis for restricting suffrage? And what legitimate mechanism other than election could be used for deciding who will rule?

The only example in the contemporary world of liberal autocracy that Zakaria explicitly cites is British-ruled Hong Kong. Yet he certainly does not seem prepared to recommend a revival of colonialism. Earlier in this decade, there was a flurry of discussion of the problem of "failed states"—former client states of the superpowers during the Cold War that threatened to collapse once the support of their patron had been withdrawn. Amid the talk of a new world order, there seemed to be some inclination to have the "international community" intervene in such cases, in effect reviving something like colonial rule under the aegis of the United Nations. Whatever the merits or the feasibility of this idea, the fiasco of the U.S. attempt at political (as opposed to humanitarian) intervention in Somalia, along with the proliferation of states that might have been candidates for such costly international reconstruction operations, quickly made it clear that the political will for this kind of policy was lacking.

The practical model that Zakaria seems to have in mind is the economically successful (at least until recently) autocracies of East Asia. Yet it would surely be questionable to assert that these autocracies are genuinely constitutional or liberal, a fact that Zakaria himself seems to recognize by characterizing Indonesia, Singapore, and Malaysia not as "liberal" but only as "liberalizing" autocracies. It would be implausible indeed to claim that these states more reliably protect individual rights or have more independent and impartial judiciaries than the Latin American democracies that Zakaria describes as "illiberal." Even the Singaporeans themselves, while claiming to practice democracy, acknowledge that their regime, to quote Singapore's U.N. Ambassador, Bilahari Kausikan, "has never pretended or aspired to be liberal." Thus, despite Zakaria's talk of constitutionalism and individual rights, he seems to wind up taking the much more familiar view that authoritarian capitalist development is the most reliable road to eventual liberal democracy.

The economic achievements of these East Asian autocracies have certainly been impressive, but so have been the economic achievements of East Asian democracies, beginning with Japan. This is not the place to enter into the complex and hotly contested argument about to what extent, if at all, authoritarian rule has been responsible for Asian economic development. What is clear, however, is that in the rest of the world the overall record of autocracies in promoting economic development, let alone the growth of constitutional liberalism, has been poor. As Mill noted, the same shortcomings that make a people poorly prepared for representative government are also likely to be found in its unelected rulers. Wise and benevolent despots are the exception, not the rule.

A LOOK INSIDE THE BALLOT BOX

IT WAS ONLY to be expected that, as countries around the world replaced their autocratic regimes with freely elected ones, they would encounter serious difficulties in making democracy work. Self-government is indeed difficult, and holding elections is merely one step in a long and arduous process that, in the best case, will culminate in a consolidated liberal democracy. Electorates can make bad choices as well as good or (most often) mediocre ones. Demagogues can use electoral campaigns to appeal to voters' worst instincts, including ethnic or religious intolerance (although the number of new democracies in which candidates have succeeded on the basis of such appeals is far fewer than might have been expected). But in any case, how often can elections themselves be plausibly cited as the cause of problems that would not have been just as likely to persist or arise under a nonelected government? African voters, for example, may often cast their ballots along ethnic or tribal lines, but in how many African countries have dictatorial governments achieved real ethnic accommodation, rather than merely the domination of some groups by others? Most new democracies are undoubtedly confronting severe challenges, but almost none of these would be overcome by abolishing elections.

It is also true that, beyond peacefully getting rid of a bad and unpopular government (which is no small accomplishment), elections by themselves do not solve most other political problems. For this and other reasons, prudence counsels against hastily pushing elections on a fairly stable, decent, and moderate nondemocratic regime, especially in a country where the strongest opposition forces are not themselves well disposed toward liberal democracy. This, however, is a lesson that most Western governments, inherently inclined toward diplomatic caution, hardly need to be taught. In fact, their adherence to such a policy is a frequent complaint of those who accuse Western governments of being too friendly with nondemocratic governments, especially in the Arab world.

There are arguably cases where elections have made things worse, as in Angola in 1992, where Jonas Savimbi's refusal to accept his defeat in a U.N.-supervised election led to a violent escalation of that country's civil war. Yet despite some serious setbacks, most recently in Cambodia, the overall record of attempts to use internationally supervised elections as a method of conflict resolution for countries embroiled in civil strife has been surprisingly positive. This relatively recent innovation, first attempted in Nicaragua in 1990, combines peacemaking with democracy-building, but is driven primarily by the former goal. Thus elections are often held under extraordinarily difficult circumstances and at times that would not have been chosen if democracy-building were the only goal. Nonetheless, such elections have not only brought a number of bloody civil wars to a halt, but in countries like Mozambique and El Salvador have had positive political results as well. Even if such countries today are merely illiberal democracies, they are manifestly much better off than if they were still racked by civil war. Afghanistan, a country that did not undergo an electoral process and faces continuing civil war and the rule of an extremist and intolerant Islamist government, does not present a very attractive alternative model.

In more typical cases of democratic transition, where an authoritarian government either is overthrown or negotiates an agreement with domestic opposition forces on the creation of a new regime, the timing of "founding elections" can be a matter of critical importance for the success of an emerging democracy. In such cases there is room for reasonable disagreement about how soon to hold elections. Amid the devastated political landscape of the post-Mobutu Congo, for example, even those committed to trying to move the country in a democratic direction are divided about both the practicability and the desirability of conducting early elections. At the same time, it is difficult to see how dispensing with elections would lead the Kabila government to move toward "constitutional liberalism," or how such unaccountable rule would be preferable to "illiberal democracy."

IF AT FIRST YOU DON'T SUCCEED

IN SUCH UNFAVORABLE SITUATIONS, of course, electoral democracies may simply be unable to endure. The history of democratization is replete with failed attempts. That is why the pattern discerned by Huntington is also characterized by "reverse waves," periods when democratic breakdowns far outnumber democratic transitions. But the overall trend, nonetheless, is for more and more countries to become and remain democratic. Moreover, the historical record shows that countries that have had an earlier experience with democracy that failed are more likely to succeed in a subsequent attempt than countries with no previous democratic experience. So even if democracy breaks down, it can leave a legacy of hope for the future.

Now that a growing number of countries lacking the standard social and economic "prerequisites" for democracy have gained the privilege of electing their own leaders, it is not surprising that these new regimes often have serious deficiencies with respect to accountability, the rule of law, and the protection of individual liberties. There is every reason for Western nations to do all they can to assist these countries in improving their electoral democracies and turning them into liberal democracies. It is precisely the illiberal democracies that Zakaria maligns that are likely to be the most receptive audience for the promotion of constitutional liberalism that he recommends. For the road to constitutional liberalism in today's world runs not through unaccountable autocracies but through freely elected governments.

disagreement

Sense and Nonsense in the Globalization Debate

Dani Rodrik

GLOBALIZATION, THOMAS FRIEDMAN of the New York Times has observed: is "the next great foreign policy debate.' Yet as the debate expands, it gets more confusing. Is globalization a source of economic growth and prosperity, as most economists and many in the policy community believe? Or is it a threat to social stability and the natural environment, as a curious mix of interests ranging from labor advocates to environmentalists-and including the unlikely trio of Ross Perot, George Soros, and Sir James Goldsmith-argue? Has globalization advanced so far that national governments are virtually powerless to regulate their economies and use their policy tools to further social ends? Is the shift of manufacturing activities to low-wage countries undermining global purchasing power, thus creating a glut in goods ranging from autos to aircraft? Or is globalization no more than a buzzword and its impact greatly exaggerated?

There are good reasons to be concerned about the quality of the globalization debate. What we are witnessing is more a dialogue of the deaf than a rational discussion. Those who favor international integration dismiss globalization's opponents as knee-jerk protectionists who do not understand the principle of comparative advantage and the complexities of trade laws and institutions. Globalization's critics, on the other hand, fault economists and trade specialists for

DANI RODRIK is Professor of International Political Economy at the John F. Kennedy School of Government at Harvard University. This article is based on the author's book, *Has Globalization Gone Too Far?* (Washington D.C.: Institute for International Economics, 1997). This article originally appeared in the Summer 1997 issue of *Foreign Policy* © 1997 Carnegie Endowment for International Peace.

their narrow, technocratic perspective. They argue that economists are too enamored with their fancy models and do not have a good handle on how the real world works. The result is that there is too much opponent bashing-and too little learning-on each side.

Both sides have valid complaints. Much of the popular discussion about globalization's effect on American wages, to pick one important example, ignores the considerable research that economists have undertaken. A reasonably informed reader of the nation's leading op-ed pages could be excused for not realizing that a substantial volume of literature on the relationship between trade and inequality exists, much of which contradicts the simplistic view that Americans or Europeans owe their deteriorating fortunes to low-wage competition from abroad. The mainstream academic view actually is that increased trade with developing countries may account for at most 20 per cent of the reduction in the earnings of low-skilled American workers (relative to highly skilled workers) but not much more. One has to look elsewhere-to technological changes and deunionization, for example-to explain most of the increase in the wage gap between skilled and unskilled workers.

It is also true, however, that economists and proponents of trade have either neglected or pooh-poohed some of the broader complications associated with international economic integration. Consider the following questions: To what extent have capital mobility and the outsourcing of production increased the *substitutability* of domestic labor across national boundaries, thereby aggravating the economic insecurity confronting workers (in addition to exerting downward pressure on their wages)? Are the distributional implications of globalization-and certainly there are some-reconcilable with domestic concepts of distributive justice? Does trade with countries that have different norms and social institutions clash with and undermine long-standing domestic social bargains? To what extent does globalization undermine the ability of national governments to provide the public goods that their citizenries have come to expect, including social insurance against economic risks?

These are serious questions that underscore the potential of globally expanding markets to come into conflict with social stability, even as these markets provide benefits to exporters, investors, and consumers. Some of these questions have not yet been seriously scrutinized by economists. Others cannot be answered with economic and statistical analysis alone. But the full story of globalization cannot be told unless these broader issues are addressed as well.

THE LIMITS OF GLOBALIZATION

EVEN WITH THE revolution in transportation and communication and the substantial progress made in trade liberalization over the last three decades, national economies remain remarkably isolated from each other. This isolation has a critical implication, which has been repeatedly emphasized by economist Paul Krugman: Most governments in the advanced industrial world are not nearly as shackled by economic globalization as is commonly believed. They retain substantial autonomy in regulating their economies, in designing their social policies, and in maintaining institutions that differ from those of their trading partners.

The supposition that domestic economies are now submerged in a seamless, unified world market is belied by various pieces of evidence. Take the case of North America. Trade between Canada and the United States is among the freest in the world and is only minimally hampered by transport and communications costs. Yet a study by Canadian economist John McCallum has documented that trade between a Canadian province and a U.S. state (that is, *international* trade) is on average 20 times smaller than trade between two Canadian provinces (that is, *intranational* trade). Clearly, the U.S. and Canadian markets remain substantially delinked from each other. And if this is true of U.S.-Canadian trade, it must be all the more true of other bilateral trade relationships.

The evidence on the mobility of physical capital also contradicts current thought. Popular discussions take it for granted that capital is now entirely free to cross national borders in its search for the highest returns. As economists Martin Feldstein and Charles Horioka have pointed out, if this were true, the level of investment that is undertaken in France would depend only on the profitability of investment in France, and it would have no relationship to the available savings in France. Actually, however, this turns out to be false. Increased savings in one country translate into increased investments in that country almost one for one. Despite substantial crossborder money flows, different rates of return among countries persist and are not equalized by capital moving to higher-return economies.

One can easily multiply the examples. U.S. portfolios tend to be remarkably concentrated in U.S. stocks. The prices of apparently identical goods differ widely from one country to another despite the fact that the goods can be traded. In reality, national economies retain a considerable degree of isolation from each other, and national policymakers enjoy more autonomy than is assumed by most recent writings on the erosion of national sovereignty.

The limited nature of globalization can perhaps be better appreciated by placing it into historical context. By many measures, the world economy was more integrated at the height of the gold standard in the late 19th century than it is now. In the United States and Europe, trade volumes peaked before World War I and then collapsed during the interwar years. Trade surged again after 1950, but neither Europe nor the United States is significantly more open today (gauging by ratios of trade to national income) than it was under the gold standard. Japan actually exports less of its total production today than it did during the interwar period.

GLOBALIZATION MATTERS

IT WOULD BE a mistake to conclude from this evidence that globalization is irrelevant. Due to the increased importance of trade, the options available to national policymakers have narrowed appreciably over the last three decades. The oft-mentioned imperative of maintaining "international competitiveness" now looms much larger and imparts a definite bias to policy making.

Consider labor market practices. As France, Germany, and other countries have shown, it is still possible to maintain labor market policies that increase the cost of labor. But globalization is raising the overall social cost of exercising this option. European nations can afford to have generous minimum wages and benefit levels if they choose to pay the costs. But the stakes-the resulting unemployment levels-have been raised by the increased international mobility of firms.

The consequences are apparent everywhere. In Japan, large corporations have started to dismantle the postwar practice of providing lifetime employment, one of Japan's most distinctive social institutions. In France and Germany, unions have been fighting government attempts to cut pension benefits. In South Korea, labor unions have taken to the streets to protest the government's relaxation of firing restrictions. Developing countries in Latin America are competing with each other in liberalizing trade, deregulating their economies, and privatizing public enterprises.

Ask business executives or government officials why these changes are necessary, and you will hear the same mantra repeated over and over again: "We need to remain (or become) competitive in a global economy." As some of these changes appear to violate long-standing social bargains in many countries, the widespread populist reaction to globalization is perhaps understandable.

The anxieties generated by globalization must be seen in the context of the demands placed on national governments, which have expanded radically since the late 19th century. At the height of the gold standard, governments were not yet expected to perform social-welfare functions on a large scale. Ensuring adequate levels of employment, establishing social safety nets, providing medical and social insurance, and caring for the poor were not parts of the government agenda. Such demands multiplied during the period following the Second World War. Indeed, a key component of the implicit postwar social bargain in the advanced industrial countries has been the provision of social insurance and safety nets at home (unemployment compensation, severance payments, and adjustment assistance, for example) in exchange for the adoption of freer trade policies.

This bargain is clearly eroding. Employers are less willing to provide the benefits of job security and stability, partly because of increased competition but also because their enhanced global mobility makes them less dependent on the goodwill of their local work force. Governments are less able to sustain social safety nets, because an important part of their tax base has become footloose because of the increased mobility of capital. Moreover, the ideological onslaught against the welfare state has paralyzed many governments and made them unable to respond to the domestic needs of a more integrated economy.

Sense and Nonsense in the Globalization Debate

MORE TRADE, MORE GOVERNMENT

THE POSTWAR PERIOD has witnessed two apparently contradictory trends: the growth of trade and the growth of government. Prior to the Second World War, government expenditures averaged around 20 per cent of the gross domestic products (GDPs) of today's advanced industrialized countries. By the mid-1990s, that figure had more than doubled to 47 per cent. The increased role of government is particularly striking in countries like the United States (from 9 to 34 per cent), Sweden (from 10 to 69 per cent), and the Netherlands (from 19 to 54 per cent). The driving force behind the expansion of government during this period was the increase in social spending-and income transfers in particular.

It is not a coincidence that social spending increased alongside international trade. For example, the small, highly open European economies like Austria, the Netherlands, and Sweden have large governments in part as a result of their attempts to minimize the social impact of openness to the international economy. It is in the most open countries like Denmark, the Netherlands, and Sweden that spending on income transfers has expanded the most.

Indeed, there is a surprisingly strong association across countries between the degree of exposure to international trade and the importance of the government in the economy. The chart on page 173 shows the relationship between trade and spending on social protection

**RELATIONSHIP BETWEEN TRADE AND SPENDING
ON SOCIAL PROTECTION (1980)**

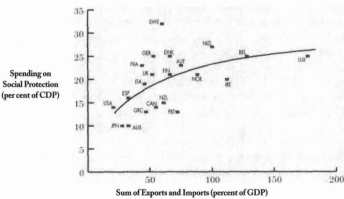

Source: Author

(including unemployment insurance, pensions, and family benefits) in 21 countries for which the Organization for Economic Cooperation and Development (OECD) publishes cross-nationally comparable data. The chart reveals an unmistakably positive correlation between a nation's openness to trade and the amount of its spending on social programs. At one end of the distribution we have the United States and Japan, which have the lowest trade shares in GDP and some of the lowest shares of spending on social protection. At the other end, Luxembourg, Belgium, and the Netherlands have economies with high degrees of openness and large income transfers. This relationship is not confined to OECD economies: Developing nations also exhibit this pattern. Furthermore, the extent to which imports and exports were important in a country's economy in the early 1960s provided a good predictor of how big its government would become in the ensuing three decades, regardless of how developed it was. All the available evidence points to the same, unavoidable conclusion: The social welfare state has been the flip side of the open economy.

International economic integration thus poses a serious dilemma: Globalization increases the demand for social insurance while simultaneously constraining the ability of governments to respond effectively to that demand. Consequently, as globalization deepens, the social consensus required to keep domestic markets open to international trade erodes.

Since the early 1980s, tax rates on capital have tended to decrease in the leading industrial nations, while tax rates on labor have continued generally to increase. At the same time, social spending has stabilized in relation to national incomes. These outcomes reflect the tradeoffs facing governments in increasingly open economies: The demands for social programs are being balanced against the need to reduce the tax burden on capital, which has become more globally mobile.

By any standard, the postwar social bargain has served the world economy extremely well. Spurred by widespread trade liberalization, world trade has soared since the 1950s. This expansion did not cause major social dislocations and did not engender much opposition in the advanced industrial countries. Today, however, the process of international economic integration is taking place against a backdrop of retreating governments and diminished social obligations. Yet the need for social insurance for the vast majority of the population that lacks international mobility has not diminished. If anything, this need has grown.

The question, therefore, is how the tension between globalization and the pressure to mitigate risks can be eased. If the vital role that social insurance played in enabling the postwar expansion of trade is neglected and social safety nets are allowed to dwindle, the domestic consensus in favor of open markets will be eroded seriously, and protectionist pressures will soar.

THE GLOBAL TRADE IN SOCIAL VALUES

IN THE MARKETS for goods, services, labor, and capital, international trade creates arbitrage-the possibility of buying (or producing) in one place at one price and selling at a higher price elsewhere. Prices thus tend to converge in the long run, this convergence being the source of the gains from trade. But trade exerts pressure toward another kind of arbitrage as well: arbitrage in national norms and social institutions. This form of arbitrage results, indirectly, as the costs of maintaining divergent social arrangements go up. As a consequence, open trade can conflict with long-standing social contracts that protect certain activities from the relentlessness of the free market. This is a key tension generated by globalization.

As the technology for manufactured goods becomes standardized and diffused internationally, nations with different sets of values, norms, institutions, and collective preferences begin to compete head on in markets for similar goods. In the traditional approach to trade policy, this trend is of no consequence: Differences in national practices and social institutions are, in effect, treated just like any other differences that determine a country's comparative advantage (such as endowments of physical capital or skilled labor).

In practice, however, trade becomes contentious when it unleashes forces that undermine the social norms implicit in domestic practices. For example, not all residents of advanced industrial countries are comfortable with the weakening of domestic institutions through the forces of trade, such as when child labor in Honduras replaces workers in South Carolina or when cuts in pension benefits in France are called for in response to the requirements of the Treaty on European

Dani Rodrik

Union. This sense of unease is one way of interpreting the demands for "fair trade." Much of the discussion surrounding the new issues in trade policy-e.g., labor standards, the environment, competition policy, and corruption-can be cast in this light of procedural fairness.

Trade usually redistributes income among industries, regions, and individuals. Therefore, a principled defense of free trade cannot be constructed without addressing the question of the fairness and legitimacy of the practices that generate these distributional "costs." How comparative advantage is created matters. Low-wage foreign competition arising from an abundance of workers is different from competition that is created by foreign labor practices that violate norms at home. Low wages that result from demography or history are very different from low wages that result from government repression of unions.

From this perspective it is easier to understand why many people are often ill at ease with the consequences of international economic integration. Automatically branding all concerned groups as self-interested protectionists does not help much. This perspective also prepares us not to expect broad popular support for trade when trade involves exchanges that clash with (and erode) prevailing domestic social arrangements.

Consider labor rules, for example. Since the 1930s, U.S. laws have recognized that restrictions on "free contract" are legitimate to counteract the effects of unequal bargaining power. Consequently, the employment relationship in the United States (and elsewhere) is subject to a multitude of restrictions, such as those that regulate working hours, workplace safety, labor/management negotiations, and so forth. Many of these restrictions have been put in place to redress the asymmetry in bargaining power that would otherwise disadvantage workers vis-a-vis employers.

Globalization upsets this balance by creating a different sort of asymmetry: Employers can move abroad, but employees cannot. There is no substantive difference between American workers being driven from their jobs by their fellow domestic workers who agree to work 12-hour days, earn less than the minimum wage, or be fired if they join a union-all of which are illegal under U.S. law-and their being similarly disadvantaged by foreign workers doing the same. If society is unwilling to accept the former, why should it countenance the latter? Globalization generates an inequality in bargaining power that 60 years of labor legislation in the United States has tried to prevent. It is in effect eroding a social understanding that has long been settled.

Whether they derive from labor standards, environmental policy, or corruption, differences in domestic practices and institutions have become matters of international controversy. That is indeed the common theme that runs the gamut of the new issues on the agenda of the World Trade Organization (WTO). Conflicts arise both when these differences create trade-as in the cases of child labor or lax environmental policies-and when they reduce it-as industrial practices in Japan are alleged to do. As the *New York Times* editorialized on July 11, 1996, in connection with the Kodak-Fuji dispute on access to the photographic film market in Japan, "the Kodak case asks the WTO, in effect, to pass judgment on the way Japan does business."

The notions of "fair trade" and "leveling the playing field" that lie behind the pressures for putting these new issues on the trade agenda have been ridiculed by economists. But once it is recognized that trade has implications for domestic norms and social arrangements and that its legitimacy rests in part on its compatibility with these, such notions are not so outlandish. These sentiments are ways of addressing the concerns to which trade gives rise. Free trade among countries with different domestic practices requires an acceptance of either an erosion of domestic structures or the need for some degree of harmonization or convergence.

If this is the appropriate context in which demands for "fair trade" or "leveling the playing field" must be understood, it should also be clear that policymakers often take too many liberties in justifying their actions along such lines. Most of the pricing policies that pass as "unfair trade" in U.S. antidumping proceedings, for example, are standard business practice in the United States and other countries. While there may not be a sharp dividing line between what is fair and unfair in international trade, one clear sign that pure protectionism is at the root of a trade dispute is the prevalence of practices within the domestic economy that are identical or similar to those being protested in the international arena. Fairness cannot be eliminated from thinking about trade policy; but neither can it be invoked to justify trade restrictions when the practice in question does not conflict with domestic norms as revealed by actual practice.

Dani Rodrik

THE TENSIONS CREATED by globalization are real. They are, however, considerably more subtle than the terminology that has come to dominate the debate. "Low-wage competition," "leveling the playing field," and "race to the bottom" are catchy phrases that often muddle the public's understanding of the real issues. A more nuanced debate and more imaginative solutions are badly needed.

A broader approach to this debate, one that takes into account some of the aspects discussed here, provides more credibility to the defenders of free trade in their attempts to clear up the misunderstandings that the opponents of trade often propagate. Journalist William Greider's recent book, *One World, Ready or Not–The Manic Logic of Global Capitalism*, illustrates the appeal that many of these misunderstandings retain in the minds of popular commentators on trade.

One of the main themes of this book–that the global expansion of markets is undermining social cohesion and is inexorably leading toward a major economic and political crisis could be viewed as a more boldly expressed version of the potential danger that is highlighted above. Many of Greider's concerns–the consequences for low-skilled workers in the advanced industrial countries, the weakening of social safety nets, and the repression of political rights in some leading exporters like China and Indonesia–are indeed valid. However, the disregard for sound economic analysis and systematic empirical evidence that characterizes

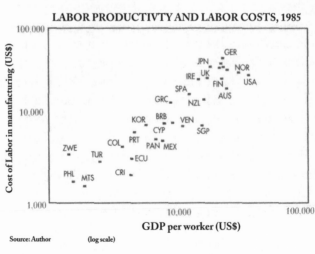

LABOR PRODUCTIVTY AND LABOR COSTS, 1985

Cost of Labor in manufacturing (US$)

GDP per worker (US$)

Source: Author   (log scale)

Greider's book makes it both a very unreliable guide to understanding what is taking place and a faulty manual for setting things right.

A popular fallacy perpetuated in works like Greider's is that low wages are the driving force behind today's global trade. If that were so, the world's most formidable exporters would be Bangladesh and a smattering of African countries. Some Mexican or Malaysian exporting plants may approach U.S. levels in labor productivity, while local wages fall far short. Yet what is true for a small number of plants does not extend to economies as a whole and therefore does not have much bearing on the bulk of world trade.

The chart on page 178 shows the relationship between economy-wide labor productivity (GDP per worker) and labor costs in manufacturing in a wide range of countries. There is almost a one-to-one relationship between these two, indicating that wages are closely related to productivity. Low-wage economies are those in which levels of labor productivity are commensurately low. This tendency is of course no surprise to anyone with common sense. Yet much of the discourse on trade presumes a huge gap between wages and productivity in the developing country exporters.

Similarly, it is a mistake to attribute the U.S. trade deficit to the restrictive commercial policies of other countries-policies that Greider calls the "unbalanced behavior" of U.S. trading partners. How then can we explain the large U.S. deficit with Canada? If trade imbalances were determined by commercial policies, then India, as one of the world's most protectionist countries until recently, would have been running large trade surpluses.

Another misconception is that export-oriented industrialization has somehow failed to improve the livelihood of workers in East and Southeast Asia. Contrary to the impression one gets from listening to the opponents of globalization, life is significantly better for the vast majority of the former peasants who now toil in Malaysian or Chinese factories. Moreover, it is generally not the case that foreign-owned companies in developing countries provide working conditions that are inferior to those available elsewhere in the particular country; in fact, the reverse is more often true.

Perhaps the most baffling of the antiglobalization arguments is that trade and foreign investment are inexorably leading to excess capacity on a global scale. This is Greider's key argument and ultimately the main reason why he believes the system will self-destruct. Consider his discussion of Boeing's outsourcing of some of its components to the Xian Aircraft Company in China:

> When new production work was moved to Xian from places like the United States, the global system was, in effect, swapping highly paid industrial workers for very cheap ones. To put the point more crudely, Boeing was exchanging a $50,000 American machinist for a Chinese machinist who earned $600 or $700 a year. Which one could buy the world's goods? Thus, even though incomes and purchasing power were expanding robustly among the new consumers of China, the overall effect was an erosion of the world's potential purchasing power. If one multiplied the Xian example across many factories and industrial sectors, as well as other aspiring countries, one could begin to visualize why global consumption was unable to keep up with global production.

An economist would rightly point out that the argument makes little sense. The Chinese worker who earns only a tiny fraction of his American counterpart is likely to be commensurately less productive. Even if the Chinese worker's wages are repressed below actual productivity, the result is a transfer in purchasing power-to Boeing's shareholders and the Chinese employers-and not a diminution of global purchasing power. Perhaps Greider is thinking that Boeing's shareholders and the Chinese employers have a lower propensity to consume than the Chinese workers. If so, where is the evidence? Where is the global surplus in savings and the secular decline in real interest rates that we would surely have observed if income is going from low savers to high savers?

It may be unfair to pick on Greider, especially since some of his other conclusions are worth taking seriously. But the misunderstandings that his book displays are commonplace in the globalization debate and do not help to advance it.

SAFETY NETS, NOT TRADE BARRIERS

ONE NEED NOT be alarmed by globalization, but neither should one take a Panglossian view of it. Globalization greatly enhances the opportunities available to those who have the skills and mobility to flourish in world markets. It can help poor countries to escape poverty. It does not constrain national autonomy nearly as much as popular discussions assume. At the same time, globalization does exert downward pressure on the wages of underskilled workers in industrialized countries, exacerbate economic insecurity, call into question accepted social arrangements, and weaken social safety nets.

There are two dangers from complacency toward the social consequences of globalization. The first and more obvious one is the potential for a political backlash against trade. The candidacy of Patrick Buchanan in the 1996 Republican presidential primaries revealed that protectionism can be a rather easy sell at a time when broad segments of American society are experiencing anxieties related to globalization. The same can be said about the political influence of Vladimir Zhirinovsky in Russia or Jean-Marie Le Pen in France-influence that was achieved, at least in part, in response to the perceived effects of globalization. Economists may complain that protectionism is mere snake oil and argue that the ailments require altogether different medicine, but intellectual arguments will not win hearts and minds unless concrete solutions are offered. Trade protection, for all of its faults, has the benefit of concreteness.

Perhaps future Buchanans will ultimately be defeated, as Buchanan himself was, by the public's common sense. Even so, a second and perhaps more serious danger remains: The accumulation of globalization's side effects could lead to a new set of class divisions-between those who prosper in the globalized economy and those who do not; between those who share its values and those who would rather not; and between those who can diversify away its risks and those who cannot. This is not a pleasing prospect even for individuals on the winning side of the globalization divide: The deepening of social fissures harms us all.

National policymakers must not retreat behind protectionist walls. Protectionism would be of limited help, and it would create its own social tensions. Policymakers ought instead to complement the external strategy of liberalization with an internal strategy of compensation, training, and social insurance for those groups who are most at risk.

In the United States, President Bill Clinton's education initiatives represent a move in the right direction. However, the August 1996 welfare reform act could weaken social safety nets precisely at a time when globalization calls for the opposite. In Europe, as well, the pruning of the welfare state may exacerbate the strains of globalization.

Contrary to widespread belief, maintaining adequate safety nets for those at the bottom of the income distribution would not break the bank. Currently, old-age insurance is the most expensive income-transfer item for the advanced industrial countries. A reorientation of public resources away from pensions and toward labor-market and antipoverty programs would be a more appropriate way to address the challenges of globalization. This shift could be achieved while reducing overall public spending. Broad segments of the population in the industrial countries are understandably nervous about changing basic social-welfare arrangements. Therefore, political leadership will be required to render such changes palatable to these groups.

At the global level, the challenge is twofold. On the one hand, a set of rules that encourages greater harmonization of social and industrial policies on a voluntary basis is needed. Such harmonization could reduce tensions that arise from differing national practices. At the same time, flexibility sufficient to allow selective disengagement from multilateral disciplines needs to be built into the rules that govern international trade.

Currently, the WTO Agreement on Safeguards allows member states to impose temporary trade restrictions following an increase in imports-but only under a stringent set of conditions. One could imagine expanding the scope of the agreement to include a broader range of circumstances, reflecting concerns over labor standards, the environment, and even ethical norms in the importing country. The purpose of such an expanded "escape clause" mechanism would be to allow countries under well-specified contingencies and subject to multi-laterally approved procedures-greater breathing room to fulfill domestic requirements that conflict with free trade. If this flexibility could be achieved in exchange for a tightening of rules on anti-dumping, which have a highly corrosive effect on the world trading system, the benefits could be substantial.

Globalization is not occurring in a vacuum: It is part of a broader trend we may call marketization. Receding government, deregulation, and the shrinking of social obligations are the domestic counterparts of the intertwining of national economies. Globalization could not have advanced this far without these complementary forces at work. The broader challenge for the 21st century is to engineer a new balance between the market and society-one that will continue to unleash the creative energies of private entrepreneurship without eroding the social bases of cooperation.

Spreading the Wealth

David Dollar and Aart Kraay

A RISING TIDE

ONE OF THE MAIN CLAIMS of the antiglobalization movement is that globalization is widening the gap between the haves and the have-nots. It benefits the rich and does little for the poor, perhaps even making their lot harder. As union leader Jay Mazur put it in these pages, "globalization has dramatically increased inequality between and within nations" ("Labor's New Internationalism," January/February 2000). The problem with this new conventional wisdom is that the best evidence available shows the exact opposite to be true. So far, the current wave of globalization, which started around 1980, has actually promoted economic equality and reduced poverty.

Global economic integration has complex effects on income, culture, society, and the environment. But in the debate over globalization's merits, its impact on poverty is particularly important. If international trade and investment primarily benefit the rich, many people will feel that restricting trade to protect jobs, culture, or the environment is worth the costs. But if restricting trade imposes further hardship on poor people in the developing world, many of the same people will think otherwise.

Three facts bear on this question. First, a long-term global trend toward greater inequality prevailed for at least 200 years; it peaked around 1975. But since then, it has stabilized and possibly even reversed. The chief reason for the change has been the accelerated growth of two large and initially poor countries: China and India.

DAVID DOLLAR and AART KRAAY are economists at the World Bank's Development Research Group. The views expressed here are their own. This article originally appeared in the January/February 2002 issue of *Foreign Affairs* © 2002 by the Council on Foreign Relations.

Second, a strong correlation links increased participation in international trade and investment on the one hand and faster growth on the other. The developing world can be divided into a "globalizing" group of countries that have seen rapid increases in trade and foreign investment over the last two decades—well above the rates for rich countries—and a "nonglobalizing" group that trades even less of its income today than it did 20 years ago. The aggregate annual per capita growth rate of the globalizing group accelerated steadily from one percent in the 1960s to five percent in the 1990s. During that latter decade, in contrast, rich countries grew at two percent and nonglobalizers at only one percent. Economists are cautious about drawing conclusions concerning causality, but they largely agree that openness to foreign trade and investment (along with complementary reforms) explains the faster growth of the globalizers.

Third, and contrary to popular perception, globalization has not resulted in higher inequality within economies. Inequality has indeed gone up in some countries (such as China) and down in others (such as the Philippines). But those changes are not systematically linked to globalization measures such as trade and investment flows, tariff rates, and the presence of capital controls. Instead, shifts in inequality stem more from domestic education, taxes, and social policies. In general, higher growth rates in globalizing developing countries have translated into higher incomes for the poor. Even with its increased inequality, for example, China has seen the most spectacular reduction of poverty in world history—which was supported by opening its economy to foreign trade and investment.

Although globalization can be a powerful force for poverty reduction, its beneficial results are not inevitable. If policymakers hope to tap the full potential of economic integration and sustain its benefits, they must address three critical challenges. A growing protectionist movement in rich countries that aims to limit integration with poor ones must be stopped in its tracks. Developing countries need to acquire the kinds of institutions and policies that will allow them to prosper under globalization, both of which may be different from place to place. And more migration, both domestic and international, must be permitted when geography limits the potential for development.

THE GREAT DIVIDE

OVER the past 200 years, different local economies around the world have become more integrated while the growth rate of the global economy has accelerated dramatically. Although it is impossible to prove causal linkage between the two developments—since there are no other world economies to be tested against—evidence suggests the arrows run in both directions. As Adam Smith argued, a larger market permits a finer division of labor, which in turn facilitates innovation and learning by doing. Some of that innovation involves transportation and communications technologies that lower costs and increase integration. So it is easy to see how integration and innovation can be mutually supportive.

Different locations have become more integrated because of increased flows of goods, capital, and knowledge. From 1820 to 1914, international trade increased faster than the global economy. Trade rose from about 2 percent of world income in 1820 to 18 percent in 1914. The globalization of trade took a step backward during the protectionist period of the Great Depression and World War II, and by 1950 trade (in relation to income) was lower than it had been in 1914. But thanks to a series of multilateral trade liberalizations under the General Agreement on Tariffs and Trade (GATT), trade dramatically expanded among industrialized countries between 1960 and 1980. Most developing countries remained largely isolated from this trade because of their own inward-focused policies, but the success of such notable exceptions as Taiwan and South Korea eventually helped encourage other developing economies to open themselves up to foreign trade and investment.

International capital flows, measured as foreign ownership of assets relative to world income, also grew during the first wave of globalization and declined during the Great Depression and World War II; they did not return to 1914 levels until 1980. But since then, such flows have increased markedly and changed their nature as well. One hundred years ago, foreign capital typically financed public infrastructure projects (such as canals and railroads) or direct investment related to natural resources. Today, in contrast, the bulk of capital flows to developing countries is direct investments tied to manufacturing and services.

The change in the nature of capital flows is clearly related to concurrent advances in economic integration, such as cheaper and faster transportation and revolutionary changes in telecommunications. Since 1920, seagoing freight charges have declined by about two-thirds and air travel costs by 84 percent; the cost of a three-minute call from New York City to London has dropped by 99 percent. Today, production in widely differing locations can be integrated in ways that simply were not possible before.

Another aspect of integration has been the movement of people. Yet here the trend is reversed: there is much more international travel than in the past but much less permanent migration. Between 1870 and 1910, about ten percent of the world's population relocated permanently from one country to another; over the past 25 years, only one to two percent have done so.

As economic integration has progressed, the annual growth rate of the world economy has accelerated, from 1 percent in the mid-nineteenth century to 3.5 percent in 1960–2000. Sustained over many years, such a jump in growth makes a huge difference in real living standards. It now takes only two to three years, for example, for the world economy to produce the same amount of goods and services that it did during the entire nineteenth century. Such a comparison is arguably a serious understatement of the true difference, since most of what is consumed today—airline travel, cars, televisions, synthetic fibers, life-extending drugs—did not exist 200 years ago. For any of these goods or services, therefore, the growth rate of output since 1820 is infinite. Human productivity has increased almost unimaginably.

All this tremendous growth in wealth was distributed very unequally up to about 1975, but since then growing equality has taken hold. One good measure of inequality among individuals worldwide is the mean log deviation—a measure of the gap between the income of any randomly selected person and a general average. It takes into account the fact that income distributions everywhere are

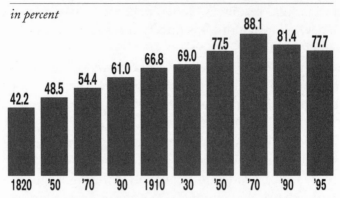

Worldwide Income Inequality, 1820–1995

in percent

1820	'50	'70	'90	1910	'30	'50	'70	'90	'95
42.2	48.5	54.4	61.0	66.8	69.0	77.5	88.1	81.4	77.7

Note: Figures represent the mean log deviation between a typical individual income and the average per capita income.

Sources: F. Bourguignon and C. Morrisson, "Inequality Among World Citizens, 1820–1992," working paper 2001-25 (Paris: Department and Laboratory of Applied and Theoretical Economics, 2001); and David Dollar, "Globalization, Inequality, and Poverty Since 1980," World Bank background paper, available at http://www.worldbank.org/research/global.

skewed in favor of the rich, so that the typical person is poorer than the group average; the more skewed the distribution, the larger the gap. Per capita income in the world today, for example, is around $5,000, whereas a randomly selected person would most likely be living on close to $1,000—80 percent less. That gap translates into a mean log deviation of 0.8.

Taking this approach, an estimate of the world distribution of income among individuals shows rising inequality between 1820 and 1975. In that period, the gap between the typical person and world per capita income increased from about 40 percent to about 80 percent. Since changes in income inequality within countries were small, the increase in inequality was driven mostly by differences in growth rates across countries. Areas that were already relatively rich in 1820 (notably, Europe and the United States) grew faster than poor areas (notably, China and India). Global inequality peaked sometime in the 1970s, but it then stabilized and even began to decline, largely because growth in China and India began to accelerate.

Another way of looking at global inequality is to examine what is happening to the extreme poor—those people living on less than $1 per day. Although the percentage of the world's population living in poverty has declined over time, the absolute number rose fairly steadily until 1980. During the Great Depression and World War II, the number of poor increased particularly sharply, and it declined somewhat immediately thereafter. The world economy grew strongly between 1960 and 1980, but the number of poor rose because growth did not occur in the places where the worst-off live. But since then, the most rapid growth has occurred in poor locations. Consequently the number of poor has declined by 200 million since 1980. Again, this trend is explained primarily by the rapid income growth in China and India, which together in 1980 accounted for about one-third of the world's population and more than 60 percent of the world's extreme poor.

UPWARD BOUND

THE SHIFT in the trend in global inequality coincides with the shift in the economic strategies of several large developing countries. Following World War II, most developing regions chose strategies that focused inward and discouraged integration with the global economy. But these approaches were not particularly successful, and throughout the 1960s and 1970s developing countries on the whole grew less rapidly than industrialized ones. The oil shocks and U.S. inflation of the 1970s created severe problems for them, contributing to negative growth, high inflation, and debt crises over the next several years. Faced with these disappointing results, several developing countries began to alter their strategies starting in the 1980s.

For example, China had an extremely closed economy until the mid-1970s. Although Beijing's initial economic reform focused on agriculture, a key part of its approach since the 1980s has involved opening up foreign trade and investment, including a drop in its tariff rates by two-thirds and its nontariff barriers by even more. These reforms have led to unprecedented economic growth in the country's coastal provinces and more moderate growth in the interior. From 1978 to 1994 the Chinese economy grew annually by 9 percent, while exports grew by 14 percent and imports by 13 percent.

Of course, China and other globalizing developing countries have pursued a wide range of reforms, not just economic openness. Beijing has strengthened property rights through land reform and moved from a planned economy toward a market-oriented one, and these measures have contributed to its integration as well as to its growth.

Other developing countries have also opened up as a part of broader reform programs. During the 1990s, India liberalized foreign trade and investment with good results; its annual per capita income growth now tops four percent. It too has pursued a broad agenda of reform and has moved away from a highly regulated, planned system. Meanwhile, Uganda and Vietnam are the best examples of very low-income countries that have increased their participation in trade and investment and prospered as a result. And in the western hemisphere, Mexico is noteworthy both for signing its free-trade agreement with the United States and Canada in 1993 and for its rapid growth since then, especially in the northern regions near the U.S. border.

These cases illustrate how openness to foreign trade and investment, coupled with complementary reforms, typically leads to faster growth. India, China, Vietnam, Uganda, and Mexico are not isolated examples; in general, countries that have become more open have grown faster. The best way to illustrate this trend is to rank developing countries in order of their increases in trade relative to national income over the past 20 years. The top third of this list can be thought of as the "globalizing" camp, and the bottom two-thirds as the "nonglobalizing" camp. The globalizers have increased their trade relative to income by 104 percent over the past two decades, compared to 71 percent for rich countries. The nonglobalizers, meanwhile, actually trade less today than they did 20 years ago. The globalizers have also cut their import tariffs by 22 percentage points on average, compared to only 11 percentage points for the nonglobalizers.

How have the globalizers fared in terms of growth? Their average annual growth rates accelerated from 1 percent in the 1960s to 3 percent in the 1970s, 4 percent in the 1980s, and 5 percent in the 1990s. Rich countries' annual growth rates, by comparison, slowed to about

2 percent in the 1990s, and the nonglobalizers saw their growth rates decline from 3 percent in the 1970s to 1 percent in the 1980s and 1990s.

The same pattern can be observed on a local level. Within both China and India, the locations that are integrating with the global economy are growing much more rapidly than the disconnected regions. Indian states, for example, vary significantly in the quality of their investment climates as measured by government efficiency, corruption, and infrastructure. Those states with better investment climates have integrated themselves more closely with outside markets and have experienced more investment (domestic and foreign) than their less-integrated counterparts. Moreover, states that were initially poor and then created good investment climates had stronger poverty reduction in the 1990s than those not integrating with the global economy. Such internal comparisons are important because, by holding national trade and macroeconomic policies constant, they reveal how important it is to complement trade liberalization with institutional reform so that integration can actually occur.

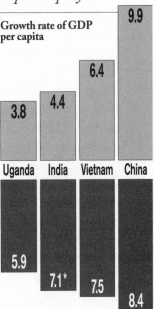

GDP Growth and Poverty Reduction *in Uganda, India, Vietnam, and China, 1992–98, in percent per year*

Growth rate of GDP per capita

| Uganda | India | Vietnam | China |

Rate of poverty reduction

*India poverty reduction figure is for 1993–99.

Source: David Dollar, "Globalization, Inequality, and Poverty Since 1980," World Bank background paper, available at http://www.worldbank.org/research/global.

The accelerated growth rates of globalizing countries such as China, India, and Vietnam are consistent with cross-country comparisons that find openness going hand in hand with faster growth. The most that these studies can establish is that more trade and investment is highly correlated with higher growth, so one needs to be careful about drawing conclusions about causality. Still, the overall evidence from individual cases and cross-country correlation is persuasive. As economists Peter Lindert and Jeffrey Williamson have written, "even though no one study can establish that openness to trade has unambiguously helped the representative Third World economy, the preponderance of evidence supports this conclusion." They go on to note that "there are no anti-global victories to report for the postwar Third World."

Contrary to the claims of the antiglobalization movement, therefore, greater openness to international trade and investment has in fact helped narrow the gap between rich and poor countries rather than widen it. During the 1990s, the economies of the globalizers, with a combined population of about 3 billion, grew more than twice as fast as the rich countries. The nonglobalizers, in contrast, grew only half as fast and nowadays lag further and further behind. Much of the discussion of global inequality assumes that there is growing divergence between the developing world and the rich world, but this is simply not true. The most important development in global inequality in recent decades is the growing divergence within the developing world, and it is directly related to whether countries take advantage of the economic benefits that globalization can offer.

THE PATH OUT OF POVERTY

THE ANTIGLOBALIZATION movement also claims that economic integration is worsening inequality within countries as well as between them. Until the mid-1980s, there was insufficient evidence to support strong conclusions on this important topic. But now more and more developing countries have begun to conduct household income and consumption surveys of reasonable quality. (In low-income countries, these surveys typically track what households actually consume because so much of their real income is self-produced and not part of the money economy.) Good surveys now exist for 137 countries, and many go back far enough to measure changes in inequality over time.

One way of looking at inequality within countries is to focus on what happens to the bottom 20 percent of households as globalization and growth proceed apace. Across all countries, incomes of the poor grow at around the same rate as GDP. Of course, there is a great deal of variation around that average relationship. In some countries, income distribution has shifted in favor of the poor; in others, against

them. But these shifts cannot be explained by any
globalization-related vari-
able. So it simply cannot be
said that inequality necessarily rises with more trade,
more foreign investment,
and lower tariffs. For many
globalizers, the overall
change in distribution was
small, and in some cases
(such as the Philippines
and Malaysia) it was even
in favor of the poor. What
changes in inequality do
reflect are country-specific
policies on education, taxes,
and social protection.

It is important not to
misunderstand this find-
ing. China is an important
example of a country that
has had a large increase in

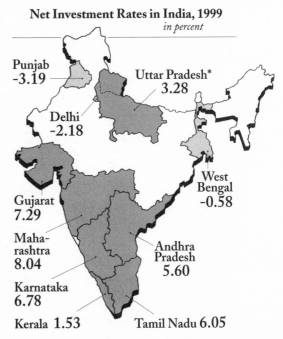

Net Investment Rates in India, 1999
in percent

Punjab
-3.19

Uttar Pradesh*
3.28

Delhi
-2.18

West
Bengal
-0.58

Gujarat
7.29

Maha-
rashtra
8.04

Andhra
Pradesh
5.60

Karnataka
6.78

Kerala 1.53

Tamil Nadu 6.05

*In September 2000, a new state, Uttaranchal, was created out of the northwestern section of Uttar Pradesh.

Note: Net investment rates represent the annual rate of growth of the capital stock of domestic and international firms. A negative rate implies that firms are pulling out.

Source: O. Goswami et al., "Competitiveness of Indian Manufacturing: Results of a Firm-Level Survey" (New Delhi: Confederation of Indian Industry, 2001).

inequality in the past decade, when the income of the bottom 20
percent has risen much less rapidly than per capita income.
This trend may be related to greater openness, although domestic liberalization is a more likely cause. China started out in the
1970s with a highly equal distribution of income, and part of its
reform has deliberately aimed at increasing the returns on education, which financially reward the better schooled. But the
Chinese case is not typical; inequality has not increased in most
of the developing countries that have opened up to foreign
trade and investment. Furthermore, income distribution in
China may have become more unequal, but the income of the
poor in China has still risen rapidly. In fact, the country's
progress in reducing poverty has been one of the most dramatic
successes in history.

Because increased trade usually accompanies more rapid growth and does not systematically change household-income distribution, it generally is associated with improved well-being of the poor. Vietnam nicely illustrates this finding. As the nation has opened up, it has experienced a large increase in per capita income and no significant change in inequality. Thus the income of the poor has risen dramatically, and the number of Vietnamese living in absolute poverty dropped sharply from 75 percent of the population in 1988 to 37 percent in 1998. Of the poorest 5 percent of households in 1992, 98 percent were better off six years later. And the improved well-being is not just a matter of income. Child labor has declined, and school enrollment has increased. It should be no surprise that the vast majority of poor households in Vietnam benefited immediately from a more liberalized trading system, since the country's opening has resulted in exports of rice (produced by most of the poor farmers) and labor-intensive products such as footwear. But the experience of China and Vietnam is not unique. India and Uganda also enjoyed rapid poverty reduction as they grew along with their integration into the global economy.

THE OPEN SOCIETIES

THESE FINDINGS have important implications for developing countries, for rich countries such as the United States, and for those who care about global poverty. All parties should recognize that the most recent wave of globalization has been a powerful force for equality and poverty reduction, and they should commit themselves to seeing that it continues despite the obstacles lying ahead.

It is not inevitable that globalization will proceed. In 1910, many believed globalization was unstoppable; they soon received a rude shock. History is not likely to repeat itself in the same way, but it is worth noting that antiglobalization sentiments are on the rise. A growing number of political leaders in the developing world realize that an open trading system is very much in their countries' interest. They would do well to heed Mexican President Vicente Fox, who said recently,

We are convinced that globalization is good and it's good when you do your homework, ... keep your fundamentals in line on the economy, build up high levels of education, respect the rule of law. ... When you do your part, we are convinced that you get the benefit.

But today the narrow interests opposed to further integration—especially those in the rich countries—appear to be much more energetic than their opponents. In Québec City last spring and in Genoa last summer, a group of democratically elected leaders gathered to discuss how to pursue economic integration and improve the lives of their peoples. Antiglobalization demonstrators were quite effective in disrupting the meetings and drawing media attention to themselves. Leaders in developed and developing countries alike must make the proglobalization case more directly and effectively or risk having their opponents dominate the discussion and stall the process.

In addition, industrialized countries still raise protectionist measures against agricultural and labor-intensive products. Reducing those barriers would help developing countries significantly. The poorer areas of the world would benefit from further openings of their own markets as well, since 70 percent of the tariff barriers that developing countries face are from other developing countries.

If globalization proceeds, its potential to be an equalizing force will depend on whether poor countries manage to integrate themselves into the global economic system. True integration requires not just trade liberalization but wide-ranging institutional reform. Many of the nonglobalizing developing countries, such as Myanmar, Nigeria, Ukraine, and Pakistan, offer an unattractive investment climate. Even if they decide to open themselves up to trade, not much is likely to happen unless other reforms are also pursued. It is not easy to predict the reform paths of these countries; some of the relative successes in recent years, such as China, India, Uganda, and Vietnam, have come as quite a surprise. But as long as a location has weak institutions and policies, people living there are going to fall further behind the rest of the world.

Through their trade policies, rich countries can make it easier for those developing countries that do choose to open up and join the global trading club. But in recent years, the rich countries have been doing just the opposite. GATT was originally built around agreements concerning trade practices. Now, institutional harmonization, such as agreement on policies toward intellectual property rights, is a requirement for joining the WTO. Any sort of regulation of labor and environmental standards made under the threat of WTO sanctions would take this requirement for harmonization much further. Such measures would be neoprotectionist in effect, because they would thwart the integration of developing countries into the world economy and discourage trade between poor countries and rich ones.

The WTO meeting in Doha was an important step forward on trade integration. More forcefully than in Seattle, leaders of industrial countries were willing to make the case for further integration and put on the table issues of central concern to developing nations: access to pharmaceutical patents, use of antidumping measures against developing countries, and agricultural subsidies. The new round of trade negotiations launched at Doha has the potential to reverse the current trend, which makes it more difficult for poor countries to integrate with the world economy.

A final potential obstacle to successful and equitable globalization relates to geography. There is no inherent reason why coastal China should be poor; the same goes for southern India, northern Mexico, and Vietnam. All of these locations are near important markets or trade routes but were long held back by misguided policies. Now, with appropriate reforms, they are starting to grow rapidly and take their natural place in the world. But the same cannot be said for Mali, Chad, or other countries or regions cursed with "poor geography"—i.e., distance from markets, inherently high transport costs, and challenging health and agricultural problems. It would be naive to think that trade and investment alone can alleviate poverty in all locations. In fact, for those locations with poor geography, trade liberalization is less important than developing proper health care systems or providing basic infrastructure—or letting people move elsewhere.

Migration from poor locations is the missing factor in the current wave of globalization that could make a large contribution to reducing poverty. Each year, 83 million people are added to the world's population, 82 million of them in the developing world. In Europe and Japan, moreover, the population is aging and the labor force is set to shrink. Migration of relatively unskilled workers from South to North would thus offer clear economic benefits to both. Most migration from South to North is economically motivated, and it raises the living standard of the migrant while benefiting the sending country in three ways. First, it reduces the South's labor force and thus raises wages for those who remain behind. Second, migrants send remittances of hard currency back home. Finally, migration bolsters transnational trade and investment networks. In the case of Mexico, for example, ten percent of its citizens live and work in the United States, taking pressure off its own labor market and raising wages there. India gets six times as much in remittances from its workers overseas as it gets in foreign aid.

Unlike trade, however, migration remains highly restricted and controversial. Some critics perceive a disruptive impact on society and culture and fear downward pressure on wages and rising unemployment in the richer countries. Yet anti-immigration lobbies ignore the fact that geographical economic disparities are so strong that illegal immigration is growing rapidly anyway, despite restrictive policies. In a perverse irony, some of the worst abuses of globalization occur because there is not enough of it in key economic areas such as labor flows. Human traffic, for example, has become a highly lucrative, unregulated business in which illegal migrants are easy prey for exploitation.

Realistically, none of the industrialized countries is going to adopt open migration. But they should reconsider their migration policies. Some, for example, have a strong bias in their immigration rules toward highly skilled workers, which in fact spurs a "brain drain" from the developing world. Such policies do little to stop the flow of unskilled workers and instead push many of these people into the illegal category. If rich countries would legally accept more unskilled workers, they could address their own looming labor shortages, improve living standards in developing countries, and reduce illegal human traffic and its abuses.

In sum, the integration of poor economies with richer ones over the past two decades has provided many opportunities for poor people to improve their lives. Examples of the beneficiaries of globalization can be found among Mexican migrants, Chinese factory workers, Vietnamese peasants, and Ugandan farmers. Many of the better-off in developing and rich countries alike also benefit. After all the rhetoric about globalization is stripped away, many of the policy questions come down to whether the rich world will make integrating with the world economy easy for those poor communities that want to do so. The world's poor have a large stake in how the rich countries answer.

Life after Pax Americana

Charles A. Kupchan

THIS DECADE HAS been a relatively easy one for American strategists. America's preponderant economic and military might has produced a unipolar international structure, which has in turn provided a
ready foundation for global stability. Hierarchy and order have devolved
naturally from power asymmetries, making less urgent the mapping of
a new international landscape and the formulation of a new grand
strategy. The Bush and Clinton administrations do deserve considerable credit for presiding over the end of the Cold War and responding
sensibly to isolated crises around the globe. But America's uncontested
hegemony has spared them the task of preserving peace and managing
competition and balancing among multiple poles of power—a
challenge that has consistently bedeviled statesmen throughout history.

The coming decade will be a far less tractable one for the
architects of U.S. foreign policy. Although the United States will
remain atop the international hierarchy for the near term, a global
landscape in which power and influence are more equally distributed
looms ahead. With this more equal distribution of power will come
a more traditional geopolitics and the return of the competitive
balancing that has been held in abeyance by America's preponderance. Economic globalization, nuclear weapons, new information
technologies, and the spread of democracy may well tame geopolitics
and dampen the rivalries likely to accompany a more diffuse

CHARLES A. KUPCHAN is Professor of International Relations
at Georgetown University and a Senior Fellow at the Council on
Foreign Relations. This article originally appeared in the Fall 1999
issue of *World Policy Journal* © 1999 World Policy Institute. He is the
author, among other works, of *The Vulnerability of Empire*.

⟶ fundamental diff. w/K.

distribution of power. But history provides sobering lessons in this respect. Time and again, postwar lulls in international competition and pronouncements about the obsolescence of war have given way to the return of power balancing and eventually to great-power conflict.

The foreign policy team that takes office in 2001 will therefore face the onerous task of piecing together a grand strategy for managing the return to multipolarity. The challenge will be as demanding politically as it is intellectually. Recognizing that new power centers are emerging and adjusting to their rise will meet political resistance after 50 years of American primacy. Politicians and strategists alike will have to engage in long-term planning and pursue policies that respond to underlying trends rather than immediate challenges. But American elites must rise to the occasion. The coming decade represents a unique window of opportunity; the United States should plan for the future while it still enjoys preponderance, and not wait until the diffusion of power has already made international politics more competitive and unpredictable.

In the next section I explain how and why a transition to a multipolar world is likely to come about in the near term. The United States will not be eclipsed by a rising challenger, as is usually the case during transitions in international hierarchy. Instead, a shrinking American willingness to be the global protector of last resort will be the primary engine of a changing global landscape. The key challenge, I then argue, will not be in preparing for battle with the next contender for hegemony but in weaning Europe and East Asia of their excessive dependence on the current hegemon, the United States. Europeans and East Asians alike have found it both comfortable and cheap to rely on American power and diplomacy to provide their security. Americans have gone along with the deal for decades because of the importance of containing the Soviet Union and the profitability of being at the center of global politics.

But now that communist regimes are a dying breed and the Cold War is receding into the past, America's protective umbrella will slowly retract. If this retrenchment in the scope of America's engagement abroad is not to result in the return of destructive power balancing to Europe and East Asia, the United States and its main regional partners must start now to prepare for life after Pax Americana.

BENIGN POWER

MOST ANALYSTS OF international politics trace change in the distribution of power to two sources: the secular diffusion over time and space of productive capabilities and material resources; and balancing against concentrations of power motivated by the search for security and prestige. Today's great powers will become tomorrow's has-beens as nodes of innovation and efficiency move from the core to the periphery of the international system. In addition, reigning hegemons threaten rising secondary states and thereby provoke the formation of countervailing coalitions. Taken together, these dynamics drive the cyclical pattern of the rise and fall of great powers.[1]

In contrast to this historical pattern, neither the diffusion of power nor balancing against the United States will be important factors driving the coming transition in the international system. It will be decades before any single state can match the United States in terms of either economic or military capability. Current power asymmetries are extreme by historical standards. The United States spends more on defense than all other great powers combined and more on defense research and development than the rest of the world combined. Its gross economic output dwarfs that of most other countries and its expenditure on R&D points to a growing qualitative edge in a global economy increasingly dominated by high-technology sectors.[2] Nor is balancing against American power likely to provoke a countervailing coalition. The United States is separated from both Europe and Asia by large expanses of water, making American power less threatening. Furthermore, it is hard to imagine that the United States would engage in behavior sufficiently aggressive to provoke opposing alliances. Even in the wake of NATO's air campaign against Yugoslavia, U.S. forces are for the most part welcomed by local powers in Europe and East Asia. Despite sporadic comments from French, Russian, and Chinese

---

1. See Robert Gilpin, *War and Change in World Politics* (Cambridge: Cambridge University Press, 1981); Paul M. Kennedy, *The Rise and Fall of the Great Powers* (New York: Random House, 1987); and Christopher Layne, "The Unipolar Illusion: Why New Great Powers Will Rise," *International Security*, vol. 17 (Spring 1993).

2. William C. Wohlforth, "The Stability of a Unipolar World," *International Security*, vol. 24 (Summer 1999).

officials about America's overbearing behavior, the United States is generally viewed as a benign power, not as a predatory hegemon.[3]

THE RISE OF EUROPE

THE WANING of unipolarity is therefore likely to stem from two novel sources: regional amalgamation in Europe and shrinking internationalism in the United States. Europe is in the midst of a long-term process of political and economic integration that is gradually eliminating the importance of borders and centralizing authority and resources. To be sure, the European Union is not yet an amalgamated polity with a single center of authority. Nor does Europe have a military capability commensurate with its economic resources.

But trend lines do indicate that Europe is heading in the direction of becoming a new pole of power. Now that its single market is accompanied by a single currency, Europe has a collective weight on matters of trade and finance rivaling that of the United States. The aggregate wealth of the European Union's 15 members is already roughly equal to America's, and the coming entry of the new democracies of Central Europe will tilt the balance in the EU's favor.

Europe has also recently embarked on efforts to forge a common defense policy and to acquire the military wherewithal to operate independently of U.S. forces. The European Union has appointed a high representative to oversee security policy, is establishing a policy planning unit, and is starting to lay the political groundwork for revamping its forces. It will be decades, if ever, before the EU becomes a unitary state, especially in light of its impending enlargement to the east, but as its resources grow and its decisionmaking becomes more centralized, power and influence will become more equally distributed between the two sides of the Atlantic.

AMERICAN RELUCTANCE

THE RISE OF Europe and its leveling effect on the global distribution of power will occur gradually. Of more immediate impact will

3. On the concept of benign power, see Charles Kupchan, "After Pax Americana: Benign Power, Regional Integration, and the Sources of a Stable Multipolarity," *International Security*, vol. 23 (Fall 1998).

Sept 11

be a diminishing appetite for robust internationalism in the United States. Today's unipolar landscape is a function not just of America's preponderant resources but also of its willingness to use them to underwrite international order. Accordingly, should the will of the body politic to bear the costs and risks of international leadership decline, so too would America's position of global primacy.

On the face of it, the appetite of the American polity for internationalism has diminished little, if at all, since the collapse of the Soviet Union. Both the Bush and Clinton administrations have pursued ambitious and activist foreign policies. The United States has taken the lead in building an open international economy and promoting financial stability, and it has repeatedly deployed its forces to trouble spots around the globe. But American internationalism is now at a high-water mark and, for three compelling reasons, it will begin to dissipate in the years ahead.

First, the internationalism of the 1990s has been sustained by a period of unprecedented economic growth in the United States. A booming stock market, an expanding economy, and substantial budget surpluses have created a political atmosphere conducive to trade liberalization, expenditure on the military, and repeated engagement in solving problems in less fortunate parts of the globe.

Yet, even under these auspicious conditions, the internationalist agenda has shown signs of faltering. Congress, for example, has mustered only a fickle enthusiasm for free trade, approving NAFTA in 1993 and the Uruguay Round in 1994, but then denying President Clinton fast-track negotiating authority in 1997. Congress has also been skeptical of America's interventions in Bosnia and Kosovo, tolerating them, but little more. When the stock market sputters and growth stalls (and this is a matter of when, not if), these inward-looking currents will grow much stronger. The little support for free trade that still exists will dwindle. And such stinginess is likely to spread into the security realm, intensifying the domestic debate over burden sharing and calls within Congress for America's regional partners to shoulder increased defense responsibilities.

Second, although the United States has pursued a very activist defense policy during the 1990s, it has done so on the cheap. Clinton has repeatedly authorized the use of force in the Balkans and in the Middle East. But he has relied almost exclusively on air power, successfully avoiding the casualties likely to accompany the introduction of ground troops in combat. In Somalia, the one case in which U.S. ground troops suffered significant losses, Clinton ordered the withdrawal of U.S. forces from the operation. In NATO's campaign against Yugoslavia, week after week of bombing only intensified the humanitarian crisis and increased the likelihood of a southward spread of the conflict. Nevertheless, the United States blocked the use of ground forces and insisted that aircraft bomb from 15,000 feet to avoid being shot down.

Congress revolted despite these operational constraints minimizing the risks to U.S. personnel. A month into the campaign, the House of Representatives voted 249 to 180 to refuse funding for sending U.S. ground troops to Yugoslavia without congressional permission. Even a resolution that merely endorsed the bombing campaign failed to win approval (the vote was 213 to 213). In short, the American polity appears to have near zero tolerance for casualties. The illusion that internationalism can be maintained with no or minimal loss of life will likely come back to haunt the United States in the years ahead, limiting its ability to use force in the appropriate manner when necessary.

Third, generational change is likely to take a toll on the character and scope of U.S. engagement abroad. The younger Americans already rising to positions of influence in the public and private sectors have not lived through the formative experiencesthe Second World War and the rebuilding of Europethat serve as historical anchors of internationalism. Individuals schooled in the 1990s and now entering the work force will not even have first-hand experience of the Cold War. These Americans will not necessarily be isolationist, but they will certainly be less interested in and knowledgeable about foreign affairs than their older colleagues-a pattern already becoming apparent in the Congress. In the absence of a manifest threat to American national security, making the case for engagement and sacrifice abroad thus promises to grow increasingly difficult with time. Trend lines clearly point to a turning inward, to a nation tiring of carrying the burdens of global leadership.

BAD NEWS AND GOOD NEWS

THE BAD NEWS is that the global stability that unipolarity has engendered will be jeopardized as power becomes more equally distributed in the international system. The good news is that this structural change will occur through different mechanisms than in the past, and therefore *may* be easier to manage peacefully.

The rising challenger is Europe, not a unitary state with hegemonic ambitions. Europe's aspirations will be moderated by the self-checking mechanisms inherent in the EU and by cultural and linguistic barriers to centralization. In addition, the United States is likely to react to a more independent Europe by stepping back and making room for an EU that appears ready to be more self reliant and more muscular. Unlike reigning hegemons in the past, the United States will not fight to the finish to maintain its primacy and prevent its eclipse by a rising challenger. On the contrary, the United States will cede leadership willingly as its economy slows and it grows weary of being the security guarantor of last resort.

The prospect is thus not one of clashing titans, but of no titans at all. Regions long accustomed to relying on American resources and leadership to preserve the peace may well be left to fend for themselves. These are the main reasons that the challenge for American grand strategy as the next century opens will be to wean Europe and East Asia of their dependence on the United States and put in place arrangements that will prevent the return of competitive balancing and regional rivalries in the wake of an American retrenchment.

EUROPE ON ITS OWN

IT IS FORTUNATE that the near-term challenge to U.S. primacy will come from Europe. After decades of close cooperation, Europe and North America enjoy unprecedented levels of trust and reciprocity. European states have gone along with U.S. leadership not just because they have not had the power and influence to do otherwise; despite cavils, they also welcome the particular brand of international order sustained by the United States. A more equal distribution of power across the Atlantic will no doubt engender increased competition

Charles A. Kupchan

between a collective Europe and the United States. But such conflict is likely to be restricted to economic matters and muted by the mutual benefits reaped from high levels of trade and investment. Furthermore, the underlying coincidence of values between North America and Europe means that even when interests diverge, geopolitical rivalry is not likely to follow. Efforts to preserve an Atlantic consensus may well lead to a lowest common denominator and produce inaction (as has occurred repeatedly in the Balkans). But it is hard to imagine the United States and Europe engaging in militarized conflict.

In this sense, the key concern for the coming decade is not the emergence of balancing between Europe and the United States, but the reemergence of balancing and rivalries within a Europe no longer under American protection. The European Union is well on its way to erecting a regional order that can withstand the retraction of American power. Through a steady process of pooling sovereignty, Europe has nurtured a supranational character and identity that make integration irreversible. Nevertheless, guaranteeing a self-sustaining and coherent European polity requires that Europe and the United States together pursue three initiatives.

A WINDOW OF OPPORTUNITY

To begin, europe must follow through with the initial steps it has taken to create a military establishment capable of carrying out major missions without the assistance of U.S. forces. The United States should be far more forthcoming in welcoming this initiative, and stop worrying that an independent European military would undercut the transatlantic security link by fueling calls in Congress for the withdrawal of U.S. troops. NATO will be in much better shape five years hence if Europe is carrying a fair load than if Congress continues to see a Europe free-riding on American soldiers. Far from expediting a U.S. departure from the continent, a serious European military will only increase the chances that a mature and balanced transatlantic partnership emerges and that America maintains a presence in Europe.

Europe now has a window of opportunity to make serious progress on the defense front. A number of factors afford this opening: British willingness to take the lead on forging a collective defense policy; recognition within the EU of Europe's excessive dependence on U.S. capability (made clear by the campaign against Yugoslavia); and the appointment of a new European Commission, with Romani Prodi as its president and Javier Solana as its high representative for security policy.

The top priorities for EU members include moving to all-volunteer forces so that defense expenditures can go toward buying capability and force-projection assets, not paying poorly trained conscripts. Europe's defense industry must be consolidated to improve economies of scale, and more funding should go toward research and development and improving the technological sophistication of weapons and intelligence systems. Europe must also make tough decisions about an appropriate division of labor among its member states if it is to build a balanced and capable force structure.

Promoting a stable peace in southeastern Europe is the second key piece of unfinished business for Europe and the United States. The task of halting ethnic conflict in the Balkans repeatedly paralyzed both NATO and the EU throughout the decade. The European enterprise would have been set back grievously had NATO failed to act in Bosnia and Kosovo. Now that the fighting has stopped, the international community must take advantage of the opportunity to construct a lasting peace. That goal ultimately means drawing the Balkans into the European Union. Rapprochement between Greece and Turkey and resolution of the Cyprus problem are no less important if Europe is to avoid being engulfed in persistent crises in its southeast. In its quest to help ensure that Europe does not again fall prey to national rivalries, the United States should make southeastern Europe a top regional priority.

Embracing Russia in a wider Europe is the third step needed to prevent the return of rivalries and shifting balances of power to the continent. Russia in the years ahead will gradually reassume its position as one of Europe's great powers. If Russia is included in the European enterprise, its resources and influence will likely be directed toward furthering continent-wide integration. If it is excluded from the European project, Russia will likely seek a coalition to balance against Europe. Indeed, the enlargement of NATO has already increased the likelihood of such balancing by raising the prospect that Russia's entire western flank will abut the Atlantic Alliance.

Instead of using NATO to protect against a threat that no longer exists, its members should use the organization as a vehicle for anchoring Russia in Europe.[4] The EU is the more appropriate vehicle for this task, but its enlargement is lagging way behind NATO's because of the institutional changes and financial costs entailed in adding new members. Furthermore, the integration of Russia into the Atlantic community, in part because of European resistance on cultural grounds, will require considerable American influence and leadership-assets that NATO provides. While it is still Europe's chief peacemaker and protector, the United States needs to ensure that Russia is included in Europe's historic process of pacification and integration.

EAST ASIA ESTRANGED

PREPARING EAST ASIA to rely less on American power is far more complicated and dangerous than the parallel task in Europe. The key difference is that European states took advantage of America's protective umbrella to pursue reconciliation, rapprochement, and an ambitious agenda of regional cooperation and integration. Europeans have accordingly succeeded in fashioning a regional order that is likely to withstand the retraction of American power. In contrast, states in East Asia have hidden behind America's presence, pursuing neither reconciliation nor regional integration. East Asia's major powers remain estranged.

The United States therefore faces a severe tradeoff in East Asia between the balancing provoked by its predominant role in the region and the intraregional balancing that would ensue in the wake of an American retrenchment. America's sizable military presence in East Asia keeps the peace and checks regional rivalries. But it also alienates China and holds in place a polarized political landscape.

As China's economy and military capability grow, its efforts to balance against the United States could become more pronounced. Were the United States to back off from its role as regional arbiter and protector, relations with China would improve, but at the

---

4. See Charles Kupchan, "Rethinking Europe," *The National Interest*, no. 56 (Summer 1999).

expense of regional stability. Japan and Korea would no doubt increase their own military capabilities, risking a regionwide arms race and spiraling tensions.

If the United States is to escape the horns of this dilemma, it must help repair the region's main cleavage and facilitate rapprochement between East Asia's two major powers: Japan and China. Just as reconciliation between France and Germany was the critical ingredient in building a stable zone of peace in Europe, Sino-Japanese rapprochement is the sine qua non of a self-sustaining regional order in East Asia.

Primary responsibility for improving Sino-Japanese ties lies with Japan. With an economy and political system much more developed than China's, Japan has far more latitude in exploring openings in the relationship. Japan can also take a major step forward by finally acknowledging and formally apologizing for its behavior during the Second World War. The United States can further this process by welcoming and helping to facilitate overtures between Tokyo and Beijing.

Washington should also help dislodge the inertia that pervades politics in Tokyo by making it clear to the Japanese that they cannot indefinitely rely on American guarantees to ensure their security. Japan therefore needs to take advantage of America's protective umbrella while it lasts, pursuing the policies of reconciliation and integration essential to constructing a regional security order resting on cooperation rather than deterrence.

If overtures from Tokyo succeed in reducing tensions between China and Japan, the United States would be able to play a less prominent role in the region, making possible an improvement in its own relations with China. As it buys time for Sino Japanese rapprochement to get underway, Washington should avoid the rhetoric and policies that might induce China to intensify its efforts to balance against Japan and the United States. Talk of an impending Chinese military threat is both counterproductive and misguided; the Chinese military is nowhere near world-class.[5] The United States should also avoid provocative moves,

---

5. See Bates Gill and Michael O'Hanlon, "China's Hollow Military," *The National Interest*, no. 56 (Summer 1999); and Gerald Segal, "Does China Matter?" *Foreign Affairs*, vol. 78 (September/October 1999).

Charles A. Kupchan

such as deploying antimissile defenses in the Western Pacific theater or supporting a Taiwanese policy of moving toward formal independence. China can do its part to strengthen its relationship with the United States by containing saber-rattling over Taiwan, halting the export of weapons to rogue states, and avoiding actions and rhetoric that could inflame territorial disputes in the region.

A GLOBAL DIRECTORATE

IF MY ANALYSIS is correct, the most dangerous consequence of a return to multipolarity is not balancing between North America, Europe, and East Asia, but the reemergence of national rivalries and competitive balancing within Europe and East Asia as American retrenchment proceeds. It is for this reason that American grand strategy should focus on facilitating regional integration in Europe and East Asia as a means of preparing both areas to assume far more responsibility for managing their own affairs.

The ultimate vision that should guide U.S. grand strategy is the construction of a concert-like directorate of the major powers in North America, Europe, and East Asia. These major powers would together manage developments and regulate relations both within and among their respective regions.

Mustering the political will and the foresight to pursue this vision will be a formidable task. The United States will need to begin ceding influence and autonomy to regions that have grown all too comfortable with American primacy. Neither American statesmen, long accustomed to calling the shots, nor statesmen in Europe and East Asia, long accustomed to passing the buck, will find the transition an easy one.

But it is far wiser and safer to get ahead of the curve and shape structural change by design, than to find unipolarity giving way to a chaotic multipolarity by default. It will take a decade, if not two, for a new international system to evolve. But the decisions taken by the first American administration of the twenty-first century will play a critical role in determining whether multipolarity reemerges peacefully or brings with it the competitive jockeying that in the past has so frequently led to great-power war.

Power and Weakness

Robert Kagan

IT IS TIME to stop pretending that Europeans and Americans share a common view of the world, or even that they occupy the same world. On the all-important question of power-the efficacy of power, the morality of power, the desirability of power-American and European perspectives are diverging. Europe is turning away from power, or to put it a little differently, it is moving beyond power into a self-contained world of laws and rules and transnational negotiation and cooperation. It is entering a post-historical paradise of peace and relative prosperity, the realization of Kant's "Perpetual Peace." The United States, meanwhile, remains mired in history, exercising power in the anarchic Hobbesian world where international laws and rules are unreliable and where true security and the defense and promotion of a liberal order still depend on the possession and use of military might. That is why on major strategic and international questions today, Americans are from Mars and Europeans are from Venus: They agree on little and understand one another less and less. And this state of affairs is not transitory-the product of one American election or one catastrophic event. The reasons for the transatlantic divide are deep, long in development, and likely to endure. When it comes to setting national priorities, determining threats, defining challenges, and fashioning and implementing foreign and defense policies, the United States and Europe have parted ways.

ROBERT KAGAN is a senior associate at the Carnegie Endowment for International Peace. He is currently based in Brussels. This article originally appeared in the June/July 2002 issue of *Policy Review* © 2002 Hoover Institute.

It is easier to see the contrast as an American living in Europe. Europeans are more conscious of the growing differences, perhaps because they fear them more. European intellectuals are nearly unanimous in the conviction that Americans and Europeans no longer share a common "strategic culture." The European caricature at its most extreme depicts an America dominated by a "culture of death," its warlike temperament the natural product of a violent society where every man has a gun and the death penalty reigns. But even those who do not make this crude link agree there are profound differences in the way the United States and Europe conduct foreign policy.

The United States, they argue, resorts to force more quickly and, compared with Europe, is less patient with diplomacy. Americans generally see the world divided between good and evil, between friends and enemies, while Europeans see a more complex picture. When confronting real or potential adversaries, Americans generally favor policies of coercion rather than persuasion, emphasizing punitive sanctions over inducements to better behavior, the stick over the carrot. Americans tend to seek finality in international affairs: They want problems solved, threats eliminated. And, of course, Americans increasingly tend toward unilateralism in international affairs. They are less inclined to act through international institutions such as the United Nations, less inclined to work cooperatively with other nations to pursue common goals, more skeptical about international law, and more willing to operate outside its strictures when they deem it necessary, or even merely useful.[1]

Europeans insist they approach problems with greater nuance and sophistication. They try to influence others through subtlety and indirection. They are more tolerant of failure, more patient when solutions don't come quickly. They generally favor peaceful responses to problems, preferring negotiation, diplomacy, and

---

1. One representative French observer describes "a U.S. mindset" that "tends to emphasize military, technical, and unilateral solutions to international problems, possibly at the expense of cooperative and political ones." See Gilles Andreani, "The Disarray of U.S. Non-Proliferation Policy," *Survival* (Winter 2999-z000).

persuasion to coercion. They are quicker to appeal to international law, international conventions, and international opinion to adjudicate disputes. They try to use commercial and economic ties to bind nations together. They often emphasize process over result, believing that ultimately process can become substance.

This European dual portrait is a caricature, of course, with its share of exaggerations and oversimplifications. One cannot generalize about Europeans: Britons may have a more "American" view of power than many of their fellow Europeans on the continent. And there are differing perspectives within nations on both sides of the Atlantic. In the United States, Democrats often seem more "European" than Republicans; Secretary of State Colin Powell may appear more "European" than Secretary of Defense Donald Rumsfeld. Many Americans, especially among the intellectual elite, are as uncomfortable with the "hard" quality of American foreign policy as any European; and some Europeans value power as much as any American.

Nevertheless, the caricatures do capture an essential truth: The United States and Europe are fundamentally different today. Powell and Rumsfeld have more in common than do Powell and Hubert Vedrine or even Jack Straw. When it comes to the use of force, mainstream American Democrats have more in common with Republicans than they do with most European Socialists and Social Democrats. During the 1990s even American liberals were more willing to resort to force and were more Manichean in their perception of the world than most of their European counterparts. The Clinton administration bombed Iraq, as well as Afghanistan and Sudan. European governments, it is safe to say, would not have done so. Whether they would have bombed even Belgrade in 1999, had the U.S. not forced their hand, is an interesting question.[2]

---

2. The case of Bosnia in the early 1990s stands out as an instance where some Europeans, chiefly British Prime Minister Tony Blair, were at times more forceful in advocating military action than first the Bush and then the Clinton administration. (Blair was also an early advocate of using air power and even ground troops in the Kosovo crisis.) And Europeans had forces on the ground in Bosnia when the United States did not, although in a U.N. peacekeeping role that proved ineffective when challenged.

What is the source of these differing strategic perspectives? The question has received too little attention in recent years, either because foreign policy intellectuals and policymakers on both sides of the Atlantic have denied the existence of a genuine difference or because those who have pointed to the difference, especially in Europe, have been more interested in assailing the United States than in understanding why the United States acts as it does—or, for that matter, why Europe acts as it does. It is past time to move beyond the denial and the insults and to face the problem head-on.

Despite what many Europeans and some Americans believe, these differences in strategic culture do not spring naturally from the national characters of Americans and Europeans. After all, what Europeans now consider their more peaceful strategic culture is, historically speaking, quite new. It represents an evolution away from the very different strategic culture that dominated Europe for hundreds of years and at least until World War I. The European governments - and peoples - who enthusiastically launched themselves into that continental war believed in *machtpolitik*. While the roots of the present European worldview, like the roots of the European Union itself, can be traced back to the Enlightenment, Europe's great-power politics for the past 300 years did not follow the visionary designs of the philosophes and the physiocrats.

As for the United States, there is nothing timeless about the present heavy reliance on force as a tool of international relations, nor about the tilt toward unilateralism and away from a devotion to international law. Americans are children of the Enlightenment, too, and in the early years of the republic were more faithful apostles of its creed. America's eighteenth and early nineteenth-century statesmen sounded much like the European statesmen of today, extolling the virtues of commerce as the soothing balm of international strife and appealing to international law and international opinion over brute force. The young United States wielded power against weaker peoples on the North American continent, but when it came to dealing with the European giants, it claimed to abjure power

and assailed as atavistic the power politics of the eighteenth-
and nineteenth-century European empires.

Two centuries later, Americans and Europeans have traded
places and perspectives. Partly this is because in those 200 years,
but especially in recent decades, the power equation has shifted
dramatically: When the United States was weak, it practiced the
strategies of indirection, the strategies of weakness; now that the
United States is powerful, it behaves as powerful nations do. When
the European great powers were strong, they believed in strength
and martial glory. Now, they see the world through the eyes of
weaker powers. These very different points of view, weak versus
strong, have naturally produced differing strategic judgments, differing
assessments of threats and of the proper means of addressing threats,
and even differing calculations of interest.

But this is only part of the answer. For along with these natural
consequences of the transatlantic power gap, there has also opened
a broad ideological gap. Europe, because of its unique historical
experience of the past half-century - culminating in the past
decade with the creation of the European Union - has developed a
set of ideals and principles regarding the utility and morality of
power different from the ideals and principles of Americans, who
have not shared that experience. If the strategic chasm between the
United States and Europe appears greater than ever today, and
grows still wider at a worrying pace, it is because these material
and ideological differences reinforce one another. The divisive
trend they together produce may be impossible to reverse.

THE POWER GAP: PERCEPTION AND REALITY

EUROPE HAS BEEN militarily weak for a long time, but until fairly recently its weakness had been obscured. World War II all but
destroyed European nations as global powers, and their postwar
inability to project sufficient force overseas to maintain colonial
empires in Asia, Africa, and the Middle East forced them to
retreat on a massive scale after more than five centuries of imperial dominance-perhaps the most significant retrenchment of global
influence in human history. For a half-century after World War II,

Robert Kagan

however, this weakness was masked by the unique geopolitical circumstances of the Cold War. Dwarfed by the two superpowers on its flanks, a weakened Europe nevertheless served as the central strategic theater of the worldwide struggle between communism and democratic capitalism. Its sole but vital strategic mission was to defend its own territory against any Soviet offensive, at least until the Americans arrived. Although shorn of most traditional measures of great-power status, Europe remained the geopolitical pivot, and this, along with lingering habits of world leadership, allowed Europeans to retain international influence well beyond what their sheer military capabilities might have afforded.

Europe lost this strategic centrality after the Cold War ended, but it took a few more years for the lingering mirage of European global power to fade. During the 1990s, war in the Balkans kept both Europeans and Americans focused on the strategic importance of the continent and on the continuing relevance of NATO. The enlargement of NATO to include former Warsaw Pact nations and the consolidation of the Cold War victory kept Europe in the forefront of the strategic discussion.

Then there was the early promise of the "new Europe." By bonding together into a single political and economic unit - the historic accomplishment of the Maastricht treaty in 1992 - many hoped to recapture Europe's old greatness but in a new political form. "Europe" would be the next superpower, not only economically and politically, but also militarily. It would handle crises on the European continent, such as the ethnic conflicts in the Balkans, and it would reemerge as a global player. In the 1990s Europeans could confidently assert that the power of a unified Europe would restore, finally, the global "multipolarity" that had been destroyed by the Cold War and its aftermath. And most Americans, with mixed emotions, agreed that superpower Europe was the future. Harvard University's Samuel P. Huntington predicted that the coalescing of the European Union would be "the single most important move" in a worldwide reaction against American hegemony and would produce a "truly multipolar" twenty-first century.[3]

---

3 Samuel P. Huntington, "The Lonely Superpower," *Foreign Affairs* (March/April 1999).

Power and Weakness

But European pretensions and American apprehensions proved unfounded. The 1990s witnessed not the rise of a European super-power but the decline of Europe into relative weakness. The Balkan conflict at the beginning of the decade revealed European military incapacity and political disarray; the Kosovo conflict at decade's end exposed a transatlantic gap in military technology and the ability to wage modern warfare that would only widen in sub-sequent years. Outside of Europe, the disparity by the close of the 1990s was even more starkly apparent as it became clear that the ability of European powers, individually or collectively, to project decisive force into regions of conflict beyond the continent was negligible. Europeans could provide peacekeeping forces in the Balkans-indeed, they could and eventually did provide the vast bulk of those forces in Bosnia and Kosovo. But they lacked the wherewithal to introduce and sustain a fighting force in potential-ly hostile territory, even in Europe. Under the best of circum-stances, the European role was limited to filling out peacekeeping forces after the United States had, largely on its own, carried out the decisive phases of a military mission and stabilized the situa-tion. As some Europeans put it, the real division of labor consisted of the United States "making the dinner" and the Europeans "doing the dishes."

This inadequacy should have come as no surprise, since these were the limitations that had forced Europe to retract its global influence in the first place. Those Americans and Europeans who proposed that Europe expand its strategic role beyond the continent set an unreasonable goal. During the Cold War, Europe's strategic role had been to defend itself. It was unrealistic to expect a return to interna-tional great-power status, unless European peoples were willing to shift significant resources from social programs to military programs.

Clearly they were not. Not only were Europeans unwilling to pay to project force beyond Europe. After the Cold War, they would not pay for sufficient force to conduct even minor military actions on the continent without American help. Nor did it seem to matter whether European publics were being asked to spend money to strengthen NATO or an independent European for-eign and defense policy. Their answer was the same. Rather than viewing the collapse of the Soviet Union as an opportunity to flex global muscles, Europeans took it as an opportunity to cash in on a sizable peace dividend. Average European defense budgets gradually fell below 2 percent of GDP. Despite talk of establishing Europe as a global superpower, therefore, European military capabilities steadily fell behind those of the United States throughout the 1990s.

The end of the Cold War had a very different effect on the other side of the Atlantic. For although Americans looked for a peace dividend, too, and defense budgets declined or remained flat during most of the 1990s, defense spending still remained above 3 percent of GDP. Fast on the heels of the Soviet empire's demise came Iraq's invasion of Kuwait and the largest American military action in a quarter-century. Thereafter American administrations cut the Cold War force, but not as dramatically as might have been expected. By historical standards, America's military power and particularly its ability to project that power to all corners of the globe remained unprecedented.

Meanwhile, the very fact of the Soviet empire's collapse vastly increased America's strength relative to the rest of the world. The sizable American military arsenal, once barely sufficient to balance Soviet power, was now deployed in a world without a single formidable adversary. This "unipolar moment" had an entirely natural and predictable consequence: It made the United States more willing to use force abroad. With the check of Soviet power removed, the United States was free to intervene practically wherever and whenever it chose–a fact reflected in the proliferation of overseas military interventions that began during the first Bush administration with the invasion of Panama in 1989, the Persian Gulf War in 1991, and the humanitarian intervention in Somalia in 1992, continuing during the Clinton years with interventions in Haiti, Bosnia, and Kosovo. While American politicians talked of pulling back from the world, the reality was an America intervening abroad more frequently than it had throughout most of the Cold War. Thanks to new technologies, the United States was also freer to use force around the world in more limited ways through air and missile strikes, which it did with increasing frequency.

Power and Weakness

How could this growing transatlantic power gap fail to create a difference in strategic perceptions? Even during the Cold War, American military predominance and Europe's relative weakness had produced important and sometimes serious disagreements. Gaullism, *Ostpolitik*, and the various movements for European independence and unity were manifestations not only of a European desire for honor and freedom of action. They also reflected a European conviction that America's approach to the Cold War was too confrontational, too militaristic, and too dangerous. Europeans believed they knew better how to deal with the Soviets: through engagement and seduction, through commercial and political ties, through patience and forbearance. It was a legitimate view, shared by many Americans. But it also reflected Europe's weakness relative to the United States, the fewer military options at Europe's disposal, and its greater vulnerability to a powerful Soviet Union. It may have reflected, too, Europe's memory of continental war. Americans, when they were not themselves engaged in the subtleties of détente, viewed the European approach as a form of appeasement, a return to the fearful mentality of the 1930s. But appeasement is never a dirty word to those whose genuine weakness offers few appealing alternatives. For them, it is a policy of sophistication.

The end of the Cold War, by widening the power gap, exacerbated the disagreements. Although transatlantic tensions are now widely assumed to have begun with the inauguration of George W. Bush in January 2001, they were already evident during the Clinton administration and may even be traced back to the administration of George H.W. Bush. By 1992, mutual recriminations were rife over Bosnia, where the United States refused to act and Europe could not act. It was during the Clinton years that Europeans began complaining about being lectured by the "hectoring hegemon." This was also the period in which Vedrine coined the term *hyperpuissance* to describe an American behemoth too worryingly powerful to be designated merely a superpower. (Perhaps he was responding to then-Secretary of State Madeleine Albright's insistence that the United States was the world's "indispensable nation.") It was also during the 1990s that the transatlantic disagreement over American plans for missile defense emerged and many Europeans began grumbling about the American propensity to choose force and punishment over diplomacy and persuasion.

The Clinton administration, meanwhile, though relatively timid and restrained itself, grew angry and impatient with European timidity, especially the unwillingness to confront Saddam Hussein. The split in the alliance over Iraq didn't begin with the 2000 election but in 1997, when the Clinton administration tried to increase the pressure on Baghdad and found itself at odds with France and (to a lesser extent) Great Britain in the United Nations Security Council. Even the war in Kosovo was marked by nervousness among some allies-especially Italy, Greece, and Germany - that the United States was too uncompromisingly militaristic in its approach. And while Europeans and Americans ultimately stood together in the confrontation with Belgrade, the Kosovo war produced in Europe less satisfaction at the successful prosecution of the war than unease at America's apparent omnipotence. That apprehension would only increase in the wake of American military action after September 11, 2001.

THE PSYCHOLOGY OF POWER AND WEAKNESS

TODAY'S TRANSATLANTIC problem, in short, is not a George Bush problem. It is a power problem. American military strength has produced a propensity to use that strength. Europe's military weakness has produced a perfectly understandable aversion to the exercise of military power. Indeed, it has produced a powerful European interest in inhabiting a world where strength doesn't matter, where international law and international institutions predominate, where unilateral action by powerful nations is forbidden, where all nations regardless of their strength have equal rights and are equally protected by commonly agreed-upon international rules of behavior. Europeans have a deep interest in devaluing and eventually eradicating the brutal laws of an anarchic, Hobbesian world where power is the ultimate determinant of national security and success.

This is no reproach. It is what weaker powers have wanted from time immemorial. It was what Americans wanted in the eighteenth and early nineteenth centuries, when the brutality of a European system of power politics run by the global giants of France, Britain, and Russia left Americans constantly vulnerable to imperial thrashing. It was what the other small powers of Europe wanted in those years, too, only to be sneered at by Bourbon kings and other powerful monarchs, who spoke instead of *raison d'état*. The great proponent of international law on the high seas in the eighteenth century was the United States; the great opponent was Britain's navy, the "Mistress of the Seas." In an anarchic world, small powers always fear they will be victims. Great powers, on the other hand, often fear rules that may constrain them more than they fear the anarchy in which their power brings security and prosperity.

This natural and historic disagreement between the stronger and the weaker manifests itself in today's transatlantic dispute over the question of unilateralism. Europeans generally believe their objection to American unilateralism is proof of their greater commitment to certain ideals concerning world order. They are less willing to acknowledge that their hostility to unilateralism is also self-interested. Europeans fear American unilateralism. They fear it perpetuates a Hobbesian world in which they may become increasingly vulnerable. The United States may be a relatively benign hegemon, but insofar as its actions delay the arrival of a world order more conducive to the safety of weaker powers, it is objectively dangerous.

This is one reason why in recent years a principal objective of European foreign policy has become, as one European observer puts it, the "multilateralising" of the United States.[4] It is not that Europeans are teaming up against the American hegemon, as Huntington and many realist theorists would have it, by creating a countervailing power. After all, Europeans are not increasing their

---

4. Steven Events, "Unilateral America, Lightweight Europe?: Managing Divergence in Transatlantic Foreign Policy," Centre for European Reform working paper (February 2001).

Robert Kagan

power. Their tactics, like their goal, are the tactics of the weak. They hope to constrain American power without wielding power themselves. In what may be the ultimate feat of subtlety and indirection, they want to control the behemoth by appealing to its conscience.

It is a sound strategy, as far as it goes. The United States *is* a behemoth with a conscience. It is not Louis XIV's France or George III's England. Americans do not argue, even to themselves, that their actions may be justified by *raison d'état*. Americans have never accepted the principles of Europe's old order, never embraced the Machiavellian perspective. The United States is a liberal, progressive society through and through, and to the extent that Americans believe in power, they believe it must be a means of advancing the principles of a liberal civilization and a liberal world order. Americans even share Europe's aspirations for a more orderly world system based not on power but on rules - after all, they were striving for such a world when Europeans were still extolling the laws of *machtpolitik*.

But while these common ideals and aspirations shape foreign policies on both sides of the Atlantic, they cannot completely negate the very different perspectives from which Europeans and Americans view the world and the role of power in international affairs. Europeans oppose unilateralism in part because they have no capacity for unilateralism. Polls consistently show that Americans support multilateral action in principle-they even support acting under the rubric of the United Nations-but the fact remains that the United States can act unilaterally, and has done so many times with reasonable success. For Europeans, the appeal to multilateralism and international law has a real practical payoff and little cost. For Americans, who stand to lose at least some freedom of action, support for universal rules of behavior really is a matter of idealism.

Even when Americans and Europeans can agree on the kind of world order they would strive to build, however, they increasingly disagree about what constitutes a threat to that international endeavor. Indeed, Europeans and Americans differ most these days in their evaluation of what constitutes a tolerable versus an intolerable threat. This, too, is consistent with the disparity of power.

Europeans often argue that Americans have an unreasonable demand for "perfect" security, the product of living for centuries shielded behind two oceans.[5] Europeans claim they know what it is like to live with danger, to exist side-by-side with evil, since they've done it for centuries. Hence their greater tolerance for such threats as may be posed by Saddam Hussein's Iraq or the ayatollahs' Iran. Americans, they claim, make far too much of the dangers these regimes pose.

Even before September 11, this argument rang a bit hollow. The United States in its formative decades lived in a state of substantial insecurity, surrounded by hostile European empires, at constant risk of being torn apart by centrifugal forces that were encouraged by threats from without: National insecurity formed the core of Washington's Farewell Address. As for the Europeans' supposed tolerance for insecurity and evil, it can be overstated. For the better part of three centuries, European Catholics and Protestants more often preferred to kill than to tolerate each other; nor have the past two centuries shown all that much mutual tolerance between Frenchmen and Germans.

Some Europeans argue that precisely because Europe has suffered so much, it has a higher tolerance for suffering than America and therefore a higher tolerance for threats. More likely the opposite is true. The memory of their horrendous suffering in World War I made the British and French publics more fearful of Nazi Germany, not more tolerant, and this attitude contributed significantly to the appeasement of the 1930s.

A better explanation of Europe's greater tolerance for threats is, once again, Europe's relative weakness. Tolerance is also very much a realistic response in that Europe, precisely because it is weak, actually faces fewer threats than the far more powerful United States.

The psychology of weakness is easy enough to understand. A man armed only with a knife may decide that a bear prowling the forest is a tolerable danger, inasmuch as the alternative-hunting the bear armed only with a knife-is actually riskier than lying low and

---

5. For that matter, this is also the view commonly found in American textbooks.

hoping the bear never attacks. The same man armed with a rifle, however, will likely make a different calculation of what constitutes a tolerable risk. Why should he risk being mauled to death if he doesn't need to?

This perfectly normal human psychology is helping to drive a wedge between the United States and Europe today. Europeans have concluded, reasonably enough, that the threat posed by Saddam Hussein is more tolerable for them than the risk of removing him. But Americans, being stronger, have reasonably enough developed a lower threshold of tolerance for Saddam and his weapons of mass destruction, especially after September 11. Europeans like to say that Americans are obsessed with fixing problems, but it is generally true that those with a greater capacity to fix problems are more likely to try to fix them than those who have no such capability. Americans can imagine successfully invading Iraq and toppling Saddam, and therefore more than 70 percent of Americans apparently favor such action. Europeans, not surprisingly, find the prospect both unimaginable and frightening.

The incapacity to respond to threats leads not only to tolerance but sometimes to denial. It's normal to try to put out of one's mind that which one can do nothing about. According to one student of European opinion, even the very focus on "threats" differentiates American policymakers from their European counterparts. Americans, writes Steven Everts, talk about foreign "threats" such as "the proliferation of weapons of mass destruction, terrorism, and `rogue states.'" But Europeans look at "challenges," such as "ethnic conflict, migration, organized crime, poverty and environmental degradation." As Everts notes, however, the key difference is less a matter of culture and philosophy than of capability. Europeans "are most worried about issues ... that have a greater chance of being solved by political engagement and huge sums of money." In other words, Europeans focus on issues—"challenges"-where European strengths come into play but not on those "threats" where European weakness makes solutions elusive. If Europe's strategic culture today places less value on power and military strength and more value on such soft-power tools as economics and trade, isn't it partly because Europe is militarily weak and economically strong? Americans are quicker to acknowledge the existence of threats, even to perceive them where others may not see any, because they can conceive of doing something to meet those threats.

The differing threat perceptions in the United States and Europe are not just matters of psychology, however. They are also grounded in a practical reality that is another product of the disparity of power. For Iraq and other "rogue" states objectively do not pose the same level of threat to Europeans as they do to the United States. There is, first of all, the American security guarantee that Europeans enjoy and have enjoyed for six decades, ever since the United States took upon itself the burden of maintaining order in farflung regions of the world-from the Korean Peninsula to the Persian Gulf-from which European power had largely withdrawn. Europeans generally believe, whether or not they admit it to themselves, that were Iraq ever to emerge as a real and present danger, as opposed to merely a potential danger, then the United States would do something about it-as it did in 1991. If during the Cold War Europe by necessity made a major contribution to its own defense, today Europeans enjoy an unparalleled measure of "free security" because most of the likely threats are in regions outside Europe, where only the United States can project effective force. In a very practical sense-that is, when it comes to actual strategic planning-neither Iraq nor Iran nor North Korea nor any other "rogue" state in the world is primarily a European problem. Nor, certainly, is China. Both Europeans and Americans agree that these are primarily American problems.

This is why Saddam Hussein is not as great a threat to Europe as he is to the United States. He would be a greater threat to the United States even were the Americans and Europeans in complete agreement on Iraq policy, because it is the logical consequence of the transatlantic disparity of power. The task of containing Saddam Hussein belongs primarily to the United States, not to Europe, and everyone agrees on this [6] - including Saddam, which is why he considers the United States, not Europe,

---

6. Notwithstanding the British contribution of patrols of the "no-fly zone."

his principal adversary. In the Persian Gulf, in the Middle East, and in most other regions of the world (including Europe), the United States plays the role of ultimate enforcer. "You are so powerful," Europeans often say to Americans. "So why do you feel so threatened?" But it is precisely America's great power that makes it the primary target, and often the only target. Europeans are understandably content that it should remain so.

Americans are "cowboys," Europeans love to say. And there is truth in this. The United States does act as an international sheriff, self-appointed perhaps but widely welcomed nevertheless, trying to enforce some peace and justice in what Americans see as a lawless world where outlaws need to be deterred or destroyed, and often through the muzzle of a gun. Europe, by this old West analogy, is more like a saloonkeeper. Outlaws shoot sheriffs, not saloonkeepers. In fact, from the saloonkeeper's point of view, the sheriff trying to impose order by force can sometimes be more threatening than the outlaws who, at least for the time being, may just want a drink.

When Europeans took to the streets by the millions after September 11, most Americans believed it was out of a sense of shared danger and common interest: The Europeans knew they could be next. But Europeans by and large did not feel that way and still don't. Europeans do not really believe they are next. They may be secondary targets-because they are allied with the U.S.- but they are not the primary target, because they no longer play the imperial role in the Middle East that might have engendered the same antagonism against them as is aimed at the United States. When Europeans wept and waved American flags after September 11, it was out of genuine human sympathy, sorrow, and affection for Americans. For better or for worse, European displays of solidarity were a product more of fellow-feeling than self-interest.

THE ORIGINS OF MODERN EUROPEAN FOREIGN POLICY

Important as the power gap may be in shaping the respective strategic cultures of the United States and Europe, it is only one part of the story. Europe in the past half-century has developed a genuinely different perspective on the role of power in internationalal relations, a perspective that springs directly from its unique historical experience since the end of World War II. It is a perspective that Americans do not share and cannot share, inasmuch as the formative historical experiences on their side of the Atlantic have not been the same.

Consider again the qualities that make up the European strategic culture: the emphasis on negotiation, diplomacy, and commercial ties, on international law over the use of force, on seduction over coercion, on multilateralism over unilateralism. It is true that these are not traditionally European approaches to international relations when viewed from a long historical perspective. But they are a product of more recent European history. The modern European strategic culture represents a conscious rejection of the European past, a rejection of the evils of European *machtpolitik*. It is a reflection of Europeans' ardent and understandable desire never to return to that past. Who knows better than Europeans the dangers that arise from unbridled power politics, from an excessive reliance on military force, from policies produced by national egoism and ambition, even from balance of power and *raison d'état*? As German Foreign Minister Joschka Fischer put it in a speech outlining his vision of the European future at Humboldt University in Berlin (May 12, 2000), "The core of the concept of Europe after 1945 was and still is a rejection of the European balance-of-power principle and the hegemonic ambitions of individual states that had emerged following the Peace of Westphalia in 1648." The European Union is itself the product of an awful century of European warfare.

Of course, it was the "hegemonic ambitions" of one nation in particular that European integration was meant to contain. And it is the integration and taming of Germany that is the great accomplishment of Europe—viewed historically, perhaps the greatest feat of international politics ever achieved. Some Europeans recall, as Fischer does, the central role played by the United States in solving the "German problem." Fewer like to recall that the military destruction of Nazi Germany was the prerequisite for the European peace that followed. Most Europeans believe that it was the transformation of European politics, the deliberate abandonment and rejection of centuries of *machtpolitik*, that in the end made possible the "new order." The Europeans, who invented power politics, turned themselves into born-again idealists by an act of will, leaving behind them what Fischer called "the old system of balance with its continued national orientation, constraints of coalition, traditional interest-led, politics and the permanent danger of nationalist ideologies and confrontations."

Fischer stands near one end of the spectrum of European idealism. But this is not really a right-left issue in Europe. Fischer's principal contention—that Europe has moved beyond the old system of power politics and discovered a new system for preserving peace in international relations-is widely shared across Europe. As senior British diplomat Robert Cooper recently wrote in the *Observer* (April 7, 2002), Europe today lives in a "postmodern system" that does not rest on a balance of power but on "the rejection of force" and on "self-enforced rules of behavior." In the "postmodern world," writes Cooper, "*raison d'état* and the amorality of Machiavelli's theories of statecraft ... have been replaced by a moral consciousness" in international affairs.

American realists might scoff at this idealism. George F. Kennan assumed only his naive fellow Americans succumbed to such "Wilsonian" legalistic and moralistic fancies, not those war-tested, historically minded European Machiavels. But, really, why shouldn't Europeans be idealistic about international affairs, at least as they are conducted in Europe's "postmodern system"? Within the confines of Europe, the age-old laws of international relations have been repealed. Europeans have stepped out of the Hobbesian world of anarchy into the Kantian world of perpetual peace. European life during the more than five decades since the end of World War II has been shaped not by the brutal laws of power politics but by the unfolding of a geopolitical fantasy, a miracle of world-historical importance: The German lion has laid down with the French lamb. The conflict that ravaged Europe ever since the violent birth of Germany in the nineteenth century has been put to rest.

The means by which this miracle has been achieved have understandably acquired something of a sacred mystique for Europeans, especially since the end of the Cold War. Diplomacy, negotiations, patience, the forging of economic ties, political engagement, the use of inducements rather than sanctions, the taking of small steps and tempering ambitions for success-these were the tools of Franco-German rapprochement and hence the tools that made European integration possible. Integration was not to be based on military deterrence or the balance of power. Quite the contrary. The miracle came from the rejection of military power and of its utility as an instrument of international affairs-at least within the confines of Europe. During the Cold War, few Europeans doubted the need for military power to deter the Soviet Union. But within Europe the rules were different.

Collective security was provided from without, meanwhile, by the deus ex machina of the United States operating through the military structures of NATO. Within this wall of security, Europeans pursued their new order, freed from the brutal laws and even the mentality of power politics. This evolution from the old to the new began in Europe during the Cold War. But the end of the Cold War, by removing even the external danger of the Soviet Union, allowed Europe's new order, and its new idealism, to blossom fully. Freed from the requirements of any military deterrence, internal or external, Europeans became still more confident that their way of settling international problems now had universal application.

"The genius of the founding fathers," European Commission President Romano Prodi commented in a speech at the Institute d'Etudes Politiques in Paris (May 29, 2001), "lay in translating extremely high political ambitions ... into a series of more specific, almost technical decisions. This indirect approach made further action possible. Rapprochement took place gradually. From confrontation we moved to willingness to cooperate in the economic sphere and then on to integration." This is what many Europeans believe they have to offer the world: not power, but the transcendence of power. The "essence" of the European Union, writes Everts, is "all about subjecting inter-state relations to the rule of

Robert Kagan

law," and Europe's experience of successful multilateral governance has in turn produced an ambition to convert the world. Europe "has a role to play in world `governance,'" says Prodi, a role based on replicating the European experience on a global scale. In Europe "the rule of law has replaced the crude interplay of power . . . power politics have lost their influence." And by "making a success of integration we are demonstrating to the world that it is possible to create a method for peace."

No doubt there are Britons, Germans, French, and others who would frown on such exuberant idealism. But many Europeans, including many in positions of power, routinely apply Europe's experience to the rest of the world. For is not the general European critique of the American approach to "rogue" regimes based on this special European insight? Iraq, Iran, North Korea, Libya-these states may be dangerous and unpleasant, even evil. But might not an "indirect approach" work again, as it did in Europe? Might it not be possible once more to move from confrontation to rapprochement, beginning with cooperation in the economic sphere and then moving on to peaceful integration? Could not the formula that worked in Europe work again with Iran or even Iraq? A great many Europeans insist that it can.

The transmission of the European miracle to the rest of the world has become Europe's new mission civilisatrice. Just as Americans have always believed that they had discovered the secret to human happiness and wished to export it to the rest of the world, so the Europeans have a new mission born of their own discovery of perpetual peace.

Thus we arrive at what may be the most important reason for the divergence in views between Europe and the United States. America's power, and its willingness to exercise that power-unilaterally if necessary-represents a threat to Europe's new sense of mission. Perhaps the greatest threat. American policymakers find it hard to believe, but leading officials and politicians in Europe worry more about how the United States might handle or mishandle the problem of Iraq-by undertaking unilateral and extralegal military action-than they worry about Iraq itself and Saddam Hussein's weapons of mass destruction. And while it is true that they fear such action might destabilize the Middle East and lead to the unnecessary loss of life, there is a deeper concern.[7] Such American action represents an assault on the essence of "postmodern" Europe. It is an assault on Europe's new ideals, a denial of their universal validity, much as the monarchies of eighteenth- and nineteenth-century Europe were an assault on American republican ideals. Americans ought to be the first to understand that a threat to one's beliefs can be as frightening as a threat to one's physical security.

As Americans have for two centuries, Europeans speak with great confidence of the superiority of their global understanding, the wisdom they have to offer other nations about conflict resolution, and their way of addressing international problems. But just as in the first decade of the American republic, there is a hint of insecurity in the European claim to "success," an evident need to have their success affirmed and their views accepted by other nations, particularly by the mighty United States. After all, to deny the validity of the new European idealism is to raise profound doubts about the viability of the European project. If international problems cannot, in fact, be settled the European way, wouldn't that suggest that Europe itself may eventually fall short of a solution, with all the horrors this implies?

And, of course, it is precisely this fear that still hangs over Europeans, even as Europe moves forward. Europeans, and particularly the French and Germans, are not entirely sure that the problem once known as the "German problem" really has been solved. As their various and often very different proposals for the future constitution of Europe suggest, the French are still not confident they can trust the Germans, and the Germans are still not sure they can trust themselves. This fear can at times hinder

---

7. The common American argument that European policy toward Iraq and Iran is dictated by financial considerations is only partly right. Are Europeans greedier than Americans? Do American corporations not influence American policy in Asia and Latin America, as well as in the Middle East? The difference is that American strategic judgments sometimes conflict with and override financial interests. For the reasons suggested in this essay, that conflict is much less common for Europeans.

progress toward deeper integration, but it also propels the European project forward despite innumerable obstacles. The European project must succeed, for how else to overcome what Fischer, in his Humboldt University speech, called "the risks and temptations objectively inherent in Germany's dimensions and central situation"? Those historic German "temptations" play at the back of many a European mind. And every time Europe contemplates the use of military force, or is forced to do so by the United States, there is no avoiding at least momentary consideration of what effect such a military action might have on the "German question."

Perhaps it is not just coincidence that the amazing progress toward European integration in recent years has been accompanied not by the emergence of a European superpower but, on the contrary, by a diminishing of European military capabilities relative to the United States. Turning Europe into a global superpower capable of balancing the power of the United States may have been one of the original selling points of the European Union-an independent European foreign and defense policy was supposed to be one of the most important byproducts of European integration. But, in truth, the ambition for European "power" is something of an anachronism. It is an atavistic impulse, inconsistent with the ideals of postmodern Europe, whose very existence depends on the rejection of power politics. Whatever its architects may have intended, European integration has proved to be the enemy of European military power and, indeed, of an important European global role.

This phenomenon has manifested itself not only in flat or declining European defense budgets, but in other ways, too, even in the realm of "soft" power. European leaders talk of Europe's essential role in the world. Prodi yearns "to make our voice heard, to make our actions count." And it is true that Europeans spend a great deal of money on foreign aid-more per capita, they like to point out, than does the United States. Europeans engage in overseas military missions, so long as the missions are mostly limited to peacekeeping. But while the EU periodically dips its fingers into troubled international waters in the Middle East or

the Korean Peninsula, the truth is that EU foreign policy is probably the most anemic of all the products of European integration.
As Charles Grant, a sympathetic observer of the EU, recently
noted, few European leaders "are giving it much time or energy."[8]
EU foreign policy initiatives tend to be short-lived and are rarely
backed by sustained agreement on the part of the various
European powers. That is one reason they are so easily rebuffed,
as was the case in late March when Israeli Prime Minister Ariel
Sharon blocked EU foreign policy chief Javier Solana from meeting with Yasser Arafat (only to turn around the next day and
allow a much lower-ranking American negotiator to meet with
the Palestinian leader).

It is obvious, moreover, that issues outside of Europe don't
attract nearly as much interest among Europeans as purely
European issues do. This has surprised and frustrated Americans
on all sides of the political and strategic debate: Recall the profound disappointment of American liberals when Europeans
failed to mount an effective protest against Bush's withdrawal
from the ABM treaty. But given the enormous and difficult
agenda of integration, this European tendency to look inward is
understandable. EU enlargement, the revision of the common economic and agricultural policies, the question of national sovereignty versus supranational governance, the so-called democracy
deficit, the jostling of the large European powers, the dissatisfac-
tion of the smaller powers, the establishment of a new European
constitution - all of these present serious and unavoidable challenges. The difficulties of moving forward might seem insupera-
ble were it not for the progress the project of European
integration has already demonstrated.

American policies that are unwelcome on substance-on a missile defense system and the ABM treaty, belligerence toward Iraq,
support for Israel-are all the more unwelcome because for Europe,
they are a distraction. Europeans often point to American insularity
and parochialism. But Europeans themselves have turned intensely

---

8. Charles Grant, "A European View of ESDP," Centre for European
Policy Studies working paper (April 2001).

introspective. As Dominique Moisi noted in the *Financial Times* (March 11, 2002), the recent French presidential campaign saw "no reference ... to the events of September 11 and their far-reaching consequences." No one asked, "What should be the role of France and Europe in the new configuration of forces created after September 11? How should France reappraise its military budget and doctrine to take account of the need to maintain some kind of parity between Europe and the United States, or at least between France and the UK?" The Middle East conflict became an issue in the campaign because of France's large Arab and Muslim population, as the high vote for Le Pen demonstrated. But Le Pen is not a foreign policy hawk. And as Moisi noted, "for most French voters in 2002, security has little to do with abstract and distant geopolitics. Rather, it is a question of which politician can best protect them from the crime and violence plaguing the streets and suburbs of their cities."

Can Europe change course and assume a larger role on the world stage? There has been no shortage of European leaders urging it to do so. Nor is the weakness of EU foreign policy today necessarily proof that it must be weak tomorrow, given the EU's record of overcoming weaknesses in other areas. And yet the political will to demand more power for Europe appears to be lacking, and for the very good reason that Europe does not see a mission for itself that requires power. Its mission is to oppose power. It is revealing that the argument most often advanced by Europeans for augmenting their military strength these days is not that it will allow Europe to expand its strategic purview. It is merely to rein in and "multilateralize" the United States. "America," writes the pro-American British scholar Timothy Garton Ash in the *New York Times* (April 9, 2002), "has too much power for anyone's good, including its own." Therefore Europe must amass power, but for no other reason than to save the world and the United States from the dangers inherent in the present lopsided situation.

Whether that particular mission is a worthy one or not, it seems unlikely to rouse European passions. Even Vedrine has stopped talking about counterbalancing the United States. Now he shrugs and declares there "is no reason for the Europeans to match a country that can fight four wars at once." It was one thing for Europe in the 1990s to increase its collective expenditures on defense from $150 billion per year to $180 billion when the United States was spending $280 billion per year. But now the United States is heading toward spending as much as $500 billion per year, and Europe has not the slightest intention of keeping up. European analysts lament the continent's "strategic irrelevance." NATO Secretary General George Robertson has taken to calling Europe a "military pygmy" in an effort to shame Europeans into spending more and doing so more wisely. But who honestly believes Europeans will fundamentally change their way of doing business? They have many reasons not to.

THE U.S. RESPONSE

IN THINKING ABOUT the divergence of their own views and Europeans', Americans must not lose sight of the main point: The new Europe is indeed a blessed miracle and a reason for enormous celebration-on both sides of the Atlantic. For Europeans, it is the realization of a long and improbable dream: a continent free from nationalist strife and blood feuds, from military competition and arms races. War between the major European powers is almost unimaginable. After centuries of misery, not only for Europeans but also for those pulled into their conflicts-as Americans were twice in the past century-the new Europe really has emerged as a paradise. It is something to be cherished and guarded, not least by Americans, who have shed blood on Europe's soil and would shed more should the new Europe ever fail.

Nor should we forget that the Europe of today is very much the product of American foreign policy stretching back over six decades. European integration was an American project, too, after World War II. And so, recall, was European weakness. When the Cold War dawned, Americans such as Dean Acheson hoped to create in Europe a powerful partner against the Soviet Union. But that was not the only American vision of Europe underlying U.S. policies during the twentieth century. Predating it was Franklin

Robert Kagan

Delano Roosevelt's vision of a Europe that had been rendered, in effect, strategically irrelevant. As the historian John Lamberton Harper has put it, he wanted "to bring about a radical reduction in the weight of Europe" and thereby make possible "the retirement of Europe from world politics."[9]

Americans who came of age during the Cold War have always thought of Europe almost exclusively in Achesonian terms-as the essential bulwark of freedom in the struggle against Soviet tyranny. But Americans of Roosevelt's era had a different view. In the late 1930s the common conviction of Americans was that "the European system was basically rotten, that war was endemic on that continent, and the Europeans had only themselves to blame for their plight."[10] By the early 1940s Europe appeared to be nothing more than the overheated incubator of world wars that cost America dearly. During World War II Americans like Roosevelt, looking backward rather than forward, believed no greater service could be performed than to take Europe out of the global strategic picture once and for all. "After Germany is disarmed," FDR pointedly asked, "what is the reason for France having a big military establishment?" Charles DeGaulle found such questions "disquieting for Europe and for France." Even though the United States pursued Acheson's vision during the Cold War, there was always a part of American policy that reflected Roosevelt's vision, too. Eisenhower undermining Britain and France at Suez was only the most blatant of many American efforts to cut Europe down to size and reduce its already weakened global influence.

But the more important American contribution to Europe's current world-apart status stemmed not from anti-European but from pro-European impulses. It was a commitment to Europe, not hostility to Europe, that led the United States in the immediate

---

9. John Lamberton Harper, *American Visions of Europe: Franklin D. Roosevelt, George F. Kennan, and Dean G. Acheson* (Cambridge University Press, 1996), p.3. The following discussion of the differing American perspectives on Europe owes much to Harper's fine book.

10. William L. Langer and S. Everett Gleason, *The Challenge to Isolation, 1937-1940* (Harper Bros., 1952), p.14.

postwar years to keep troops on the continent and to create NATO. The presence of American forces as a security guarantee in Europe was, as it was intended to be, the critical ingredient to begin the process of European integration.

Europe's evolution to its present state occurred under the mantle of the U.S. security guarantee and could not have occurred without it. Not only did the United States for almost half a century supply a shield against such external threats as the Soviet Union and such internal threats as may have been posed by ethnic conflict in places like the Balkans. More important, the United States was the key to the solution of the German problem and perhaps still is. Germany's Fischer, in the Humboldt University speech, noted two "historic decisions" that made the new Europe possible: "the USA's decision to stay in Europe" and "France's and Germany's commitment to the principle of integration, beginning with economic links." But of course the latter could never have occurred without the former. France's willingness to risk the reintegration of Germany into Europe-and France was, to say the least, highly dubious-depended on the promise of continued American involvement in Europe as a guarantee against any resurgence of German militarism. Nor were postwar Germans unaware that their own future in Europe depended on the calming presence of the American military.

The United States, in short, solved the Kantian paradox for the Europeans. Kant had argued that the only solution to the immoral horrors of the Hobbesian world was the creation of a world government. But he also feared that the "state of universal peace" made possible by world government would be an even greater threat to human freedom than the Hobbesian international order, inasmuch as such a government, with its monopoly of power, would become "the most horrible despotism."[11] How nations could achieve perpetual peace without destroying human freedom was a problem Kant could not solve. But for Europe the problem was

---

11. See Thomas L. Pangle and Peter J. Ahrensdorf, *Justice Among Nations: On the Moral Basis of Power and Peace* (University Press of Kansas, 1999), 200-200-201.

solved by the United States. By providing security from outside, the United States has rendered it unnecessary for Europe's supranational government to provide it. Europeans did not need power to achieve peace and they do not need power to preserve it.

The current situation abounds in ironies. Europe's rejection of power politics, its devaluing of military force as a tool of international relations, have depended on the presence of American military forces on European soil. Europe's new Kantian order could flourish only under the umbrella of American power exercised according to the rules of the old Hobbesian order. American power made it possible for Europeans to believe that power was no longer important. And now, in the final irony, the fact that United States military power has solved the European problem, especially the "German problem," allows Europeans today to believe that American military power, and the "strategic culture" that has created and sustained it, are outmoded and dangerous.

Most Europeans do not see the great paradox: that their passage into post-history has depended on the United States not making the same passage. Because Europe has neither the will nor the ability to guard its own paradise and keep it from being overrun, spiritually as well as physically, by a world that has yet to accept the rule of "moral consciousness," it has become dependent on America's willingness to use its military might to deter or defeat those around the world who still believe in power politics.

Some Europeans do understand the conundrum. Some Britons, not surprisingly, understand it best. Thus Robert Cooper writes of the need to address the hard truth that although "within the postmodern world [i.e., the Europe of today], there are no security threats in the traditional sense," nevertheless, throughout the rest of the world-what Cooper calls the "modern and pre-modern zones"-threats abound. If the postmodern world does not protect itself, it can be destroyed. But how does Europe protect itself without discarding the very ideals and principles that undergird its pacific system?

"The challenge to the postmodern world," Cooper argues, "is to get used to the idea of double standards." Among themselves, Europeans may "operate on the basis of laws and open cooperative security." But when dealing with the world outside Europe, "we need to revert to the rougher methods of an earlier era-force, preemptive attack, deception, whatever is necessary." This is Cooper's principle for safeguarding society: "Among ourselves, we keep the law but when we are operating in the jungle, we must also use the laws of the jungle."

Cooper's argument is directed at Europe, and it is appropriately coupled with a call for Europeans to cease neglecting their defenses, "both physical and psychological." But what Cooper really describes is not Europe's future but America's present. For it is the United States that has had the difficult task of navigating between these two worlds, trying to abide by, defend, and further the laws of advanced civilized society while simultaneously employing military force against those who refuse to abide by those rules. The United States is already operating according to Cooper's double standard, and for the very reasons he suggests. American leaders, too, believe that global security and a liberal order-as well as Europe's "postmodern" paradise-cannot long survive unless the United States does use its power in the dangerous, Hobbesian world that still flourishes outside Europe.

What this means is that although the United States has played the critical role in bringing Europe into this Kantian paradise, and still plays a key role in making that paradise possible, it cannot enter this paradise itself. It mans the walls but cannot walk through the gate. The United States, with all its vast power, remains stuck in history, left to deal with the Saddams and the ayatollahs, the Kim Jong Its and the Jiang Zemins, leaving the happy benefits to others.

AN ACCEPTABLE DIVISION?

Is this situation tolerable for the United States? In many ways, it is. Contrary to what many believe, the United States can shoulder the burden of maintaining global security without much help from Europe. The United States spends a little over 3 percent of its GDP on defense today. Were Americans to increase that to 4 percent-meaning a defense budget in excess of $500 billion per year-it would still represent a smaller percentage of national wealth than Americans spent on defense throughout most of the past half-century. Even Paul Kennedy, who invented the term "imperial overstretch" in the late 1980s (when the United States was spending around 7 percent of its GDP on defense), believes the United States can sustain its current military spending levels and its current global dominance far into the future. Can the United States handle the rest of the world without much help from Europe? The answer is that it already does. The United States has maintained strategic stability in Asia with no help from Europe. In the Gulf War, European help was token; so it has been more recently in Afghanistan, where Europeans are once again "doing the dishes"; and so it would be in an invasion of Iraq to unseat Saddam. Europe has had little to offer the United States in strategic military terms since the end of the Cold War - except, of course, that most valuable of strategic assets, a Europe at peace.

The United States can manage, therefore, at least in material terms. Nor can one argue that the American people are unwilling to shoulder this global burden, since they have done so for a decade already. After September 11, they seem willing to continue doing so for a long time to come. Americans apparently feel no resentment at not being able to enter a "postmodern" utopia. There is no evidence most Americans desire to. Partly because they are so powerful, they take pride in their nation's military power and their nation's special role in the world.

Americans have no experience that would lead them to embrace fully the ideals and principles that now animate Europe. Indeed, Americans derive their understanding of the world from a very different set of experiences. In the first half of the twentieth century, Americans had a flirtation with a certain kind of internationalist idealism. Wilson's "war to end all wars" was followed a decade later by an American secretary of state putting his signature to a treaty outlawing war. FDR in the 1930s put his faith in non-aggression pacts and asked merely that Hitler promise not to attack a list of countries Roosevelt presented to him. But then came Munich and Pearl Harbor, and then, after a fleeting moment of renewed idealism, the plunge into the Cold War. The "lesson of Munich" came to dominate American strategic thought, and although it was supplanted for a time by the "lesson of Vietnam," today it remains the dominant paradigm. While a small segment of the American elite still yearns for "global governance" and eschews military force, Americans from Madeleine Albright to Donald Rumsfeld, from Brent Scowcroft to Anthony Lake, still remember Munich, figuratively if not literally. And for younger generations of Americans who do not remember Munich or Pearl Harbor, there is now September 11. After September 11, even many American globalizers demand blood.

Americans are idealists, but they have no experience of promoting ideals successfully without power. Certainly, they have no experience of successful supranational governance; little to make them place their faith in international law and international institutions, much as they might wish to; and even less to let them travel, with the Europeans, beyond power. Americans, as good children of the Enlightenment, still believe in the perfectibility of man, and they retain hope for the perfectibility of the world. But they remain realists in the limited sense that they still believe in the necessity of power in a world that remains far from perfection. Such law as there may be to regulate international behavior, they believe, exists because a power like the United States defends it by force of arms. In other words, just as Europeans claim, Americans can still sometimes see themselves in heroic terms-as Gary Cooper at high noon. They will defend the townspeople, whether the townspeople want them to or not.

The problem lies neither in American will or capability, then, but precisely in the inherent moral tension of the current international situation. As is so often the case in human affairs, the real question is one of intangibles-of fears, passions, and beliefs. The problem is that the United States must sometimes play by the rules of a Hobbesian world, even though in doing so it violates European norms. It must refuse to abide by certain international conventions that may constrain its ability to fight effectively in Robert Cooper's jungle. It must support arms control, but not always for itself. It must live by a double standard. And it must sometimes act unilaterally, not out of a passion for unilateralism but, given a weak Europe that has moved beyond power, because the United States has no choice but to act unilaterally.

Few Europeans admit, as Cooper does implicitly, that such American behavior may redound to the greater benefit of the civilized world, that American power, even employed under a double standard, may be the best means of advancing human progress-and perhaps the only means. Instead, many Europeans today have come to consider the United States itself to be the outlaw, a rogue colossus. Europeans have complained about President Bush's "unilateralism," but they are coming to the deeper realization that the problem is not Bush or any American president. It is systemic. And it is incurable.

Given that the United States is unlikely to reduce its power and that Europe is unlikely to increase more than marginally its own power or the will to use what power it has, the future seems certain to be one of increased transatlantic tension. The danger-if it is a danger-is that the United States and Europe will become positively estranged. Europeans will become more shrill in their attacks on the United States. The United States will become less inclined to listen, or perhaps even to care. The day could come, if it has not already, when Americans will no more heed the pronouncements of the EU than they do the pronouncements of ASEAN or the Andean Pact.

To those of us who came of age in the Cold War, the strategic decoupling of Europe and the United States seems frightening. DeGaulle, when confronted by FDR'S vision of a world where Europe was irrelevant, recoiled and suggested that this vision "risked endangering the Western world." If Western Europe was to be considered a "secondary matter" by the United States, would not FDR only "weaken the very cause he meant to serve—that of civilization?" Western Europe, DeGaulle insisted, was "essential to the West. Nothing can replace the value, the power, the shining example of the ancient peoples." Typically, DeGaulle insisted this was "true of France above all." But leaving aside French *amour propre*, did not DeGaulle have a point? If Americans were to decide that Europe was no more than an irritating irrelevancy, would

American society gradually become unmoored from what we now call the West? It is not a risk to be taken lightly, on either side of the Atlantic.

So what is to be done? The obvious answer is that Europe should follow the course that Cooper, Ash, Robertson, and others recommend and build up its military capabilities, even if only marginally. There is not much ground for hope that this will happen. But, then, who knows? Maybe concern about America's overweening power really will create some energy in Europe. Perhaps the atavistic impulses that still swirl in the hearts of Germans, Britons, and Frenchmen-the memory of power, international influence, and national ambition-can still be played upon. Some Britons still remember empire; some Frenchmen still yearn for *la gloire*; some Germans still want their place in the sun. These urges are now mostly channeled into the grand European project, but they could find more traditional expression. Whether this is to be hoped for or feared is another question. It would be better still if Europeans could move beyond fear and anger at the rogue colossus and remember, again, the vital necessity of having a strong America-for the world and especially for Europe.

Americans can help. It is true that the Bush administration came into office with a chip on its shoulder. It was hostile to the new Europe-as to a lesser extent was the Clinton administration-seeing it not so much as an ally but as an albatross. Even after September 11, when the Europeans offered their very limited military capabilities in the fight in Afghanistan, the United States resisted, fearing that European cooperation was a ruse to tie America down. The Bush administration viewed NATO's historic decision to aid the United States under Article V less as a boon than as a booby trap. An opportunity to draw Europe into common battle out in the Hobbesian world, even in a minor role, was thereby unnecessarily lost.

Americans are powerful enough that they need not fear Europeans, even when bearing gifts. Rather than viewing the United States as a Gulliver tied down by Lilliputian threads, American leaders should realize that they are hardly constrained at all, that Europe is not really capable of constraining the United States. If the United States could move past the anxiety engendered by this inaccurate sense of constraint, it could begin to show more understanding for the sensibilities of others, a little generosity of spirit. It could pay its respects to multilateralism and the rule of law and try to build some international political capital for those moments when multilateralism is impossible and unilateral action unavoidable. It could, in short, take more care to show what the founders called a "decent respect for the opinion of mankind."

These are small steps, and they will not address the deep problems that beset the transatlantic relationship today. But, after all, it is more than a cliché that the United States and Europe share a set of common Western beliefs. Their aspirations for humanity are much the same, even if their vast disparity of power has now put them in very different places. Perhaps it is not too naively optimistic to believe that a little common understanding could still go a long way.

American Primacy in Perspective

Stephen G. Brooks and William C. Wohlforth

FROM STRENGTH TO STRENGTH

MORE THAN A DECADE AGO, political columnist Charles Kraut-hammer proclaimed in these pages the arrival of what he called a "unipolar moment," a period in which one superpower, the United States, stood clearly above the rest of the international community ("The Unipolar Moment," America and the World 1990/91). In the following years the Soviet Union collapsed, Russia's economic and military decline accelerated, and Japan stagnated, while the United States experienced the longest and one of the most vigorous economic expansions in its history. Yet toward the close of the century readers could find political scientist Samuel Huntington arguing here that unipolarity had already given way to a "uni-multipolar" structure, which in turn would soon become unambiguously multipolar ("The Lonely Superpower," March/April 1999). And despite the boasting rhetoric of American officials, Huntington was not alone in his views. Polls showed that more than 40 percent of Americans had come to agree that the United States was now merely one of several leading powers—a number that had risen steadily for several years.

Why did the unipolarity argument seem less persuasive to many even as U.S. power appeared to grow? Largely because the goal posts

STEPHEN G. BROOKS is an Assistant Professor and WILLIAM C. WOHLFORTH an Associate Professor in the Department of Government at Dartmouth College. This article originally appeared in the July/August 2002 issue of *Foreign Affairs* © 2002 by the Council on Foreign Relations.

were moved. Krauthammer's definition of unipolarity, as a system with only one pole, made sense in the immediate wake of a Cold War that had been so clearly shaped by the existence of two poles. People sensed intuitively that a world with no great power capable of sustaining a focused rivalry with the United States would be very different in important ways.

But a decade later what increasingly seemed salient was less the absence of a peer rival than the persistence of a number of problems in the world that Washington could not dispose of by itself. This was the context for Huntington's new definition of unipolarity, as a system with "one superpower, no significant major powers, and many minor powers." The dominant power in such a system, he argued, would be able to "effectively resolve important international issues alone, and no combination of other states would have the power to prevent it from doing so." The United States had no such ability and thus did not qualify.

The terrorist attacks last fall appeared to some to reinforce this point, revealing not only a remarkable degree of American vulnerability but also a deep vein of global anti-American resentment. Suddenly the world seemed a more threatening place, with dangers lurking at every corner and eternal vigilance the price of liberty. Yet as the success of the military campaign in Afghanistan demonstrated, vulnerability to terror has few effects on U.S. strength in more traditional interstate affairs. If anything, America's response to the attacks—which showed its ability to project power in several places around the globe simultaneously, and essentially unilaterally, while effortlessly increasing defense spending by nearly $50 billion—only reinforced its unique position.

If today's American primacy does not constitute unipolarity, then nothing ever will. The only things left for dispute are how long it will last and what the implications are for American foreign policy.

PICK A MEASURE, ANY MEASURE

To UNDERSTAND JUST how dominant the United States is today, one needs to look at each of the standard components of national power in succession. In the military arena, the United States is poised to spend more on defense in 2003 than the next 15–20 biggest spenders combined. The United States has overwhelming nuclear superiority, the world's dominant air force, the only truly blue-water navy, and a unique capability to project power around the globe. And its military advantage is even more apparent in quality than in quantity. The United States leads the world in exploiting the military applications of advanced communications and information technology and it has demonstrated an unrivaled ability to coordinate and process information about the battlefield and destroy targets from afar with extraordinary precision. Washington is not making it easy for others to catch up, moreover, given the massive gap in spending on military research and development (R&D), on which the United States spends three times more than the next six powers combined. Looked at another way, the United States currently spends more on military R&D than Germany or the United Kingdom spends on defense in total.

No state in the modern history of international politics has come close to the military predominance these numbers suggest. And the United States purchases this preeminence with only 3.5 percent of its GDP. As historian Paul Kennedy notes, "being Number One at great cost is one thing; being the world's single superpower on the cheap is astonishing."

America's economic dominance, meanwhile—relative to either the next several richest powers or the rest of the world combined—surpasses that of any great power in modern history, with the sole exception of its own position after 1945 (when World War II had temporarily laid waste every other major economy). The U.S. economy is currently twice as large as its closest rival, Japan. California's economy alone has risen to become the fifth largest in the world (using market exchange-rate estimates), ahead of France and just behind the United Kingdom.

It is true that the long expansion of the 1990s has ebbed, but it would take an experience like Japan's in that decade—that is, an extraordinarily deep and prolonged domestic recession juxtaposed with robust growth elsewhere—for the United States just to fall back to the economic position it occupied in 1991. The odds against such relative decline are long, however, in part because the United States is the country in the best position to take advantage of globalization. Its status as the preferred destination for scientifically trained foreign workers solidified during the 1990s, and it is the most popular destination for foreign firms. In 1999 it attracted more than one-third of world inflows of foreign direct investment.

U.S. military and economic dominance, finally, is rooted in the country's position as the world's leading technological power. Although measuring national R&D spending is increasingly difficult in an era in which so many economic activities cross borders, efforts to do so indicate America's continuing lead. Figures from the late 1990s showed that U.S. expenditures on R&D nearly equaled those of the next seven richest countries combined.

Measuring the degree of American dominance in each category begins to place things in perspective. But what truly distinguishes the current international system is American dominance in all of them simultaneously. Previous leading states in the modern era were either great commercial and naval powers or great military powers on land, never both. The British Empire in its heyday and the United States during the Cold War, for example, each shared the world with other powers that matched or exceeded them in some areas. Following the Napoleonic Wars, the United Kingdom was clearly the world's leading commercial and naval power. But even at the height of the Pax Britannica, the United Kingdom was outspent, outmanned, and outgunned by both France and Russia. And its 24 percent share of GDP among the six leading powers in the early 1870s was matched by the United States, with Russia and Germany following close behind. Similarly, at the dawn of the Cold War the United States was clearly dominant economically as well as in air and naval capabilities. But the Soviet Union retained overall military parity, and thanks to geography and investment in land power it had a superior ability to seize territory in Eurasia.

Today, in contrast, the United States has no rival in any critical dimension of power. There has never been a system of sovereign states that contained one state with this degree of dominance. The recent tendency to equate unipolarity with the ability to achieve desired outcomes single-handedly on all issues only reinforces this point; in no previous international system would it ever have occurred to anyone to apply such a yardstick.

CAN IT LAST?

MANY WHO ACKNOWLEDGE the extent of American power, however, regard it as necessarily self-negating. Other states traditionally band together to restrain potential hegemons, they say, and this time will be no different. As German political commentator Josef Joffe has put it, "the history books say that Mr. Big always invites his own demise. Nos. 2, 3, 4 will gang up on him, form countervailing alliances and plot his downfall. That happened to Napoleon, as it happened to Louis XIV and the mighty Hapsburgs, to Hitler and to Stalin. Power begets superior counterpower; it's the oldest rule of world politics."

What such arguments fail to recognize are the features of America's post–Cold War position that make it likely to buck the historical trend. Bounded by oceans to the east and west and weak, friendly powers to the north and south, the United States is both less vulnerable than previous aspiring hegemons and also less threatening to others. The main potential challengers to its unipolarity, meanwhile—China, Russia, Japan, and Germany—are in the opposite position. They cannot augment their military capabilities so as to balance the United States without simultaneously becoming an immediate threat to their neighbors. Politics, even international politics, is local. Although American power attracts a lot of attention globally, states are usually more concerned with their own neighborhoods than with the global equilibrium. Were any of the potential challengers to make a serious run at the United States, regional balancing efforts would almost certainly help contain them, as would the massive latent power capabilities of the United States, which could be mobilized as necessary to head off an emerging threat.

When analysts refer to a historical pattern of balancing against potentially preponderant powers, they rarely note that the cases in question—the Hapsburg ascendancy, Napoleonic France, the Soviet Union in the Cold War, and so forth—featured would-be hegemons that were vulnerable, threatening, centrally located, and dominant in only one or two components of power. Moreover, the would-be hegemons all specialized in precisely the form of power—the ability to seize territory—most likely to scare other states into an antihegemonic coalition. American capabilities, by contrast, are relatively greater and more comprehensive than those of past hegemonic aspirants, they are located safely offshore, and the prospective balancers are close regional neighbors of one another. U.S. power is also at the command of one government, whereas the putative balancers would face major challenges in acting collectively to assemble and coordinate their military capabilities.

Previous historical experiences of balancing, moreover, involved groups of status quo powers seeking to contain a rising revisionist one. The balancers had much to fear if the aspiring hegemon got its way. Today, however, U.S. dominance is the status quo. Several of the major powers in the system have been closely allied with the United States for decades and derive substantial benefits from their position. Not only would they have to forego those benefits if they tried to balance, but they would have to find some way of putting together a durable, coherent alliance while America was watching. This is a profoundly important point, because although there may be several precedents for a coalition of balancers preventing a hegemon from emerging, there is none for a group of subordinate powers joining to topple a hegemon once it has already emerged, which is what would have to happen today.

The comprehensive nature of U.S. power, finally, also skews the odds against any major attempt at balancing, let alone a successful one. The United States is both big and rich, whereas the potential challengers are all either one or the other. It will take at least a generation for today's other big countries (such as China and India) to become rich, and given declining birth rates the other rich powers are not about to get big, at least in relative terms. During the 1990s, the U.S. population increased by 32.7 million—a figure equal to more than half the current population of France or the United Kingdom.

Some might argue that the European Union is an exception to the big-or-rich rule. It is true that if Brussels were to develop impressive military capabilities and wield its latent collective power like a state, the EU would clearly constitute another pole. But the creation of an autonomous and unified defense and defense-industrial capacity that could compete with that of the United States would be a gargantuan task. The EU is struggling to put together a 60,000-strong rapid reaction force that is designed for smaller operations such as humanitarian relief, peacekeeping, and crisis management, but it still lacks military essentials such as capabilities in intelligence gathering, airlift, air-defense suppression, air-to-air refueling, sea transport, medical care, and combat search and rescue—and even when it has those capacities, perhaps by the end of this decade, it will still rely on NATO command and control and other assets.

Whatever capability the EU eventually assembles, moreover, will matter only to the extent that it is under the control of a statelike decision-making body with the authority to act quickly and decisively in Europe's name. Such authority, which does not yet exist even for international financial matters, could be purchased only at the price of a direct frontal assault on European nations' core sovereignty. And all of this would have to occur as the EU expands to add ten or more new member states, a process that will complicate further deepening. Given these obstacles, Europe is unlikely to emerge as a dominant actor in the military realm for a very long time, if ever.

Most analysts looking for a future peer competitor to the United States, therefore, focus on China, since it is the only power with the potential to match the size of the U.S. economy over the next several decades. Yet even if China were eventually to catch up to the United States in terms of aggregate GDP, the gaps in the two states' other power capabilities—technological, military, and geographic—would remain.

Since the mid-1990s, Chinese strategists themselves have become markedly less bullish about their country's ability to close the gap in what they call "comprehensive national power" any time soon. The latest estimates by China's intelligence agency project that in 2020 the country will possess between slightly more than a third and slightly more than half of U.S. capabilities. Fifty percent of China's labor force is employed in agriculture, and relatively little of its economy is geared toward high technology. In the 1990s, U.S. spending on technological development was more than 20 times China's. Most of China's weapons are decades old. And nothing China can do will allow it to escape its geography, which leaves it surrounded by countries that have the motivation and ability to engage in balancing of their own should China start to build up an expansive military force.

These are not just facts about the current system; they are recognized as such by the major players involved. As a result, no global challenge to the United States is likely to emerge for the foreseeable future. No country, or group of countries, wants to maneuver itself into a situation in which it will have to contend with the focused enmity of the United States.

Two of the prime causes of past great-power conflicts—hegemonic rivalry and misperception—are thus not currently operative in world politics. At the dawn of the twentieth century, a militarily powerful Germany challenged the United Kingdom's claim to leadership. The result was World War I. In the middle of the twentieth century, American leadership seemed under challenge by a militarily and ideologically strong Soviet Union. The result was the Cold War. U.S. dominance today militates against a comparable challenge, however, and hence against a comparable global conflict. Because the United States is too powerful to balance, moreover, there is far less danger of war emerging from the misperceptions, miscalculations, arms races, and so forth that have traditionally plagued balancing attempts. Pundits often lament the absence of a post–Cold War Bismarck. Luckily, as long as unipolarity lasts, there is no need for one.

UNIPOLAR POLITICS AS USUAL

THE CONCLUSION THAT balancing is not in the cards may strike many as questionable in light of the parade of ostensibly anti-U.S. diplomatic combinations in recent years: the "European troika" of

France, Germany, and Russia; the "special relationship" between Germany and Russia; the "strategic triangle" of Russia, China, and India; the "strategic partnership" between China and Russia; and so on. Yet a close look at any of these arrangements reveals their rhetorical as opposed to substantive character. Real balancing involves real economic and political costs, which neither Russia, nor China, nor indeed any other major power has shown any willingness to bear.

The most reliable way to balance power is to increase defense outlays. Since 1995, however, military spending by most major powers has been declining relative to GDP, and in the majority of cases in absolute terms as well. At most, these opposing coalitions can occasionally succeed in frustrating U.S. policy initiatives when the expected costs of doing so remain conveniently low. At the same time, Beijing, Moscow, and others have demonstrated a willingness to cooperate with the United States periodically on strategic matters and especially in the economic realm. This general tendency toward bandwagoning was the norm before September 11 and has only become more pronounced since then.

Consider the Sino-Russian "strategic partnership," the most prominent instance of apparent balancing to date. The easy retort to overheated rhetoric about a Moscow-Beijing "axis" would involve pointing out how it failed to slow, much less stop, President Vladimir Putin's geopolitical sprint toward Washington in the aftermath of the September 11 attacks. More telling, however, is just how tenuous the shift was even before it was thrown off track. At no point did the partnership entail any costly commitment or policy coordination against Washington that might have risked a genuine confrontation. The keystone of the partnership—Russia's arms sales to China—reflects a symmetry of weaknesses, rather than the potential of combined strengths. The sales partially offset China's backward military technology while helping to slow the decline of Russia's defense industries. Most of the arms in question are legacies of the R&D efforts of the Soviet military-industrial complex, and given Moscow's paltry R&D budget today, few of these systems will long remain competitive with their U.S. or NATO analogues.

Even as the two neighbors signed cooperative agreements, moreover, deep suspicions continued to plague their relationship, economic ties between them remained anemic and unlikely to grow dramatically, and both were highly dependent on inflows of capital and technology that could come only from the West. Russian and Chinese leaders highlighted their desire for a world of reduced U.S. influence not because this was a goal toward which they had actually started moving, but because it was one general principle on which they could agree.

Balancing rhetoric is obviously partly the reflection of genuine sentiment. The world finds it unfair, undemocratic, annoying, and sometimes downright frightening to have so much power concentrated in the hands of one state, especially when the United States aggressively goes its own way. But given the weight and prominence of U.S. power on the world stage, some unease among other countries is inevitable no matter what Washington does. Foreign governments frequently rail against what they regard as excessive U.S. involvement in their affairs. Yet inflated expectations about what the United States can do to solve global problems (such as the Israeli-Palestinian conflict) can lead to frustration with supposed U.S. underengagement as well. Nothing the United States could do short of abdicating its power would solve the problem completely.

Local and regional politics also contribute to balancing rhetoric, although not to its substance. Even nondemagogic leaders face incentives to play on anti-American resentment for domestic audiences. And simple math dictates the need for more regional cooperation today than previously, much of which can take on an anti-American coloring. The nineteenth-century international system featured six to eight poles among roughly 30 states. In the early Cold War, there were two poles, but the number of states had doubled to just over 70. Today there is one pole in a system in which the population has trebled to nearly 200. Inevitably, therefore, much activity will take place at a regional level, and it can often be in the interests of the parties involved to use balancing rhetoric as a rallying point for stimulating cooperation, even if that is not the chief driver of their actions.

Such maneuvering has the potential to backfire, however, by reinforcing the perception that the countries in question are too weak to act individually, something that can have harmful consequences at home and abroad. Thus, other powers have to find a way of reminding Washington that they have somewhere else to turn, but without talking down their own capabilities or foreclosing promising bilateral arrangements with the United States. The result—balancing that is rhetorically grand but substantively weak—is politics as usual in a unipolar world.

SO WHAT?

THE FIRST AND most important practical consequence of unipolarity for the United States is notable for its absence: the lack of hegemonic rivalry. During the Cold War the United States confronted a military superpower with the potential to conquer all the industrial power centers of Europe and Asia. To forestall that catastrophic outcome, for decades the United States committed between 5 and 14 percent of its GDP to defense spending and maintained an extended nuclear deterrent that put a premium on the credibility of its commitments. Largely to maintain a reputation for resolve, 85,000 Americans lost their lives in two Asian wars while U.S. presidents repeatedly engaged in brinkmanship that ran the risk of escalation to global thermo-nuclear destruction.

Today the costs and dangers of the Cold War have faded into history, but they need to be kept in mind in order to assess unipolarity accurately. For decades to come, no state is likely to combine the resources, geography, and growth rates necessary to mount a hegemonic challenge on such a scale—an astonishing development. Crowns may generally lie uneasy, but America's does not.

Some might question the worth of being at the top of a unipolar system if that means serving as a lightning rod for the world's malcontents. When there was a Soviet Union, after all, it bore the brunt of Osama bin Laden's anger, and only after its collapse did he shift his focus to the United States (an indicator of the demise of bipolarity that was ignored at the time but looms larger in retrospect). But terrorism has been a perennial problem in history, and multipolarity did not save the leaders of several great powers from assassination by anarchists around the turn of the twentieth century. In fact, a slide back toward multipolarity would actually be the worst of all worlds for the United States. In such a scenario it would continue to lead the pack and serve as a focal point for resentment and hatred by both state and nonstate actors, but it would have fewer carrots and sticks to use in dealing with the situation. The threats would remain, but the possibility of effective and coordinated action against them would be reduced.

The second major practical consequence of unipolarity is the unique freedom it offers American policymakers. Many decision-makers labor under feelings of constraint, and all participants in policy debates defend their preferred courses of action by pointing to the dire consequences that will follow if their advice is not accepted. But the sources of American strength are so varied and so durable that U.S. foreign policy today operates in the realm of choice rather than necessity to a greater degree than any other power in modern history. Whether the participants realize it or not, this new freedom to choose has transformed the debate over what the U.S. role in the world should be.

Historically, the major forces pushing powerful states toward restraint and magnanimity have been the limits of their strength and the fear of overextension and balancing. Great powers typically checked their ambitions and deferred to others not because they wanted to but because they had to in order to win the cooperation they needed to survive and prosper. It is thus no surprise that today's champions of American moderation and international benevolence stress the constraints on American power rather than the lack of them. Political scientist Joseph Nye, for example, insists that "[the term] unipolarity is misleading because it exaggerates the degree to which the United States is able to get the results it wants in some dimensions of world politics... American power is less effective than it might first appear." And he cautions that if the United States "handles its hard power in an overbearing, unilateral manner," then others might be provoked into forming a balancing coalition.

Such arguments are unpersuasive, however, because they fail to acknowledge the true nature of the current international system. The United States cannot be scared into meekness by warnings of inefficacy or potential balancing. Isolationists and aggressive unilateralists see this situation clearly, and their domestic opponents need to as well. Now and for the foreseeable future, the United States will have immense power resources it can bring to bear to force or entice others to do its bidding on a case-by-case basis.

But just because the United States is strong enough to act heedlessly does not mean that it should do so. Why not? Because it can afford to reap the greater gains that will eventually come from magnanimity. Aside from a few cases in a few issue areas, ignoring others' concerns avoids hassles today at the cost of more serious trouble tomorrow. Unilateralism may produce results in the short term, but it is apt to reduce the pool of voluntary help from other countries that the United States can draw on down the road, and thus in the end to make life more difficult rather than less. Unipolarity makes it possible to be the global bully—but it also offers the United States the luxury of being able to look beyond its immediate needs to its own, and the world's, long-term interests.

RESISTING TEMPTATION

CONSIDER THE QUESTION that preoccupied many observers before September 11: whether to engage or contain potential great-power challengers such as China. Supporters of engagement argued that the best way to moderate Chinese behavior (both internal and external) was to tie the country into the international political and economic system as thoroughly as possible. Supporters of containment, meanwhile, argued that this course was far too risky, because it might hasten the emergence of a strong but still tyrannical power. To the extent that the above analysis of unipolarity is correct, however, the risks that accompany engagement are minor, because the margin of U.S. superiority is so great that China is unlikely to pose a significant challenge to U.S. dominance for decades, no matter what policy is followed. Although engagement may not succeed, therefore, the chance that it might makes it worth a try, and there will be plenty of time to reverse course if it fails.

The same applies with even more force to Russia. The aftermath of the September 11 attacks demonstrated the benefits of having a stable friend in Eurasia's heartland, and the preceding three centuries demonstrated the high costs that could come from an autocratic Russia that is extracting military capabilities from its vast territory. Integrating Russia fully into the reigning international order would represent a major step toward eliminating the perennial "Russia problem." Russia's political and economic institutions have a long road to travel before such integration becomes feasible, of course, but thanks to unipolarity there is plenty of time to wait, and there are plenty of resources to deploy in helping.

Washington also needs to be concerned about the level of resentment that an aggressive unilateral course would engender among its major allies. After all, it is influence, not power, that is ultimately most valuable. The further one looks beyond the immediate short term, the clearer become the many issues—the environment, disease, migration, and the stability of the global economy, to name a few—that the United States cannot solve on its own. Such issues entail repeated dealings with many partners over many years. Straining relationships now will lead only to a more challenging policy environment later on.

As for the developing world, if the United States could help improve political, social, and economic conditions there, practically everybody would benefit—the locals directly, and the rest of the world indirectly. No magic wand can transform the situation overnight, but the United States can nevertheless take a variety of measures that would help on the margins. The most important would be to lower the high protectionist trade barriers Washington maintains for agricultural products, clothing, and textiles—all crucial for the economic prospects of much of the developing world. Opening up U.S. markets to developing-country exports in these areas would not guarantee rapid economic development abroad, and even if it did, rapid development is not a panacea for all ills. But there is little doubt that it would help the exporting countries' economies and societies along with America's image.

President George W. Bush recently said, "To be serious about fighting poverty, we must be serious about expanding trade...

Greater access to the markets of wealthy countries has a direct and immediate impact on the economies of developing nations." But deeds are more important than words. Lowering domestic trade barriers would be precisely the kind of U.S. policy that could reduce the inevitable frictions and resentments unipolarity generates. It would mean going beyond reacting to security challenges once they became critical and trying to forestall their emergence in the first place. Implemented fully and expanded to other cases, this approach could serve as the velvet glove covering the iron fist of American power, demonstrating that the United States was interested in not just its own special interests but the interests of others as well.

Magnanimity and restraint in the face of temptation are tenets of successful statecraft that have proved their worth from classical Greece onward. Standing taller than leading states of the past, the United States has unprecedented freedom to do as it pleases. It can play the game for itself alone or for the system as a whole; it can focus on small returns today or larger ones tomorrow. If the administration truly wants to be loved as well as feared, the policy answers are not hard to find.

Why Do They Hate Us?

Fareed Zakaria

To THE QUESTION "Why do the terrorists hate us?" Americans could be pardoned for answering, "Why should we care?" The immediate reaction to the murder of 5,000 innocents is anger, not analysis. Yet anger will not be enough to get us through what is sure to be a long struggle. For that we will need answers. The ones we have heard so far have been comforting but familiar. We stand for freedom and they hate it. We are rich and they envy us. We are strong and they resent this. All of which is true. But there are billions of poor and weak and oppressed people around the world. They don't turn planes into bombs. They don't blow themselves up to kill thousands of civilians. If envy were the cause of terrorism, Beverly Hills, Fifth Avenue and Mayfair would have become morgues long ago. There is something stronger at work here than deprivation and jealousy. Something that can move men to kill but also to die.

Osama bin Laden has an answer-religion. For him and his followers, this is a holy war between Islam and the Western world. Most Muslims disagree. Every Islamic country in the world has condemned the attacks of September. 11. To many, bin Laden belongs to a long line of extremists who have invoked religion to justify mass murder and spur men to suicide. The words "thug," "zealot" and "assassin" all come from ancient terror cults-Hindu, Jewish and Muslim, respectively-that believed they were doing the work of God. The terrorist's mind is its own place, and like Milton's Satan, can make a hell of heaven, a heaven of hell. Whether it is the Unabomber, Aum Shinrikyo or Baruch Goldstein (who killed scores

FAREED ZAKARIA is Editor of *Newsweek* magazine's overseas editions. This article originally appeared in the October 15, 2001 issue of *Newsweek* © 2001 Newsweek, Inc.

of unarmed Muslims in Hebron), terrorists are almost always misfits who place their own twisted morality above mankind's.

Admiration for bin Laden

But bin Laden and his followers are not an isolated cult like Aum Shinrikyo or the Branch Davidians or demented loners like Timothy McVeigh and the Unabomber. They come out of a culture that reinforces their hostility, distrust and hatred of the West-and of America in particular. This culture does not condone terrorism but fuels the fanaticism that is at its heart. To say that al Qaeda is a fringe group may be reassuring, but it is false. Read the Arab press in the aftermath of the attacks and you will detect a not-so-hidden admiration for bin Laden. Or consider this from the Pakistani newspaper *The Nation*: "September 11 was not mindless terrorism for terrorism's sake. It was reaction and revenge, even retribution." Why else is America's response to the terror attacks so deeply constrained by fears of an "Islamic backlash" on the streets? Pakistan will dare not allow Washington the use of its bases. Saudi Arabia trembles at the thought of having to help us publicly. Egypt pleads that our strikes be as limited as possible. The problem is not that Osama bin Laden believes that this is a religious war against America. It's that millions of people across the Islamic world seem to agree.

This awkward reality has led some in the West to dust off old essays and older prejudices predicting a "clash of civilizations" between the West and Islam. The historian Paul Johnson has argued that Islam is intrinsically an intolerant and violent religion. Other scholars have disagreed, pointing out that Islam condemns the slaughter of innocents and prohibits suicide. Nothing will be solved by searching for "true Islam" or quoting the Quran. The Quran is a vast, vague book, filled with poetry and contradictions (much like the Bible). You can find in it condemnations of war and incitements to struggle, beautiful expressions of tolerance and stern strictures against unbelievers. Quotations from it usually tell us more about the person who selected the passages than about Islam. Every religion is compatible with the best and the worst of humankind. Through its long history, Christianity has supported inquisitions and anti-Semitism, but also human rights and social welfare.

Searching the history books is also of limited value. From the Crusades of the 11th century to the Turkish expansion of the 15th century to the colonial era in the early 20th century, Islam and the West have often battled militarily. This tension has existed for hundreds of years, during which there have been many periods of peace and even harmony. Until the 1950s, for example, Jews and Christians lived peaceably under Muslim rule. In fact, Bernard Lewis, the preeminent historian of Islam, has argued that for much of history religious minorities did better under Muslim rulers than they did under Christian ones. All that has changed in the past few decades. So surely the relevant question we must ask is, Why are we in a particularly difficult phase right now? What has gone wrong in the world of Islam that explains not the conquest of Constantinople in 1453 or the siege of Vienna of 1683 but September 11, 2001?

Let us first peer inside that vast Islamic world. Many of the largest Muslim countries in the world show little of this anti-American rage. The biggest, Indonesia, had, until the recent Asian economic crisis, been diligently following Washington's advice on economics, with impressive results. The second and third most populous Muslim countries, Pakistan and Bangladesh, have mixed Islam and modernity with some success. While both countries are impoverished, both have voted a woman into power as prime minister, before most Western countries have done so. Next is Turkey, the sixth largest Muslim country in the world, a flawed but functioning secular democracy and a close ally of the West (being a member of NATO).

Only when you get to the Middle East do you see in lurid colors all the dysfunctions that people conjure up when they think of Islam today. In Iran, Egypt, Syria, Iraq, Jordan, the occupied territories and the Persian Gulf, the resurgence of Islamic fundamentalism is virulent, and a raw anti-Americanism seems to be everywhere. This is the land of suicide bombers, flag-burners and fiery mullahs. As we strike Afghanistan it is worth remembering that not a single Afghan has been tied to a terrorist attack against the United States. Afghanistan is the campground from which an Arab army is battling America.

But even the Arab rage at America is relatively recent. In the 1950s and 1960s it seemed unimaginable that the United States and the Arab world would end up locked in a cultural clash. Egypt's most powerful journalist, Mohamed Heikal, described the mood at the time: "The whole picture of the United States… was a glamorous one. Britain and France were fading, hated empires. The Soviet Union was 5,000 miles away and the ideology of communism was anathema to the Muslim religion. But America had emerged from World War II richer, more powerful and more appealing than ever." I first traveled to the Middle East in the early 1970s, and even then the image of America was of a glistening, approachable modernity: fast cars, Hilton hotels and Coca-Cola. Something happened in these lands. To understand the roots of anti-American rage in the Middle East, we need to plumb not the past 300 years of history but the past 30.

CHAPTER 1: THE RULERS

IT IS DIFFICULT to conjure up the excitement in the Arab world in the late 1950s as Gamal Abdel Nasser consolidated power in Egypt. For decades Arabs had been ruled by colonial governors and decadent kings. Now they were achieving their dreams of independence, and Nasser was their new savior, a modern man for the postwar era. He was born under British rule, in Alexandria, a cosmopolitan city that was more Mediterranean than Arab. His formative years were spent in the Army, the most Westernized segment of the society. With his tailored suits and fashionable dark glasses, he cut an energetic figure on the world stage. "The Lion of Egypt," he spoke for all the Arab world.

Nasser believed that Arab politics needed to be fired by modern ideas like self-determination, socialism and Arab unity. And before oil money turned the Gulf states into golden geese, Egypt was the undisputed leader of the Middle East. So Nasser's vision became the region's. Every regime, from the Baathists in Syria and Iraq to the conservative monarchies of the Gulf, spoke in similar terms and tones. It wasn't that they were just aping Nasser. The Middle East desperately wanted to become modern. It failed. For all their energy these regimes chose bad ideas and implemented them in worse ways. Socialism produced bureaucracy and stagnation. Rather than adjusting to the failures of central planning, the economies never really moved on. The republics calcified into dictatorships. Third World "nonalignment" became pro-Soviet propaganda. Arab unity cracked and crumbled as countries discovered their own national interests and opportunities. Worst of all, Israel humiliated the Arabs in the wars of 1967 and 1973. When Saddam Hussein invaded Kuwait in 1990, he destroyed the last remnants of the Arab idea.

Egypt's Quiet Nightmare

Look at Egypt today. The promise of Nasserism has turned into a quiet nightmare. The government is efficient in only one area: squashing dissent and strangling civil society. In the past 30 years Egypt's economy has sputtered along while its population has doubled. Unemployment is at 25 percent, and 90 percent of those searching for jobs hold college diplomas. Once the heart of Arab intellectual life, the country produces just 375 books every year (compared with Israel's 4,000). For all the angry protests to foreigners, Egyptians know all this.

Shockingly, Egypt has fared better than its Arab neighbors. Syria has become one of the world's most oppressive police states, a country where 25,000 people can be rounded up and killed by the regime with no consequences. (This in a land whose capital, Damascus, is the oldest continuously inhabited city in the world.) In 30 years Iraq has gone from being among the most modern and secular of Arab countries—with women working, artists thriving, journalists writing—into a squalid playpen for Saddam Hussein's megalomania. Lebanon, a diverse, cosmopolitan society with a capital, Beirut, that was once called the Paris of the East, has become a hellhole of war and terror. In an almost unthinkable reversal of a global pattern, almost every Arab country today is less free than it was 30 years ago. There are few countries in the world of which one can say that.

We think of Africa's dictators as rapacious, but those in the Middle East can be just as greedy. And when contrasted with the success of Israel, Arab failures are even more humiliating. For all its flaws, out of the same desert Israel has created a functioning democracy, a modern society with an increasingly high-technology economy and thriving artistic and cultural life. Israel now has a per capita GDP that equals that of many Western countries.

If poverty produced failure in most of Arabia, wealth produced failure in the rest of it. The rise of oil power in the 1970s gave a second wind to Arab hopes. Where Nasserism failed, petroleum would succeed. But it didn't. All that the rise of oil prices has done over three decades is to produce a new class of rich, superficially Western gulf Arabs, who travel the globe in luxury and are despised by the rest of the Arab world. Look at any cartoons of Gulf sheiks in Egyptian, Jordanian or Syrian newspapers. They are portrayed in the most insulting, almost racist manner: as corpulent, corrupt and weak. Most Americans think that Arabs should be grateful for our role in the Gulf War, for we saved Kuwait and Saudi Arabia. Most Arabs think that we saved the Kuwaiti and Saudi *royal families*. Big difference.

Wealth's Negative Effects
The money that the gulf sheiks have frittered away is on a scale that is almost impossible to believe. Just one example: a favored prince of Saudi Arabia, at the age of 25, built a palace in Riyadh for $300 million and, as an additional bounty, was given a $1 billion commission on the kingdom's telephone contract with AT&T. Far from producing political progress, wealth has actually had some negative effects. It has enriched and empowered the gulf governments so that, like their Arab brethren, they, too, have become more repressive over time. The Bedouin societies they once ruled have become gilded cages, filled with frustrated, bitter and discontented young men—some of whom now live in Afghanistan and work with Osama bin Laden. (Bin Laden and some of his aides come from privileged backgrounds in Saudi Arabia.)

By the late 1980s, while the rest of the world was watching old regimes from Moscow to Prague to Seoul to Johannesburg crack, the Arabs were stuck with their aging dictators and corrupt kings. Regimes that might have seemed promising in the 1960s were now exposed as tired, corrupt kleptocracies, deeply unpopular and thoroughly illegitimate. One has to add that many of them are close American allies.

CHAPTER II: FAILED IDEAS

How does a region that once yearned for modernity reject it so dramatically?

About a decade ago, in a casual conversation with an elderly Arab intellectual, I expressed my frustration that governments in the Middle East had been unable to liberalize their economies and societies in the way that the East Asians had done. "Look at Singapore, Hong Kong and Seoul," I said, pointing to their extraordinary economic achievements.

The man, a gentle, charming scholar, straightened up and replied sharply, "Look at them. They have simply aped the West. Their cities are cheap copies of Houston and Dallas. That may be all right for fishing villages. But we are heirs to one of the great civilizations of the world. We cannot become slums of the West."

This disillusionment with the West is at the heart of the Arab problem. It makes economic advance impossible and political progress fraught with difficulty. Modernization is now taken to mean, inevitably, uncontrollably, Westernization and, even worse, Americanization. This fear has paralyzed Arab civilization. In some ways the Arab world seems less ready to confront the age of globalization than even Africa, despite the devastation that continent has suffered from AIDS and economic and political dysfunction. At least the Africans want to adapt to the new global economy. The Arab world has not yet taken that first step.

Past or Future?

The question is how a region that once yearned for modernity could reject it so dramatically. In the Middle Ages the Arabs studied Aristotle (when he was long forgotten in the West) and invented algebra. In the 19th century, when the West set ashore in Arab lands, in the form of Napoleon's conquest of Egypt, the locals were fascinated by this powerful civilization. In fact, as the historian Albert Hourani has documented, the 19th century saw European-inspired liberal political and social thought flourish in the Middle East.

The colonial era of the late 19th and early 20th centuries raised hopes of British friendship that were to be disappointed, but still Arab elites remained fascinated with the West. Future kings and generals attended Victoria College in Alexandria, learning the speech and manners of British gentlemen. Many then went on to Oxford, Cambridge and Sandhurst—a tradition that is still maintained by Jordan's royal family, though now they go to Hotchkiss or Lawrenceville. After World War I, a new liberal age flickered briefly in the Arab world, as ideas about opening up politics and society gained currency in places like Egypt, Lebanon, Iraq and Syria. But since they were part of a world of kings and aristocrats, these ideas died with those old regimes. The new ones, however, turned out to be just as Western.

Nasser thought his ideas for Egypt and the Arab world were modern. They were also Western. His "national charter" of 1962 reads as if it were written by left-wing intellectuals in Paris or London. (Like many Third World leaders of the time, Nasser was a devoted reader of France's *Le Monde* and Britain's *New Statesman*.) Even his most passionately held project, Pan-Arabism, was European. It was a version of the nationalism that had united Italy and Germany in the 1870s—that those who spoke one language should be one nation.

One Failure After Another

America thinks of modernity as all good—and it has been almost all good for America. But for the Arab world, modernity has been one failure after another. Each path followed—socialism, secularism, nationalism—has turned into a dead end. While other countries adjusted to their failures, Arab regimes got stuck in their ways. And those that reformed economically could not bring themselves to ease up politically. The Shah of Iran, the Middle Eastern ruler who tried to move his country into the modern era fastest, reaped the most violent reaction in the Iranian revolution of 1979. But even the shah's modernization—compared, for example, with the East Asian approach of hard work, investment and thrift—was an attempt to buy modernization with oil wealth.

It turns out that modernization takes more than strongmen and oil money. Importing foreign stuff—Cadillacs, Gulfstreams and McDonald's—is easy. Importing the inner stuffings of modern society—a free market, political parties, accountability and the rule of law—is difficult and dangerous. The Gulf states, for example, have gotten modernization lite, with the goods and even the workers imported from abroad. Nothing was homegrown; nothing is even now. As for politics, the Gulf governments offered their people a bargain: we will bribe you with wealth, but in return let us stay in power. It was the inverse slogan of the American revolution—no taxation, but no representation either.

The new age of globalization has hit the Arab world in a very strange way. Its societies are open enough to be disrupted by modernity, but not so open that they can ride the wave. They see the television shows, the fast foods and the fizzy drinks. But they don't see genuine liberalization in the society, with increased opportunities and greater openness. Globalization in the Arab world is the critic's caricature of globalization—a slew of Western products and billboards with little else. For some in their societies it means more things to buy. For the regimes it is an unsettling, dangerous phenomenon. As a result, the people they rule can look at globalization but for the most part not touch it.

Unstoppable Globalization
America stands at the center of this world of globalization. It seems unstoppable. If you close the borders, America comes in through the mail. If you censor the mail, it appears in the fast food and faded jeans. If you ban the products, it seeps in through satellite television. Americans are so comfortable with global capitalism and consumer culture that we cannot fathom just how revolutionary these forces are.

Disoriented young men, with one foot in the old world and another in the new, now look for a purer, simpler alternative. Fundamentalism searches for such people everywhere; it, too, has been globalized. One can now find men in Indonesia who regard the Palestinian cause as their own. (Twenty years ago an Indonesian Muslim would barely have known where Palestine was.) Often they learned about this path away from the West while they were in the West. As did Mohamed Atta, the Hamburg-educated engineer who drove the first plane into the World Trade Center.

The Arab world has a problem with its Attas in more than one sense. Globalization has caught it at a bad demographic moment. Arab societies are going through a massive youth bulge, with more than half of most countries' populations under the age of 25. Young men, often better educated than their parents, leave their traditional villages to find work. They arrive in noisy, crowded cities like Cairo, Beirut and Damascus or go to work in the oil states. (Almost 10 percent of Egypt's working population worked in the Gulf at one point.) In their new world they see great disparities of wealth and the disorienting effects of modernity; most unsettlingly, they see women, unveiled and in public places, taking buses, eating in cafes and working alongside them.

A huge influx of restless young men in any country is bad news. When accompanied by even small economic and social change, it usually produces a new politics of protest. In the past, societies in these circumstances have fallen prey to a search for revolutionary solutions. (France went through a youth bulge just before the French Revolution, as did Iran before its 1979 revolution.) In the case of the Arab world, this revolution has taken the form of an Islamic resurgence.

CHAPTER III: ENTER RELIGION
THE ORIGINS OF "ISLAMIC FUNDAMENTALISM"

NASSER WAS A REASONABLY DEVOUT MUSLIM, but he had no interest in mixing religion with politics. It struck him as moving backward. This became apparent to the small Islamic parties that supported Nasser's rise to power. The most important one, the Muslim Brotherhood, began opposing him vigorously, often violently. Nasser cracked down on it in 1954, imprisoning more than a thousand of its leaders and executing six. One of those jailed, Sayyid Qutub, a frail man with a fiery pen, wrote a book in prison called "Signposts on the Road," which in some ways marks the beginnings of modern political Islam or what is often called "Islamic fundamentalism."

In his book, Qutub condemned Nasser as an impious Muslim and his regime as un-Islamic. Indeed, he went on, almost every modern Arab regime was similarly flawed. Qutub envisioned a better, more virtuous polity that was based on strict Islamic principles, a core goal of orthodox Muslims since the 1880s. As the regimes of the Middle East grew more distant and oppressive and hollow in the decades following Nasser, fundamentalism's appeal grew. It flourished because the Muslim Brotherhood and organizations like it at least tried to give people a sense of meaning and purpose in a changing world, something no leader in the Middle East tried to do.

In his seminal work, "The Arab Predicament," Fouad Ajami explains, "The fundamentalist call has resonance because it invited men to participate ... [in] contrast to a political culture that reduces citizens to spectators and asks them to leave things to their rulers. At a time when the future is uncertain, it connects them to a tradition that reduces bewilderment." Fundamentalism gave Arabs who were dissatisfied with their lot a powerful language of opposition.

Few Pathways for Dissent

On that score, Islam had little competition. The Arab world is a political desert with no real political parties, no free press, few pathways for dissent. As a result, the mosque turned into the place to discuss politics. And fundamentalist organizations have done more than talk. From the Muslim Brotherhood to Hamas to Hizbullah, they actively provide social services, medical assistance, counseling and temporary housing. For those who treasure civil society, it is disturbing to see that in the Middle East these illiberal groups *are* civil society.

I asked Sheri Berman, a scholar at Princeton who studies the rise of fascist parties in Europe, whether she saw any parallels. "Fascists were often very effective at providing social services," she pointed out. "When the state or political parties fail to provide a sense of legitimacy or purpose or basic services, other organizations have often been able to step into the void. In Islamic countries there is a ready-made source of legitimacy in the religion. So it's not surprising that this is the foundation on which these groups have flourished. The particular form—Islamic fundamentalism—is specific to this region, but the basic dynamic is similar to the rise of Nazism, fascism and even populism in the United States."

Islamic fundamentalism got a tremendous boost in 1979 when Ayatollah Ruhollah Khomeini toppled the Shah of Iran. The Iranian revolution demonstrated that a powerful ruler could be taken on by groups within society. It also revealed how in a broken society even seemingly benign forces of progress—education and technology—can add to the turmoil. Until the 1970s most Muslims in the Middle East were illiterate and lived in villages and towns. They practiced a kind of street-Islam that had adapted itself to the local culture. Pluralistic and tolerant, these people often worshiped saints, went to shrines, sang religious hymns and cherished religious art, all technically disallowed in Islam. (This was particularly true in Iran.) By the 1970s, however, people had begun moving out of the villages and their religious experience was not rooted in a specific place. At the same time they were learning to read and they discovered that a new Islam was being preached by the fundamentalists, an abstract faith not rooted in historical experience but literal, puritanical and by the book. It was Islam of the High Church as opposed to Islam of the village fair.

Against 'Westoxification'
In Iran, Ayatollah Khomeini used a powerful technology—the audiocassette. His sermons were distributed throughout the country and became the vehicle of opposition to the shah's repressive regime. But Khomeini was not alone in using the language of Islam as a political tool. Intellectuals, disillusioned by the half-baked or overrapid modernization that was throwing their world into turmoil, were writing books against "Westoxification" and calling the modern Iranian man—half Western, half Eastern—rootless. Fashionable intellectuals, often writing from the comfort of London or Paris, would critique American secularism and consumerism and endorse an Islamic alternative. As theories like these spread across the Arab world, they appealed not to the poorest of the poor, for whom Westernization was magical (it meant food and medicine). They appealed to the half-educated hordes entering the cities of the Middle East or seeking education and jobs in the West.

The fact that Islam is a highly egalitarian religion for the most part has also proved an empowering call for people who felt powerless. At the same time it means that no Muslim really has the authority to question whether someone who claims to be a proper Muslim is one. The fundamentalists, from Sayyid Qutub on, have jumped into that the void. They ask whether people are "good Muslims." It is a question that has terrified the Muslim world. And here we come to the failure not simply of governments but intellectual and social elites. Moderate Muslims are loath to criticize or debunk the fanaticism of the fundamentalists. Like the moderates in Northern Ireland, they are scared of what would happen to them if they speak their mind.

The biggest Devil's bargain has been made by the moderate monarchies of the Persian Gulf, particularly Saudi Arabia. The Saudi regime has played a dangerous game. It deflects attention from its shoddy record at home by funding religious schools (*madrasas*) and centers that spread a rigid, puritanical brand of Islam—Wahhabism. In the past 30 years Saudi-funded schools have churned out tens of thousands of half-educated, fanatical Muslims who view the modern world and non-Muslims with great suspicion. America in this world view is almost always evil.

Allied with Fundamentalism

This exported fundamentalism has in turn infected not just other Arab societies but countries outside the Arab world, like Pakistan. During the 11-year reign of Gen. Zia ul-Haq, the dictator decided that as he squashed political dissent he needed allies. He found them in the fundamentalists. With the aid of Saudi financiers and functionaries, he set up scores of *madrasas* throughout the country. They bought him temporary legitimacy but have eroded the social fabric of Pakistan.

If there is one great cause of the rise of Islamic fundamentalism, it is the total failure of political institutions in the Arab world. Muslim elites have averted their eyes from this reality. Conferences at Islamic centers would still rather discuss "Islam and the Environment" than examine the dysfunctions of the current regimes. But as the moderate majority looks the other way, Islam is being taken over by a small poisonous element, people who advocate cruel attitudes toward women, education, the economy and modern life in general. I have seen this happen in India, where I grew up. The rich, colorful, pluralistic and easygoing Islam of my youth has turned into a dour, puritanical faith, policed by petty theocrats and religious commissars. The next section deals with what the United States can do to help the Islamic world. But if Muslims do not take it upon themselves to stop their religion from falling prey to medievalists, nothing any outsider can do will save them.

CHAPTER IV: WHAT TO DO

AMERICA'S greatest sins toward the arab world are sins of omission

If almost any Arab were to have read this essay so far, he would have objected vigorously by now. "It is all very well to talk about the failures of the Arab world," he would say, "but what about the failures of the West? You speak of long-term decline, but our problems are with specific, cruel American policies." For most Arabs, relations with the United States have been filled with disappointment.

While the Arab world has long felt betrayed by Europe's colonial powers, its disillusionment with America begins most importantly with the creation of Israel in 1948. As the Arabs see it, at a time when colonies were winning independence from the West, here was a state largely composed of foreign people being imposed on a region with Western backing. The anger deepened in the wake of America's support for Israel during the wars of 1967 and 1973, and ever since in its relations with the Palestinians. The daily exposure to Israel's iron-fisted rule over the occupied territories has turned this into the great cause of the Arab—and indeed the broader Islamic—world. Elsewhere, they look at American policy in the region as cynically geared to America's oil interests, supporting thugs and tyrants without any hesitation. Finally, the bombing and isolation of Iraq have become fodder for daily attacks on the United States. While many in the Arab world do not like Saddam Hussein, they believe that the United States has chosen a particularly inhuman method of fighting him—a method that is starving an entire nation.

There is substance to some of these charges, and certainly from the point of view of an Arab, American actions are never going to seem entirely fair. Like any country, America has its interests. In my view, America's greatest sins toward the Arab world are sins of omission. We have neglected to press any regime there to open up its society. This neglect turned deadly in the case of Afghanistan. Walking away from that fractured country after 1989 resulted in the rise of bin Laden and the Taliban. This is not the gravest error a great power can make, but it is a common American one. As F. Scott Fitzgerald explained of his characters in "The Great Gatsby," "They were careless people, Tom and Daisy—they smashed things up and creatures and then retreated back into their money, or their vast carelessness ... and let other people clean up the mess." America has not been venal in the Arab world. But it has been careless.

Explaining Arab Rage

Yet carelessness is not enough to explain Arab rage. After all, if concern for the Palestinians is at the heart of the problem, why have their Arab brethren done nothing for them? (They cannot resettle in any Arab nation but Jordan, and the aid they receive from the Gulf states is minuscule.) Israel treats its 1 million Arabs as second-class citizens, a disgrace on its democracy. And yet the tragedy of the Arab world is that Israel accords them more political rights and dignities than most Arab nations give to their own people. Why is the focus of Arab anger on Israel and not those regimes?

The disproportionate feelings of grievance directed at America have to be placed in the overall context of the sense of humiliation, decline and despair that sweeps the Arab world. After all, the Chinese vigorously disagree with most of America's foreign policy and have fought wars with U.S. proxies. African states feel the same sense of disappointment and unfairness. But they do not work it into a rage against America. Arabs, however, feel that they are under siege from the modern world and that the United States symbolizes this world. Thus every action America takes gets magnified a thousandfold. And even when we do not act, the rumors of our gigantic powers and nefarious deeds still spread. Most Americans would not believe how common the rumor is throughout the Arab world that either the CIA or Israel's Mossad blew up the World Trade Center to justify attacks on Arabs and Muslims. This is the culture from which the suicide bombers have come.

America must now devise a strategy to deal with this form of religious terrorism. As is now widely understood, this will be a long war, with many fronts and battles small and large. Our strategy must be divided along three lines: military, political and cultural. On the military front—by which I mean war, covert operations and other forms of coercion—the goal is simple: the total destruction of al Qaeda. Even if we never understand all the causes of apocalyptic terror, we must do battle against it. Every person who plans and helps in a terrorist operation must understand that he will be tracked and punished. Their operations will be disrupted, their finances drained, their hideouts destroyed. There will be associated costs to pursuing such a strategy, but they will all fade if we succeed. Nothing else matters on the military front.

The New New World Order
The political strategy is more complex and more ambitious. At the broadest level, we now have a chance to reorder the international system around this pressing new danger. The degree of cooperation from around the world has been unprecedented. We should not

look on this trend suspiciously. Most governments feel threatened by the rise of subnational forces like al Qaeda. Even some that have clearly supported terrorism in the past, like Iran, seem interested in re-entering the world community and reforming their ways.

We can define a strategy for the post-Cold War era that addresses America's principal national-security need and yet is sustained by a broad international consensus. To do this we will have to give up some Cold War reflexes, such as an allergy to multilateralism, and stop insisting that China is about to rival us militarily or that Russia is likely to re-emerge as a new military threat. (For 10 years now, our defense forces have been aligned for everything but the real danger we face. This will inevitably change.)

The purpose of an international coalition is practical and strategic. Given the nature of this war, we will need the constant cooperation of other governments—to make arrests, shut down safe houses, close bank accounts and share intelligence. Alliance politics has become a matter of high national security. But there is a broader imperative. The United States dominates the world in a way that inevitably arouses envy or anger or opposition. That comes with the power, but we still need to get things done. If we can mask our power in—sorry, work with—institutions like the United Nations Security Council, U.S. might will be easier for much of the world to bear. Bush's father understood this, which is why he ensured that the United Nations sanctioned the Gulf War. The point here is to succeed, and international legitimacy can help us do that.

Now we get to Israel. It is obviously one of the central and most charged problems in the region. But it is a problem to which we cannot offer the Arab world support for its solution—the extinction of the state. We cannot in any way weaken our commitment to the existence and health of Israel. Similarly, we cannot abandon our policy of containing Saddam Hussein. He is building weapons of mass destruction.

Broken Policy in Iraq
However, we should not pursue mistaken policies simply out of spite. Our policy toward Saddam is broken. We have no inspectors in Iraq, the sanctions are—for whatever reason—starving Iraqis, and he continues to build chemical and biological weapons. There

is a way to reorient our policy to focus our pressure on Saddam and not his people, contain him militarily but not harm common Iraqis economically. Colin Powell has been trying to do this; he should be given leeway to try again. In time we will have to address the broader question of what to do about Saddam, a question that, unfortunately, does not have an easy answer. (Occupying Iraq, even if we could do it, does not seem a good idea in this climate.)

On Israel we should make a clear distinction between its right to exist and its occupation of the West Bank and Gaza. On the first we should be as unyielding as ever; on the second we should continue trying to construct a final deal along the lines that Bill Clinton and Ehud Barak outlined. I suggest that we do this less because it will lower the temperature in the Arab world—who knows if it will?—than because it's the right thing to do. Israel cannot remain a democracy and continue to occupy and militarily rule 3 million people against their wishes. It's bad for Israel, bad for the Palestinians and bad for the United States.

But policy changes, large or small, are not at the heart of the struggle we face. The third, vital component to this battle is a cultural strategy. The United States must help Islam enter the modern world. It sounds like an impossible challenge, and it certainly is not one we would have chosen. But America—indeed the whole world—faces a dire security threat that will not be resolved unless we can stop the political, economic and cultural collapse that lies at the roots of Arab rage. During the Cold War the West employed myriad ideological strategies to discredit the appeal of communism, make democracy seem attractive and promote open societies. We will have to do something on that scale to win this cultural struggle.

Fresh Thinking in the Arab World

First, we have to help moderate Arab states, but on the condition that they embrace moderation. For too long regimes like Saudi Arabia's have engaged in a deadly dance with religious extremism. Even Egypt, which has always denounced fundamentalism, allows its controlled media to rant crazily about America and Israel. (That way they don't rant about the dictatorship they live under.) But more broadly, we must persuade Arab moderates to make the case to their people that Islam is compatible with modern society, that it does allow women to work, that it encourages education and that it has welcomed people of other faiths and creeds. Some of this they will do—September 11 has been a wake-up call for many. The Saudi regime denounced and broke its ties to the Taliban (a regime that it used to glorify as representing pure Islam). The Egyptian press is now making the case for military action. The United States and the West should do their own work as well. We can fund moderate Muslim groups and scholars and broadcast fresh thinking across the Arab world, all aimed at breaking the power of the fundamentalists.

Obviously we will have to help construct a new political order in Afghanistan after we have deposed the Taliban regime. But beyond that we have to press the nations of the Arab world—and others, like Pakistan, where the virus of fundamentalism has spread—to reform, open up and gain legitimacy. We need to do business with these regimes; yet, just as we did with South Korea and Taiwan during the Cold War, we can ally with these dictatorships and still push them toward reform. For those who argue that we should not engage in nation-building, I would say foreign policy is not theology. I have myself been skeptical of nation-building in places where our interests were unclear and it seemed unlikely that we would stay the course. In this case, stable political development is the key to reducing our single greatest security threat. We have no option but to get back into the nation-building business.

It sounds like a daunting challenge, but there are many good signs. Al Qaeda is not more powerful than the combined force of many determined governments. The world is indeed uniting around American leadership, and perhaps we will see the emergence, for a while, of a new global community and consensus, which could bring progress in many other areas of international life. Perhaps most important, Islamic fundamentalism still does not speak to the majority of the Muslim people. In Pakistan, fundamentalist parties have yet to get more than 10 percent of the vote. In Iran, having experienced the brutal puritanism of the mullahs, people are yearning for normalcy. In Egypt, for all the repression, the fundamentalists are a potent force but so far not dominant. If the West can help Islam enter modernity in dignity and peace, it will have done more than achieved security. It will have changed the world.

Somebody Else's Civil War

Michael Scott Doran

Call it a city on four legs
heading for murder...
New York is a woman
holding, according to history,
a rag called liberty with one hand
and strangling the earth with the other.
                    -Adonis [Ali Ahmed Said],
                    "The Funeral of New York," 1971

IN THE WEEKS after the attacks of September 11, Americans repeatedly asked, "Why do they hate us?" To understand what happened, however, another question may be even more pertinent: "Why do they want to provoke us?"

David Fromkin suggested the answer in *Foreign Affairs* back in 1975. "Terrorism," he noted, "is violence used in order to create fear; but it is aimed at creating fear in order that the fear, in turn, will lead somebody else—not the terrorist—to embark on some quite different program of action that will accomplish whatever it is that the terrorist really desires." When a terrorist kills, the goal is not murder itself but something else—for example, a police crackdown

MICHAEL SCOTT DORAN taught for three years at the University of Central Florida and is now Professor of Near Eastern Studies at Princeton University. He is the author of *Pan-Arabism Before Nasser: Egyptian Power Politics and the Palestine Question*. This article is adapted from his chapter in *How Did This Happen? Terrorism and the New War*, published by PublicAffairs and *Foreign Affairs* with the support of the Council on Foreign Relations.

that will create a rift between government and society that the terrorist can then exploit for revolutionary purposes. Osama bin Laden sought—and has received—an international military crackdown, one he wants to exploit for his particular brand of revolution.

Bin Laden produced a piece of high political theater he hoped would reach the audience that concerned him the most: the *umma*, or universal Islamic community. The script was obvious: America, cast as the villain, was supposed to use its military might like a cartoon character trying to kill a fly with a shotgun. The media would see to it that any use of force against the civilian population of Afghanistan was broadcast around the world, and the *umma* would find it shocking how Americans nonchalantly caused Muslims to suffer and die. The ensuing outrage would open a chasm between state and society in the Middle East, and the governments allied with the West—many of which are repressive, corrupt, and illegitimate—would find themselves adrift. It was to provoke such an outcome that bin Laden broadcast his statement following the start of the military campaign on October 7, in which he said, among other things, that the Americans and the British "have divided the entire world into two regions—one of faith, where there is no hypocrisy, and another of infidelity, from which we hope God will protect us."

Polarizing the Islamic world between the *umma* and the regimes allied with the United States would help achieve bin Laden's primary goal: furthering the cause of Islamic revolution within the Muslim world itself, in the Arab lands especially and in Saudi Arabia above all. He had no intention of defeating America. War with the United States was not a goal in and of itself but rather an instrument designed to help his brand of extremist Islam survive and flourish among the believers. Americans, in short, have been drawn into somebody else's civil war.

Washington had no choice but to take up the gauntlet, but it is not altogether clear that Americans understand fully this war's true dimensions. The response to bin Laden cannot be left to soldiers and police alone. He has embroiled the United States in an intra-Muslim ideological battle, a struggle for hearts and minds in which al Qaeda had already scored a number of victories—as the reluctance of America's Middle Eastern allies to offer public support for the campaign against it demonstrated. The first step toward weakening the hold of bin Laden's ideology, therefore, must be to comprehend the symbolic universe into which he has dragged us.

AMERICA, THE HUBAL OF THE AGE

BIN LADEN'S October 7 statement offers a crucial window onto his conceptual world and repays careful attention. In it he states, "Hypocrisy stood behind the leader of global idolatry, behind the Hubal of the age—namely, America and its supporters." Because the symbolism is obscure to most Americans, this sentence was widely mistranslated in the press, but bin Laden's Muslim audience understood it immediately.

In the early seventh century, when the Prophet Muhammad began to preach Islam to the pagan Arab tribes in Mecca, Hubal was a stone idol that stood in the Kaaba—a structure that Abraham, according to Islamic tradition, originally built on orders from God as a sanctuary of Islam. In the years between Abraham and Muhammad, the tradition runs, the Arabs fell away from true belief and began to worship idols, with Hubal the most powerful of many. When bin Laden calls America "the Hubal of the age," he suggests that it is the primary focus of idol worship and that it is polluting the Kaaba, a symbol of Islamic purity. His imagery has a double resonance: it portrays American culture as a font of idolatry while rejecting the American military presence on the Arabian peninsula (which is, by his definition, the holy land of Islam, a place barred to infidels).

Muhammad's prophecy called the Arabs of Mecca back to their monotheistic birthright. The return to true belief, however, was not an easy one, because the reigning Meccan oligarchy persecuted the early Muslims. By calling for the destruction of Hubal, the Prophet's message threatened to undermine the special position that Mecca enjoyed in Arabia as a pagan shrine city. With much of their livelihood at stake, the oligarchs punished Muhammad's followers and conspired to kill him. The Muslims therefore fled from Mecca to Medina, where they established the *umma* as a political and religious community. They went on to fight and win a war against Mecca that ended with the destruction of Hubal and the spread of true Islam around the world.

Before the Prophet could achieve this success, however, he encountered the *Munafiqun,* the Hypocrites of Medina. Muhammad's acceptance of leadership over the Medinese reduced the power of a number of local tribal leaders. These men outwardly accepted Islam in order to protect their worldly status, but in their hearts they bore malice toward both the Prophet and his message. Among other misdeeds, the treacherous *Munafiqun* abandoned Muhammad on the battlefield at a moment when he was already woefully outnumbered. The Hypocrites were apostates who accepted true belief but then rejected it, and as such they were regarded as worse than the infidels who had never embraced Islam to begin with. Islam can understand just how difficult it is for a pagan to leave behind all the beliefs and personal connections that he or she once held dear; it is less forgiving of those who accept the truth and then subvert it.

In bin Laden's imagery, the leaders of the Arab and Islamic worlds today are Hypocrites, idol worshippers cowering behind America, the Hubal of the age. His sword jabs simultaneously at the United States and the governments allied with it. His attack was designed to force those governments to choose: You are either with the idol-worshiping enemies of God or you are with the true believers.

The al Qaeda organization grew out of an Islamic religious movement called the Salafiyya—a name derived from *al-Salaf al-Salih,* "the venerable forefathers," which refers to the generation of the Prophet Muhammad and his companions. Salafis regard the Islam that most Muslims practice today as polluted by idolatry; they seek to reform the religion by emulating the first generation of Muslims, whose pristine society they consider to have best reflected God's wishes for humans. The Salafiyya is not a unified movement, and it expresses itself in many forms, most of which do not approach the extremism of Osama bin Laden or the Taliban. The Wahhabi ideology of the Saudi state, for example, and the religious doctrines of the Muslim Brotherhood in Egypt and a host of voluntary religious organizations around the Islamic world are all

Salafi. These diverse movements share the belief that Muslims have deviated from God's plan and that matters can be returned to their proper state by emulating the Prophet.

Like any other major religious figure, Muhammad left behind a legacy that his followers have channeled in different directions. An extremist current in the Salafiyya places great emphasis on jihad, or holy war. Among other things, the Prophet Muhammad fought in mortal combat against idolatry, and some of his followers today choose to accord this aspect of his career primary importance. The devoted members of al Qaeda display an unsettling willingness to martyr themselves because they feel that, like the Prophet, they are locked in a life-or-death struggle with the forces of unbelief that threaten from all sides. They consider themselves an island of true believers surrounded by a sea of iniquity and think the future of religion itself, and therefore the world, depends on them and their battle against idol worship.

In almost every Sunni Muslim country the Salafiyya has spawned Islamist political movements working to compel the state to apply the *shari`a*—that is, Islamic law. Extremist Salafis believe that strict application of the *shari`a* is necessary to ensure that Muslims walk on the path of the Prophet. The more extremist the party, the more insistent and violent the demand that the state must apply the *shari`a* exclusively. In the view of extremist Salafis, the *shari`a* is God's thunderous commandment to Muslims, and failure to adopt it constitutes idolatry. By removing God from the realm of law, a domain that He has clearly claimed for Himself alone, human legislation amounts to worshiping a pagan deity. Thus it was on the basis of failure to apply the *shari`a* that extremists branded Egyptian President Anwar al-Sadat an apostate and then killed him. His assassins came from a group often known as Egyptian Islamic Jihad, the remnants of which have in recent years merged with al Qaeda. In fact, investigators believe that Egyptian Islamic Jihad's leaders, Ayman al-Zawahiri and Muhammad Atef (who was killed in the U.S. air campaign), masterminded the attacks of September 11. In his 1996 "Declaration of War against the Americans," bin Laden showed that he and his Egyptian associates are cut from the same cloth. Just as Zawahiri and Atef considered the current regime of Hosni Mubarak in Egypt to be a nest of apostates, so bin Laden considered the Saudi monarchy (its Wahhabi doctrines notwithstanding) to have renounced Islam. According to bin Laden, his king adopted "polytheism," which bin Laden defined as the acceptance of "laws fabricated by men... permitting that which God has forbidden." It is the height of human arrogance and irreligion to "share with God in His sole right of sovereignty and making the law."

Extremist Salafis, therefore, regard modern Western civilization as a font of evil, spreading idolatry around the globe in the form of secularism. Since the United States is the strongest Western nation, the main purveyor of pop culture, and the power most involved in the political and economic affairs of the Islamic world, it receives particularly harsh criticism. Only the apostate Middle Eastern regimes themselves fall under harsher condemnation.

It is worth remembering, in this regard, that the rise of Islam represents a miraculous case of the triumph of human will. With little more than their beliefs to gird them, the Prophet Muhammad and a small number of devoted followers started a movement that brought the most powerful empires of their day crashing to the ground. On September 11, the attackers undoubtedly imagined themselves to be retracing the Prophet's steps. As they boarded the planes with the intention of destroying the Pentagon and the World Trade Center, they recited battle prayers that contained the line "All of their equipment, and gates, and technology will not prevent [you from achieving your aim], nor harm [you] except by God's will." The hijackers' imaginations certainly needed nothing more than this sparse line to remind them that, as they attacked America, they rode right behind Muhammad, who in his day had unleashed forces that, shortly after his death, destroyed the Persian Empire and crippled Byzantium—the two superpowers of the age.

AMERICA, LAND OF THE CRUSADERS

WHEN THINKING ABOUT the world today and their place in it, the extremist Salafis do not reflect only on the story of the foundation of Islam. They also scour more than a millennium of Islamic history in search of parallels to the present predicament. In his "Declaration of War," for instance, bin Laden states that the stationing of American forces on the soil of the Arabian peninsula constitutes the greatest aggression committed against the Muslims since the death of the Prophet in AD 632.

To put this claim in perspective, it is worth remembering that in the last 1,300 years Muslims have suffered a number of significant defeats, including but not limited to the destruction of the Abbasid caliphate by the Mongols, an episode of which bin Laden is well aware. In 1258 the ruthless Mongol leader Hulegu sacked Baghdad, killed the caliph, and massacred hundreds of thousands of inhabitants, stacking their skulls, as legend has it, in a pyramid outside the city walls. Whatever one thinks about U.S. policy toward Iraq, few in America would argue that the use of Saudi bases to enforce the sanctions against Saddam Hussein's regime constitutes a world-historical event on a par with the Mongol invasion of the Middle East. Before September 11, one might have been tempted to pass off as nationalist hyperbole bin Laden's assumption that U.S. policy represents the pinnacle of human evil. Now we know he is deadly serious.

The magnitude of the attacks on New York and Washington make it clear that al Qaeda does indeed believe itself to be fighting a war to save the *umma* from Satan, represented by secular Western culture. Extreme though they may be, these views extend far beyond al Qaeda's immediate followers in Afghanistan. Even a quick glance at the Islamist press in Arabic demonstrates that many Muslims who do not belong to bin Laden's terrorist network consider the United States to be on a moral par with Genghis Khan. Take, for instance, Muhammad Abbas, an Egyptian Islamist who wrote the following in the newspaper *Al Shaab* on September 21:

> Look! There is the master of democracy whom they have so often sanctified but who causes criminal, barbaric, bloody oppression that abandons the moral standards of even the most savage empires in history. In my last column I listed for readers the five million killed (may God receive them as martyrs) because of the crimes committed by this American civilization that America leads. These five million were killed in the last few decades alone.

Similar feelings led another *Al Shaab* columnist that day, Khalid al-Sharif, to describe the shock and delight that he felt while watching the World Trade Center crumbling:

> Look at that! America, master of the world, is crashing down. Look at that! The Satan who rules the world, east and west, is burning. Look at that! The sponsor of terrorism is itself seared by its fire.

THE FANATICS OF al Qaeda see the world in black and white and advance a particularly narrow view of Islam. This makes them a tiny minority among Muslims. But the basic categories of their thought flow directly from the mainstream of the Salafiyya, a perspective that has enjoyed a wide hearing over the last 50 years. Familiarity thus ensures bin Laden's ideas a sympathetic reception in many quarters.

In Salafi writings, the United States emerges as the senior member of a "Zionist-Crusader alliance" dedicated to subjugating Muslims, killing them, and, most important, destroying Islam. A careful reading reveals that this alliance represents more than just close relations between the United States and Israel today. The international cooperation between Washington and Jerusalem is but one nefarious manifestation of a greater evil of almost cosmic proportions. Thus in his "Declaration of War" bin Laden lists 10 or 12 world hot spots where Muslims have recently died (including Bosnia, Chechnya, and Lebanon) and attributes all of these deaths to a conspiracy led by the United States, even though Americans actually played no role in pulling the trigger. And thus, in another document, "Jihad Against Jews and Crusaders," bin Laden describes U.S. policies toward the Middle East as "a clear declaration of war on God, His messenger, and Muslims."

As strange as it may sound to an American audience, the idea that the United States has taken an oath of enmity toward God has deep roots in the Salafi tradition. It has been around for more than 50 years and has reached a wide public through the works of, among others, Sayyid Qutb, the most important Salafi thinker of the last half-century and a popular author in the Muslim world even today, nearly 40 years after his death. A sample passage taken from his writings in the early 1950s illustrates the point. Addressing the reasons why the Western powers had failed to support Muslims against their enemies in Pakistan, Palestine, and elsewhere, Qutb canvassed a number of common explanations such as Jewish financial influence and British imperial trickery but concluded,

> All of these opinions overlook one vital element in the question... the Crusader spirit that runs in the blood of all Occidentals. It is this that colors all their thinking, which is responsible for their imperialistic fear of the spirit of Islam and for their efforts to crush the strength of Islam. For the instincts and the interests of all Occidentals are bound up together in the crushing of that strength. This is the common factor that links together communist Russia and capitalist America. We do not forget the role of international Zionism in plotting against Islam and in pooling the forces of the Crusader imperialists and communist materialists alike. This is nothing other than a continuation of the role played by the Jews since the migration of the Prophet to Medina and the rise of the Islamic state.

Sayyid Qutb, Osama bin Laden, and the entire extremist Salafiyya see Western civilization, in all periods and in all guises, as innately hostile to Muslims and to Islam itself. The West and Islam are locked in a prolonged conflict. Islam will eventually triumph, of course, but only after enduring great hardship. Contemporary history, defined as it is by Western domination, constitutes the darkest era in the entire history of Islam.

AMERICA AND THE MONGOL THREAT

WHEN ATTEMPTING TO come to grips with the nature of the threat the modern West poses, extremist Salafis fall back on the writings of Ibn Taymiyya for guidance. A towering figure in the history of Islamic thought, he was born in Damascus in the thirteenth century, when Syria stood under the threat of invasion from the Mongols. Modern radicals find him attractive because he too faced the threat of a rival civilization. Ibn Taymiyya the firebrand exhorted his fellow Muslims to fight the Mongol foe, while Ibn Taymiyya the intellectual guided his community through the problems Muslims face when their social order falls under the shadow of non-Muslim power. It is only natural that bin Laden himself looks to such a master in order to legitimate his policies. Using Ibn Taymiyya to target America, however, marks an interesting turning point in the history of the radical Salafiyya.

Bin Laden's "Declaration of War" uses the logic of Ibn Taymiyya to persuade others in the Salafiyya to abandon old tactics for new ones. The first reference to him arises in connection with a discussion of the "Zionist-Crusader alliance," which according to bin Laden has been jailing and killing radical preachers—men such as Sheikh Omar Abdel Rahman, in prison for plotting a series of bombings in New York City following the 1993 bombing of the World Trade Center. Bin Laden argues that the "iniquitous Crusader movement under the leadership of the U.S.A." fears these preachers because they will successfully rally the Islamic community against the West, just as Ibn Taymiyya did against the Mongols in his day. Having identified the United States as a threat to Islam equivalent to the Mongols, bin Laden then discusses what to do about it. Ibn Taymiyya provides the answer: "To fight in the defense of religion and belief is a collective duty; there is no other duty after belief than fighting the enemy who is corrupting the life and the religion." The next most important thing after accepting the word of God, in other words, is fighting for it.

By calling on the *umma* to fight the Americans as if they were the Mongols, bin Laden and his Egyptian lieutenants have taken the extremist Salafiyya down a radically new path. Militants have long identified the West as a pernicious evil on a par with the Mongols, but they have traditionally targeted the internal enemy, the Hypocrites and apostates, rather than Hubal itself. Aware that he is shifting the focus considerably, bin Laden quotes Ibn Taymiyya at length to establish the basic point that "people of Islam should join forces and support each other to get rid of the main infidel," even if that means that the true believers will be forced to fight alongside Muslims of dubious piety. In the grand scheme of things, he argues, God often uses the base motives of impious Muslims as a means of advancing the cause of religion. In effect, bin Laden calls upon his fellow Islamist radicals to postpone the Islamic revolution, to stop fighting Hypocrites and apostates:

"An internal war is a great mistake, no matter what reasons there are for it," because discord among Muslims will only serve the United States and its goal of destroying Islam.

The shift of focus from the domestic enemy to the foreign power is all the more striking given the merger of al Qaeda and Egyptian Islamic Jihad. The latter's decision to kill Sadat in 1981 arose directly from the principle that the cause of Islam would be served by targeting lax Muslim leaders rather than by fighting foreigners, and here, too, Ibn Taymiyya provided the key doctrine. In his day Muslims often found themselves living under Mongol rulers who had absorbed Islam in one form or another. Ibn Taymiyya argued that such rulers—who outwardly pretended to be Muslims but who secretly followed non-Islamic, Mongol practices—must be considered infidels. Moreover, he claimed, by having accepted Islam but having also failed to observe key precepts of the religion, they had in effect committed apostasy and thereby written their own death sentences. In general, Islam prohibits fighting fellow Muslims and strongly restricts the right to rebel against the ruler; Ibn Taymiyya's doctrines, therefore, were crucial in the development of a modern Sunni Islamic revolutionary theory.

Egyptian Islamic Jihad views leaders such as Sadat as apostates. Although they may outwardly display signs of piety, they do not actually have Islam in their hearts, as their failure to enforce the *shari`a* proves. This non-Islamic behavior demonstrates that such leaders actually serve the secular West, precisely as an earlier generation of outwardly Muslim rulers had served the Mongols, and as the Hypocrites had served idolatry. Islamic Jihad explained itself back in the mid-1980s in a long, lucid statement titled "The Neglected Duty." Not a political manifesto like bin Laden's tracts, it is a sustained and learned argument that targets the serious believer rather than the angry, malleable crowd. Unlike bin Laden's holy war, moreover, Islamic Jihad's doctrine, though violent, fits clearly in the mainstream of Salafi consciousness, which historically has been concerned much more with the state of the Muslims themselves than with relations between Islam and the outside world. The decision to target America, therefore, raises the question of whether, during the 1990s, Egyptian Islamic Jihad changed its ideology entirely. Did its leaders decide that the foreign enemy was in fact the real enemy? Or was the 1993 bombing in New York tactical rather than strategic?

The answer would seem to be the latter. Bin Laden's "Declaration of War" itself testifies to the tactical nature of his campaign against America. Unlike "The Neglected Duty," which presents a focused argument, the "Declaration of War" meanders from topic to topic, contradicting itself along the way. On the one hand, it calls for unity in the face of external aggression and demands an end to internecine warfare; on the other, it calls in essence for revolution in Saudi Arabia. By presenting a litany of claims against the Saudi ruling family and by discussing the politics of Saudi Arabia at length and in minute detail, bin Laden protests too much: he reveals that he has not, in fact, set aside the internal war among the believers. Moreover, he also reveals that the ideological basis for that internal war has not changed. The members of the Saudi elite, like Sadat, have committed apostasy. Like the Hypocrites of Medina, they serve the forces of irreligion in order to harm the devotees of the Prophet and his message:

> You know more than anybody else about the size, intention, and
> the danger of the presence of the U.S. military bases in the area.
> The [Saudi] regime betrayed the *umma* and joined the infidels,
> assisting them ... against the Muslims. It is well known that this
> is one of the ten "voiders" of Islam, deeds of de-Islamization.
> By opening the Arabian Peninsula to the crusaders, the regime
> disobeyed and acted against what has been enjoined by the
> messenger of God.

OSAMA BIN LADEN undoubtedly believes that Americans are Crusader-Zionists, that they threaten his people even more than did the Mongols—in short, that they are the enemies of God Himself. But he also sees them as obstacles to his plans for his native land. The "Declaration of War" provides yet more testimony to the old saw that ultimately all politics is local.

THE FAILURE OF POLITICAL ISLAM

IF THE ATTACKS on the United States represented a change in radical Salafi tactics, then one must wonder what prompted bin

Laden and Zawahiri to make that change. The answer is that the attacks were a response to the failure of extremist movements in the Muslim world in recent years, which have generally proved incapable of taking power (Sudan and Afghanistan being the major exceptions). In the last two decades, several violent groups have challenged regimes such as those in Egypt, Syria, and Algeria, but in every case the government has managed to crush, co-opt, or marginalize the radicals. In the words of the "Declaration of War,"

> the Zionist-Crusader alliance moves quickly to contain and abort any "corrective movement" appearing in Islamic countries. Different means and methods are used to achieve their target. Sometimes officials from the Ministry of the Interior, who are also graduates of the colleges of the *shari`a*, are [unleashed] to mislead and confuse the nation and the *umma*... and to circulate false information about the movement, wasting the energy of the nation in discussing minor issues and ignoring the main one that is the unification of people under the divine law of Allah.

GIVEN THAT IN Egypt, Algeria, and elsewhere regimes have resorted to extreme violence to protect themselves, it is striking that bin Laden emphasizes here not the brutality but rather the counterpropaganda designed to divide and rule. Consciously or not, he has put his finger on a serious problem for the extremist Salafis: the limitations of their political and economic theories.

Apart from insisting on the implementation of the *shari`a*, demanding social justice, and turning the *umma* into the only legitimate political community, radical Salafis have precious little to offer in response to the mundane problems that people and governments face in the modern world. Extremist Islam is profoundly effective in mounting a protest movement: it can produce a cadre of activists whose devotion to the cause knows no bounds, it can galvanize people to fight against oppression. But it has serious difficulties when it comes to producing institutions and programs that can command the attention of diverse groups in society over the long haul. Its success relies mainly on the support of true believers, but they tend to fragment in disputes over doctrine, leadership, and agenda.

The limitations of extremist Salafi political theory and its divisive tendencies come to light clearly if one compares the goals of al

Qaeda with those of the Palestinian terrorist group Hamas, whose suicide bombers have also been in the headlines recently. The ideology of Hamas also evolved out of the Egyptian extremist Salafiyya milieu, and it shares with al Qaeda a paranoid view of the world: the *umma* and true Islam are threatened with extinction by the spread of Western secularism, the policies of the Crusading West, and oppression by the Zionists. Both Hamas and al Qaeda believe that the faithful must obliterate Israel. But looking more closely at Hamas and its agenda, one can see that it parts company with al Qaeda in many significant ways. This is because Hamas operates in the midst of nationalistic Palestinians, a majority of whom fervently desire, among other things, an end to the Israeli occupation and the establishment of a Palestinian state in part of historic Palestine.

The nationalist outlook of Hamas' public presents the organization with a number of thorny problems. Nationalism, according to the extremist Salafiyya, constitutes *shirk*—that is, polytheism or idolatry. If politics and religion are not distinct categories, as extremist Salafis argue, then political life must be centered around God and God's law. Sovereignty belongs not to the nation but to God alone, and the only legitimate political community is the *umma*. Pride in one's ethnic group is tolerable only so long as it does not divide the community of believers, who form an indivisible unit thanks to the sovereignty of the *shari`a*. One day, extremist Salafis believe, political boundaries will be erased and all Muslims will live in one polity devoted to God's will. At the moment, however, the priority is not to erase boundaries but to raise up the *shari`a* and abolish secular law. Nationalism is idolatry because it divides the *umma* and replaces a *shari`a*-centered consciousness with ethnic pride.

If Hamas were actually to denounce secular Palestinian nationalists as apostates, however, it would immediately consign itself to political irrelevance. To skirt this problem, the organization has developed an elaborate view of Islamic history that in effect elevates the Palestinian national struggle to a position of paramount importance for the *umma* as a whole. This allows Hamas activists to function in the day-to-day political world as fellow travelers with the nationalists. Thus one of the fascinating aspects of Palestinian extremist Salafiyya is a dog that hasn't barked: in contrast to its sibling movements in neighboring countries, Hamas has refrained from labeling the secular leaders in the Palestinian Authority as apostates. Even at the height of Yasir Arafat's crackdown against Hamas, the movement never openly branded him as an idolater.

Like al Qaeda, Hamas argues that a conspiracy between Zionism and the West has dedicated itself to destroying Islam, but for obvious reasons it magnifies the role of Zionism in the alliance. The Hamas Covenant, for example, sees Zionism as, among other things, a force determining many of the greatest historical developments of the modern period:

> [Zionists] were behind the French Revolution, the communist
> revolution... They were behind World War I, when they were
> able to destroy the Islamic caliphate [i.e., the Ottoman Empire]...
> They obtained the Balfour Declaration [favoring establishment of
> a Jewish homeland in Palestine], [and] formed the League of
> Nations, through which they could rule the world. They were
> behind World War II, through which they made huge financial
> gains by trading in armaments, and paved the way for the establish-
> ment of their state. It was they who instigated the replacement
> of the League of Nations with the United Nations and the
> Security Council... There is no war going on anywhere, without
> [them] having their finger in it.

DO A NUMBER of intelligent and educated people actually believe this? Yes, because they must; their self-understanding hinges on it. Since their political struggle must be for the greater good of the *umma* and of Islam as a whole, their enemy must be much more than just one part of the Jewish people with designs on one sliver of Muslim territory. The enemy must be the embodiment of an evil that transcends time and place.

Although the sanctity of Jerusalem works in Hamas' favor, in Islam Jerusalem does not enjoy the status of Mecca and Medina and is only a city, not an entire country. To reconcile its political and religious concerns, therefore, Hamas must inflate the significance of Palestine in Islamic history: "The present Zionist onslaught," the covenant says, "has also been preceded by Crusading raids from the West and other Tatar [Mongol] raids from the East." The references here are to Saladin, the Muslim leader who defeated the Crusaders in Palestine at the battle of Hattin in 1187, and to the Muslim armies that defeated the Mongols at another Palestinian site called Ayn Jalut in 1260. On this basis Hamas argues that Palestine has always been the bulwark against the enemies of Islam; the *umma*, therefore, must rally behind the Palestinians to destroy Israel, which represents the third massive onslaught against the true religion since the death of the Prophet.

Despite the similarities in their perspectives, therefore, al Qaeda and Hamas have quite different agendas. Al Qaeda justifies its political goals on the basis of the holiness of Mecca and Medina and on the claim that the presence of U.S. forces in Arabia constitutes the greatest aggression that the Muslims have ever endured. Hamas sees its own struggle against Israel as the first duty of the *umma*. The two organizations undoubtedly share enough in common to facilitate political cooperation on many issues, but at some point their agendas diverge radically, a divergence that stems from the different priorities inherent in their respective Saudi and Palestinian backgrounds.

The differences between al Qaeda and Hamas demonstrate how local conditions can mold the universal components of Salafi consciousness into distinct world views. They display the creativity of radical Islamists in addressing a practical problem similar to that faced by communists in the early twentieth century: how to build a universal political movement that can nevertheless function effectively at the local level. This explains why, when one looks at the political map of the extremist Salafiyya, one finds a large number of organizations all of which insist that they stand for the same principles. They do, in fact, all insist on the implementation of the *shari`a*, but the specific social and political forces fueling that insistence differ greatly from place to place. They all march to the beat of God's drummer, but the marchers tend to wander off in different directions.

The new tactic of targeting America is designed to overcome precisely this weakness of political Islam. Bin Laden succeeded in attacking Hubal, the universal enemy: he identified the only target that all of the Salafiyya submovements around the world can claim equally as their own, thereby reflecting and reinforcing the collective belief that the *umma* actually is the political community. He and his colleagues adopted this strategy not from choice but from desperation, a desperation born of the fact that in recent years the extremist Salafis had been defeated politically almost everywhere in the Arab and Muslim world. The new tactic, by tapping into the deepest emotions of the political community, smacks of brilliance, and—much to America's chagrin—will undoubtedly give political Islam a renewed burst of energy.

EXPLAINING THE ECHO

THE DECISION TO target the United States allows al Qaeda to play the role of a radical "Salafi International." It resonates beyond the small community of committed extremists, however, reaching not just moderate Salafis but, in addition, a broad range of disaffected citizens experiencing poverty, oppression, and power-lessness across the Muslim world. This broader resonance of what appears to us as such a wild and hateful message is the dimension of the problem that Americans find most difficult to understand.

One reason for the welcoming echo is the extent to which Salafi political movements, while failing to capture state power, have nevertheless succeeded in capturing much cultural ground in Muslim countries. Many authoritarian regimes (such as Mubarak's Egypt) have cut a deal with the extremists: in return for an end to assassinations, the regime acquiesces in some of the demands regarding implementation of the *shari`a*. In addition, it permits the extremist groups to run networks of social welfare organizations that often deliver services more efficiently than does a state sector riddled with corruption and marred by decay. This powerful cultural presence of the Salafis across the Islamic world means not only that their direct ranks have grown but also that their symbolism is more familiar than ever among a wider public.

But the attack on America also resonates deeply among secular groups in many countries. The immediate response in the secular

Arab press, for example, fell broadly into three categories. A minority denounced the attacks forcefully and unconditionally, another minority attributed them to the Israelis or to American extremists like Timothy McVeigh, and a significant majority responded with a version of "Yes, but"—yes, the terrorist attacks against you were wrong, but you must understand that your own policies in the Middle East have for years sown the seeds of this kind of violence.

This rationalization amounts to a political protest against the perceived role of the United States in the Middle East. Arab and Islamic commentators, and a number of prominent analysts of the Middle East in this country, point in particular to U.S. enforcement of the sanctions on Iraq and U.S. support for Israel in its struggle against Palestinian nationalism. Both of these issues certainly cause outrage, and if the United States were to effect the removal of Israeli settlements from the West Bank and alleviate the suffering of the Iraqi people, some of that outrage would certainly subside. But although a change in those policies would dampen some of bin Laden's appeal, it would not solve the problem of the broader anger and despair that he taps, because the sources of those feelings lie beyond the realm of day-to-day diplomacy.

Indeed, secular political discourse in the Islamic world in general and the Arab world in particular bears a striking resemblance to the Salafi interpretation of international affairs, especially insofar as both speak in terms of Western conspiracies. The secular press does not make reference to Crusaders and Mongols but rather to a string of "broken promises" dating back to World War I, when the European powers divided up the Ottoman Empire to suit their own interests. They planted Israel in the midst of the Middle East, so the analysis goes, in order to drive a wedge between Arab states, and the United States continues to support Israel for the same purpose. Bin Laden played to this sentiment in his October 7 statement when he said,

> What the United States tastes today is a very small thing compared to what we have tasted for tens of years. Our nation has been tasting this humiliation and contempt for more than eighty years. Its sons are being killed, its blood is being shed, its holy places are being attacked, and it is not being ruled according to what God has decreed.

Michael Scott Doran

For 80 years—that is, since the destruction of the Ottoman Empire—the Arabs and the Muslims have been humiliated. Although they do not share bin Laden's millenarian agenda, when secular commentators point to Palestine and Iraq today they do not see just two difficult political problems; they see what they consider the true intentions of the West unmasked.

Arab commentators often explain, for instance, that Saddam Hussein and Washington are actually allies. They ridicule the notion that the United States tried to depose the dictator. After all, it is said, the first Bush administration had the forces in place to remove the Baath Party and had called on the Iraqi populace to rise up against the tyrant. When the people actually rose, however, the Americans watched from the sidelines as the regime brutally suppressed them. Clearly, therefore, what the United States really wanted was to divide and rule the Arabs in order to secure easy access to Persian Gulf oil—a task that also involves propping up corrupt monarchies in Kuwait and Saudi Arabia. Keeping Saddam on a leash was the easiest way to ensure that Iran could not block the project.

Needless to say, this world view is problematic. Since World War I, Arab societies have been deeply divided among themselves along ethnic, social, religious, and political lines. Regardless of what the dominant Arab discourse regarding broken promises has to say, most of these divisions were not created by the West. The European powers and the United States have sometimes worked to divide the Arabs, sometimes to unify them. Mostly they have pursued their own interests, as have all the other actors involved. Bin Laden is a participant in a profoundly serious civil war over Arab and Muslim identity in the modern world. The United States is also a participant in that war, because whether it realizes it or not, its policies affect the fortunes of the various belligerents. But Washington is not a primary actor, because it is an outsider in cultural affairs and has only a limited ability to define for believers the role of Islam in public life.

The war between extremist Salafis and the broader populations around them is only the tip of the iceberg. The fight over religion among Muslims is but one of a number of deep and enduring regional struggles that originally had nothing to do with the United

States and even today involve it only indirectly. Nonetheless, U.S. policies can influence the balance of power among the protagonists in these struggles, sometimes to a considerable degree.

Until the Arab and Muslim worlds create political orders that do not disenfranchise huge segments of their own populations, the civil war will continue and will continue to touch the United States. Washington can play an important role in fostering authentic and inclusive polities, but ultimately Arabs and Muslims more generally must learn to live in peace with one another so as to live comfortably with outsiders. Whether they will do so is any-body's guess.

It is a stark political fact that in the Arab and Muslim worlds today economic globalization and the international balance of power both come with an American face, and neither gives much reason for optimism. Osama bin Laden's rhetoric, dividing the world into two camps—the *umma* versus the United States and puppet regimes—has a deep resonance because on some levels it conforms, if not to reality, then at least to its appearances. This is why, for the first time in modern history, the extremist Salafis have managed to mobilize mass popular opinion.

This development is troubling, but the United States still has some cards to play. Its policies, for instance, on both West Bank settlements and Iraq, are sorely in need of review—but only after bin Laden has been vanquished. These policy changes might help, but the root problem lies deeper. Once al Qaeda has been annihilated without sparking anti-American revolutions in the Islamic world, the United States should adopt a set of policies that ensure that significant numbers of Muslims—not Muslim regimes but Muslims—identify their own interests with those of the United States, so that demagogues like bin Laden cannot aspire to speak in the name of the entire *umma*. In 1991, millions of Iraqis consti-tuted just such a reservoir of potential supporters, yet America turned its back on them. Washington had its reasons, but they were not the kind that can be justified in terms of the American values that we trumpet to the world. Today we are paying a price for that hypocrisy. This is not to say that we caused or deserved the attacks of September 11 in any way. It is to say, however, that we are to some extent responsible for the fact that so few in the Arab and Muslim worlds express vocal and unequivocal support for our cause, even when that cause is often their cause as well.

Since the events of September 11, innumerable articles have appeared in the press discussing America's loss of innocence. To foreigners, this view of Americans as naive bumpkins, a band of Forrest Gumps who just arrived in town, is difficult to fathom. Whether the MTV generation knows it or not, the United States has been deeply involved in other peoples' civil wars for a long time. A generation ago, for example, we supposedly lost our innocence in Vietnam. Back then, Adonis, the poet laureate of the Arab world, meditated on the ambivalence Arabs feel toward America. In the aftermath of the September 11 attacks, his poem seems prophetic:

> New York, you will find in my land
> …the stone of Mecca and the waters of the Tigris.
> In spite of all this,
> you pant in Palestine and Hanoi.
> East and west you contend with people
> whose only history is fire.
> These tormented people knew us before we were virgins.

Terror, Islam,
and Democracy

Ladan Boroumand and Roya Boroumand

"WHY?" THAT IS the question that people in the West have been asking ever since the terrible events of September 11. What are the attitudes, beliefs, and motives of the terrorists and the movement from which they sprang? What makes young men from Muslim countries willing, even eager, to turn themselves into suicide bombers? How did these men come to harbor such violent hatred of the West, and especially of the United States? What are the roots—moral, intellectual, political, and spiritual—of the murderous fanaticism we witnessed that day?

As Western experts and commentators have wrestled with these questions, their intellectual disarray and bafflement in the face of radical Islamist (notice we do not say "Islamic") terrorism have become painfully clear. This is worrisome, for however necessary an armed response might seem in the near term, it is undeniable that a successful long-term strategy for battling Islamism and its terrorists will require a clearer understanding of who these foes are, what they think, and how they understand their own motives. For terrorism is first and foremost an ideological and moral challenge to liberal democracy. The sooner the defenders of democracy realize this and grasp its implications, the sooner democracy can prepare itself to win the long-simmering war of ideas and values that exploded into full fury last September 11.

LADAN BOROUMAND is a former visiting fellow at the International Forum for Democratic Studies and a historian from Iran. Her sister ROYA BOROUMAND has been a consultant for Human Rights Watch and is a historian from Iran specializing in contemporary Iranian history. This article originally appeared in the April 2002 issue of *Journal of Democracy* © 2002 by the National Endowment for Democracy and The Johns Hopkins University Press. Reprinted with permission of The Johns Hopkins University Press.

Ladan Boroumand and Roya Boroumand

The puzzlement of liberal democracies in the face of Islamist terrorism seems odd. After all, since 1793, when the word "terror" first came into use in its modern political sense with the so-called Terror of the French Revolution, nearly every country in the West has had some experience with a terrorist movement or regime. Why then does such a phenomenon, which no less than liberal democracy itself is a product of the modern age, appear in this instance so opaque to Western analysts?

Islamist terror first burst onto the world scene with the 1979 Iranian Revolution and the seizure of the U.S. embassy in Tehran in November of that year. Since then, Islamism has spread, and the ideological and political tools that have helped to curb terrorism throughout much of the West have proven mostly ineffective at stopping it. Its presence is global, and its influence is felt not only in the lands of the vast Islamic crescent that extends from Morocco and Nigeria in the west to Malaysia and Mindanao in the east but also in many corners of Europe, India, the former Soviet world, the Americas, and even parts of western China.

Before the Iranian Revolution, terrorism was typically seen as a straightforward outgrowth of modern ideologies. Islamist terrorists, however, claim to fight on theological grounds: A few verses from the Koran and a few references to the *sunna* ("deeds of the Prophet") put an Islamic seal on each operation. The whole ideological fabric appears to be woven from appeals to tradition, ethnicity, and historical grievances both old and new, along with a powerful set of religious-sounding references to "infidels," "idolaters," "crusaders," "martyrs," "holy wars," "sacred soil," "enemies of Islam," "the party of God," and "the great Satan."

But this religious vocabulary hides violent Islamism's true nature as a modern totalitarian challenge to both traditional Islam and modern democracy. If terrorism is truly as close to the core of Islamic belief as both the Islamists and many of their enemies claim, why does international Islamist terrorism date only to 1979? This question finds a powerful echo in the statements of the many eminent Islamic scholars and theologians who have consistently condemned the actions of the Islamist networks.

This is not to say that Islamic jurisprudence and philosophy propound a democratic vision of society or easily accommodate the principles of democracy and human rights. But it does expose the fraudulence of the terrorists' references to Islamic precepts. There is in the history of Islam no precedent for the utterly unrestrained violence of al Qaeda or the Hezbollah. Even the Shi'ite Ismaili sect known as the Assassins, though it used men who were ready to die to murder its enemies, never descended to anything like the random mass slaughter in which the Hezbollah, Osama bin Laden, and his minions glory.[1] To kill oneself while wantonly murdering women, children, and people of all religions and descriptions—let us not forget that Muslims too worked at the World Trade Center—has nothing to do with Islam, and one does not have to be a learned theologian to see this. The truth is that contemporary Islamist terror is an eminently modern practice thoroughly at odds with Islamic traditions and ethics.[2]

A striking illustration of the tension between Islam and terrorism was offered by an exchange that took place between two Muslims in the French courtroom where Fouad Ali Saleh was being tried for his role in a wave of bombings that shook Paris in 1985–86. One of his victims, a man badly burned in one of these attacks, said to Saleh: "I am a practicing Muslim... Did God tell you to bomb babies and pregnant women?" Saleh responded, "You are an Algerian. Remember what [the French] did to your fathers."[3] Challenged regarding the religious grounds of his actions, the terrorist replied not with Koranic verses but with secular nationalist grievances.

The record of Saleh's trial makes fascinating reading. He was a Sunni Muslim, originally from Tunisia, who spent the early 1980s

---

1. Bernard Lewis, *The Assassins: A Radical Sect in Islam* (New York: Oxford University Press, 1987), p.133–34.

2. On the heterodoxy of the Islamists' references to Muslim jurisprudent Ibn Taymiyya (1263–1328), see Olivier Carré, *Mystique et politique: Lecture révolutionnaire du Coran par Sayyid Qutb, Frère musulman radical* (Paris: Cerf, 1984), p.16–17. On Ibn Taymiyya's theology and life, see Henri Laoust, *Pluralisme dans l'Islam* (Paris: Librairie Orientaliste Paul Geuthner, 1983).

3. This account of the Saleh case is based on reports in *Le Monde* (Paris), April 8 and 10 1992.

"studying" at Qom, the Shi'ite theological center in Iran. He received weapons training in Libya and Algeria, and got his explosives from the pro-Iranian militants of Hezbollah. In his defense, he invoked not only the Koran and the Ayatollah Khomeini but also Joan of Arc—who is, among other things, a heroine of the French far right—as an example of someone who "defended her country against the aggressor." After this he read out long passages from *Revolt Against the Modern World* by Julius Evola (1898–1974), an Italian author often cited by European extreme rightists. This strange ideological brew suggests the importance of exploring the intellectual roots of Islamist terrorism.[4]

THE GENEALOGY OF ISLAMISM

THE IDEA OF a "pan-Islamic"[5] movement appeared in the late nineteenth and early twentieth centuries concomitantly with the rapid transformation of traditional Muslim polities into nation-states. The man who did more than any other to lend an Islamic cast to totalitarian ideology was an Egyptian schoolteacher named

---

4. For an overview of the career of Islamist terror networks, see Xavier Raufer, *La Nebuleuse: Le terrorisme du Moyen-Orient* (Paris: Fayard, 1987); Roland Jacquard, *Au nom d'Oussama Ben Laden: Dossier secret sur le terroriste le plus recherché du monde* (Paris: Jean Picollec, 2001); Yossef Bodansky, *Bin Laden: The Man Who Declared War on America* (Rocklin, Calif.: Prima, 1999); Gilles Kepel, *Jihad: Expansion et déclin de l'islamisme* (Paris: Galli-mard, 2000); and Yonah Alexander and Michael S. Swetnam, *Usama Bin Laden's al-Qaida: Profile of a Terrorist Network* (New York: Transnational Publishers, 2001).

5. To confront Western colonialism, Muslim intellectuals and religious scholars such as Sayyid Jamal al-Din 'al-Afghani of Iran and Muhammad Abduh of Egypt concluded that a reformation and a new interpretation of Islam were needed in Muslim societies. The reforms that they advocated were aimed at reconciling Islam and modernity. They sought to promote individual freedom, social justice, and political liberalism. After the First World War, however, this movement was succeeded by one that was hostile to political liberalism. On Afghani, see Nikki K. Keddie, *An Islamic Response to Imperialism: Political and Religious Writings of Sayyid Jamal al-Din 'al-Afghani* (Berkeley: University of California Press, 1983). On Abduh, see Yvonne Haddad, "Muhammad Abduh: Pioneer of Islamic Reform," in Ali Rahnema, ed., *Pioneers of Islamic Revival* (London: Zed, 1994), pp.31–63.

Hassan al-Banna (1906–49). Banna was not a theologian by training. Deeply influenced by Egyptian nationalism, he founded the
Muslim Brotherhood in 1928 with the express goal of counteract-
ing Western influences.[6]

By the late 1930s, Nazi Germany had established contacts
with revolutionary junior officers in the Egyptian army, including
many who were close to the Muslim Brothers. Before long the
Brothers, who had begun by pursuing charitable, associational, and
cultural activities, also had a youth wing, a creed of unconditional
loyalty to the leader, and a paramilitary organization whose slogan
"action, obedience, silence" echoed the "believe, obey, fight" motto
of the Italian Fascists. Banna's ideas were at odds with those of the
traditional *ulema* (theologians), and he warned his followers as early
as 1943 to expect "the severest opposition" from the traditional
religious establishment.[7]

From the Fascists—and behind them, from the European tradition of putatively "transformative" or "purifying" revolutionary
violence that began with the Jacobins—Banna also borrowed the
idea of heroic death as a political art form. Although few in the
West may remember it today, it is difficult to overstate the degree
to which the aestheticization of death, the glorification of armed
force, the worship of martyrdom, and faith in "the propaganda of
the deed" shaped the antiliberal ethos of both the far right and
elements of the far left earlier in the twentieth century. Following
Banna, today's Islamist militants embrace a terrorist cult of martyrdom that has more to do with Georges Sorel's *Réflexions sur la
violence* than with anything in either Sunni or Shi'ite Islam.[8]

After the Allied victory in World War II, Banna's assassination
in early 1949, and the Egyptian Revolution of 1952–54, the Muslim
Brothers found themselves facing the hostility of a secularizing
military government and sharp ideological competition from

---

6. This section draws on David Dean Commins, "Hassan al-Banna
(1906–49)," in Ali Rahnema, ed., *Pioneers of Islamic Revival*, 146–47; as well
as Richard P. Mitchell, *The Society of the Muslim Brothers* (London: Oxford
University Press, 1969). See also Gilles Kepel, *Muslim Extremism in Egypt*
(Berkeley: University of California Press, 1993).

7. Richard P. Mitchell, *The Society of the Muslim Brothers, p.*29.

Egyptian communists. Sayyid Qutb (1906–66), the Brothers' chief spokesman and also their liaison with the communists, framed an ideological response that would lay the groundwork for the Islamism of today.

Qutb was a follower not only of Banna but of the Pakistani writer and activist Sayyid Abu'l-A'la Mawdudi (1903–79), who in 1941 founded the Jamaat-e-Islami-e-Pakistan (Pakistan Islamic Assembly), which remains an important political force in Pakistan, though it cannot claim notable electoral support.[9] Mawdudi's rejection of nationalism, which he had earlier embraced, led to his interest in the political role of Islam. He denounced all nationalism, labeling it as *kufr* (unbelief). Using Marxist terminology, he advocated a struggle by an Islamic "revolutionary vanguard" against both the West and traditional Islam, attaching the adjectives "Islamic" to such distinctively Western terms as "revolution," "state," and "ideology." Though strongly opposed by the Muslim religious authorities, his ideas influenced a whole generation of "modern" Islamists.

Like both of his preceptors, Qutb lacked traditional theological training. A graduate of the state teacher's college, in 1948 he went to study education in the United States. Once an Egyptian nationalist,

---

8. The widespread but mistaken impression that a Shi'ite cult of martyrdom serves as a religious inspiration for suicide attacks is one of the illusions about themselves that the terrorists skillfully cultivate. It is true that Shi'ites revere Hussein (d. 680 C.E.), the third Imam and a grandson of the Prophet, as a holy martyr. Yet Shi'ite teaching also enjoins the avoidance of martyrdom, even recommending *taqieh* ("hiding one's faith") as a way of saving one's life from murderous persecutors. Moreover, Sunnis are not noted for devotion to Hussein, and yet when it comes to suicide attacks, there is little difference between the Sunnis of al Qaeda and the mostly Shi'ite cadres of Hezbollah. There are striking similarities between the Islamist justification for violence and martyrdom and the discourse of German and Italian Marxist terrorists from the 1970s. On this subject see Philippe Raynaud, "Les origines intellectuelles du terrorisme," in François Furet et al., eds., *Terrorisme et démocratie* (Paris: Fayard, 1985), p.65ff.

9. On Mawdudi, see Seyyed Vali Reza Nasr, *The Vanguard of the Islamic Revolution: The Jama'at-i Islami of Pakistan* (Berkeley: University of California Press, 1994); and Seyyed Vali Reza Nasr, *Mawdudi and the Making of Islamic Revivalism* (New York: Oxford University Press, 1996).

he joined the Muslim Brothers soon after returning home in 1950. Qutb's brand of Islamism was informed by his knowledge of both the Marxist and fascist critiques of modern capitalism and representative democracy.[10] He called for a monolithic state ruled by a single party of Islamic rebirth. Like Mawdudi and various Western totalitarians, he identified his own society (in his case, contemporary Muslim polities) as among the enemies that a virtuous, ideologically self-conscious, vanguard minority would have to fight by any means necessary, including violent revolution, so that a new and perfectly just society might arise. His ideal society was a classless one where the "selfish individual" of liberal democracies would be banished and the "exploitation of man by man" would be abolished. God alone would govern it through the implementation of Islamic law *(shari'a)*. This was Leninism in Islamist dress.

When the authoritarian regime of President Gamel Abdel Nasser suppressed the Muslim Brothers in 1954 (it would eventually get around to hanging Qutb in 1966), many went into exile in Algeria, Saudi Arabia,[11] Iraq, Syria, and Morocco. From there, they spread their revolutionary Islamist ideas—including the organizational and ideological tools borrowed from European totalitarianism— by means of a network that reached into numerous religious schools and universities. Most young Islamist cadres today are the direct intellectual and spiritual heirs of the Qutbist wing of the Muslim Brotherhood.

---

10 Olivier Carré, *Mystique et politique, pp.*206–7.

11 Muhammad Qutb, Sayyid Qutb's brother, was among the Muslim Brothers who were welcomed in Saudi Arabia. He was allowed to supervise the publication and distribution of his brother's works, and became ideologically influential in his own right: The official justification for the Saudi penal code uses his definition of secular and liberal societies as a "new era of ignorance." Exiled Muslim Brothers became influential in Saudi Arabia. Wahabism, the intolerant and fanatical brand of Islam that prevails in Saudi Arabia, was not in its origins a modern totalitarian ideology, but it provides fertile ground for the dissemination of terrorist ideology and facilitates the attraction of young Saudis to terrorist groups. See Olivier Carré, *L'utopie islamique dans l'Orient arabe* (Paris: Presses de la Fondation Nationale des Sciences Politiques, 1991), pp.112–14; and Gilles Kepel, *Jihad, pp.*72–75.

Ladan Boroumand and Roya Boroumand

THE IRANIAN CONNECTION

BANNA AND THE BROTHERHOOD advocated the creation of a solidarity network that would reach across the various schools of Islam.[12] Perhaps in part because of this ecumenism, we can detect the Brothers' influence as early as 1945 in Iran, the homeland of most of the world's Shi'ites.

Returning home from Iraq that year, a young Iranian cleric named Navab Safavi started a terrorist group that assassinated a number of secular Iranian intellectuals and politicians. In 1953, Safavi visited Egypt at the Brothers' invitation and presumably met with Qutb. Although Safavi's group was crushed and he was executed after a failed attempt on the life of the prime minister in 1955, several of its former members would become prominent among those who lined up with the Ayatollah Khomeini (1900–89) to mastermind the Islamic Revolution of 1979.

Khomeini himself first took a political stand in 1962, joining other ayatollahs to oppose the shah's plans for land reform and female suffrage. At this point, Khomeini was not a revolutionary but a traditionalist alarmed by modernization and anxious to defend the privileges of his clerical caste. When his followers staged an urban uprising in June 1963, he was arrested and subsequently exiled, first to Turkey, then to Iraq. The turning point came in 1970, when Khomeini, still in Iraq, became one of the very few Shi'ite religious authorities to switch from traditionalism to totalitarianism. Much like Mawdudi,[13] he called for a revolution to create an Islamic state, and inspired by Qutb, he condemned all nontheocratic regimes as idolatrous. His followers in Iran were active in Islamist cultural associations that spread, among others, the ideas of Qutb and Mawdudi. Qutb's ideology was used by Khomeini's students to recapture for the Islamist movement a whole generation influenced by the world's predominant revolutionary culture—Marxism-Leninism.

---

12. Banna's followers recalled that he often said, "Each of the four schools [of Islam] is respectable," and urged, "Let us cooperate in those things on which we can agree and be lenient in those on which we cannot." Richard P. Mitchell, *The Society of the Muslim Brothers, p.217.*

13. Mawdudi, *The Process of Islamic Revolution* (Lahore, 1955).

Khomeini became a major figure in the history of Islamist terrorism because he was the first truly eminent religious figure to lend it his authority. For despite all its influence on the young, Islamism before the Iranian Revolution was a marginal heterodoxy. Qutb and Mawdudi were theological dabblers whom Sunni scholars had refuted and dismissed. Even the Muslim Brothers had officially rejected Qutb's ideas. As an established clerical scholar, Khomeini gave modern Islamist totalitarianism a religious respectability that it had sorely lacked.

Once in power, the onetime opponent of land reform and women's suffrage became a "progressivist," launching a massive program of nationalization and expropriation and recruiting women for campaigns of revolutionary propaganda and mobilization. The Leninist characteristics of his rule—his policy of terror, his revolutionary tribunals and militias, his administrative purges, his cultural revolution, and his accommodating attitude toward the USSR—alienated the majority of his fellow clerics but also gained him the active support of the Moscow-aligned Iranian Communist Party, which from 1979 to 1983 put itself at the service of the new theocracy.

Khomeini's revolution was not an exclusively Shi'ite phenomenon. Not accidentally, one of the first foreign visitors who showed up to congratulate him was the Sunni Islamist Mawdudi; before long, Qutb's face was on an Iranian postage stamp. Khomeini's successor, Ali Khamenei, translated Qutb into Persian.[14] Khomeini's own interest in creating an "Islamist International"—it would later be known by the hijacked Koranic term Hezbollah ("party of God")—was apparent as early as August 1979.

THE ISLAMIST "COMINTERN"

AS THESE TIES SUGGEST, Islamism is a self-consciously pan-Muslim phenomenon. It is a waste of time and effort to try to distinguish Islamist terror groups from one another according

---

14. See Baqer Moin, *Khomeini: Life of the Ayatollah* (London: I.B. Tauris, 1999), p.246.

to their alleged differences along a series of traditional religious, ethnic, or political divides (Shi'ite versus Sunni, Persian versus Arab, and so on). The reason is simple: *In the eyes of the Islamist groups themselves, their common effort to strike at the West while seizing control of the Muslim world is immeasurably more important than whatever might be seen as "dividing" them from one another.*

The Lebanese-based, Iranian-supported Hezbollah is a case in point. Its Iranian founder was a hardcore Khomeini aide who drew his inspiration from a young Egyptian Islamist—an engineer by training, not a theologian—who was the first to politicize what had been a purely religious term. A closer look at the organization reveals the strong influence of Marxism-Leninism on the ideology of its founders and leadership. The group's current leader, Mohammad Hosein Fadlallah, influenced by Marx's and Nietzsche's theories on violence,[15] has openly advocated terrorist methods and tactical alliances with leftist organizations.[16] Hezbollah is a successful creation of the Islamist "Comintern." "We must," says Sheikh Fadlallah, "swear allegiance to the leader of the [Iranian] revolution and to the revolutionaries as to God himself," because "this revolution is the will of God."[17] One indication of the extent of this allegiance is the fact that all the negotiations over the fate of the hostages held in Lebanon ended up being carried out by Tehran. Similarly, the head of Iran's Revolutionary Guards boasted about having sponsored the attack against French and American peacekeeping forces in Lebanon.[18] Hezbollah's chief military planner, Imad Mughaniyyah, is an Arab who operates from Iran. Western intelligence agencies suspect that Hezbollah has been working with bin Laden on international operations since the

---

15. Cited in Olivier Carré, *L'utopie islamique dans l'Orient arabe*, p.197.

16. Cited in Olivier Carré, *L'utopie islamique dans l'Orient arabe*, p.231–32.

17.Olivier Carré, *L'utopie islamique dans l'Orient arabe*, p.232.

18. The then-head of the Iranian Revolutionary Guards, Mohsen Rafiqdoust, said that "both the TNT and the ideology which in one blast sent to hell 400 officers, NCOs, and soldiers at the Marine headquarters have been provided by Iran." *Resalat* (Tehran), July 20, 1987.

early 1990s.[19] Hezbollah's terrorist network in Lebanon contains both Shi'ite and Sunni groups, and there is also a Saudi Arabian wing that was involved in the Khobar Towers bombing, which killed 19 U.S. troops in 1996.

Also inspired by the Iranian Revolution was the independent Sunni terrorist network that later became the basis of al-Qaeda. The Tehran regime began forming propaganda organs to sway opinion among Sunni religious authorities as early as 1982.[20] Among the supranational institutions created was the World Congress of Friday Sermons Imams, which at one time had a presence in no fewer than 40 countries. The overarching goal of these efforts has been to mobilize the "Islam of the people" against the "reactionary Islam of the establishment."[21]

For a variety of reasons this network has remained loosely organized, but all of its branches spring from and are fed by the same ideological taproot.

The influence of Iran's Islamist revolution was also cited by the members of Egyptian Islamic Jihad who gunned down President Anwar Sadat in October 1981. Their theoretician was an engineer, Abdessalam Faraj, who was also fond of quoting Qutb to justify terror.[22] The conspirators—including the junior army officers who did the actual shooting—were inspired by the Iranian model, and expected the death of Sadat to trigger a mass uprising that would replay in Cairo the same sort of events which had taken place two years earlier in Tehran[23] (where the Iranian authorities would

---

19. On March 22, 1998, the *Times of London* reported that bin Laden and the Iranian Revolutionary Guards had signed a pact the previous February 16 to consolidate their operations in Albania and Kosovo. Roland Jacquard adds that in September 1999, the Turkish intelligence services learned of an Islamist group financed by bin Laden in the Iranian city of Tabriz. See Roland Jacquard, *Au nom d'Oussama Ben Laden*, pp.287–88.

20. The first conference on the unification of Islamist movements was organized under Iranian auspices in January 1982. See the speeches of Khamenei and Mohammad Khatami (who is now the elected president of the Islamic Republic) in *Etela'at* (Tehran), January 9, 1982.

21. Xavier Rauffer, *La Nebuleuse*, p.175.

22. Charles Tripp, "Sayyid Qutb: The Political Vision," in Ali Rahnema, ed., *Pioneers of Islamic Revival*, pp.178–79.

23. Gilles Kepel, *Jihad*, pp.122–23.

subsequently name a street after Sadat's killer). Among those impris-
oned in connection with the plot was a Cairo physician named
Ayman al-Zawahiri. He became Egyptian Islamic Jihad's leader after
serving his three-year prison term, met bin Laden in 1985, and then
joined him in Sudan in the early 1990s. Zawahiri, who would become
al-Qaeda's top operational planner, is reported to have said publicly
that Osama is "the new Che Guevara."[24]

The Islamization of the Palestinian question is also partly due
to Khomeini's influence on the Palestinian branch of Islamic
Jihad. Its founder was another physician, this one named Fathi
Shqaqi. His 1979 encomium *Khomeini: The Islamic Alternative* was
dedicated to both the Iranian ruler and Hassan al-Banna ("the two
men of this century"). The first press run of 10,000 sold out in a
few days.[25] Shqaqi, who was of course a Sunni, had nonetheless
traveled to Tehran to share the Friday sermon podium with Ali
Khameini, denouncing the Mideast peace process and accusing
Yasser Arafat of treason.[26]

DISTORTING ISLAM'S HISTORY AND TEACHINGS

AS THESE EXAMPLES SHOW, such distinctions as may exist among
these terrorist groups are overshadowed by their readiness to coalesce
and collaborate according to a common set of ideological beliefs.
These beliefs are properly called "Islamist" rather than "Islamic"
because they are actually in conflict with Islam—a conflict that we
must not allow to be obscured by the terrorists' habit of commandeer-
ing Islamic religious terminology and injecting it with their own distorted content. One illustration is the Islamists' interpretation of the
hijra—Mohammed's journey, in September 622 C.E., from Mecca to
Medina to found the first fully realized and autonomous Islamic
community *(umma)*. Despite a wealth of historical and doctrinal evidence to the contrary, half-educated Islamists insist on portraying this
journey as a revolutionary rupture with existing society that licenses

---

24. Roland Jacquard, *Au nom d'Oussama Ben Laden*, 76.
25. Gilles Kepel, *Jihad*, 187 and 579.
26. As reported in *Jomhouri-e Islami* (Tehran), 5 March 1994 (14 esfand
1372), 14 and 2.

their desire to excommunicate contemporary Muslim societies in favor of their own radically utopian vision.

The Islamic Republic of Iran also rests on heterodoxy, in this case Khomeini's novel and even idiosyncratic theory of the absolute power of the single, supreme Islamic jurisprudent *(faqih)*. It was not a coincidence that one of the first uprisings against Khomeini's regime took place under the inspiration of a leading ayatollah, Shariat Madari.[27] Officials of the regime have admitted that most Iranian clerics have always taken a wary view of Khomeinism. It is important to realize that the religious references which Khomeini used to justify his rule were literally the same as those invoked a century earlier by an eminent ayatollah who was arguing for the legitimacy of parliamentarism and popular sovereignty on Islamic grounds.[28] Koranic verses lend themselves to many different and even contradictory interpretations. It is thus to something other than Islamic religious sources that we must look if we want to understand Islamism and the war that it wages on its own society, a war in which international terrorism is only one front.

In a brief article on bin Laden's 1998 declaration of *jihad* against the United States, Bernard Lewis showed brilliantly how bin Laden travestied matters not only of fact (for instance, by labeling the invited U.S. military presence in Saudi Arabia a "crusader" invasion) but also of Islamic doctrine, by calling for the indiscriminate butchery of any and all U.S. citizens, wherever they can be found in the world. Reminding his readers that Islamic law *(shari'a)* holds *jihad* to be nothing but a regular war and subject to the rules that limit such conflicts, Lewis concluded, "At no point do the basic texts of Islam enjoin terrorism and murder. At no point do they even consider the random slaughter of uninvolved bystanders."[29]

---

27. Reported in the daily *Khalq-e Mosalman*, December 4 and 9, 1979.

28. M.H. Naïni, *Tanbih al-Omma va Tanzih al-mella*, 5th ed. (Tehran, 1979), pp.75–85.

29. Bernard Lewis, "License to Kill: Usama bin Ladin's Declaration of Jihad," *Foreign Affairs* (November/December 1998): p.19. Bin Laden's declaration of *jihad* mentions Ibn Taymiyya's authority and yet clearly contradicts the latter's ideas on *jihad.* Ibn Taymiyya explicitly forbids the murder of civilians and submits *jihad* to strict rules and regulations. See Henri Laoust, *Le traité de droit public d'Ibn Taimiya* (annotated translation of *Siyasa shar'iya*) (Beirut, 1948), p.122–35.

What gives force to the terrorist notion of *jihad* invented by the Iranians and later embraced by bin Laden is not its Koranic roots— there are none—but rather the brute success of terrorist acts. Bin Laden has spoken with particular admiration of the Iranian-sponsored suicide truck bombing that killed 241 U.S. Marines and others in Beirut on October 23, 1983, precipitating the U.S. withdrawal from Lebanon.[30] Bin Laden was also not the first to think of setting up training camps for international terrorists—the Tehran authorities were there before him.[31]

A Friday sermon given in 1989 by one of these authorities, Ali-Akbar Hashemi Rafsanjani, then president of the Islamic Parliament, reveals better than any other the logic of Islamist terrorism. Attacking the existence of Israel as another front in the pervasive war of unbelief *(kufr)* against Islam, Rafsanjani added:

> If for each Palestinian killed today in Palestine five Americans, English, or French were executed, they would not commit such acts anymore... [T]here are Americans everywhere in the world... [They] protect Israel. Does their blood have any value? Scare them outside Palestine, so that they don't feel safe... There are a hundred thousand Palestinians in a country. They are educated, and they work... [T]he factories that serve the enemies of Palestine function thanks to the work of the Palestinians. Blow up the factory. Where you work, you can take action... Let them call you terrorists... They [the "imperialism of information and propaganda"] commit crimes and call it human rights. We call it the defense of rights and of an oppressed people... They will say the president of the Parliament officially incites to terror... [L]et them say it.[32]

THERE IS NO reference here to religion; Rafsanjani's appeal is purely political. The West's offense he calls human rights; against it he urges Muslims to wield terror as the best weapon for defending

---

30. See "Declaration of war against the Americans occupying the land of the two holy places: A Message from Usama bin Muhammad bin Laden unto his Muslim Brethren all over the world generally and in the Arab Peninsula specifically" (23 August 1996), in Yonah Alexander and Michael S. Swetnam, *Usama Bin Laden's al-Qaida*, 13.

31. In 1989, the vice-president of Parliament, Hojatol-Eslam Karoubi, proposed the creation of training camps for the "anti-imperialist struggle in the region." Quoted in the daily *Jomhouri-e Eslami* (Tehran) May 9, 1989 p.9.

32. *Jomhouri-e Eslami* (Tehran), May 7, 1989, 11.

the rights of an oppressed people. Rafsanjani, moreover, proudly commends "terror" by name, using the English word and not a Persian or Arabic equivalent. Thus he employs the very term that Lenin had borrowed from *la Terreur* of the French Revolution. The line from the guillotine and the Cheka to the suicide bomber is clear.

With this in mind, let us look for a moment at the French Revolution, where the modern concept of political terror was invented, to find the explanation that the Islamic tradition cannot give. When it announced its policy of terror in September 1793, the "virtuous minority" which then ran the revolutionary government of France was declaring war on its own society. At the heart of this war was a clash between two understandings of "the people" in whose name this government claimed to rule. One was a group of 25 million actually existing individuals, each endowed with inherent rights. The other was an essentially ideological construct, an abstraction, an indivisible and mystical body, its power absolute. The Terror of the French Revolution was neither a mistake nor an unfortunate accident; it was meant to purify this mystical body of what the terrorist elite regarded as corrupting influences, among which they numbered the notion that individual human beings had unalienable rights.[33]

The spokesmen of the Islamist revolution echo the terrorists of Jacobin France. The denigration of human rights marks the spot where the internal war on Muslim society meets the terrorist war against the West. Suffice it to hear bin Laden's comments on the destruction of the World Trade Center: "Those awesome symbolic towers that speak of liberty, human rights, and humanity have been destroyed. They have gone up in smoke."[34] Every Islamist terror campaign against Westerners during the last 20 years has had as its cognate an Islamist effort to tyrannize over a

33. In this connection, it is worth noting that after the end of the Terror, the Declaration of the Rights of Man and the Citizen was not officially restored to constitutional status in France until 1946.

34. Howard Kurtz, "Interview Sheds Light on Bin Laden's Views," *Washington Post*, February 7, 2002, A12. Bin Laden gave this interview to Tayseer Alouni of the Arabiclanguage satellite television network al-Jazeera in October 2001.

Muslim population somewhere in the world. Think of the ordeal to which the Taliban and al Qaeda subjected the people of Afghanistan, or of what ordinary Algerians suffered during the savage Islamist civil wars of the 1990s. Or think of the state terror that daily labors to strangle any hope for recognition of human rights in Iran. To explore fully this correlation between terror against the West and tyranny against Muslims would take a separate essay. Yet we can get an idea of its nature by considering the first instance of Islamist terrorism against the United States, the 1979 hostage-taking in Tehran.

HOLDING DEMOCRACY HOSTAGE TO TERROR

As THEY RELEASED the hostages in January 1981, the Tehran authorities crowed over their victory, which Prime Minster Mohammad Ali Rajai called "the greatest political gain in the social history of the world" and an act that "had forced the greatest satanic power to its knees." At first glance this claim might seem foolish, for the United States had said no to the revolutionary government's demands to hand over the shah and unfreeze Iranian assets. But a closer look shows that the Iranian Islamists had in fact scored a big political and ideological victory over both the United States and their domestic opponents, and thus had ample cause for jubilation.

The seizure of the U.S. embassy took place at a time when Khomeini and his allies had not yet consolidated their tyrannical regime. An Assembly of Experts was drafting the constitution of the Islamic Republic. Opposition was gaining strength daily in religious as well as in moderate secular circles. The Marxist-Leninist left, angered by a ban on its press, was growing restive. Open rebellions were breaking out in sensitive border regions populated by ethnic Kurds and Azeris. By sending in its cadres of radical students to take over the U.S. embassy and hold its staff hostage, the regime cut through the Gordian knot of these challenges at a single blow and even put itself in a position to ram through its widely criticized Constitution. Rafsanjani's assessment of what the act meant is instructive:

In the first months of the revolution, the Washington White House decided in favor of a coup d'état in Iran. The idea was to infiltrate Iranian groups and launch a movement to annihilate the revolution. But the occupation of the embassy and the people's assault against the U.S.A. neutralized this plan, pushing the U.S. into a defensive stand.[35]

ONE COULD DESCRIBE this version of the facts as a parody: The U.S. government in 1979 clearly had neither the will nor the ability to stage a coup against the Islamic Republic. But totalitarians typically speak an esoteric language of their own devising. Those who administered the Terror in revolutionary France painted some of their country's best known republicans with the label "monarchist" before sending them off to be guillotined. The Bolsheviks called striking workers and the sailors of Kronstadt "bandits" and "counterrevolutionaries" before slaughtering them. In 1979, promoting human rights was a prominent aspect of how the United States described its foreign policy. By Rafsanjani's logic, therefore, any Iranian group that spoke of human rights was thereby revealing itself as a tool of the United States.

And indeed, as muddled negotiations over the hostages dragged on, the administration of President Jimmy Carter dropped any talk of supporting democracy in Iran[36]—the very cause for which Carter had taken the risk of ending U.S. support for the shah. Meanwhile, the revolutionary regime began using the Stalinist tactic of claiming that anyone who spoke in favor of a more representative government was really a U.S. agent.[37] With the hostage crisis, the Islamist regime was able to make

---

35. Ali-Akbar Hashemi Rafsanjani, *Enqelabe va defa'e Moqadass* (Revolution and its sacred defense) (Tehran: Press of the Foundation of 15 Khordad, 1989), pp.63–64.

36. Russell Leigh Moses, *Freeing the Hostages: Reexamining U.S.-Iranian Negotiations and Soviet Policy, 1979–1981* (Pittsburgh: University of Pittsburgh Press, 1996), pp.174–75.

37. In an interview that ran in the Tehran daily *Jomhouri-e Eslami* on November 4, 1981 to mark the second anniversary of the embassy seizure, student-radical leader Musavi Khoeiniha remarked that the neutralization of Iranian liberals and democrats was the hostage-taking's most important result.

anti-Americanism such a leading theme that Iranian Marxists rallied to its support, while Moscow extended its tacit protection to the new theocracy.

After the failure of the U.S. military's "Desert One" rescue attempt on April 25, 1980 and eight more months of negotiations, the United States at last succeeded in obtaining the release of the hostages. To do so, it had to agree to recognize the legitimacy of the Iranian revolutionary regime, and it had to promise not to file any complaints against Iran before international authorities, despite the gross violations of human rights and international law that had occurred. Though these concessions may have appeared necessary at the time, in retrospect we can see that they emboldened the Islamists to sink to new levels of hatred and contempt for the West and its talk of human rights. For had not the revolutionary students and clerics in Tehran forced the Great Satan to abandon its principles and brought it to its knees?

The terrorists accurately assessed the extent of their victory and drew conclusions from it. They used terror to achieve their goal, and upon the continued use of terror their survival depends. "[America] is on the defensive. If tomorrow it feels safe, then it will think to implement its imperialistic projects."[38] Among these projects are human rights, which a representative of the Islamic Republic denounced before the U.N. Human Rights Committee as an "imperialist myth."[39]

From the taking of the hostages in Tehran in 1979 until the terrorist attacks of last September, Western policymakers too often implicitly downgraded the claims of justice and shirked their duty both to their own citizens and to the cause of human rights by refusing to pursue the terrorists with any real determination. Considerations of "pragmatism" and "prudence" were put forward to justify a sellout of justice which, in one of the cruelest ironies revealed by the harsh light of September 11, proved not to have been prudent at all.

---

38. Ali-Akbar Hashemi Rafsanjani, *Enqelabe va defa'e Moqadass,* p.64.

39. *Amnesty International Newsletter,* September 1982. The representative was Hadi Khosroshahi, another translator of Sayyid Qutb.

Since the impunity granted to the hostage-takers of Tehran, terrorist outrages have increased both in frequency and in scale. In addition to all the questions raised about security measures, intelligence failures, accountability in foreign-policy decision making, and the like, the atrocity of September 11 also forces citizens of democratic countries to ask themselves how strongly they are committed to democratic values. Their enemies may believe in a chimera, but it is one for which they have shown themselves all too ready to die. In the mirror of the terrorists' sacrifice, the citizens of the free world are called to examine their consciences; they must reevaluate the nature of their loyalty to fragile and imperfect democracy. In particular, the strongly solidaristic networks that the Islamist totalitarians have created should make citizens in democratic societies ask how much they and their governments have done to help prodemocracy activists who have been persecuted for years in Iran, in Algeria, in Afghanistan, in Sudan, and elsewhere. Unarmed, they stand on the front lines of the struggle against terror and tyranny, and they deserve support. Here is moral, political, and even philosophical challenge upon which the minds and hearts of the West should focus.

WHITHER THE MUSLIM WORLD?

ISLAMIST TERROR POSES a different but no less grave problem for those of us (including the authors of this essay) who come from Islamic countries, and it carries a special challenge for Muslim intellectuals. Public opinion in the Muslim world has largely—if perhaps too quietly—condemned the massacres of September 11. In Iran, young people poured spontaneously into the streets, braving arrest and police violence in order to hold candlelight vigils for the victims. But there were also outbursts of celebration in some Muslim countries, and sizeable anti-American demonstrations in Pakistan. Perhaps more disturbing still have been the persistent and widespread rumors going around Muslim societies that somehow an Israeli conspiracy was behind the attack. The force and pervasiveness of this rumor are symptoms of a collective flight from an uncontrollable reality. It is true that the Palestinian question is a painful and complicated one that requires an equitable solution. But it is equally true that reaching for foreign conspiracies has become an easy way of evading responsibility for too many of us from Muslim countries.

For the last several centuries, the Islamic world has been undergoing a traumatizing encounter with the West. Since this encounter began, our history has been a story of irreversible modernization, but also of utter domination on the one side, and humiliation and resentment on the other. To Muslim minds the West and its ways have become a powerful myth—evil, impenetrable, and incomprehensible. Whatever the Western world's unfairness toward Muslims, it remains true that Western scholars have at least made the effort to learn about and understand the Islamic world. But sadly, the great and brilliant works of the West's "Orientalists" have found no echo in a Muslim school of "Occidentalism."

We have been lacking the ability or the will to open up to others. We have opted for an easy solution, that of disguising in the clothes of Islam imported Western intellectual categories and concepts. In doing so we have not only failed to grasp the opportunity to understand the West, we have also lost the keys to our own culture. Otherwise, how could a degenerate Leninism aspire today to pass itself off as the true expression of a great monotheistic religion? The Islamists see themselves as bold warriors against modernity and the West, but in fact it is they who have imported and then dressed up in Islamic-sounding verbiage some of the most dubious ideas that ever came out of the modern West, ideas which now—after much death and suffering—the West itself has generally rejected. Had we not become so alien to our own cultural heritage, our theologians and intellectuals might have done a better job of exposing the antinomy between what the Islamists say and what Islam actually teaches. They might have more effectively undercut the terrorists' claim to be the exclusive and immediate representatives of God on earth, even while they preach a doctrine that does nothing but restore human sacrifice, as if God had never sent the angel to stop Abraham from slaying his son.

Our incapacity to apprehend reality lies at the root of our paranoia. If we were to take a clear and careful look at the West, we would see that it draws its strength from its capacity for introspection and its intransigent self-criticism. We would know that Western culture has never stopped calling on us, on the figure of the stranger, to help it understand itself and fight its vices. When it could not find the other, it invented it: Thomas More imagined a faraway island called Utopia to mirror the social problems of his time; Michel de Montaigne couched his criticisms of French politics in the form of a conversation with an Indian chief from Brazil; and Montesquieu invented letters from a Persian tourist to denounce the vices of Europe.

Had we had our own eminent experts on Western civilization, we might know that the West is a diverse, plural, and complex entity. Its political culture has produced horrors but also institutions that protect human dignity. One of these horrors was the imperialism imposed on Muslim and other lands, but even that did as much harm to the Europeans themselves as it did to us, as anyone familiar with the casualty figures from the First World War will know. Our experts might have helped us understand that Qutb and Khomeini's denunciations of human rights were remarkably similar to Pope Pius VI's denunciation of the French Declaration of the Rights of Man of 1789. We might have grasped that, not long ago, Westerners faced the same obstacles that we face today on the road to democracy. Citizens in the West fought for their freedoms; in this fight they lost neither their souls nor their religion. We too must roll up our sleeves to fight for freedom, remembering that we are first and foremost free and responsible human beings whom God has endowed with dignity.

ACKNOWLEDGEMENTS

We would like to thank Hormoz Hekmat for his useful comments and critiques and Laith Kubba for providing some useful information.

Beyond bin Laden: Reshaping U.S. Foreign Policy

Stephen M. Walt

THE TERRORIST ATTACKS that destroyed the World Trade Center and damaged the Pentagon triggered the most rapid and dramatic change in the history of U.S. foreign policy.[1] On September 10, 2001, there was not the slightest hint that the United States was about to embark on an all-out campaign against "global terrorism." Indeed, apart from an explicit disdain for certain multilateral agreements and a fixation on missile defense, the foreign policy priorities of George W. Bush and his administration were not radically different from those of their predecessors. Bush had already endorsed continued NATO expansion, reluctantly agreed to keep U.S. troops in the Balkans, reaffirmed the existing policy of wary engagement with Russia and China, and called for further efforts to liberalize global markets. The administration's early attention focused primarily on domestic issues, and new international initiatives were notably absent.

The business-as-usual approach to foreign policy vanished on September 11. Instead of education reform and tax cuts, the war on terrorism dominated the administration's agenda. The United States quickly traced the attacks to al Qaeda—the network of Islamic extremists led by Saudi exile Osama bin Laden—whose leaders had

---

STEPHEN M. WALT is Robert and Renee Belfer Professor of International Affairs at the John F. Kennedy School of Government, Harvard University. This article was originally published in the Winter 2001/2002 issue of *International Security* © 2001 by the President and Fellows of Harvard College and the Massachusetts Institute of Technology.

been operating from Afghanistan since 1996. When the Taliban government in Afghanistan rejected a U.S. ultimatum to turn over bin Laden, the United States began military efforts to eradicate al Qaeda and overthrow the Taliban itself.[2] The United States also began a sustained diplomatic campaign to enlist foreign help in rooting out any remaining terrorist organizations "with global." U.S. officials emphasized that this campaign would be prolonged and warned that military action against suspected terrorist networks might continue after the initial assault on al-Qaeda and its Taliban hosts.[3]

This article analyzes how the campaign against global terrorism alters the broad agenda of U.S. foreign policy. I focus primarily on the diplomatic aspects of this campaign and do not address military strategy, homeland defense, or the need for improved intelligence in much detail. These issues are obviously important but lie outside the bounds of this essay.

---

1. Germany's decision to resume unrestricted submarine warfare in January 1917 brought the United States into World War 1, but the United States had come close to war the previous year, and the submarine campaign was merely the final straw. The Japanese attack on Pearl Harbor in December 1941 was as shocking as were the events o f September 11, but the United States and Japan were already on a collision course, and the attack merely facilitated President Franklin Roosevelt's efforts to enter the war. The Soviet testing of an atomic bomb in 1949 and the North Korean invasion of South Korea in 1950 combined to trigger U.S. rearmament, but the basic architecture of containment was already in place when the Korean War broke out, and the U.S. response did not involve a compete reversal of policy. The most comparable event is the U.S. response to the fall of France in 1940, which reversed the tide of isolationism and began the movement toward entry into World War II.

2. In an apparent effort to split the Taliban and to accommodate Pakistan's desire that any postwar Afghani regime be friendly to Pakistan, U.S. officials have indicated that "moderate" members of the current regime might be incorporated into a postwar coalition government. See "U.S. and Pakistan 'Share Afghan Goal,' " *BBC News Online/South Asia,* October 16, 2001, http://www.news.bbc.co.uk/english/world/south_asia; and "Afghan King Said to Agree to Role in Kabul for Taliban," *New York Times,* October 19, 2001, p. B4.

3. In a letter to the United Nations Security Council, U.S. Ambassador John Negroponte stated that the U.S. inquiry into the September 11 attacks was "in the early stages" and noted that "we may find that our self-defense requires further actions with respect to other organizations and other states." See Christopher S. Wren, "U.S. Advises U.N. Council More Strikes Could Come," *New York Times,* October 9, 2001, p. B5.

I proceed in three stages. The first section considers what the events of September 11 tell us about the U.S. position in the world and identifies four lessons that should inform U.S. policy in the future. The second section explores how the campaign on terrorism should alter the foreign policy agenda in the near-to-medium term: What new policies should the United States pursue, and what prior goals should be downgraded or abandoned? The third section addresses the long-term implications, focusing on whether the United States will be willing to accept the increased costs of its current policy of global engagement. I argues that this decisions will depend in part on the success of the current campaign, but also on whether the United States can make its dominant global position more palatable to other countries.

WHAT DID WE LEARN ON SEPTEMBER 11?

THE ATTACK ON the United States did not alter every aspect of world politics, but it did underscore several aspects of U.S. foreign policy that have received insufficient attention in recent years. Understanding these lessons will be essential both to the immediate campaign against al-Qaeda and to any subsequent effort to reduce the overall danger from global terrorism.

LESSON #1: U.S. FOREIGN POLICY IS NOT COST-FREE

SINCE THE EARLY 1990S, U.S. leaders have acted as if the United States could pursue ambitious foreign policy goals without having to make significant sacrifices.[4] The public at large seems to have

---

4. Among other things, the United States has taken the following actions: (1) expanded the core alliances created during the Cold War; (2) fought a brief but intense war to liberate Kuwait after the Iraqi invasion of August 1990; (3) sought to compel Iraqi compliance with the U.N. weapons inspection regime through a combination of economic sanctions and coercive bombings; (4) intervened in civil conflicts in Haiti, Bosnia, Kosovo, and Somalia; (5) attempted to broker a final peace agreement between Israel and the Palestinians; and (6) sought to foster a more liberal world economy through the creation of the World Trade Organization and the negotiation of the North American Free Trade Association.

shared this view, to judge by the low importance it has attached to international issues since the 1980s.[5] With an economy that produces one-quarter of gross world product and defense spending equal to the next seven countries combined, and protected by two oceanic moats, it is not surprising that Americans thought they could act with relative impunity.

This sense of hubris grew with the U.S. victory in the Cold War and was reinforced even more by the record of the past ten years. Although U.S. military forces have been remarkably busy, the human and economic costs of these activities to the United States have been extraordinarily low. Casualties in the 1991 Persian Gulf War were far lower than expected, and the U.S. Air Force has patrolled the no-fly zone in Iraq and conducted intermittent bombing raids there for nearly a decade without losing a single plane. Subsequent U.S. interventions in Haiti, Somalia, Bosnia, and Kosovo led to fewer than fifty U.S. deaths (the greatest number of them in the ill-fated attempt to capture Somali warlord Mohammed Farah Aideed). This record is an admirable military achievement, but it reinforced the belief that the United States could run the world without risking much of its own blood or treasure. Anti-American terrorists did stage several costly attacks on U.S. forces overseas (most recently the bombing of the USS *Cole* in October 2000), but previous attempts on U.S. soil failed to do extensive damage and probably

---

5. According to a 1998 survey by the Chicago Council on Foreign Relations, American did not place any foreign policy issue among the top-seven "biggest problems facing the nation." When Americans were asked to identify "two or three biggest foreign policy problems facing the United States today," the most common answer (at 21 percent) was "don't know." See John E. Rielly, ed., *American Public Opinion and U.S. Foreign Policy, 1999* (Chicago: Chicago Council on Foreign Relations, 1999), pp.2-8. Ole Holsti recently analyzed a diverse array of survey results and concluded that there is still broad public support for an active U.S. role in the world, but he also found "compelling evidence that foreign an defense policy have lost a good deal of their salience for the general public." See Holsti, "Public Opinion and Foreign Policy," in Robert J. Lieber, ed., *Eagle Rules? Foreign Policy and American Primacy in the Twenty-first Century* (Upper Saddle River, N.J.: Prentice-Hall, 2001), p.41.

contributed to the sense of complacency.[6] The 1990s was also a period of sustained economic growth, which reinforced U.S. self-confidence and made it easier to bear international burdens without feeling a fiscal pinch.[7]

LESSON #2: THE UNITED STATES IS LESS POPULAR THAN IT THINKS

AMERICANS ARE PRONE to see their country as a "shining city on a hill" (as President Ronald Reagan liked to say) and often assume that other societies admire the United States and appreciate its global role. Yet both the September 11 attacks and the international response to them underscore the degree to which many people outside the United States are actually ambivalent about the U.S. position in the world. At one extreme, terrorist organizations such as al Qaeda are inspired by an intense antipathy toward the United States and its global dominance. Some of this antipathy arises from a particular vision of the United Sates as a corrupt and godless society, but it is also fueled by America's close relationship with Israel, its support for several conservative Arab regimes, and its seemingly endless conflict with Iraq. In the eyes of these radical anti-U.S. extremists, the United States

---

6. The February 1993 attempt to blow up the World Trade Center killed six people but did not bring down the buildings. Elementary blunders led to the rapid apprehension of several of the perpetrators, which may have caused the United States to underestimate the ability of similar groups to stage more sophisticated attacks.

7. Even sophisticated scholars of international politics succumbed to this optimistic vision of U.S. global dominance. Thus William C. Wohlforth argued that U.S. dominance was (1) a major cause of great power peace; (2) unlikely to provoke significant oppositions; and (3) relatively easy maintain. See Wohlforth, "The Stability of a Unipolar World," *International Security*, Vol. 24, No.1 (Summer 1999), p. 5-41. Similarly, Joseph S. Nye's emphasis on America's, "soft power" implied that the U.S. ability to shape the world was even greater than its material preponderance suggested. See Nye, *Bound to Lead: The Chasing Nature of American Power* (New York: Basic Books, 1990). The recent growth of anti-U.S. attitudes has led Nye to qualify his views somewhat; see especially Nye, *The Paradox of American Power* (New York: Oxford University Press, forthcoming).

is a global bully whose interference in the Islamic world must be resisted by any means necessary.[8]

Although the vast majority of Arabs and Muslims reject al Qaeda's methods, hostility toward the United States is widespread in the Arab and Islamic world. This phenomenon explains why Arab support for the war on terrorism has been relatively limited and why Afghanistan's neighbors have been reluctant to give the U.S. military forces unqualified access to their own territory.

Concerns about the U.S. role are not confined to the Arab or Islamic world, however. Throughout the 1990s, Russia, China, and India accused the United States of ignoring their interests and trying to impose its own preferences on the rest of the world.[9] Such worries led Russia and China to negotiate a friendship treaty in July 2001, which one Russian commentator described as an "act of friendship against America."[10] Even traditional U.S. allies have been concerned about the concentration of power in U.S. hands and Washington's penchant for unilateralism, and they have searched

---

8. See Fareed Zakaria, "Why Do They Hate Us?" *Newsweek*, October 15, 2001, pp. 22-40; Martin Davis, "Bin Laden, the Believer," *National Journal*, September 29, 2001, pp. 2982-2983; Roula Khalaf, "Why They Hate," *Financial Times*, October 5, 2001, p. 20; and David Gardner, "An Eye for an Eye for..." *Financial Times*, October 13, 2001, p.1.

9. For example, the "National Security Blueprint" of the Russian Federation, published in January 2000, warned of "attempts to create an international relations structure based on domination by developed Western countries in the international community, under U.S. leadership and designed for unilateral solutions (including the use of military force) to key issues in world politics." See "Russia's National Security Concept," *Arms Control Today*, Vol. 30 No1 (January/February 2002), p. 15 and Sergey M. Rogov, *The New Russian Security Concept* (Alexandria, Va.: Center for Naval Analyses, 2000).

10. See Patrick E. Tyler, "Russia and China Sign 'Friendship Pact'", *New York Times*, July 17, 2001, p. A1. For additional background on Russian and Chinese perceptions of the United States prior to September 11, see Celeste A. Wallander, "Wary of the West: Russian Security Policy at the Millennium," *Arms Control Today*, Vol. 30, No.2 (March 2000), pp. 7-12; and David Shambaugh, "China's Military View the World: Ambivalent Security," *International Security*, Vol. 24, No. 3 (Winter 1999/2000), pp. 52-79; and Lanxin Xiang, "Washington's Misguided China Policy," *Survival*, Vol. 43, No. 3 (Autumn 2001), pp. 7-23.

for ways to constrain U.S. freedom of action.[11] Although many of these countries appreciated the stabilizing effects of the global presence of the United States, they resent Washington's tendency to impose its will on others and worry that it will use its power unwisely.[12]

These concerns did not vanish when the twin towers fell. Although the United States has enjoyed considerable international sympathy in the aftermath of the September attacks, international support has not been unconditional, and key U.S. allies have made it clear that they wanted the U.S. response to be restrained. U.S. allies were especially concerned that the United States would seize this opportunity to attack Iraq, and a group of heads of state from the European Union emphasized that the U.S. response would have to be "proportional." Similarly, the NATO decision to invoke Article 5 of the NATO treaty, thereby identifying the September 11 events as an attack on all NATO members, was accompanied by European insistence that the United States consult with its allies before taking action.[13]

This lesson also warns us not to exaggerate the depth of international support that the United States presently enjoys. Other states have backed the United States because they agree that terrorism is a threat and because Washington has made it clear that neutrality is not an option, but also because they see this crisis as an opportunity to advance their own interests. Thus, Russia has sought to strike a deal over missile defense and gain U.S. acquiescence to its own campaign

11. Thus, French Foreign Minister Hubert Védrine famously described the United States as a "hyperpower" and stated that the "entire foreign policy of France... is aimed at making the world of tomorrow composed of several poles, not just one." German Chancellor Gerhard Schröder also warned that the danger of "unilateralism" by the United States was "undeniable." Quoted in Craig R. Whitney, "NATO at Fifty: Is It a Misalliance?" *New York Times*, February 15, 1999, p. A7. See also Suzanne Daley, "Europe's Dim View of U.S. Is Evolving into Frank Hostility," *New York Times*, April 9, 2000, pp. A1, A8.

12. See Hubert Védrine with Dominique Moisi, *France in an Age of Globalization*, trans. Philip H. Gordon (Washington, D.C.; Brookings Institute, 2001); Martin Walker, "What Europeans Think of America," *World Policy*, Vol. 17, No.2 (Summer 2000), pp. 26-38; François Heisbourg, "American Hegemony? Perceptions of the U.S. Abroad," *Survival*, Vol. 41, No.4 (Winter 1999-2000), pp. 5-19; Peter W. Rodman, *Drifting Apart? Trends in U.S.-European Relations* (Washington, D>C.: Nixon Center, June 1999); and Peter W. Rodman, *Uneasy Giant: The Challenges to American Predominance* (Washington, D.C.: Nixon Center, June 2000).

Beyond bin Laden: Reshaping U.S. Foreign Policy

against Islamic "terrorists" in Chechnya, Pakistan has gained important economic concessions, and Uzbekistan has bargained for a security guarantee. But support for U.S. policy in Afghanistan does not mean that other states are comfortable with U.S. power or that they agree with the United States on other issues.[14] If U.S. leaders assume that the current surge in international support will enable them to ignore the interests of other states in the future they will squander the diplomatic capital that the United States now enjoys and increase the risk of a backlash when the immediate challenge recedes.

LESSON #3: FAILED STATES ARE
A NATIONAL SECURITY PROBLEM

WHEN GOVERNMENTS COLLAPSE, the resulting anarchy often triggers large-scale migration, economic chaos, and mass violence. Although these effects often spread to neighboring countries, the challenge of "failed states" such as Somalia, Sierra Leone, Liberia, Rwanda, and Afghanistan has usually been seen as a humanitarian issue. As a result, international responses have generally been half-hearted and only partly successful.[15]

---

13. See Steven Erlanger, "So Far, Europe Breathes Easier over Free Hand Given the United States," *New York Times*, September 29, 2001, pp. B1, B6. Concern that allied participation might constrain its freedom of action led the Bush administration to declare that it welcomed allied support but intended to conduct military operations only in league with Great Britain. As one senior official put it, "The fewer people you have to rely on, the fewer permissions you have to get." Quoted in Elaine Sciolino and Steven Lee Meyers, "Bush Says 'Time Is Running out'; U.S. Plans to Act Largely Alone," *New York Times*, October 7, 2001, p. A1; and Rebecca Johnson and Micah Zenko, "All Dressed Up and No Place to Go: Why NATO Should br at the Front Lines of the War against Terrorism," November 2001, p.3.

14. To note but one example, China remains unwilling to sign an agreement prohibiting the export of missile parts and missile-making technology, despite what one U.S. official called a "full court press" prior to the Asia-Pacific Economic Conference summit in Shanghai in October 2001. See Craig S. Smith, "Frustrating U.S., China Balks at Pact to Stem Missile Sales," *New York Times*, October 20,2001, p. B4.

15. On the problems of failed states, see Robert I. Rotberg, ed., "Why States Fail (and How to Resuscitate Them)," 2001, unpublished ms.; and I. William Zartman, *Collapsed States: The Disintegration and Restoration of Legitimate Authority* (Boulder, Colo.: Lynne Rienner, 1995)

The attacks on September 11 demonstrate that failed states are more than a humanitarian tragedy; they can also be a major national security problem.[16] The Taliban government and the al Qaeda movement arose from the protracted civil conflict within Afghanistan, and bin Laden has used failed states for refuge since the mid-1990s. Indeed if Afghanistan had been governed by a more capable and moderate regime over the past decade, bin Laden would not have found sanctuary there, and the attacks on the United States might never have occurred.

The danger that some failed states pose also remind us that unresolved conflicts are always a potential danger. Protracted conflicts generated hatred and the desire for revenge, foster the emergence of groups whose main aim is to wage war, and empower leaders who depend on a climate of fear to justify their own rule. These conditions provide ideal breeding grounds for precisely the sort of people who willingly engage in mass terror. The terrorist network that the United States now seeks to eradicate is a product of the protracted conflicts in Afghanistan and Kashmir, and on the West Bank and Gaza Strip. The September 11 attacks on the United States might never have occurred has these violent struggles been resolved. Thus, helping to settle protracted civil conflicts is not merely good for the world in general; it can also make the United States safer.[17]

LESSON # 4: THE UNITED STATES CANNOT "GO IT ALONE"

FINALLY, THE U.S. response to the terrorist attacks is a forceful reminder that even a superpower needs support from other countries. During its first months in office, the Bush administration often acted as if the opinions of other countries did not matter very much, an attitude revealed by its uncompromising pursuit of missile

---

16. Recognizing this problem does not eliminate the need to make judgments about which failed states are potential threats to U.S. interests and which are not. The United States cannot rebuild every failed state, but the attacks on September 11 suggest that doing nothing will sometimes be costly.

17. There are trade-offs here as well, however. Trying to settle bitter civil conflicts is never easy, and getting involved can provoke intense and enduring resentments. A prudential rule would be to remain disengaged unless (1) vital U.S. interests are involved; and (2) U.S. leaders have a clear blueprint for resolving the conflict and restoring a workable government.

defenses and brusque rejection of several prominent international conventions.[18] Although these policies led to widespread criticism at home and abroad, there was no sign that the Bush administration was rethinking its basic approach prior to September 11.

Once the United States was attacked, however, the Bush administration suddenly discovered that international support was indispensable. The military effort against al Qaeda requires access to foreign territory and permission to use foreign airspace, and as discussed below, the campaign to dismantle far-flung terrorist networks cannot succeed without extensive and enduring support from many other countries. Broad international support also legitimates the use of force against al Qaeda and the Taliban and reduces the tendency for others to see the United States as a trigger-happy imperial power.

The irony is obvious: A president whose initial approach to foreign policy was decidedly unilateralist is now being judged in large part on his ability to muster an unprecedented degree of international cooperation.[19] To its credit, the Bush team changed course rapidly and has done an excellent job of rounding up support from a diverse set of foreign powers. That support is likely to wane, however, if the fighting in Afghanistan drags on and if the United States cannot replace the Taliban with a viable ruling coalition. Indeed, keeping the coalition against terrorism intact will be a daunting challenge.

---

18. In its first months in office, the Bush administration rejected the Kyoto Protocol on global warming and the inspection protocol to the Biological Weapons Convention, and forced the other participants to water down a U.N. agreement to limit the global trade in small arms. The administration also declared that it would not attempt to ratify the Comprehensive Test Ban Treaty or the treaty to create an international criminal court, and reiterated U.S. opposition to the global ban on land mines.

19. As Secretary of State Colin Powell put it, "Nobody's calling us unilateral anymore. That's kind of gone away for the time being; we're so multilateral it keeps me up 24 hours a day checking on everybody." Quoted in Patrick E. Tyler, "Russia and U.S. Optimistic on Defense Issues," *New York Times*, October 19, 2001, pp. A1, B4. It remains to be seen whether this constitutes a true shift in approach or merely a tactical adjustment for a skeptical forecast, see Steven E. Miller, "The End of Unilateralism? Or Unilateralism Redux?" *Washington Quarterly*, Vol. 25, No. 1 (Winter 2001-2002).

Stephen M. Walt

WAGING THE WAR ON TERRORISM:
IMPLICATIONS FOR U.S. FOREIGN POLICY

ALTHOUGH TRAGIC IN purely human terms, the losses that the
United States has suffered to date have not affected its material
position or its core national interests. The United States is still the
leading economic and military power in the world, and the global
consensus that terrorism is a serious problem may have enhanced
the U.S. influence in the short term. Basic U.S. foreign policy goals
are also unaffected: The United States still wants to discourage
security competition in Europe and Asia, prevent the emergence of
hostile great powers, promote a more open world economy, inhibit
the spread of weapons of mass destruction (WMD), and expand
democracy and respect for human rights.[20] Even the new war on
terrorism in not an entirely novel objective, insofar as the United
States and al Qaeda has already attacked each other on several
occasions in the past.[21]

What has changed, of course, is the priority attached to these
different goals. The campaign against global terrorism is now the
central aim of U.S. foreign and defense policy, and other international goals will be subordinated to this broad objective.

In the short term, the campaign has two main objectives. The
first goal is to eradicate al Qaeda, both by attacking it in Afghanistan and by eliminating its cells in other countries. The second goal

---

20. These goals are enunciated in numerous official and unofficial statements, including William J. Clinton, *A National Security Strategy for a New
Century* (Washington, D.C.: The White House, May 1997); *America's
National Interests* (Cambridge, Mass.: Commission on America's National
Interests, 2000); and George W. Bush, "A Distinctly American Internationalism," speech at the Ronald Reagan Presidential Library, November 19,
1999, http://www.georgewbush.com.

21. Al Qaeda has been linked to the February 1993 bombing of the World
Trade Center, the June 1996 bombing of a U.S. barracks in Saudi Arabia,
the August 1998 attacks on the U.S. embassies in Kenya and Tanzania, and
the October 2000 assault on USS *Cole*. The United States bombed al Qaeda
bases in Afghanistan in August 1998 and has undertaken a host of other
measures against al Qaeda over the past five years. See Kenneth Katzman,
Terrorism: Near Eastern Groups and State Sponsors, 2001 (Washington, D.C.:
Congressional Research Service, 2001).

is to replace the Taliban government, both to deny al Qaeda a safe haven and to demonstrate to other government what will happen to them if they permit attacks on the United States to be organized from their territory.[22]

Over the longer term, the United States must also take steps to ensure that new al Qaedas do not emerge and make it more difficult for potential enemies to acquire even more lethal means (such as nuclear weapons). To achieve these ends, U.S. foreign policy must focus on (1) managing the antiterrorist coalition; (2) enhancing control over weapons of mass destruction; (3) reconstructing Afghanistan; and (4) rebuilding relations with the Arab and Islamic world.

MANAGING THE COALITION

As SUGGESTED ABOVE, the key to victory against global terrorism lies in the U.S. ability to create and sustain a broad international coalition. International support has been a prerequisite for military action against al Qaeda and the Taliban, but cooperation from other states is even more crucial to the effort to dismantle al Qaeda's far-flung network of terrorist cells. Other states must be willing to share intelligence information with the United States, cooperate in exposing the covert money flows that nourish terrorist networks; and invest the time, resources, and political capital to suppress anti-American extremists within their own societies.

Unfortunately, keeping this coalition together will not be easy. Some Arab and Muslim states are already reluctant to cooperate with Washington, given their fears of domestic instability and the popular belief that the United States is insensitive to Arab and Muslim concerns. There are also serious rifts between some of the putative allies of the United States (most obviously in the simmering conflict between India and Pakistan), and these conflicts are certain to regain their salience as time goes on. History also warns that support for the campaign against terrorism is likely to fade with

---

22. As of this writing, there is no convincing evidence linking any other governments to the September 11 attacks or the subsequent anthrax attacks in several U.S. cities. Obviously, if other states are found to have been involved in these operations, the focus of the U.S. campaign would shift.

time, once the shock on the initial attacks wears off and as the costs of the campaign become more apparent. Even close U.S. allies may be tempted to pass the buck in the months ahead, especially if full compliance with U.S. requests requires real sacrifices.[23]

Given the importance of maintaining broad international support, the United States is likely to subordinate other foreign policy goals to the broader task of keeping its coalition intact. In the short-to-medium term, therefore, the following adjustments are in order.

First, the United States must continue its efforts to support Pervez Musharraf and his regime in Pakistan. This policy is necessary to facilitate the military campaign in Afghanistan, prepare the way for a successor regime in Kabul, and make sure that Islamic extremists do not overthrow Musharraf and gain access to Pakistan's nuclear arsenal. Lifting sanctions and pledging new economic aid (including debt relief) was a good first step, but the United States should also take immediate action to open the U.S. market to Pakistani exports.[24] Pressing India to begin meaningful negotiations on Kashmir would also give Musharraf an immediate political boost and reduce Pakistan's interest in maintaining close ties with various Islamic extremists.[25]

Second, because the United States needs help from a number of states and groups with poor human rights records, including Uzbekistan

---

23. For example, some states will be unable or unwilling to comply fully with U.S. requests to clean up the secret bank accounts and covert money flows that nurture global terrorist networks, especially if this involves significant economic costs. On the difficult of controlling these flows, see Tim Weiner and David Cay Johnston, "Roadblocks Cited in Effort to Trace Bin Laden's Money," *New York Times,* September 20, 2001, pp. A1, B2; Robert M. Morgenthau, "Cutting Off the Funds for Terror," *New York Times,* October 22, 2001, p. A21; Jimmy Burns, William Hall, Harvey Morris, and Richard Wolffe, "Huge Obstacles in Global Search for Terrorist Paper Trail, "*Financial Times,* September 24, 2001, p. 6; and Hugh Williamson, "Global Financial Taskforce Needs Overhaul to Fight Terrorism," *Financial Times,* October 3, 2001, p. 4.

24. See Helene Cooper, "Pakistan's Textile Bind Presents Bush Team with a Tough Choice," *Wall Street Journal,* October 29, 2001, pp. A1, A8.

25. Pakistan has used Islamic guerrillas (including some Afghan *mujahdeen*) to conduct an insurgency against Indian control of Kashmir. For background on this conflict, See Šumit Ganguly, "Explaining the Kashmir Insurgency: Political Mobilization and Institutional Decay," *International Security,* Vol. 21, No.2 (Fall 1996), pp. 76-107; and Raju G. C. Thomas, ed., *Perspectives on Kashmir: Roots of Conflict in South Asia* (Boulder, Colo.: Westview, 1992).

and the Afghan Northern Alliance, the war on terrorism will require it to downgrade its concern for human rights temporarily. But Washington should make it clear to its new partners that it does not condone their past behavior and encourage them to improve these policies over time.

Third, the crisis also provides an ideal opportunity to improve relations with Russia. The United States has behaved with scant regard for Russia's concerns over the past decade, but it now needs Russian support on a variety of fronts. To get it, the Bush administration should either abandon the process of NATO expansion or pursue it in a way that is acceptable to Russia. Russian President Vladimir Putin has recently indicated that expansion might be acceptable under certain conditions, but it is still a red flag to many Russians and does little to further the antiterrorist campaign. At the very least, expansion should be conducted in a manner that takes due account of Russian sensitivities, possibly by opening the door to Russia's entry into NATO sooner rather than later. The United States should also follow a similar policy toward missile defenses and move ahead only in the context of a mutually acceptable revision of the 1972 Antiballistic Missile Treaty. Improved relations with Moscow would also be furthered by continued efforts to stabilize the Russian economy and more generous support for cooperative denuclearization programs in Russia. The United States must also recognize that Russia is likely to regard a U.S. military presence in Central Asia with some misgivings, and reassure Moscow that it is not seeking a new sphere of influence in Russia's backyard.

Fourth, this crisis behooves the United States to keep relations with other major powers tranquil. China has tacitly supported the antiterrorist campaign (in part because it faces the threat of Islamic unrest in its western provinces) and has not tried to exploit the situation by raising other issues (such as Taiwan). Here the proper U.S. course is quiet diplomacy in Beijing and Taiwan, letting both parties know that any provocations would jeopardize future relations with the United States.

Finally, the United States would be wise to reciprocate the foreign support that it has recently sought by making some concessions of its own. Committing itself to a serious effort to negotiate a replacement for the Kyoto Protocol on global warming would be an ideal first step and would go a long way toward defusing lingering fears of U.S. unilateralism. Similarly, the United States could accelerate preparations for a new global trade round and declare that it was especially interested in lowering its barriers against exports from the developing world, even if this hurt some interests at home. Such a step may be difficult to take in the midst of a global recession, but that is precisely when reducing obstacles to trade is most needed.

CONTROLLING WEAPONS OF MASS DESTRUCTION

THE EVENTS OF September 11 showed that international terrorists are more capable and ruthless than many experts had believed. Given their willingness to sacrifice themselves and their indifference to the killing of innocent people, the most ominous danger is the possibility that al Qaeda or some like-minded group might acquire a weapon of mass destruction and use it to full effect.[26] Who can seriously doubt that bin Laden would love to get his hands on such a weapon, or that he would use it if he did?[27]

Reducing this threat requires a new effort to bring existing stockpiles of nuclear, chemical, and biological weapons under reliable control.[28] The most immediate and obvious risk is in Russia, whose vast arsenal of WMD remains under unacceptably loose supervision. There are also potentially dangerous stockpiles of nuclear,

---

26. By confirming that some groups are willing and able to use biological agents, the series of anthrax attacks in several U.S. cities that started in October 2001 underscores the potential danger of this new form of terrorism. For background, see Jonathan B. Tucker, *Toxic Terror: Assessing the Terrorist Use of Chemical and Biological Weapons* (Cambridge, Mass.: MIT Press, 2000).

27. In a 1999 interview, bin Laden states that "it would be a sin for Muslims not to try to possess the weapons that would prevent infidels from inflicting harm on Muslims. Hostility towards Americans is a religious duty and we hope to be rewarded for it by God." See "Interview with Bin Laden," *Time*, January 11, 1999. There is unconfirmed testimony from former bin Laden associates regarding his efforts to obtain nuclear materials. See Kimberly McCloud and Matthew Osborne, "Osama Bin Laden and WMD Terrorism," *CNS Reports* (Monterey, Calif.: Center for Non-proliferation Studies, Monterey Institute for International Studies, 2001), http://www.cns.miis.edu/ pub/reports/binladen.htm.

chemical, and biological materials in many other countries, and some of these supplies are poorly monitored or protected. Thus, the effort to control Russia's "loose nukes" must be accompanied by a global campaign to prevent terrorists from acquiring weapons of mass destruction from any other source.

To accomplish this vital task, the Bush administration should move swiftly to implement the recommendations of the January 2001 baker-Cutler report on nonproliferation programs in Russia, and encourage Congress to fund the necessary programs much more generously that it has in the past.[29] Earlier efforts to denuclearize several post-Soviet republics and to establish reliable control over Russia's loose nukes did make real progress, but the overall effort has been hobbled by mismanagement, bureaucratic infighting, pork-barrel politics, and presidential and congressional fecklessness. Given the potential danger that these weapons would pose in the wrong hands, this half-hearted effort constitutes a dramatic policy failure.[30] Yet neither the Bush administration nor the U.S. Congress has yet shown that it appreciates the seriousness of this problem, despite the promises made during the 2000 presidential campaign and the wake-up call the United States received on September 11.[31] The administration should also help the Pakistanis

---

28. According to former Senator Sam Nunn, "our number one national security priority is to keep weapons of mass destruction out of the hands of terrorist groups." Quoted in Albert R. Hunt, "An Accelerated Agenda for the Terrorism Threat," *Wall Street Journal*, October 25, 2001, p. A21. See also Graham T. Allison, "Could Worse Be Yet to Come?" *Economist, November 1, 2001, pp. 19-21.*

29. Among other things, the report recommends that the United States and Russia develop a strategic plan to "secure and/or neutralize in the next eight to ten years all nuclear weapons-usable material located in Russia"; appoint a senior official to manage the various programs; and accelerate joint efforts to manage, control, and account for nuclear materials. See Howard Baker and Lloyd Cutler, co-chairs, *A Report Card on the Department of Energy's Nonproliferation Programs with Russia* (Washington, D.C.: U.S. Department of Energy, Secretary of Energy Advisory Board, January 10, 2001), *http://www.hr.doe.gov/seab/rusrpt.pdf*. For additional recommendations, see Matthew Bunn, *The Next Wave: Urgently Needed New Steps to Control Warheads and Fissile Material* (Washington, D.C. , and Cambridge, Mass.: Carnegie Endowment for International Peace and Managing to Atom Project, Belfer Center for Science and International Affairs, John F. Kennedy School of Government, Harvard University, 2000).

secure the nuclear arsenal more reliably, possibly by providing them with permissive action links and other technical measure to prevent unauthorized use.[32]

At the same time, the United States should recommit itself to the difficult but essential business of multilateral arms control. Other states will not accept new restrictions on their own conduct and new monitoring procedures over their stockpiles if the United States refuses to constrain its own behavior. The Bush administration should therefore reconsider its opposition to the Comprehensive Test Ban Treaty and the inspections protocol of the Biological Weapons Convention, and immediately announce its desire to negotiate new arrangements to deny potential terrorist access to WMD materials.

Needless to say, this approach will require the Bush administration to abandon its aversion to arms control. But the administration has already shown an admirable ability to change course in other areas, and a direct attack on U.S. soil is the sort of event that inspires fresh thinking. Al Qaeda's attack suggests that the threat of catastrophic terrorism is more serious than previously believed, which makes this an ideal time to launch a major effort to limit the danger from weapons of mass destruction. If the United States is serious about reducing the treat from global terrorism, a sustained

---

30. Assessments of the various cooperative threat reduction efforts within the former Soviet Union include Matthew Bunn, Oleg Bukharin, and Kenneth Luongo, *Renewing the Partnership: Recommendations for Accelerated Action to Secure Nuclear Material in the Former Soviet Union* (Princeton, N.J.: Russian-American Nuclear Security Advisory Council, 2000); "Special Report: Assessing U.S. Non-Proliferation Assistance to the NIS, "*Nonproliferation Review*, Vol. 7, No.1 (Spring 2000), pp. 55-124, Jason D. Ellis, *Defense by Other Means: The Politics of U.S.-NIS Threat Reduction and Nuclear Security Cooperation* (Westport, Conn.: Prague, 2001); and Sam Nunn, chairman, *Managing the Global Nuclear Materials Threat: Policy Recommendations* (Washington, D.C.: Center for Strategic and International Studies, 2000).

31. The Bush administration's initial list of priorities for spending the $40 billion in emergency funding authorized by Congress after the September 11 attacks did not include any money for additional WMD control efforts overseas. See *Supplemental Appropriations: How the Money Is Allocated* (Washington, D.C.: Council for a Livable World, 2001), http://www.clw.org/sept11/suuanalysis.html.

32. See Bruce G. Blair, "The Ultimate Hatred Is Nuclear," *New York Times*, October 22, 2001, p. A21.

effort to deny such groups access to truly fearsome weapons should be a key element of its strategy.

FIXING A FAILED STATE

As a candidate for president, George W. Bush repeatedly criticized the Clinton administration for its attempts at "nation building." Within a month of the attacks on the United States, however, the Bush administration was openly acknowledging that its campaign to topple the Taliban would have to be accompanied by a serious effort to create a viable Afghan government and rebuild this war-torn country.[33] Nation building, it seems, is not such a bad idea after all.

As discussed above, this shift in policy reflects both the lesson that failed states such as Afghanistan have been breeding grounds and safe havens for anti-American extremists and the knowledge that the United States is partly responsible for Afghanistan's current condition. The U.S. failure to rebuild Afghanistan after the 1989 Soviet withdrawal led to the progressive radicalization of Afghan society and the ultimate triumph of the Taliban.[34] If the United States repeats this error once the Taliban are defeated, new bin Ladens are more likely to emerge. To reduce the long-term threat from terrorism, in short, nation building in Afghanistan is an unavoidable responsibility.

---

33. See Robert Cotterell, Stephen Fidler, Richard McGregor, and Andrew Parker, "U.S. Expects Long-Term Role in Afghanistan," *Financial Times*, October 11, 2001, p.1; and David E. Sanger, "A New, Uneasy Burden," *New York Times*, October 12, 2001, pp.A1, B2.

34. As Ahmed Rashid wrote well before the September 11 attacks: "By walking away from Afghanistan as early as it did, the USA faced within a few years dead diplomats, destroyed embassies, bombs in New York and cheap heroin on its streets... In the 1980s the USA was prepared 'to fight to the last Afghan' to get even with the Soviet Union, but when the Soviets left, Washington was not prepared to help bring peace or feed a hungry people." See Rashid, *Taliban: Militant Islam, Oil, and Fundamentalism in Central Asia* (New Haven, Conn.: Yale University Press, 2000), p. 209 and chap. 13.

Stephen M. Walt

REBUILDING RELATIONS WITH
THE ARAB AND ISLAMIC WORLD

ARAB AND ISLAMIC reaction to al Qaeda's attack and to the initial U.S. military response highlights the degree to which the United States has become estranged from theses societies. Although many Arab and Islamic leaders were quick to condemn the attack and to reject bin Laden's call for a new *jihad,* or holy war, Arab and Muslim opinion remains sharply critical of U.S. policy in the Middle East.[35] These attitudes make it more difficult for moderate Arab governments to support the war on terrorism and make it more likely that the U.S. campaign against al Qaeda will create new sympathizers.

To make it less risky for Arab and Islamic governments to back the U.S. effort and to isolate anti-American extremists within the Islamic world, the United States will have to rebuild its relations with these societies. Over the long term, the United States cannot rely solely on the friendship of Arab governments; it must also improve its image with the broader population.

The obvious first step-which the Bush administration has been inching toward-is to take a less one-sided approach to the conflict between Israel and the Palestinians. The United States is not as reflexively pro-Israel as many Arabs believe, but its policies in the past have not been evenhanded. While reaffirming its unshakable commitment to Israel's security within its pre-1967 borders, therefore, the United States should make it clear that it is dead-set against Israel's expansionist settlements policy and does not think that this policy is in the long-term interests of the United States or Israel.[36] The United States should also clarify its position on the requirements for a Palestinian state and emphasize that a viable state will require Israel to offer more generous terms than it proposed at

---

35. Meeting in Qatar on October 10, 2001, the Organization of the Islamic Conference "strongly condemned the brutal terror and expressed its condolences to the U.S. people and the families of the victims." But it also declared that "international initiative toward achieving security and stability... must include the achievement of security and justice for the Palestinian people." See "Final Communiqué of the Ninth Extraordinary Session of the Islamic Conference and Foreign Ministers," Doha, Qatar, October 10, 2001, http://www.oic-oci.org.

Camp David in July 2000. Specifically, Israel should offer to withdraw from virtually all territories it occupied in June 1967 in exchange for full peace.[37] The aborted Israeli-Palestinian negotiations at Taba in January 2001 showed that there was still some change for a final deal, but the progress achieved there proved to be tragically late.[38]

---

36. Israel is far more secure now than it was when it occupied the West Bank and Gaza Strip in June 1967, and its continued occupation of these territories is the primary source of the lingering dangers that it faces. In 1967 Israel's defense spending was less than half the combined defense expenditures of Egypt, Iraq, Jordan, and Syria; today Israel's defense expenditures are 30 percent larger than the combined defense spending of these four Arab states. Several of Israel's adversaries had strong support from the Soviet Union in 1967, but the Soviet Union no longer exists, and Israel's ties to the United States are far more extensive today. Israel had no nuclear weapons in 1967 but has a substantial (albeit undeclared) nuclear arsenal today. Within its pre-1967 borders, in short, Israel is more secure than it has ever been. By continuing to occupy the West Bank, Gaza Strip, and the Islamic holy sites in Jerusalem, however, Israel further inflames Arab opinion and forces Israelis and Palestinians to live together, thereby facilitating the low-level violence that has been occurring since the collapse of the Oslo peace process. In short, Israel's presence outside the Green Line now reduces its security, and the costs of denying the Palestinians a viable state of their own have never been greater. The above figures on defense spending are drawn from *World Military Expenditures and Arms Transfers, 1966-1975* (Washington, D.C.: U.S. Arms Control and Disarmament Agency, 1976); and *The Military Balance, 2000-2001* (London: International Institute for Strategic Studies, 2001). See also Shai Feldman, "Middle East Strategic Assessment," in Feldman and Yiftah Shapir, eds., *The Middle East Military Balance, 2000-2001* (Cambridge, Mass.: MIT Press, 2001). pp. 15-79, especially pp. 63-71.

37. Israel did make important concessions at Camp David, but their actual significance depends on the baseline from which they are compared. Israel's final offer would have entailed the annexation of 8-9 percent of the occupied territories (mostly to accommodate its illegal settlements), and the Palestinians would have ended up with only some 22 percent of the territory of pre-1947 Palestine-hardly a generous outcome. Furthermore, the Israeli proposals would have created a Palestinian state that was bisected by several Israeli-controlled corridors. These arrangements would have left the new state in a condition of permanent vulnerability and force Palestinians to endure the humiliation of passing through Israeli checkpoints in order to travel within their own country. The failure of the post-Oslo peace process is not due solely to Israeli intransigence, however; for an evenhanded analysis by an Israeli participant, see Ron Pundak, "From Oslo to Taba: What Went Wrong?" *Survival,* Vol. 43, No.3 (Autumn 2001), pp. 31-45.

Adjusting the U.S. position will require careful and deft diplomacy, so that Washington does not appear to be backing down to terrorist pressure and does not sacrifice important national values. Among other things, the United States should point out that the U.S. leaders supported the creation of a Palestinian state well before the September 11attacks and emphasize that the Clinton administration went to considerable effort to bring such a state into existence. To restart the peace process itself, the United States should press Israel to accept the recommendations of the Mitchell Commission (including a compete halt to additional Israeli settlements), and encourage both sides to resume talks at the point where they were broken off in January 2001.[39]

Given the recent violence and especially the reciprocal assassinations of Israeli and Palestinian leaders in the fall of 2001, these measures are unlikely to yield an immediate agreement by themselves. But they would remove a major irritant between the United States and the Arab world and dilute one of the extremists' main charges against the United States.[40] And because it will take time to erase the negative image that is now deeply etched ion the minds of Arabs and Muslims, the United States cannot simply issue a few presidential statements and then revert to its previous policies.

---

38. For a summary of these negotiations, see "Deconstructing the TabaTalks," *Report on Israeli Settlement in the Occupied Territories*, Vol. 11, No.2 (March/April 2001), pp.4,7, published by the Foundation for Middle East Peace, Washington, D.C. As Pundak, "From Oslo to Taba," pp.44-45, observes, "The Taba negotiations... proved that a Permanent Status Agreement between Israel and the Palestinians was within reach. The distance between the two sides narrowed during the last week at Taba, and the climate of the discussions was reminiscent of the approach adopted during the Oslo talks. This led to dramatic progress on almost all the most important issues."

39. Israel and the Palestinians will also have to reach an agreement on the right of displaced Palestinians to return to their homes. Allowing this right to be exercised in its entirety would threaten Israel's viability and is obviously infeasible, but the Palestinians have made it clear that the basic principle is an essential issue of justice. A possible solution would be for the two sides to acknowledge the "Right" of return, while the Palestinians agree to forgo exercising that right in exchange for compensation. The United States could then organize and help finance a generous program of reconstruction assistance, which would be understood to end all subsequent claims for the physical return of Palestinians to what is now Israeli territory.

Rather, it will have to take a principled position and stick with it through what is likely to be a long and contentious process.

Adjusting the U.S. stance in the Middle East should also include a reassessment of U.S. relations with certain Arab governments. To preserve access to oil at affordable prices, the United States has long supported traditional monarchies such as Saudi Arabia despite their financial support to Islamic radicals, their domestic fragility, and their reluctance to support U.S. diplomatic efforts openly. Concern for oil supplies has also made the United States reluctant to encourage greater pluralism within these societies, thereby increasing the danger that these societies will turn against the United States should the existing order collapse. Over time, the United States should strive to reduce its military presence in the Persian Gulf and encourage these regimes to open the doors to greater political participation. The United States should also stop regarding the Islamic world as a "democracy-free zone" where Islamist movements are consistently barred from meaningful political participation. If Islamist groups cannot participate openly in politics, they will be driven to adopt violent and radical methods. If allowed to participate along with other social groups, however, they are more likely to become a constructive force within these societies.[41] Such a policy has risks, of course, but so does U.S. single-minded dependence on a set of fragile and unreliable autocrats.

Finally, the United States needs to enhance its ability to communicate directly with Arab and Muslim communities around the world. Arab and Islamic hatred is partly a reaction to specific U.S. actions, but it is also fueled by a combination of myths and accusations promoted by anti-American groups and governments.[42]

---

40. Such a shift will undoubtedly make U.S. supporters of Israel uneasy. But the time has come to recognize that it is in neither Israel's nor America's interest for the United States to be estranged from the Arab and Islamic worlds. Americans and Israelis should also recognize that denying the Palestinians their legitimate rights has not made Israel safer.

41. On this point, see Glenn E. Robinson, "Can Islamists Be Democrats? The Case of Jordan," *Middle East Journal*, Vol. 51, No.3 (Summer 1997), pp.373-387; and Yaroslav Trofimov, "Bahrain's Bold Rebuff to Its Islamic Rebels: Democracy and Rights," *Wall Street Journal*, October 25, 2001, pp. A1, A10.

42. See Roula Khalaf and Gerard Baker, "A Different Script," *Financial Times*, October 13-14, 2001, p.9.

For example, many Arabs believe that U.S. sanctions against Iraq are responsible for the deaths of thousands of Iraqis (many of them children), unaware that these deaths are actually due to Saddam Hussein's ruthless refusal to use the U.N. oil-for-food program from 1991 to 1996 and his subsequent abuses of that program. Similarly, the United States gets little credit for its efforts to help the Muslim populations of Bosnia, Kosovo, Somalia and northern Iraq, or for its stewardship of the peace process between Israel, Egypt, Jordan, and the Palestinians. It will do little good to adjust U.S. policies in this region if these shifts are ignored or misunderstood by the hearts and minds that the United States is trying to reach.

To overcome this problem, the United States must launch a broad-based public information campaign, using every instrument and channel at its disposal.[43] It must train a cadre of diplomats and spokespeople who can speak to these societies effectively, and make them readily available to media outlets such as al-Jazeera (the Qatari-based news network that reaches 35 million viewers in the Arab world).[44] The United States should also expand its own Arabic-language broadcast activities in this region, so that local populations are not as dependent on official sources, and develop Arabic-language web sites to reach the growing internet-savvy populations in these countries. This does not mean simply purveying pro-U.S. propaganda (which would probably be discounted); it means monitoring what foreign populations are begin told and providing them with the information they need to form accurate judgments for themselves.

---

43. As former U.N. Ambassador Richard Holbrooke recently put it, "Incredible as it seems... a mass murderer seems to be winning the fight for the hearts and minds of the Muslim world." If this persists, he warned, the United States could "win the battle but lose the war." See Hunt, "An Accelerated Agenda for the Terrorism Threat."

44. In the first months after the September 11 attacks, only two U.S. officials (Secretary of State Powell and National Security Adviser Condoleezza Rice) gave interviews to al-Jazeera. Given the critical importance of persuading the Arab world that the U.S. cause is just, this minimal effort testifies to the low priority that the United States has attached to public diplomacy in this region. The U.S. government has recently increased its efforts in this regard, but has a long period of neglect to overcome.

Beyond bin Laden: Reshaping U.S. Foreign Policy

A FINAL RISK

THE AGENDA OUTLINED above is obviously ambitious. To support its military operations in Afghanistan (and possibly elsewhere), the United States has taken on new security obligations in Pakistan and Uzbekistan. To keep the coalition together and rebuild relations with the Arab world, the United States will have to convince both Israel and the Palestinians to make additional concessions after a year of bloody violence. To stabilize the Musharraf government and encourage it to sever its ties to Islamic extremists, Washington will have to provide it with economic aid and press for genuine negotiations on Kashmir, a dispute that has defied resolution for more than half a century. Once its efforts to topple the Taliban succeed, the United States must then take on the challenge of nation building in an impoverished region where it has little background or prior experience. Efforts to cut off the financial flows that sustain terrorism will require continued pressure on other governments and overseas financial institutions. Keeping weapons of mass destruction out of terrorist hands will take a protracted diplomatic campaign and many difficult compromises. Accomplishing any one of these goals would be difficult, and to advocate the entire agenda may seem wildly utopian. Yet these measures are all consistent with the stated aim of reducing the danger from global terrorism, and they provide a set of benchmarks by which to judge the U.S. performance in the future.

There is a final danger, however. By requiring the United States to become even more forcefully engaged around the world, and especially in the Middle East and Central Asia, the effort to combat global terrorism is likely to reinforce the fears and resentment that gave rise to al Qaeda in the first place. The longer this effort takes and the more it required the United States to interfere in other countries' business, the great the change of a hostile backlash later on.[45] This risk raises the final issue: Can these policies be sustained over the longer term?

---

45. For an insightful and provocative analysis of this phenomenon, see Chalmers A. Johnson, *Blowback: The Costs and Consequences of American Empire* (New York: Metropolitan, 2000).

Stephen M. Walt

THE NEXT DEBATE: ENGAGEMENT OR RETRENCHMENT?

PUBLIC DEBATE ON the central principles of U.S. foreign policy
has been muted since September 11. Disagreements have emerged
over the best way to respond to the immediate threat, but few Americans have questioned the need for a vigorous response or called for a
more far-reaching reassessment of the U.S. role in the world. As the
campaign proceeds, however, these more fundamental issues are
likely to resurface and could rekindle a long-dormant debate on U.S.
grand strategy.

The central issue is whether the United States should continue
to maintain its current array of global military commitments-and
especially its large forward military presence-or move back to its
earlier positions as an "offshore balancer."[46] For the past fifty years,
the United States has maintained large military forces in Europe
and Asia and been actively engaged in virtually every corner of the
world. This policy originated in the Cold War struggle against
the Soviet Union, and it has been sustained by the belief that
U.S. engagement helps keep the peace in Europe and Asia,
encourages the spread of liberal values, and facilitates the maintenance of an open world economy. This belief explains why the
United States did not liquidate its Cold War alliances after the Soviet
Union collapsed, and eventually took on additional commitments in
Central Europe, the Balkans, and the Persian Gulf.

As already discussed, it is increasingly clear that this policy entails
significantly greater costs than Americans have thought. In addition
to the lives already lost and the need to devote greater resources to
homeland defense, the international campaign against global terrorism

---

46. For representative statements of these two positions, see Robert J. Art,
Selective Engagement: American Grand Strategy and World Politics (Ithaca,
N.Y.: Cornell University Press, forthcoming); Nye, *Bound to Lead;* Nye, *Para-
dox of American Power;* John J. Mearsheimer, *The Tragedy of Great Power
Politics* (New York: W.W. Norton, 2001); Christopher Layne, "From Prepon-
derance to Offshore Balancing: America's Future Grand Strategy," *Interna-
tional Security,* Vol. 22, No.1 (Summer 1997), pp. 86-124 and Eugene Gholz,
Daryl G. Press, and Harvey M. Sapolsky, "Come Home, America: The Strategy of Restraint in the Face of Temptation,." *International Security,* Vol.21,
No. 4 (Spring 1997), pp. 5-48.

is forcing the United States to shoulder a breathtaking array of international burdens. As the campaign against terrorism unfolds, Americans are likely to ask whether all this effort is really worth it. And if the threat from global terrorism is at least partly a reaction to the looming global presence of the United States, then some Americans are likely to ask if the danger might also be reduced if it were not as visibly and actively engaged in trying to run the world. These voices will be muted if the current campaign continues to go well, and if the short-term costs are not too great. If it goes poorly, however, and if groups such as al-Qaeda prove to be more resilient than expected, pressure to retrench is likely to increase.

What does this mean for U.S. foreign policy? It means that the ability of the United States to remain actively engaged at an acceptable cost will depend in large part on whether it can reduce these costs by making its dominant position more acceptable to the rest of the world. Over the long term, what changes in policy and attitude does this imply?

First, the United States should rely more heavily on multilateral institutions, even if this policy reduces its freedom of action in the short term. Institutions are useful not because they are power restraints on state behavior (they are not), but because they diffuse responsibility for international backlash. U.S. critics of the United Nations and other multilateral institutions have mistakenly focused on the restrictions that these institutions might impose, and they have ignored how these institutions make it easier for the United States to achieve its goals without provoking unnecessary foreign resentment.

Second, the United States must act with great forbearance and generosity in its dealings with other states. The United States enjoys enormous wealth and power and a favorable geopolitical position. It is only natural that other states resent its good fortune, and especially when it appears overweening, self-congratulatory, or selfish. When President Bush explains his rejection of the Kyoto Protocol by saying he was not going to do anything that might hurt American workers, or when the United States rejects useful arms control treaties to appease special interests at home, the United States appears both selfish and short-sighted. When Washington caves in to domestic lobbies and reneges on its earlier pledges to phase out restrictions on textile imports (which make it more difficult for poor countries to develop), it is being both fickle and irresponsible. If the United States wants to make its positioning of primacy more palatable to others, in short, it will have to use its wealth and power in ways that serve the interests of others as well as its own.[47]

Finally, the United States should begin to devolve responsibility for regional security onto other countries or regional associations and gradually reduce its forward military presence. There were some indications that the Bush administration intended to move in this direction before September 11, and there have been a few hints that it will resume this course once the current crisis is over.[48] For example, the demands of the war in Afghanistan may provide the pretext for removing U.S. troops from the Balkans, and they are unlikely to go back when the crisis is over. In effect, this step means that the United States will be turning responsibility for Europe's security back to the Europeans.[49] The United States will not retreat into isolationism but will try to reduce global resentment by shrinking its forward military presence and allowing other states greater freedom to chart their own course. This process will be a gradual one, but it is a logical long-term response to the new structure of world politics.

---

47. The obvious precedent is U.S. behavior after World War II, when the United States helped rebuild Europe and Asia (including its former enemies) and worked to create a number of enduring international institutions. These steps were clearly in the U.S. national interest, but they were also farsighted and generous acts. On the historical precedent, see John Gerard Ruggie, *Winning the Peace: America and World Order in the New Era* (New York: Columbia University Press, 1996), especially chap. 2.

48. See Greg Jaffe, "Rumsfeld Aides Seek Deep Personnel Cuts in Armed Forces to Pay for New Weaponry," *Wall Street Journal,* August 8, 2001, p. A3; Lisa Burgess, "Review Suggests Making Military Leaner, More Mobile to Face Changing Threats," *Stars and Stripes,* June 24, 2001; and James Dao, "Americans Plead to Remain in Bosnia," *New York Times,* October 22, 2001, p. B3.

49. Indeed, the administration's decision to minimize NATO's role in the war in Afghanistan suggests that NATO is continuing to evolve from a military alliance into a loose political association. This process will also make it easier to accommodate Russia in the future, which may explain why President Putin no longer opposes NATO expansion strenuously. See James Kurth, "The Next NATO: Building an American Commonwealth of Nations," *National Interest,* No. 65 (Fall 2001), pp. 5-16.

CONCLUSION

DEALING WITH THE world in the manner just described will require a level of foresight, restraint, and maturity that has rarely been evident in the recent conduct of U.S. foreign policy.[50] If the United States wants to make its privileged position palatable to others, the American body politic must acquire a more serious and disciplined attitude toward the management of international affairs. In the past, seemingly secure behind its nuclear deterrent and oceanic moats, and possessing unmatched economic and military power, the United States has allowed its foreign policy to be distorted by partisan sniping, hijacked by foreign lobbyists and narrow domestic special interests, and held hostage by irresponsible and xenophobic members of Congress. Despite its pretensions as the world's only superpower, the United States has starved its intelligence services, gutted its international affairs budget, done little to attract the ablest members of its society to government service, neglected the study of foreign languages and cultures, and basically behaved as though it simply did not matter if U.S. foreign policy were well run or not.[51] If al Qaeda's horrible act convinces the United States that it is finally time to grow up and take the business of being a great power seriously, then the people bin Laden's minions killed will not have died in vain.

---

50. For an extended argument along similar lines, see Henry A. Kissinger, *Does America Need a Foreign Policy" Toward a Diplomacy for the Twenty-first Century* (New York: Simon and Schuster, 2001).

51. By way of illustration, nonmilitary spending on international affairs (State Department, foreign aid, United Nations, information programs, etc.) has declined 20 percent in real terms since 1986. The United States spent 1.0 percent of gross domestic product on these programs in 1962, but only 0.2 percent of GDP in 2000. These are not the budgetary priorities of a great power that is really serious about how it conducts diplomacy. See Robert J. Lieber, "Three Propositions About America's World Role," in Lieber, *Eagle Rules*, p. 10.

The New Threat
of Mass Destruction

Richard K. Betts

WHAT IF MCVEIGH HAD USED ANTHRAX?

DURING THE COLD WAR, weapons of mass destruction were the centerpiece of foreign policy. Nuclear arms hovered in the background of every major issue in East-West competition and alliance relations. The highest priorities of U.S. policy could almost all be linked in some way to the danger of World War III and the fear of millions of casualties in the American homeland.

Since the Cold War, other matters have displaced strategic concerns on the foreign policy agenda, and that agenda itself is now barely on the public's radar screen. Apart from defense policy professionals, few Americans still lose sleep over weapons of mass destruction (WMD). After all, what do normal people feel is the main relief provided by the end of the Cold War? It is that the danger of nuclear war is off their backs.

Yet today, WMD present more and different things to worry about than during the Cold War. For one, nuclear arms are no longer the only concern, as chemical and biological weapons have come to the fore. For another, there is less danger of complete annihilation, but more danger of mass destruction. Since the Cold War is over and American and Russian nuclear inventories are much smaller, there is

RICHARD K. BETTS is Director of National Security Studies at the Council on Foreign Relations and the Leo A. Shifrin Professor of War and Peace Studies Director, Program in International Security Policy Director, Institute of War and Peace Studies at Columbia University. This article originally appeared in the January/February 1998 issue of *Foreign Affairs* © 1998 by the Council on Foreign Relations.

less chance of an apocalyptic exchange of many thousands of weapons. But the probability that some smaller number of WMD will be used is growing. Many of the standard strategies and ideas for coping with WMD threats are no longer as relevant as they were when Moscow was the main adversary. But new thinking has not yet congealed in as clear a form as the Cold War concepts of nuclear deterrence theory.

The new dangers have not been ignored inside the Beltway. "Counterproliferation" has become a cottage industry in the Pentagon and the intelligence community, and many worthwhile initiatives to cope with threats are under way. Some of the most important implications of the new era, however, have not yet registered on the public agenda. This in turn limits the inclination of politicians to push some appropriate programs. Even the defense establishment has directed its attention mainly toward countering threats WMD pose to U.S. military forces operating abroad rather than to the more worrisome danger that mass destruction will occur in the United States, killing large numbers of civilians.

The points to keep in mind about the new world of mass destruction are the following. First, the roles such weapons play in international conflict are changing. They no longer represent the technological frontier of warfare. Increasingly, they will be weapons of the weak—states or groups that militarily are at best second-class. The importance of the different types among them has also shifted. Biological weapons should now be the most serious concern, with nuclear weapons second and chemicals a distant third.

Second, the mainstays of Cold War security policy—deterrence and arms control—are not what they used to be. Some new threats may not be deterrable, and the role of arms control in dealing with WMD has been marginalized. In a few instances, continuing devotion to deterrence and arms control may have side effects that offset the benefits.

Third, some of the responses most likely to cope with the threats in novel ways will not find a warm welcome. The response that should now be the highest priority is one long ignored, opposed, or ridiculed: a serious civil defense program to blunt the effects of WMD if they are unleashed within the United States. Some of the most effective measures to prevent attacks within the United States may also challenge traditional civil liberties if pursued to the maximum. And the most troubling conclusion for foreign policy as a whole is that reducing the odds of attacks in the United States might require pulling back from involvement in some foreign conflicts. American activism to guarantee international stability is, paradoxically, the prime source of American vulnerability.

This was partly true in the Cold War, when the main danger that nuclear weapons might detonate on U.S. soil sprang from strategic engagement in Europe, Asia, and the Middle East to deter attacks on U.S. allies. But engagement then assumed a direct link between regional stability and U.S. survival. The connection is less evident today, when there is no globally threatening superpower or transnational ideology to be contained—only an array of serious but entirely local disruptions. Today, as the only nation acting to police areas outside its own region, the United States makes itself a target for states or groups whose aspirations are frustrated by U.S. power.

FROM MODERN TO PRIMITIVE

WHEN NUCLEAR WEAPONS were born, they represented the most advanced military applications of science, technology, and engineering. None but the great powers could hope to obtain them. By now, however, nuclear arms have been around for more than half a century, and chemical and biological weapons even longer. They are not just getting old. In the strategic terms most relevant to American security, they have become primitive. Once the military cutting edge of the strong, they have become the only hope for so-called rogue states or terrorists who want to contest American power. Why? Because the United States has developed overwhelming superiority in conventional military force—something it never thought it had against the Soviet Union.

The Persian Gulf War of 1991 demonstrated the American advantage in a manner that stunned many abroad. Although the U.S. defense budget has plunged, other countries are not closing the gap. U.S. military spending remains more than triple that of any potentially hostile power and higher than the combined defense budgets of Russia, China, Iran, Iraq, North Korea, and Cuba.

More to the point, there is no evidence that those countries' level of military professionalism is rising at a rate that would make them competitive even if they were to spend far more on their forces. Rolling along in what some see as a revolution in military affairs, American forces continue to make unmatched use of state-of-the-art weapons, surveillance and information systems, and the organizational and doctrinal flexibility for managing the integration of these complex innovations into "systems of systems" that is the key to modern military effectiveness. More than ever in military history, brains are brawn. Even if hostile countries somehow catch up in an arms race, their military organizations and cultures are unlikely to catch up in the competence race for management, technology assimilation, and combat command skills.

If it is infeasible for hostile states to counter the United States in conventional combat, it is even more daunting for smaller groups such as terrorists. If the United States is lucky, the various violent groups with grievances against the American government and society will continue to think up schemes using conventional explosives. Few terrorist groups have shown an interest in inflicting true mass destruction. Bombings or hostage seizures have generally threatened no more than a few hundred lives. Let us hope that this limitation has been due to a powerful underlying reason, rather than a simple lack of capability, and that the few exceptions do not become more typical.

There is no sure reason to bet on such restraint. Indeed, some have tried to use WMD, only to see them fizzle. The Japanese Aum Shinrikyo cult released sarin nerve gas in Tokyo in 1995 but killed only a few people, and some analysts believe that those who attacked the World Trade Center in 1993 laced their bomb with cyanide, which burned up in the explosion (this was not confirmed, but a large amount of cyanide was found in the perpetrators' possession). Eventually such a group will prove less incompetent. If terrorists decide that they want to stun American policymakers by inflicting enormous damage, WMD become more attractive at the same time that they are becoming more accessible.

Finally, unchallenged military superiority has shifted the attention of the U.S. military establishment away from WMD. During the Cold War, nuclear weapons were the bedrock of American war capabilities. They were the linchpin of defense debate, procurement programs, and arms control because the United States faced another superpower—one that conventional wisdom feared could best it in conventional warfare. Today, no one cares about the MX missile or B-1 bomber, and hardly anyone really cares about the Strategic Arms Reduction Treaty. In a manner that could only have seemed ludicrous during the Cold War, proponents now rationalize the $2 billion B-2 as a weapon for conventional war. Hardly anyone in the Pentagon is still interested in how the United States could use WMD for its own strategic purposes.

What military planners are interested in is how to keep adversaries from using WMD as an "asymmetric" means to counter U.S. conventional power, and how to protect U.S. ground and naval forces abroad from WMD attacks. This concern is all well and good, but it abets a drift of attention away from the main danger. The primary risk is not that enemies might lob some nuclear or chemical weapons at U.S. armored battalions or ships, awful as that would be. Rather, it is that they might attempt to punish the United States by triggering catastrophes in American cities.

CHOOSE YOUR WEAPONS WELL

UNTIL THE PAST DECADE, the issue was nuclear arms, period. Chemical weapons received some attention from specialists, but never made the priority list of presidents and cabinets. Biological weapons were almost forgotten after they were banned by the 1972 Biological Weapons Convention. Chemical and biological arms have received more attention in the 1990s. The issues posed by the trio lumped under the umbrella of mass destruction differ, however. Most significantly, biological weapons have received less attention than the others but probably represent the greatest danger.

Chemical weapons have been noticed more in the past decade, especially since they were used by Iraq against Iranian troops in the 1980-88 Iran-Iraq War and against Kurdish civilians in 1988. Chemicals are far more widely available than nuclear weapons because the technology required to produce them is far simpler, and large numbers of countries have undertaken chemical weapons programs. But chemical weapons are not really in the same class as other weapons of mass destruction, in the sense of ability to inflict a huge number of civilian casualties in a single strike. For the tens of thousands of fatalities as in, say, the biggest strategic bombing raids of World War II, it would be very difficult logistically and operationally to deliver chemical weapons in necessary quantities over wide areas.

Nevertheless, much attention and effort have been lavished on a campaign to eradicate chemical weapons. This may be a good thing, but the side effects are not entirely benign. For one, banning chemicals means that for deterrence, nuclear weapons become even more important than they used to be. That is because a treaty cannot assuredly prevent hostile nations from deploying chemical weapons, while the United States has forsworn the option to retaliate in kind.

In the past, the United States had a no-first-use policy for chemical weapons but reserved the right to strike back with them if an enemy used them first. The 1993 Chemical Weapons Convention (cwc), which entered into force last April, requires the United States to destroy its stockpile, thus ending this option. The United States did the same with biological arms long ago, during the Nixon administration. Eliminating its own chemical and biological weapons practically precludes a no-first-use policy for nuclear weapons, since they become the only WMD available for retaliation.

Would the United States follow through and use nuclear weapons against a country or group that had killed several thousand Americans with deadly chemicals? It is hard to imagine breaking the post-Nagasaki taboo in that situation. But schemes for conventional military retaliation would not suffice without detracting from the force of American deterrent threats. There would be a risk for the United States in setting a precedent that someone could use WMD against Americans without suffering similar destruction in return. Limiting the range of deterrent alternatives available to U.S. strategy will not necessarily cause deterrence to fail, but it will certainly not strengthen it.

The ostensible benefit of the cwc is that it will make chemical arms harder to acquire and every bit as illegal and stigmatized as biological weapons have been for a quarter-century. If it has that benefit, what effect will the ban have on the choices of countries or groups who want some kind of WMD in any case, whether for purposes of deterrence, aggression, or revenge? At the margin, the ban will reduce the disincentives to acquiring biological weapons, since they will be no less illegal, no harder to obtain or conceal, and far more damaging than chemical weapons. If major reductions in the chemical threat produce even minor increases in the biological threat, it will be a bad trade.

One simple fact should worry Americans more about biological than about nuclear or chemical arms: unlike either of the other two, biological weapons combine maximum destructiveness and easy availability. Nuclear arms have great killing capacity but are hard to get; chemical weapons are easy to get but lack such killing capacity; biological agents have both qualities. A 1993 study by the Office of Technology Assessment concluded that a single airplane delivering 100 kilograms of anthrax spores—a dormant phase of a bacillus that multiplies rapidly in the body, producing toxins and rapid hemorrhaging—by aerosol on a clear, calm night over the Washington, D.C., area could kill between one million and three million people, 300 times as many fatalities as if the plane had delivered sarin gas in amounts ten times larger.[1]

Like chemical weapons but unlike nuclear weapons, biologicals are relatively easy to make. Innovations in biotechnology have obviated many of the old problems in handling and preserving biological agents, and many have been freely available for scientific research. Nuclear weapons are not likely to be the WMD of choice for non-state terrorist groups. They require huge investments and targetable infrastructure, and are subject to credible threats by the United States. An aggrieved group that decides it wants to kill huge numbers of Americans will find the mission easier to accomplish with anthrax than with a nuclear explosion.

Inside the Pentagon, concern about biological weapons has picked up tremendously in the past couple of years, but there is little serious attention to the problem elsewhere. This could be a good thing if

---

1. U.S. Congress, Office of Technology Assessment, *Proliferation of Weapons of Mass Destruction: Assessing the Risks,* Washington: Government Printing Office, 1993, p. 54.

nothing much can be done, since publicity might only give enemies ideas. But it is a bad thing if it impedes efforts to take steps—such as civil defense—that could blunt nuclear, chemical, or biological attacks.

DETERRENCE AND ARMS CONTROL IN DECLINE

AN OLD VOCABULARY still dominates policy discussion of WMD. Rhetoric in the defense establishment falls back on the all-purpose strategic buzzword of the Cold War: deterrence. But deterrence now covers fewer of the threats the United States faces than it did during the Cold War.

The logic of deterrence is clearest when the issue is preventing unprovoked and unambiguous aggression, when the aggressor recognizes that it is the aggressor rather than the defender. Deterrence is less reliable when both sides in a conflict see each other as the aggressor. When the United States intervenes in messy Third World conflicts, the latter is often true. In such cases, the side that the United States wants to deter may see itself as trying to deter the United States. Such situations are ripe for miscalculation.

For the country that used to be the object of U.S. deterrence— Russia—the strategic burden has been reversed. Based on assumptions of Soviet conventional military superiority, U.S. strategy used to rely on the threat to escalate—to be the first to use nuclear weapons during a war—to deter attack by Soviet armored divisions. Today the tables have turned. There is no Warsaw Pact, Russia has half or less of the military potential of the Soviet Union, and its current conventional forces are in disarray, while NATO is expanding eastward. It is now Moscow that has the incentive to compensate for conventional weakness by placing heavier reliance on nuclear capabilities. The Russians adopted a nuclear no-first-use policy in the early 1980s, but renounced it after their precipitous post–Cold War decline.

Today Russia needs to be reassured, not deterred. The main danger from Russian WMD is leakage from vast stockpiles to anti-American groups elsewhere—the "loose nukes" problem. So long as the United States has no intention of attacking the Russians, their greater reliance on nuclear forces is not a problem. If the United States has an interest in reducing nuclear stockpiles, however, it is.

Richard K. Betts

The traditional American approach—thinking in terms of its own deterrence strategies—provides no guidance. Indeed, noises some Americans still make about deterring the Russians compound the problem by reinforcing Moscow's alarm.

Similarly, U.S. conventional military superiority gives China an incentive to consider more reliance on an escalation strategy. The Chinese have a long-standing no-first-use policy but adopted it when their strategic doctrine was that of "people's war," which relied on mass mobilization and low-tech weaponry. Faith in that doctrine was severely shaken by the American performance in the Persian Gulf War. Again, the United States might assume that there is no problem as long as Beijing only wants to deter and the United States does not want to attack. But how do these assumptions relate to the prospect of a war over Taiwan? That is a conflict that no one wants but that can hardly be ruled out in light of evolving tensions. If the United States decides openly to deter Beijing from attacking Taiwan, the old lore from the Cold War may be relevant. But if Washington continues to leave policy ambiguous, who will know who is deterring whom? Ambiguity is a recipe for confusion and miscalculation in a time of crisis. For all the upsurge of attention in the national security establishment to the prospect of conflict with China, there has been remarkably little discussion of the role of nuclear weapons in a Sino-American collision.

The main problem for deterrence, however, is that it still relies on the corpus of theory that undergirded Cold War policy, dominated by reliance on the threat of second-strike retaliation. But retaliation requires knowledge of who has launched an attack and the address at which they reside. These requirements are not a problem when the threat comes from a government, but they are if the enemy is anonymous. Today some groups may wish to punish the United States without taking credit for the action—a mass killing equivalent to the 1988 bombing of Pan Am Flight 103 over Lockerbie, Scotland. Moreover, the options the defense establishment favors have shifted over entirely from deterrence to preemption. The majority of those who dealt with nuclear weapons policy during the Cold War adamantly opposed developing first-strike options. Today, scarcely anyone looks to that old logic when thinking about rogues or terrorists, and most hope to be able to mount a disarming action against any group with WMD.

Finally, eliminating chemical weapons trims some options for deterrence. Arms control restrictions on the instruments that can be used for deterrent threats are not necessarily the wrong policy, but they do work against maximizing deterrence. Overall, however, the problem with arms control is not that it does too much but that it now does relatively little.

From the Limited Test Ban negotiations in the 1960s through the Strategic Arms Limitation Talks, Strategic Arms Reduction Talks, and Intermediate-range Nuclear Forces negotiations in the 1970s and 1980s, arms control treaties were central to managing WMD threats. Debates about whether particular agreements with Moscow were in the United States' interest were bitter because everyone believed that the results mattered. Today there is no consensus that treaties regulating armaments matter much. Among national security experts, the corps that pays close attention to START and Conventional Forces in Europe negotiations has shrunk. With the exception of the Chemical Weapons Convention, efforts to control WMD by treaty have become small potatoes. The biggest recent news in arms control has not been any negotiation to regulate WMD, but a campaign to ban land mines.

The United States' Cold War partner in arms control, Russia, has disarmed a great deal voluntarily. But despite standard rhetoric, the United States has not placed a high priority on convincing Moscow to divest itself of more of its nuclear weapons; the Clinton administration has chosen to promote NATO expansion, which pushes the Russians in the opposite direction.

The 1968 Nuclear Nonproliferation Treaty remains a hallowed institution, but it has nowhere new to go. It will not convert the problem countries that want to obtain WMD—unless, like Iraq and North Korea in the 1980s, they sign and accept the legal obligation and then simply cheat. The NPT regime will continue to impede access to fissile materials on the open market, but it will not do so in novel or more effective ways. And it does not address the problem of Russian "loose nukes" any better than the Russian and American governments do on their own.

Richard K. Betts

CIVIL DEFENSE

DESPITE ALL THE new limitations, deterrence remains an important aspect of strategy. There is not much the United States needs to do to keep up its deterrence capability, however, given the thousands of nuclear weapons and the conventional military superiority it has. Where capabilities are grossly underdeveloped, however, is the area of responses for coping should deterrence fail.

Enthusiasts for defensive capability, mostly proponents of the Strategic Defense Initiative from the Reagan years, remain fixated on the least relevant form of it: high-tech active defenses to intercept ballistic missiles. There is still scant interest in what should now be the first priority: civil defense preparations to cope with uses of WMD within the United States. Active defenses against missiles would be expensive investments that might or might not work against a threat the United States probably will not face for years, but would do nothing against the threat it already faces. Civil defense measures are extremely cheap and could prove far more effective than they would have against a large-scale Soviet attack.

During the Cold War, debate about antimissile defense concerned whether it was technologically feasible or cost-effective and whether it would threaten the Soviets and ignite a spiraling arms race between offensive and defensive weapons. One need not refight the battles over SDI to see that the relevance to current WMD threats is tenuous. Iraq, Iran, or North Korea will not be able to deploy intercontinental missiles for years. Nor, if they are strategically cunning, should they want to. For the limited number of nuclear warheads these countries are likely to have, and especially for biological weapons, other means of delivery are more easily available. Alternatives to ballistic missiles include aircraft, ship-launched cruise missiles, and unconventional means, such as smuggling, at which the intelligence agencies of these countries have excelled. Non-state perpetrators like those who bombed the World Trade Center will choose clandestine means of necessity.

A ballistic missile defense system, whether it costs more or less than the $60 billion the Congressional Budget Office recently estimated would be required for one limited option, will not counter these modes of attack. Indeed, if a larger part of the worry about WMD these days is about their use by terrorist states or groups, the odds are higher that sometime, somewhere in the country, some of these weapons will go off, despite the best efforts to stop them. If that happens, the United States should have in place whatever measures can mitigate the consequences.

By the later phases of the Cold War it was hard to get people interested in civil defense against an all-out Soviet attack that could detonate thousands of high-yield nuclear weapons in U.S. population centers. To many, the lives that would have been saved seemed less salient than the many millions that would still have been lost. It should be easier to see the value of civil defense, however, in the context of more limited attacks, perhaps with only a few low-yield weapons. A host of minor measures can increase protection or recovery from biological, nuclear, or chemical effects. Examples are stockpiling or distribution of protective masks; equipment and training for decontamination; standby programs for mass vaccinations and emergency treatment with antibiotics; wider and deeper planning of emergency response procedures; and public education about hasty sheltering and emergency actions to reduce individual vulnerability.

Such programs would not make absorbing a WMD attack tolerable. But inadequacy is no excuse for neglecting actions that could reduce death and suffering, even if the difference in casualties is small. Civil defenses are especially worthwhile considering that they are extraordinarily cheap compared with regular military programs or active defense systems. Yet until recently, only half a billion dollars—less than two-tenths of one percent of the defense budget and less than $2 a head for every American—went to chemical and biological defense, while nearly $4 billion was spent annually on ballistic missile defense.[2] Why haven't policymakers attended to first things first—cheap programs that can cushion the effects of a disaster—before undertaking expensive programs that provide no assurance they will be able to prevent it?

---

2. John F. Sopko, "The Changing Proliferation Threat," Foreign Policy, Spring 1997, pp. 3-20.

One problem is conceptual inertia. The Cold War accustomed strategists to worrying about an enemy with thousands of WMD, rather than foes with a handful. For decades the question of strategic defense was also posed as a debate between those who saw no alternative to relying on deterrence and those who hoped that an astrodome over the United States could replace deterrence with invulnerability. None of these hoary fixations address the most probable WMD threats in the post–Cold War world.

Opposition to Cold War civil defense programs underlies psychological aversion to them now. Opponents used to argue that civil defense was a dangerous illusion because it could do nothing significant to reduce the horror of an attack that would obliterate hundreds of cities, because it would promote a false sense of security, and because it could even be destabilizing and provoke attack in a crisis. Whether or not such arguments were valid then, they are not now. But both then and now, there has been a powerful reason that civil defense efforts have been unpopular: they alarm people. They remind them that their vulnerability to mass destruction is not a bad dream, not something that strategic schemes for deterrence, preemption, or interception are sure to solve.

Civil defense can limit damage but not minimize it. For example, some opponents may be able to develop biological agents that circumvent available vaccines and antibiotics. (Those with marginal technical capabilities, however, might be stopped by blocking the easier options.) Which is worse—the limitations of defenses, or having to answer for failure to try? The moment that WMD are used somewhere in a manner that produces tens of thousands of fatalities, there will be hysterical outbursts of all sorts. One of them will surely be, "Why didn't the government prepare us for this?" It is not in the long-term interest of political leaders to indulge popular aversion. If public resistance under current circumstances prevents widespread distribution, stockpiling, and instruction in the use of defensive equipment or medical services, the least that should be done is to optimize plans and preparations to rapidly implement such activities when the first crisis ignites demand.

As threats of terrorism using WMD are taken more seriously, interest will grow in preemptive defense measures—the most obvious of which is intensified intelligence collection. Where this involves targeting groups within the United States that might seem to be potential breeding grounds for terrorists (for example, supporters of Palestinian militants, home-grown militias or cults, or radicals with ties to Iran, Iraq, or Libya), controversies will arise over constitutional limits on invasion of privacy or search and seizure. So long as the WMD danger remains hypothetical, such controversies will not be easily resolved. They have not come to the fore so far because U.S. law enforcement has been unbelievably lucky in apprehending terrorists. The group arrested in 1993 for planning to bomb the Lincoln Tunnel happened to be infiltrated by an informer, and Timothy McVeigh happened to be picked up in 1995 for driving without a license plate. Those who fear compromising civil liberties with permissive standards for government snooping should consider what is likely to happen once such luck runs out and it proves impossible to identify perpetrators. Suppose a secretive radical Islamic group launches a biological attack, kills 100,000 people, and announces that it will do the same thing again if its terms are not met. (The probability of such a scenario may not be high, but it can no longer be consigned to science fiction.) In that case, it is hardly unthinkable that a panicked legal system would roll over and treat Arab-Americans as it did the Japanese-Americans who were herded into concentration camps after Pearl Harbor. Stretching limits on domestic surveillance to reduce the chances of facing such choices could be the lesser evil.

IS RETREAT THE BEST DEFENSE?

No PROGRAMS AIMED at controlling adversaries' capabilities can eliminate the dangers. One risk is that in the more fluid politics of the post–Cold War world, the United States could stumble into an unanticipated crisis with Russia or China. There are no well-established rules of the game to brake a spiraling conflict over the Baltic states or Taiwan, as there were in the superpower competition after the Cuban missile crisis. The second danger is that some angry group that blames the United States for its problems may decide to coerce Americans, or simply exact vengeance, by inflicting devastation on them where they live.

If steps to deal with the problem in terms of capabilities are limited, can anything be done to address intentions—the incentives of any foreign power or group to lash out at the United States? There are few answers to this question that do not compromise the fundamental strategic activism and internationalist thrust of U.S. foreign policy over the past half-century. That is because the best way to keep people from believing that the United States is responsible for their problems is to avoid involvement in their conflicts.

Ever since the Munich agreement and Pearl Harbor, with only a brief interruption during the decade after the Tet offensive, there has been a consensus that if Americans did not draw their defense perimeter far forward and confront foreign troubles in their early stages, those troubles would come to them at home. But because the United States is now the only superpower and weapons of mass destruction have become more accessible, American intervention in troubled areas is not so much a way to fend off such threats as it is what stirs them up.

Will U.S. involvement in unstable situations around the former U.S.S.R. head off conflict with Moscow or generate it? Will making NATO bigger and moving it to Russia's doorstep deter Russian pressure on Ukraine and the Baltics or provoke it? With Russia and China, there is less chance that either will set out to conquer Europe or Asia than that they will try to restore old sovereignties and security zones by reincorporating new states of the former Soviet Union or the province of Taiwan. None of this means that NATO expansion or support for Taiwan's autonomy will cause nuclear war. It does mean that to whatever extent American activism increases those countries' incentives to rely on WMD while intensifying political friction between them and Washington, it is counterproductive.

The other main danger is the ire of smaller states or religious and cultural groups that see the United States as an evil force blocking their legitimate aspirations. It is hardly likely that Middle Eastern radicals would be hatching schemes like the destruction of the World Trade Center if the United States had not been identified for so long as the mainstay of Israel, the shah of Iran, and conservative Arab regimes and the source of a cultural assault on Islam. Cold War triumph magnified the problem. U.S. military and cultural hegemony—the basic threats to radicals seeking to challenge the status quo—are directly linked to the imputation of American responsibility for maintaining world order. Playing Globocop feeds the urge of aggrieved groups to strike back.

Is this a brief for isolationism? No. It is too late to turn off foreign resentments by retreating, even if that were an acceptable course. Alienated groups and governments would not stop blaming Washington for their problems. In addition, there is more to foreign policy than dampening incentives to hurt the United States. It is not automatically sensible to stop pursuing other interests for the sake of uncertain reductions in a threat of uncertain probability. Security is not all of a piece, and survival is only part of security.

But it is no longer prudent to assume that important security interests complement each other as they did during the Cold War. The interest at the very core—protecting the American homeland from attack—may now often be in conflict with security more broadly conceived and with the interests that mandate promoting American political values, economic interdependence, social Westernization, and stability in regions beyond Western Europe and the Americas. The United States should not give up all its broader political interests, but it should tread cautiously in areas—especially the Middle East— where broader interests grate against the core imperative of preventing mass destruction within America's borders.

West Point
Commencement Speech

President George W. Bush

THE PRESIDENT: Thank you very much, General Lennox. Mr. Secretary, Governor Pataki, members of the United States Congress, Academy staff and faculty, distinguished guests, proud family members, and graduates: I want to thank you for your welcome. Laura and I are especially honored to visit this great institution in your bicentennial year.

In every corner of America, the words "West Point" command immediate respect. This place where the Hudson River bends is more than a fine institution of learning. The United States Military Academy is the guardian of values that have shaped the soldiers who have shaped the history of the world.

A few of you have followed in the path of the perfect West Point graduate, Robert E. Lee, who never received a single demerit in four years. Some of you followed in the path of the imperfect graduate, Ulysses S. Grant, who had his fair share of demerits, and said the happiest day of his life was "the day I left West Point." During my college years I guess you could say I was a Grant man.

You walk in the tradition of Eisenhower and MacArthur, Patton and Bradley—the commanders who saved a civilization. And you walk in the tradition of second lieutenants who did the same, by fighting and dying on distant battlefields.

Graduates of this academy have brought creativity and courage

GEORGE W. BUSH is President of the United States of America. These remarks were originally made at the 2002 Graduation Exercise of the United States Military Academy, West Point, New York.

to every field of endeavor. West Point produced the chief engineer of the Panama Canal, the mind behind the Manhattan Project, the first American to walk in space. This fine institution gave us the man they say invented baseball, and other young men over the years who perfected the game of football.

You know this, but many in America don't, George C. Marshall, a VMI graduate, is said to have given this order: "I want an officer for a secret and dangerous mission. I want a West Point football player."

As you leave here today, I know there's one thing you'll never miss about this place: Being a plebe. But even a plebe at West Point is made to feel he or she has some standing in the world. I'm told that plebes, when asked whom they outrank, are required to answer this: "Sir, the Superintendent's dog, the Commandant's cat, and all the admirals in the whole damn Navy." I probably won't be sharing that with the Secretary of the Navy.

West Point is guided by tradition, and in honor of the "Golden Children of the Corps," I will observe one of the traditions you cherish most. As the Commander-in-Chief, I hereby grant amnesty to all cadets who are on restriction for minor conduct offenses. Those of you in the end zone might have cheered a little early. Because, you see, I'm going to let General Lennox define exactly what "minor" means.

Every West Point class is commissioned to the Armed Forces. Some West Point classes are also commissioned by history, to take part in a great new calling for their country. Speaking here to the class of 1942 six months after Pearl Harbor General Marshall said, "We're determined that before the sun sets on this terrible struggle, our flag will be recognized throughout the world as a symbol of freedom on the one hand, and of overwhelming power on the other."

Officers graduating that year helped fulfill that mission, defeating Japan and Germany, and then reconstructing those nations as allies. West Point graduates of the 1940s saw the rise of a deadly new challenge the challenge of imperial communism and opposed it from Korea to Berlin, to Vietnam, and in the Cold War, from beginning to end. And as the sun set on their struggle, many of those West Point officers lived to see a world transformed.

History has also issued its call to your generation. In your last year,

America was attacked by a ruthless and resourceful enemy. You graduate from this Academy in a time of war, taking your place in an American military that is powerful and is honorable. Our war on terror is only begun, but in Afghanistan it was begun well.

I am proud of the men and women who have fought on my orders. America is profoundly grateful for all who serve the cause of freedom, and for all who have given their lives in its defense. This nation respects and trusts our military, and we are confident in your victories to come.

This war will take many turns we cannot predict. Yet I am certain of this: Wherever we carry it, the American flag will stand not only for our power, but for freedom. Our nation's cause has always been larger than our nation's defense. We fight, as we always fight, for a just peace, a peace that favors human liberty. We will defend the peace against threats from terrorists and tyrants. We will preserve the peace by building good relations among the great powers. And we will extend the peace by encouraging free and open societies on every continent.

Building this just peace is America's opportunity, and America's duty. From this day forward, it is your challenge, as well, and we will meet this challenge together. You will wear the uniform of a great and unique country. America has no empire to extend or utopia to establish. We wish for others only what we wish for ourselves: safety from violence, the rewards of liberty, and the hope for a better life.

In defending the peace, we face a threat with no precedent. Enemies in the past needed great armies and great industrial capabilities to endanger the American people and our nation. The attacks of September the 11th required a few hundred thousand dollars in the hands of a few dozen evil and deluded men. All of the chaos and suffering they caused came at much less than the cost of a single tank. The dangers have not passed. This government and the American people are on watch, we are ready, because we know the terrorists have more money and more men and more plans.

The gravest danger to freedom lies at the perilous crossroads of radicalism and technology. When the spread of chemical and biological and nuclear weapons, along with ballistic missile technology when that occurs, even weak states and small groups could attain a catastrophic power to strike great nations. Our enemies have declared this very intention, and have been caught seeking these terrible weapons. They want the capability to blackmail us, or to harm us, or to harm our friends and we will oppose them with all our power.

For much of the last century, America's defense relied on the Cold War doctrines of deterrence and containment. In some cases, those strategies still apply. But new threats also require new thinking. Deterrence, the promise of massive retaliation against nations, means nothing against shadowy terrorist networks with no nation or citizens to defend. Containment is not possible when unbalanced dictators with weapons of mass destruction can deliver those weapons on missiles or secretly provide them to terrorist allies.

We cannot defend America and our friends by hoping for the best. We cannot put our faith in the word of tyrants, who solemnly sign non-proliferation treaties, and then systemically break them. If we wait for threats to fully materialize, we will have waited too long.

Homeland defense and missile defense are part of stronger security, and they're essential priorities for America. Yet the war on terror will not be won on the defensive. We must take the battle to the enemy, disrupt his plans, and confront the worst threats before they emerge. In the world we have entered, the only path to safety is the path of action. And this nation will act.

Our security will require the best intelligence, to reveal threats hidden in caves and growing in laboratories. Our security will require modernizing domestic agencies such as the FBI, so they're prepared to act, and act quickly, against danger. Our security will require transforming the military you will lead, a military that must be ready to strike at a moment's notice in any dark corner of the world. And our security will require all Americans to be forward-looking and resolute, to be ready for preemptive action when necessary to defend our liberty and to defend our lives.

The work ahead is difficult. The choices we will face are complex. We must uncover terror cells in 60 or more countries, using every tool of finance, intelligence and law enforcement. Along with our friends and allies, we must oppose proliferation and confront regimes that sponsor terror, as each case requires. Some nations need military training to fight terror, and we'll provide it. Other nations oppose terror, but tolerate the hatred that leads to terror—and that must change. We will send diplomats where they are needed, and we will send you, our soldiers, where you're needed.

All nations that decide for aggression and terror will pay a price. We will not leave the safety of America and the peace of the planet at the mercy of a few mad terrorists and tyrants. We will lift this dark threat from our country and from the world.

Because the war on terror will require resolve and patience, it will also require firm moral purpose. In this way our struggle is similar to the Cold War. Now, as then, our enemies are totalitarians, holding a creed of power with no place for human dignity. Now, as then, they seek to impose a joyless conformity, to control every life and all of life.

America confronted imperial communism in many different ways, diplomatic, economic, and military. Yet moral clarity was essential to our victory in the Cold War. When leaders like John F. Kennedy and Ronald Reagan refused to gloss over the brutality of tyrants, they gave hope to prisoners and dissidents and exiles, and rallied free nations to a great cause.

Some worry that it is somehow undiplomatic or impolite to speak the language of right and wrong. I disagree. Different circumstances require different methods, but not different moralities. Moral truth is the same in every culture, in every time, and in every place. Targeting innocent civilians for murder is always and everywhere wrong. Brutality against women is always and everywhere wrong. There can be no neutrality between justice and cruelty, between the innocent and the guilty. We are in a conflict between good and evil, and America will call evil by its name. By confronting evil and lawless regimes, we do not create a problem, we reveal a problem. And we will lead the world in opposing it.

As we defend the peace, we also have an historic opportunity to preserve the peace. We have our best chance since the rise of the nation state in the 17th century to build a world where the great powers compete in peace instead of prepare for war. The history of the last century, in particular, was dominated by a series of destructive national rivalries that left battlefields and graveyards across the Earth. Germany fought France, the Axis fought the Allies, and then the East fought the West, in proxy wars and tense standoffs, against a backdrop of nuclear Armageddon.

Competition between great nations is inevitable, but armed conflict in our world is not. More and more, civilized nations find ourselves on the same side, united by common dangers of terrorist violence and chaos. America has, and intends to keep, military strengths beyond challenge thereby, making the destabilizing arms races of other eras pointless, and limiting rivalries to trade and other pursuits of peace.

Today the great powers are also increasingly united by common values, instead of divided by conflicting ideologies. The United States, Japan and our Pacific friends, and now all of Europe, share a deep commitment to human freedom, embodied in strong alliances such as NATO. And the tide of liberty is rising in many other nations.

Generations of West Point officers planned and practiced for battles with Soviet Russia. I've just returned from a new Russia, now a country reaching toward democracy, and our partner in the war against terror. Even in China, leaders are discovering that economic freedom is the only lasting source of national wealth. In time, they will find that social and political freedom is the only true source of national greatness.

When the great powers share common values, we are better able to confront serious regional conflicts together, better able to cooperate in preventing the spread of violence or economic chaos. In the past, great power rivals took sides in difficult regional problems, making divisions deeper and more complicated. Today, from the Middle East to South Asia, we are gathering broad international coalitions to increase the pressure for peace. We must build strong and great power relations when times are good; to help manage crisis when times are bad. America needs partners to preserve the peace, and we will work with every nation that shares this noble goal.

And finally, America stands for more than the absence of war. We have a great opportunity to extend a just peace, by replacing poverty, repression, and resentment around the world with hope of a better day. Through most of history, poverty was persistent, inescapable, and almost universal. In the last few decades, we've seen nations from Chile to South Korea build modern economies and freer societies, lifting millions of people out of despair and want. And there's no mystery to this achievement.

The 20th century ended with a single surviving model of human progress, based on non-negotiable demands of human dignity, the rule of law, limits on the power of the state, respect for women and private property and free speech and equal justice and religious tolerance. America cannot impose this vision, yet we can support and reward governments that make the right choices for their own people. In our development aid, in our diplomatic efforts, in our international broadcasting, and in our educational assistance, the United States will promote moderation and tolerance and human rights. And we will defend the peace that makes all progress possible.

When it comes to the common rights and needs of men and women, there is no clash of civilizations. The requirements of freedom apply fully to Africa and Latin America and the entire Islamic world. The peoples of the Islamic nations want and deserve the same freedoms and opportunities as people in every nation. And their governments should listen to their hopes.

A truly strong nation will permit legal avenues of dissent for all groups that pursue their aspirations without violence. An advancing nation will pursue economic reform, to unleash the great entrepreneurial energy of its people. A thriving nation will respect the rights of women, because no society can prosper while denying opportunity to half its citizens. Mothers and fathers and children across the Islamic world, and all the world, share the same fears and aspirations. In poverty, they struggle. In tyranny, they suffer. And as we saw in Afghanistan, in liberation they celebrate.

America has a greater objective than controlling threats and containing resentment. We will work for a just and peaceful world beyond the war on terror.

The bicentennial class of West Point now enters this drama. With all in the United States Army, you will stand between your fellow citizens and grave danger. You will help establish a peace that allows millions around the world to live in liberty and to grow in prosperity. You will face times of calm, and times of crisis. And every test will find you prepared—because you're the men and women of West Point. You leave here marked by the character of this Academy, carrying with you the highest ideals of our nation.

Toward the end of his life, Dwight Eisenhower recalled the first day he stood on the plain at West Point. "The feeling came over me," he said, "that the expression 'the United States of America' would now and henceforth mean something different than it had ever before. From here on, it would be the nation I would be serving, not myself."

Today, your last day at West Point, you begin a life of service in a career unlike any other. You've answered a calling to hardship and purpose, to risk and honor. At the end of every day you will know that you have faithfully done your duty. May you always bring to that duty the high standards of this great American institution. May you always be worthy of the long gray line that stretches two centuries behind you.

On behalf of the nation, I congratulate each one of you for the commission you've earned and for the credit you bring to the United States of America. May God bless you all.

America's Imperial Ambition

G. John Ikenberry

THE LURES OF PREEMPTION

In the shadows of the Bush administration's war on terrorism, sweeping new ideas are circulating about U.S. grand strategy and the restructuring of today's unipolar world. They call for American unilateral and preemptive, even preventive, use of force, facilitated if possible by coalitions of the willing—but ultimately unconstrained by the rules and norms of the international community. At the extreme, these notions form a neoimperial vision in which the United States arrogates to itself the global role of setting standards, determining threats, using force, and meting out justice. It is a vision in which sovereignty becomes more absolute for America even as it becomes more conditional for countries that challenge Washington's standards of internal and external behavior. It is a vision made necessary—at least in the eyes of its advocates—by the new and apocalyptic character of contemporary terrorist threats and by America's unprecedented global dominance. These radical strategic ideas and impulses could transform today's world order in a way that the end of the Cold War, strangely enough, did not.

The exigencies of fighting terrorism in Afghanistan and the debate over intervening in Iraq obscure the profundity of this geopolitical challenge. Blueprints have not been produced, and Yalta-style summits have not been convened, but actions are afoot to dramatically alter the

G. John Ikenberry is Peter F. Krogh Professor of Geopolitics and Global Justice, with a joint affiliation in the Department of Government, at the Edmund A. Walsh School of Foreign Service, Georgetown University. This article originally appeared in the September/October 2002 issue of *Foreign Affairs* © 2002 by the Council on Foreign Relations.

political order that the United States has built with its partners since the 1940s. The twin new realities of our age—catastrophic terrorism and American unipolar power—do necessitate a rethinking of the organizing principles of international order. America and the other major states do need a new consensus on terrorist threats, weapons of mass destruction (WMD), the use of force, and the global rules of the game. This imperative requires a better appreciation of the ideas coming out of the administration. But in turn, the administration should understand the virtues of the old order that it wishes to displace.

America's nascent neoimperial grand strategy threatens to rend the fabric of the international community and political partnerships precisely at a time when that community and those partnerships are urgently needed. It is an approach fraught with peril and likely to fail. It is not only politically unsustainable but diplomatically harmful. And if history is a guide, it will trigger antagonism and resistance that will leave America in a more hostile and divided world.

PROVEN LEGACIES

THE MAINSTREAM of American foreign policy has been defined since the 1940s by two grand strategies that have built the modern international order. One is realist in orientation, organized around containment, deterrence, and the maintenance of the global balance of power. Facing a dangerous and expansive Soviet Union after 1945, the United States stepped forward to fill the vacuum left by a waning British Empire and a collapsing European order to provide a counter-weight to Stalin and his Red Army.

The touchstone of this strategy was containment, which sought to deny the Soviet Union the ability to expand its sphere of influence. Order was maintained by managing the bipolar balance between the American and Soviet camps. Stability was achieved through nuclear deterrence. For the first time, nuclear weapons and the doctrine of mutual assured destruction made war between the great powers irrational. But containment and global power-balancing ended with the collapse of the Soviet Union in 1991. Nuclear deterrence is no longer the defining logic of the existing order, although it remains a recessed feature that continues to impart stability in relations among China, Russia, and the West.

This strategy has yielded a bounty of institutions and partnerships for America. The most important have been the NATO and U.S.-Japan alliances, American-led security partnerships that have survived the end of the Cold War by providing a bulwark for stability through commitment and reassurance. The United States maintains a forward presence in Europe and East Asia; its alliance partners gain security protection as well as a measure of regularity in their relationship with the world's leading military power. But Cold War balancing has yielded more than a utilitarian alliance structure; it has generated a political order that has value in itself.

This grand strategy presupposes a loose framework of consultations and agreements to resolve differences: the great powers extend to each other the respect of equals, and they accommodate each other until vital interests come into play. The domestic affairs of these states remain precisely that—domestic. The great powers compete with each other, and although war is not unthinkable, sober statecraft and the balance of power offer the best hope for stability and peace.

George W. Bush ran for president emphasizing some of these themes, describing his approach to foreign policy as "new realism": the focus of American efforts should shift away from Clinton-era preoccupations with nation building, international social work, and the promiscuous use of force, and toward cultivating great-power relations and rebuilding the nation's military. Bush's efforts to integrate Russia into the Western security order have been the most important manifestation of this realist grand strategy at work. The moderation in Washington's confrontational rhetoric toward China also reflects this emphasis. If the major European and Asian states play by the rules, the great-power order will remain stable. (In a way, it is precisely because Europe is not a great power—or at least seems to eschew the logic of great-power politics—that it is now generating so much discord with the United States.)

The other grand strategy, forged during World War II as the United States planned the reconstruction of the world economy, is liberal in orientation. It seeks to build order around institutionalized political relations among integrated market democracies, supported by an opening of economies. This agenda was not simply an inspiration of American businessmen and economists, however. There have always been geopolitical goals as well. Whereas America's realist grand strategy was aimed at countering Soviet power, its liberal grand strategy was aimed at avoiding a return to the 1930s, an era of regional blocs, trade conflict, and strategic rivalry. Open trade, democracy, and multilateral institutional relations went together. Underlying this strategy was the view that a rule-based international order, especially one in which the United States uses its political weight to derive congenial rules, will most fully protect American interests, conserve its power, and extend its influence.

This grand strategy has been pursued through an array of postwar initiatives that look disarmingly like "low politics": the Bretton Woods institutions, the World Trade Organization (WTO), and the Organization for Economic Cooperation and Development are just a few examples. Together, they form a complex layer cake of integrative initiatives that bind the democratic industrialized world together. During the 1990s, the United States continued to pursue this liberal grand strategy. Both the first Bush and the Clinton administrations attempted to articulate a vision of world order that was not dependent on an external threat or an explicit policy of balance of power. Bush the elder talked about the importance of the transatlantic community and articulated ideas about a more fully integrated Asia-Pacific region. In both cases, the strategy offered a positive vision of alliance and partnership built around common values, tradition, mutual self-interest, and the preservation of stability. The Clinton administration likewise attempted to describe the post–Cold War order in terms of the expansion of democracy and open markets. In this vision, democracy provided the foundation for global and regional community, and trade and capital flows were forces for political reform and integration.

The current Bush administration is not eager to brandish this Clinton-looking grand strategy, but it still invokes that strategy's ideas in various ways. Support for Chinese entry into the WTO is based on the liberal anticipation that free markets and integration into the Western economic order will create pressures for Chinese political reform and discourage a belligerent foreign policy. Administration support for last year's multilateral trade-negotiating round in Doha, Qatar, also was premised on the economic and political benefits of freer trade. After September 11, U.S. Trade Representative Robert Zoellick even linked trade expansion authority to the fight against terrorism: trade, growth, integration, and political stability go together. Richard Haass, policy planning director at the State Department, argued recently that "the principal aim of American foreign policy is to integrate other countries and organizations into arrangements that will sustain a world consistent with U.S. interests and values"—again, an echo of the liberal grand strategy. The administration's recent protectionist trade actions in steel and agriculture have triggered such a loud outcry around the world precisely because governments are worried that the United States might be retreating from this postwar liberal strategy.

AMERICA'S HISTORIC BARGAINS

THESE TWO GRAND STRATEGIES are rooted in divergent, even antagonistic, intellectual traditions. But over the last 50 years they have worked remarkably well together. The realist grand strategy created a political rationale for establishing major security commitments around the world. The liberal strategy created a positive agenda for American leadership. The United States could exercise its power and achieve its national interests, but it did so in a way that helped deepen the fabric of international community. American power did not destabilize world order; it helped create it. The development of rule-based agreements and political-security partnerships was good both for the United States and for much of the world. By the end of the 1990s, the result was an international political order of unprecedented size and success: a global coalition of democratic states tied together through markets, institutions, and security partnerships.

This international order was built on two historic bargains. One was the U.S. commitment to provide its European and Asian partners with security protection and access to American markets, technology, and supplies within an open world economy. In return, these countries agreed to be reliable partners providing diplomatic, economic, and logistical support for the United States as it led the wider Western postwar order. The other is the liberal bargain that addressed the uncertainties of American power. East Asian and European states agreed to accept American leadership and operate within an agreed-upon political-economic system. The United States, in response, opened itself up and bound itself to its partners. In effect, the United States built an institutionalized coalition of partners and reinforced the stability of these mutually beneficial relations by making itself more "user-friendly"—that is, by playing by the rules and creating ongoing political processes that facilitated consultation and joint decision-making. The United States made its power safe for the world, and in return the world agreed to live within the U.S. system. These bargains date from the 1940s, but they continue to shore up the post–Cold War order. The result has been the most stable and prosperous international system in world history. But new ideas within the Bush administration—crystallized by September 11 and U.S. dominance—are unsettling this order and the political bargains behind it.

A NEW GRAND STRATEGY

FOR THE FIRST TIME since the dawn of the Cold War, a new grand strategy is taking shape in Washington. It is advanced most directly as a response to terrorism, but it also constitutes a broader view about how the United States should wield power and organize world order. According to this new paradigm, America is to be less bound to its partners and to global rules and institutions while it steps forward to play a more unilateral and anticipatory role in attacking terrorist threats and confronting rogue states seeking WMD. The United States will use its unrivaled military power to manage the global order.

This new grand strategy has seven elements. It begins with a fundamental commitment to maintaining a unipolar world in which the United States has no peer competitor. No coalition of great powers without the United States will be allowed to achieve hegemony. Bush made this point the centerpiece of American security policy in his West Point commencement address in June: "America has, and intends to keep, military strengths beyond challenges—thereby making the destabilizing arms races of other eras pointless, and limiting rivalries to trade and other pursuits of peace." The United States will not seek security through the more modest realist strategy of operating within a global system of power balancing, nor will it pursue a liberal strategy in which institutions, democracy, and integrated markets reduce the importance of power politics altogether. America will be so much more powerful than other major states that strategic rivalries and security competition among the great powers will disappear, leaving everyone—not just the United States—better off.

This goal made an unsettling early appearance at the end of the first Bush administration in a leaked Pentagon memorandum written by then Assistant Secretary of Defense Paul Wolfowitz. With the collapse of the Soviet Union, he wrote, the United States must act to prevent the rise of peer competitors in Europe and Asia. But the 1990s made this strategic aim moot. The United States grew faster than the other major states during the decade, it reduced military spending more slowly, and it dominated investment in the technological advancement of its forces. Today, however, the new goal is to make these advantages permanent—a fait accompli that will prompt other states to not even try to catch up. Some thinkers have described the strategy as "breakout," in which the United States moves so quickly to develop technological advantages (in robotics, lasers, satellites, precision munitions, etc.) that no state or coalition could ever challenge it as global leader, protector, and enforcer.

The second element is a dramatic new analysis of global threats and how they must be attacked. The grim new reality is that small groups of terrorists—perhaps aided by outlaw states—may soon acquire highly destructive nuclear, chemical, and biological weapons that can inflict catastrophic destruction. These terrorist groups cannot be appeased or deterred, the administration believes, so they must be eliminated. Secretary of Defense Donald Rumsfeld has articulated this frightening view with elegance: regarding the threats that confront the United States, he said, "There are things we know that we know. There are known unknowns. That is to say, there are things that we know we don't know. But there are also unknown unknowns. There are things we don't know we don't know. ... Each year, we discover a few more of those unknown unknowns." In other words, there could exist groups of terrorists that no one knows about. They may have nuclear, chemical, or biological weapons that the United States did not know they could get, and they might be willing and able to attack without warning. In the age of terror, there is less room for error. Small networks of angry people can inflict unimaginable harm on the rest of the world. They are not nation-states, and they do not play by the accepted rules of the game.

The third element of the new strategy maintains that the Cold War concept of deterrence is outdated. Deterrence, sovereignty, and the balance of power work together. When deterrence is no longer viable, the larger realist edifice starts to crumble. The threat today is not other great powers that must be managed through second-strike nuclear capacity but the transnational terrorist networks that have no home address. They cannot be deterred because they are either willing to die for their cause or able to escape retaliation. The old defensive strategy of building missiles and other weapons that can survive a first strike and be used in a retaliatory strike to punish the attacker will no longer ensure security. The only option, then, is offense.

The use of force, this camp argues, will therefore need to be preemptive and perhaps even preventive—taking on potential threats before they can present a major problem. But this premise plays havoc with the old international rules of self-defense and United Nations norms about the proper use of force. Rumsfeld has articulated the justification for preemptive action by stating that the "absence of evidence is not evidence of absence of weapons of mass destruction." But such an approach renders international norms of self-defense—enshrined by Article 51 of the UN Charter—almost meaningless. The administration should remember that when Israeli jets bombed the Iraqi nuclear reactor at Osirak in 1981 in what Israel described as an act of self-defense, the world condemned it as an act of aggression. Even British Prime Minister Margaret Thatcher and the American ambassador to the UN, Jeane

Kirkpatrick, criticized the action, and the United States joined in passing a UN resolution condemning it.

The Bush administration's security doctrine takes this country down the same slippery slope. Even without a clear threat, the United States now claims a right to use preemptive or preventive military force. At West Point, Bush put it succinctly when he stated that "the military must be ready to strike at a moment's notice in any dark corner of the world. All nations that decide for aggression and terror will pay a price." The administration defends this new doctrine as a necessary adjustment to a more uncertain and shifting threat environment. This policy of no regrets errs on the side of action—but it can also easily become national security by hunch or inference, leaving the world without clear-cut norms for justifying force.

As a result, the fourth element of this emerging grand strategy involves a recasting of the terms of sovereignty. Because these terrorist groups cannot be deterred, the United States must be prepared to intervene anywhere, anytime to preemptively destroy the threat. Terrorists do not respect borders, so neither can the United States. Moreover, countries that harbor terrorists, either by consent or because they are unable to enforce their laws within their territory, effectively forfeit their rights of sovereignty. Haass recently hinted at this notion in *The New Yorker:*

> What you are seeing in this administration is the emergence of a new principle or body of ideas ... about what you might call the limits of sovereignty. Sovereignty entails obligations. One is not to massacre your own people. Another is not to support terrorism in any way. If a government fails to meet these obligations, then it forfeits some of the normal advantages of sovereignty, including the right to be left alone inside your own territory. Other governments, including the United States, gain the right to intervene. In the case of terrorism, this can even lead to a right of preventive ... self-defense. You essentially can act in anticipation if you have grounds to think it's a question of when, and not if, you're going to be attacked.

Here the war on terrorism and the problem of the proliferation of WMD get entangled. The worry is that a few despotic states—Iraq in particular, but also Iran and North Korea—will develop capabilities to produce weapons of mass destruction and put these weapons in the hands of terrorists. The regimes themselves may be deterred from using such capabilities, but they might pass along these weapons to terrorist networks that are not deterred. Thus another emerging principle within the Bush administration: the possession of WMD by unaccountable, unfriendly, despotic governments is itself a threat that must be countered. In the old era, despotic regimes were to be lamented but ultimately tolerated. With the rise of terrorism and weapons of mass destruction, they are now unacceptable threats. Thus states that are not technically in violation of any existing international laws could nevertheless be targets of American force—if Washington determines that they have a prospective capacity to do harm.

The recasting of sovereignty is paradoxical. On the one hand, the new grand strategy reaffirms the importance of the territorial nation-state. After all, if all governments were accountable and capable of enforcing the rule of law within their sovereign territory, terrorists would find it very difficult to operate. The emerging Bush doctrine enshrines this idea: governments will be held responsible for what goes on inside their borders. On the other hand, sovereignty has been made newly conditional: governments that fail to act like respectable, law-abiding states will lose their sovereignty.

In one sense, such conditional sovereignty is not new. Great powers have willfully transgressed the norms of state sovereignty as far back as such norms have existed, particularly within their traditional spheres of influence, whenever the national interest dictated. The United States itself has done this within the western hemisphere since the nineteenth century. What is new and provocative in this notion today, however, is the Bush administration's inclination to apply it on a global basis, leaving to itself the authority to determine when sovereign rights have been forfeited, and doing so on an anticipatory basis.

The fifth element of this new grand strategy is a general depreciation of international rules, treaties, and security partnerships. This point relates to the new threats themselves: if the stakes are rising and the margins of error are shrinking in the war on terrorism, multilateral norms and agreements that sanction and limit the use of force are just annoying distractions. The critical task is to eliminate the threat. But the emerging unilateral strategy is also informed by a deeper suspicion about the suspect value of international agreements themselves. Part of this view arises from a deeply felt and authentically American belief that the United States should not get entangled in the corrupting and constraining world of multilateral rules and institutions. For some Americans, the belief that American sovereignty is politically sacred leads to a preference for isolationism. But the more influential view—particularly after September 11—is not that the United States should withdraw from the world but that it should operate in the world on its own terms. The Bush administration's repudiation of a remarkable array of treaties and institutions—from the Kyoto Protocol on global warming to the International Criminal Court to the Biological Weapons Convention—reflects this new bias. Likewise, the United States signed a formal agreement with Russia on the reduction of deployed nuclear warheads only after Moscow's insistence; the Bush administration wanted only a "gentlemen's agreement." In other words, the United States has decided it is big enough, powerful enough, and remote enough to go it alone.

Sixth, the new grand strategy argues that the United States will need to play a direct and unconstrained role in responding to threats. This conviction is partially based on a judgment that no other country or coalition—even the European Union—has the force-projection capabilities to respond to terrorist and rogue states around the world. A decade of U.S. defense spending and modernization has left allies of the United States far behind. In combat operations, alliance partners are increasingly finding it difficult to mesh with U.S. forces. This view is also based on the judgment that joint operations and the use of force through coalitions tend to hinder effective operations. To some observers, this lesson became clear in the allied bombing campaign over Kosovo. The sentiment was also expressed during the U.S. and allied military actions in Afghanistan. Rumsfeld explained this point earlier this year, when he said, "The mission must determine the coalition; the coalition must not determine the mission. If it does, the mission will be dumbed down to the lowest common denominator, and we can't afford that."

No one in the Bush administration argues that NATO or the U.S.-Japan alliance should be dismantled. Rather, these alliances are now seen as less useful to the United States as it confronts today's threats. Some officials argue that it is not that the United States chooses to depreciate alliance partnerships, but that the Europeans are unwilling to keep up. Whether that is true, the upgrading of the American military, along with its sheer size relative to the forces of the rest of the world, leaves the United States in a class by itself. In these circumstances, it is increasingly difficult to maintain the illusion of true alliance partnership. America's allies become merely strategic assets that are useful depending on the circumstance. The United States still finds attractive the logistical reach that its global alliance system provides, but the pacts with countries in Asia and Europe become more contingent and less premised on a vision of a common security community.

Finally, the new grand strategy attaches little value to international stability. There is an unsentimental view in the unilateralist camp that the traditions of the past must be shed. Whether it is withdrawal from the Anti-Ballistic Missile Treaty or the resistance to signing other formal arms-control treaties, policymakers are convinced that the United States needs to move beyond outmoded Cold War thinking. Administration officials have noted with some satisfaction that America's withdrawal from the ABM Treaty did not lead to a global arms race but actually paved the way for a historic arms-reduction agreement between the United States and Russia. This move is seen as a validation that moving beyond the old paradigm of great-power relations will not bring the international house down. The world can withstand radically new security approaches, and it will accommodate American unilateralism as well. But stability is not an end in itself. The administration's new hawkish policy toward North Korea, for example, might be destabilizing to the region, but such instability might be the necessary price for dislodging a dangerous and evil regime in Pyongyang.

In this brave new world, neoimperial thinkers contend that the older realist and liberal grand strategies are not very helpful. American security will not be ensured, as realist grand strategy assumes, by the preservation of deterrence and stable relations among the major powers. In a world of asymmetrical threats, the global balance of power is not the linchpin of war and peace. Likewise, liberal strategies of building order around open trade and democratic institutions might have some long-term impact on terrorism, but they do not address the immediacy of the threats. Apocalyptic violence is at our doorstep, so efforts at strengthening the rules and institutions of the international community are of little practical value. If we accept the worst-case imagining of "we don't know what we don't know," everything else is secondary: international rules, traditions of partnership, and standards of legitimacy. It is a war. And as Clausewitz famously remarked, "War is such a dangerous business that the mistakes which come from kindness are the very worst."

IMPERIAL DANGERS

PITFALLS ACCOMPANY this neoimperial grand strategy, however. Unchecked U.S. power, shorn of legitimacy and disentangled from the postwar norms and institutions of the international order, will usher in a more hostile international system, making it far harder to achieve American interests. The secret of the United States' long brilliant run as the world's leading state was its ability and willingness to exercise power within alliance and multinational frameworks, which made its power and agenda more acceptable to allies and other key states around the world. This achievement has now been put at risk by the administration's new thinking.

The most immediate problem is that the neoimperialist approach is unsustainable. Going it alone might well succeed in removing Saddam Hussein from power, but it is far less certain that a strategy of counterproliferation, based on American willingness to use unilateral force to confront dangerous dictators, can work over the long term. An American policy that leaves the United States alone to decide which states are threats and how best to deny them weapons of mass destruction will lead to a diminishment of multilateral mechanisms—most important of which is the nonproliferation regime.

The Bush administration has elevated the threat of WMD to the top of its security agenda without investing its power or prestige in fostering, monitoring, and enforcing nonproliferation commitments. The tragedy of September 11 has given the Bush administration the authority and willingness to confront the Iraqs of the world. But that will not be enough when even more complicated cases come along—when it is not the use of force that is needed but concerted multilateral action to provide sanctions and inspections. Nor is it certain that a preemptive or preventive military intervention will go well; it might trigger a domestic political backlash to American-led and military-focused interventionism. America's well-meaning imperial strategy could undermine the principled multilateral agreements, institutional infrastructure, and cooperative spirit needed for the long-term success of nonproliferation goals.

The specific doctrine of preemptive action poses a related problem: once the United States feels it can take such a course, nothing will stop other countries from doing the same. Does the United States want this doctrine in the hands of Pakistan, or even China or Russia? After all, it would not require the intervening state to first provide evidence for its actions. The United States argues that to wait until all the evidence is in, or until authoritative international bodies support action, is to wait too long. Yet that approach is the only basis that the United States can use if it needs to appeal for restraint in the actions of others. Moreover, and quite paradoxically, overwhelming American conventional military might, combined with a policy of preemptive strikes, could lead hostile states to accelerate programs to acquire their only possible deterrent to the United States: WMD. This is another version of the security dilemma, but one made worse by a neoimperial grand strategy.

Another problem follows. The use of force to eliminate WMD capabilities or overturn dangerous regimes is never simple, whether it is pursued unilaterally or by a concert of major states. After the military intervention is over, the target country has to be put back together. Peacekeeping and state building are inevitably required, as are long-term strategies that bring the UN, the World Bank, and the major powers together to orchestrate aid and other forms of assistance. This is not heroic work, but it is utterly necessary. Peacekeeping troops may be required for many years, even after a new regime is built. Regional conflicts inflamed by outside military intervention must also be calmed. This is the "long tail" of burdens and commitments that comes with every major military action.

When these costs and obligations are added to America's imperial military role, it becomes even more doubtful that the neoimperial strategy can be sustained at home over the long haul—the classic problem of imperial overstretch. The United States could keep its military predominance for decades if it is supported by a growing and increasingly productive economy. But the indirect burdens of cleaning up the political mess in terrorist-prone failed states levy a hidden cost. Peacekeeping and state building will require coalitions of states and multilateral agencies that can be brought into the process only if the initial decisions about military intervention are hammered out in consultation with other major states. America's older realist and liberal grand strategies suddenly become relevant again.

A third problem with an imperial grand strategy is that it cannot generate the cooperation needed to solve practical problems at the heart of the U.S. foreign policy agenda. In the fight on terrorism, the United States needs cooperation from European and Asian countries in intelligence, law enforcement, and logistics. Outside the security sphere, realizing U.S. objectives depends even more on a continuous stream of amicable working relations with major states around the world. It needs partners for trade liberalization, global financial stabilization, environmental protection, deterring transnational organized crime, managing the rise of China, and a host of other thorny challenges. But it is impossible to expect would-be partners to acquiesce to America's self-appointed global security protectorate and then pursue business as usual in all other domains.

The key policy tool for states confronting a unipolar and unilateral America is to withhold cooperation in day-to-day relations with the United States. One obvious means is trade policy; the European response to the recent American decision to impose tariffs on imported steel is explicable in these terms. This particular struggle concerns specific trade issues, but it is also a struggle over how Washington exercises power. The United States may be a unipolar military power, but economic and political power is more evenly distributed across the globe. The major states may not have much leverage in directly restraining American military policy, but they can make the United States pay a price in other areas.

Finally, the neoimperial grand strategy poses a wider problem for the maintenance of American unipolar power. It steps into the oldest trap of powerful imperial states: self-encirclement. When the most powerful state in the world throws its weight around, unconstrained by rules or norms of legitimacy, it risks a backlash. Other countries will bridle at an international order in which the United States plays only by its own rules. The proponents of the new grand strategy have assumed that the United States can single-handedly deploy military power abroad and not suffer untoward consequences; relations will be coarser with friends and allies, they believe, but such are the costs of leadership. But history shows that powerful states tend to trigger self-encirclement by their own overestimation of their power. Charles V, Louis XIV, Napoleon, and the leaders of post-Bismarck Germany sought to expand their imperial domains and impose a coercive order on others. Their imperial orders were all brought down when other countries decided they were not prepared to live in a world dominated by an overweening coercive state. America's imperial goals and modus operandi are much more limited and benign than were those of age-old emperors. But a hard-line imperial grand strategy runs the risk that history will repeat itself.

BRING IN THE OLD

WARS CHANGE world politics, and so too will America's war on terrorism. How great states fight wars, how they define the stakes, how they make the peace in its aftermath—all give lasting shape to the international system that emerges after the guns fall silent. In mobilizing their societies for battle, wartime leaders have tended to describe the military struggle as more than simply the defeat of an enemy. Woodrow Wilson sent U.S. troops to Europe not only to stop the kaiser's army but to destroy militarism and usher in a worldwide democratic revolution. Franklin Roosevelt saw the war with Germany and Japan as a struggle to secure the "four great freedoms." The Atlantic Charter was a statement of war aims that called not just for the defeat of fascism but for a new dedication to social welfare and human rights within an open and stable world system. To advance these visions, Wilson and Roosevelt proposed new international rules and mechanisms of cooperation. Their message was clear: If you bear the burdens of war, we, your leaders, will use this dreadful conflict to usher in a more peaceful and decent order among states. Fighting the war had as much to do with building global relations as it did with vanquishing an enemy.

Bush has not fully articulated a vision of postwar international order, aside from defining the struggle as one between freedom and evil. The world has seen Washington take determined steps to fight terrorism, but it does not yet have a sense of Bush's larger, positive agenda for a strengthened and more decent international order.

This failure explains why the sympathy and goodwill generated around the world for the United States after September 11 quickly disappeared. Newspapers that once proclaimed, "We are all Americans," now express distrust toward America. The prevailing view is that the United States seems prepared to use its power to go after terrorists and evil regimes, but not to use it to help build a more stable and peaceful world order. The United States appears to be degrading the rules and institutions of international community, not enhancing them. To the rest of the world, neoimperial thinking has more to do with exercising power than with exercising leadership.

In contrast, America's older strategic orientations—balance-of-power realism and liberal multilateralism—suggest a mature world power that seeks stability and pursues its interests in ways that do not fundamentally threaten the positions of other states. They are strategies of co-option and reassurance. The new imperial grand strategy presents the United States very differently: a revisionist state seeking to parlay its momentary power advantages into a world order in which it runs the show. Unlike the hegemonic states of the past, the United States does not seek territory or outright political domination in Europe or Asia; "America has no empire to extend or utopia to establish," Bush noted in his West Point address. But the sheer power advantages that the United States possesses and the doctrines of preemption and counterterrorism that it is articulating do unsettle governments and people around the world. The costs could be high. The last thing the United States wants is for foreign diplomats and government leaders to ask, How can we work around, undermine, contain, and retaliate against U.S. power?

Rather than invent a new grand strategy, the United States should reinvigorate its older strategies, those based on the view that America's security partnerships are not simply instrumental tools but critical components of an American-led world political order that should be preserved. U.S. power is both leveraged and made more legitimate and user-friendly by these partnerships. The neoimperial thinkers are haunted by the specter of catastrophic terrorism and seek a radical reordering of America's role in the world. America's commanding unipolar power and the advent of frightening new terrorist threats feed this imperial temptation. But it is a grand strategic vision that, taken to the extreme, will leave the world more dangerous and divided—and the United States less secure.

it's ok
it's alright
nthi—